DISCOVERING YOUR
SOUL MISSION

"The first edition of Linda's book was life altering for me. In this second edition, with the addition of chapters on the inner child, the source of our deepest wound and updated information on how to navigate the times we live in, this revision takes all that I had already learned in the first book and through Linda's internship program to incredible new levels of discovery. If a joyful life is what you seek and you have the courage to look in the mirror and dive into the 'deep end of the pool,' Linda's voice will hasten your journey."

—**Darlene Elkins**, Creative Choices Internship Graduate

"I have been on many paths in pursuit of a full and more meaningful life. Meeting Linda Brady and reading her book *Discovering your Soul Mission* was the best thing that happened to me in this pursuit. Linda's book got me started on the fast track to greater self awareness and actualization. Further work with Linda and her husband, Michael, has helped me recognize and heal the stumbling blocks of my personality, and in the process I have become more fully alive with the ability to actualize my greater purpose. My path has always been one of holism, and this book pulls everything together to that end."

—**Virginia Roberts**, RN, BS, LHRM, CLC

"Linda's philosophies resonated with me on a very deep soul level from the very first day I met her back in 2003. For my entire adolescence, I couldn't explain why I felt so 'broken.' None of my life events explained the severe depression, 'irrational' fears, and bad patterns. I felt lost and crazy. Linda's guidance has completely transformed my life as she systematically helped me peel back and see the layers of my soul. She's grown with my family as she officiated my wedding and now works with my young daughter too. Meeting Linda has transformed my life in amazing ways, and I feel so fortunate to have the opportunity to work so closely with her. This book is an entry point for anyone seeking true life transformation."

—**Ashley Valarezo**, Massage Therapist, CMT

"If it's clarity you're seeking, listen to spiritual teachers Linda and Michael Brady. Their intuition and wisdom are there to help guide you down the path of meaning that your soul lovingly wants you to travel. I hope I am able to do the same for my clients as Linda and Michael have done for me and countless others."

—**Marla Chalnick**, PhD, LPC

"As one part spiritual seeker, one part skeptic, I have always used both my right and left brains to process and try out the Brady's spiritual teachings. In the end, my skeptic falls away and I am simply left with the truth. The astrological chart is a gift to us—our own personal blueprint that's been time-date stamped by the stars.

Once we tune our ears to hearing the wisdom of our charts and the whispers of our souls, we have all that we need to let go of old, unhealthy patterns of living and move toward the life of love, joy, and purpose that we crave at the deepest levels of our beings. The Brady's book offers guiding hands on the journey."

—**Suzanne Bellavista Murray**, MS, Pastoral Counseling

"As a Clinical Psychologist, I continue to be amazed at the ways in which Linda's work with Karmic Astrology has brought clarity to the patterns and processes in my own life and Soul's mission. While psychology offers people a basic understanding into their own behaviors, thoughts, issues and fears, this is often insufficient, leaving us *stuck*. Karmic Astrology provides the missing link to ultimate growth, as I have seen time and again with my clients, friends and family.

The Brady's candor and willingness to tell the truth without blame, shame or judgment is often laced with humor and a genuine love for this work and the people they help. Their book and their work are filled with timeless spiritual wisdom that is essential for all of us sharing the planet at this time."

—**Arieahn Matamonasa-Bennett**, PhD, Licensed Psychologist

DISCOVERING

YOUR SOUL

MISSION

New Rules for a New Age

Linda and Michael Brady

Partners for Karmic Freedom, Inc.

Published by Partners for Karmic Freedom, Inc., 2015
Printed in the United States of America

Cover Design by Darlene Elkins and Tarin Pratte, Memphremagog Press

ISBN-13: 978-0692566077

Second Edition

Many years ago Evan St. Lifer, my co-author of the first edition of *Discovering Your Soul Mission,* and I wrote a book proposal entitled *New Rules for a New Age.* Evan did most of the research and writing for that book, which I am happy to include in the chapters on the Age of Pisces and the Age of Aquarius. I thank him for all the work he did for that proposal and for all that he taught me about being a writer. I would not have been able to write this revised version of *Discovering Your Soul Mission* without his tutelage. I dedicate *Discovering Your Soul Mission: New Rules for a New Age* to him.

—L.B.

To my wife, Linda Brady, who has been my soul mate and inspiration for thirty-five years.

—M.B.

Acknowledgments

This new and expanded version of my original book *Discovering Your Soul Mission* continues to be a testimony to all the clients I have worked with for more than forty years. Without them the original book and this book would not have been possible. I thank them from the bottom of my heart.

I also would like to thank my friends, clients, and students who took the time to write the personal anecdotes that are scattered throughout the book. Their keen awareness and poignant insights have helped give the book life. A special thank you goes to Lynn Van Gilder for updating all of the planetary tables.

—L.B.

TABLE OF CONTENTS

PROLOGUE

OUR GOALS

Discovering Your Soul Mission offers seven fundamental goals to help you uncover and maintain your soul's own sacred covenant for a fulfilling and meaningful life:

1. *Encourage an awareness of personal responsibility as a vehicle to self-empowerment.* When we take personal responsibility, we no longer blame others; we no longer create victimization; and we are able to make lucid decisions about what we want and desire.

2. *Create a distinction between perfection as a goal and the experience of intrinsic perfection.* Cultivate an understanding that our soul always creates our life to be perfect at any given moment.

3. *Promote an optimistic belief system that life is meaningful and full of unexpected events that lead to soul growth,* and that all of life's experiences have the potential to be life-altering.

4. *Instill a philosophy that values the soul.* Recognize that our soul creates our life experience, and that if we have karmic balance, our lives will be free of paranoia, internal conflict, sadness, and fear.

5. *Learn the meaning of the symbols we create that give us information about our karmic past.*

6. *Gain access to our soul and its mission.*

7. *Teach methods leading to greater access into the unconscious through astrological evaluation.*

HOW THIS BOOK WILL HELP YOU

Discovering Your Soul Mission: New Rules for a New Age includes a new and expanded version of my original book released in 1998. I have added all of the planetary tables up to 2035 with current astrological explanations of Uranus, Neptune and Pluto. I have also included chapters on the Age of Pisces and Aquarius as well as on Chiron and Uranus. I could not have written the chapter on Chiron in 1998. I needed years of experience working with many people to determine its efficacy in aiding us to become the integrated people we wish to be.

In the past seventeen years since *Discovering Your Soul Mission* was published, my husband, Michael, and I have continued to work with our clients and students, learning and growing with them. We have developed new techniques and strategies to aid them in living a freeing, happier life.

Discovering Your Soul Mission: New Rules for a New Age will assist you in your pursuit of the ultimate destination of your soul road. Its collection of exercises will foster a deeper understanding of your soul as well as help you maintain your soul mission once you discover it. This book will also help prevent you from repeating past mistakes and teach you how to use your past as an elixir to heal your life. By the end of the book, you will be amazed at how much you know about your soul and its purpose for you.

Discovering Your Soul Mission: New Rules for a New Age presents applications that will spur you to make the most of your soul's energy, to keep your soul and personality in alignment daily, as well as to explore your relationships and experiences symbolically. In order to maximize the techniques and practicums designed to help you integrate your soul into your life on a daily basis, we suggest you purchase a blank journal that has special meaning to you. The journal will enable you to actively participate in the exercises, and review what you've learned. You are now an active participant in this book. Your soul is with you, helping you glean the information necessary for you to discover your soul mission.

Although this book represents our best collaborative effort, we felt it necessary and entirely appropriate to cast the book in Linda's first-person voice in order to truly relate the intimacy of her client relationships and the salience with which she espouses her philosophy.

Thank you for allowing us the opportunity to continue our own soul missions. As we help you reframe your old beliefs, we are rethinking our own. As we help you see your karmic past, we are reviewing our own. As we inspire you to seek your soul mission, we are pursuing our own. Our commitment is to be as clear and as concise as we can. We welcome you to make whatever commitment is necessary, so that reading *Discovering Your Soul Mission: New Rules for A New Age* becomes a personal and transformational experience for you.

THE AGE OF PISCES REVIEWED

Every two thousand years our universe enters into a distinctly different cycle of energy and fresh experiences, symbolically represented by the characteristics of an astrological sign. Beginning with the Age of Leo until the Age of Aquarius, the historical significance of each cycle clarifies man's progress into the current New Age. There were astrological periods prior to the Age of Leo, but scientists believe the last Ice Age ended shortly before the Age of Leo began, around 11,000 years B.C. There is evidence that man existed prior to the end of the last ice age, but because it is considered pre-history there is little evidence of any organized culture prior to the end of the last ice age. Cro-Magnon man's culture culminated in terms of tool making, primitive art, and the use of fire for warmth and food during the Age of Virgo (12,000-10,000 B.C.). Any evidence of culture was destroyed in the natural events prior to that time. So, an evidentiary history as a chronicle of mankind could not begin until the Ice Ages ended. To understand the present, and prepare for the future, we must examine and attempt to understand the past. This is as true astrologically as it is politically, economically, and scientifically.

The Age of Aries began in approximately 2500 B.C. and lasted until 6 A.D. Aries is symbolized by the ram. During this age, the Ram headed god, Amen-Re, became the one god replacing the polytheism of earlier eras. Great men emerged as heroes based on their courage and their ability rather than their lineage. This Age corresponds to the Old Testament and is characterized by the symbolic Moses. Moses was a desert man who challenged the Pharaoh of Egypt with a staff and the power of God. Aggressive, fearless and against all odds, he led his people back into the desert to find their freedom. God manifested Himself as a burning bush (Aries is a fire sign) and provided Moses with the Ten Commandments. God throughout the Old Testament is seen as an angry God, a jealous and unforgiving God, and an Arian God. Through this Age, humanity was struggling with emergence into self-awareness and self-actualization. There was a great deal of savagery and selfishness also. People took what they wanted by fighting each other: "might made right." Iron, which is the metal ruled by Aries and Mars, was discovered and used most often to create weapons. Aries' ruling planet, Mars, the warrior king rules by the sword! Libra, the opposing sign of Aries, influenced this age in the development of legal systems. We don't have to look any further than the Ten Commandments to see the emergence of the first written legal code for Western civilization.

THE AGE OF PISCES

The Age of Pisces began around 06 A.D. when Christ was born and lasted until 1998 A.D. Globally, the Age of Pisces introduced organized religion. Each religion has a prescription for living and consequences for ignoring or disobeying the rules. Buddha, Confucius, and Christ are examples of the spiritual teachers that symbolize the mysticism of this era. In Western culture, the Piscean Age corresponds to the New Testament, with the advent of Christianity. It comes as a direct response to the savagery of the Age of Aries. The Age of Pisces taught that humanity needs to relate to the divine and the world-at-large through a more emotional filter. In its more constructive aspect, this age brought about a newfound element of compassion and faith in society, especially within Christian society. There was an emergence of a spiritual sensibility that spoke of "turning the other cheek" rather than the smiting of one's enemies.

Jesus spoke about God, not as an angry God, but as a God of forgiveness. Christ was the son of this loving God, a lamb, and a gentle creature. In His role as a symbol of Pisces, Jesus would die for humanity's sins, which made Him both the victim and the redeemer. Pisces is the martyr, sacrificing itself for the needs of others. Christ's resurrection symbolizes the rebirth into spirit, a Piscean reality.

Pisces is a water sign, and water symbolizes the emotions that can create the level of Love associated with this age. Throughout Jesus's short ministry a plethora of Piscean symbols emerged: baptism by water, the washing of feet, disciples who were fisherman, turning water into wine, miracles, spiritual healing, drawing fish in the sand and so many more. Christ's message was that of forgiveness--what Pisces does best!

The Piscean principle is transcendence from the material to the spiritual. Its experience is personal sacrifice for the sense of redemption. It symbolizes the myth of sacrifice, which creates leaving the physical plane to enter the higher spiritual realm, followed by spiritual redemption only to return to the physical realm a spiritually transformed figure. This is accomplished by the need to enter into the suffering of human experience in order to become compassionate and empathetic to become more spiritual. Christ as the ruler of the Piscean Age is one of the archetypes of sacrifice and redemption. Pisces strives for attunement and an idealistic compassionate experience. In essence it wants to emulate the Christ! It is highly creative and artistic, using these skills to try and create a more perfect, loving world.

HEAVEN IS OUR GOAL

During the Piscean Age, when we were unclear about our choices, we had spiritual leaders and the Bible to choose our path to righteousness for us. It was comfortable to live within this predictable, unvarying model. We led an almost childlike existence: we didn't have to think as much, and we didn't have to take responsibility. Those who strayed from the conventional, black-or-white thinking of mutual exclusivity were thought of as unsettling, unconventional, and dangerous. We learned that being perfect was the ideal and that to be Christ-like, we too needed to strive for perfection. The brass ring, after all, was heaven. The promise of heaven helped motivate us to live more kindly, gently, and compassionately, which was constructive and valuable following the self-righteous Age of Aries. It also led us to be willing to accept much suffering during life on earth. That was an extreme view of what it meant to be Piscean, one that is not constructive and has become outmoded. Two thousand years later, this willingness to suffer is no longer moving us forward as individuals or as a human species.

How do we move forward? We need to know Pisces well enough that we can recognize the old, historic beliefs that no longer work for us and release them. As Churchill said, "Those who do not understand history are bound to repeat it" and he was right. I believe that as we moved into the Age of Aquarius in 1998 our souls wanted us to resolve the past in Pisces and move into this new life experience of self-empowerment, freedom, and equality.

MARTYRDOM ARISES

The crucifixion is one of the primary focuses of the Piscean Age. It symbolizes the best and the worst of Pisces. Consider that for 2,000 years we have defined our spiritual nature by a man being nailed to a cross and being tortured and killed. Negatively the crucifixion expresses qualities such as self-pity, masochism, guilt, and martyrdom. This was an era when many felt that suffering and guilt were somehow synonymous with spirituality. Many of us are still plagued by these neurotic beliefs today. The crucifixion can also be seen as the transcendence of the ego and a surrendering of "oneselfness" for a higher ideal to serve. In its most profound sense, the crucifixion means the principle of sacrifice, worship, and profound devotion. It is the water element at its most refined.

The Piscean Age was characterized to a large extent by near-sightedness, interspersed with religious bigotry, dogmatism, self-conceit, and opportunism, due largely to a lack of knowledge. During this age, a lot of atrocities have been perpetrated in the name of God and in the bid to attain salvation, coupled with so much rancor and strife between different religious sects and denominations and their various adherents on the "true and only route to God." Some lay absolute claim to the only one true God as though they have some form of copyright on the Divine, while all non-believers are automatically excluded from God's kingdom. Pisces is intensely concerned with matters of faith. However, taken to extremes, this can lead to zealotry, self-righteousness, and the urge to establish absolute guidelines for all to follow. At its worst, the Piscean Age was an era of religious intolerance, when large populations were expected to show unquestioning allegiance to a rigid belief system.

On a psychological level, the Piscean Age brought about an emotional need to take responsibility for our actions. Importantly, it taught us to value controlling our impulsive and aggressive actions, which were part of the previous, Arian experience. Unfortunately, it also brought about suffering and pain as the movement toward responsibility for one's actions tipped into the realm of feeling shame and guilt.

One young, single mother still living by the principles of the Piscean Age became so overwhelmed and exhausted by her demanding life that she would periodically develop serious sinus infections so that she could rest and take care of herself. She didn't feel right about taking care of herself unless she had a "legitimate" excuse, like being sick. The result was that she must suffer to be able to make some time for herself. True to the Piscean Age, she believed in obligations and sacrifice and not honoring herself; she deeply believed that other people's needs were always more important than her own. In fact, she was addicted to other people's opinions of her and thus wanted to maintain her façade of being a super woman so that these others would approve of her. After learning about the negative aspects of the Piscean Age, this mom's commitment now is to create rest and fun once a week. Her mantra is "what 'they' think about me is none of my business."

On a psychological level Pisces represents an attempt to reconcile the challenges intrinsic in the integration of spiritual and material paths. Often this path to redemption creates the "victim/savior" compulsion, which leads to significant problems. Relationships that are sourced by this compulsion are denigrating to both partners. There is no growth, only suffering. One person is dependent; the other enables, and no one wins.

A fifty-year-old, twice married man finally met a woman who he feels represents a real possibility for him to have a mature and loving relationship. This man called me after their first date with the woman's chart information, happy that she had consented to my looking at her chart. I was happy that he had found a woman who was open to hearing what I had to say. I was not happy, though, when the first words out of his mouth were "What are her primary issues and how can I help her?" Both of his marriages were with women who had serious addiction problems that he felt he must fix. His Piscean pattern of not considering his own needs and trying desperately to take care of his partners who were needy and addictive threatened to repeat itself.

Imagine how surprised this man was when I said that this woman's issues were none of his business. This new woman was an opportunity for him to learn to concentrate on his own emotions and take care of himself and still be in a relationship. What we did discuss was how this woman had no addiction problems, was very independent, and was available for a mature relationship. My client and I agreed that this was a wonderful "creation." He is now committed to honoring his Soul for bringing him this opportunity by not falling back into old patterns.

SPIRITUAL DEPRESSION

We have been mentally "soaked" for 2,000 years in the Piscean principles, attitudes and emotions, which at the start served a very useful purpose to rebalance us and move us toward love and compassion but over time, at their extremes, led many of us to experience spiritual depression and karmic post traumatic stress.

As Bertrand Russell explained in *Why I am Not a Christian and Other Essays on Religion and Related Subjects*, "There are a great many ways in which, at the present moment, the church, by its insistence upon what it chooses to call morality, inflicts upon all sorts of people undeserved and unnecessary suffering. And of course, as we know, it is in its major part an opponent still of progress and improvement in all the ways that diminish suffering in the world, because it has chosen to label as morality a certain narrow set of rules of conduct which have nothing to do with human happiness; and when you say that this or that ought to be done because it would make for human happiness, they think that has nothing to do with the matter at all. What has human happiness to do with morals? The object of morals is not to make people happy."

Michael and I have experienced many clients whose need to suffer borders on an addiction. When we have peeled the onion enough, we find another Piscean belief that suffering is redemptive and good for the soul. These individuals don't know what they are redeeming themselves for and it doesn't seem to matter as long as they do it.

A very sad, frustrated woman came to me because she was unable to leave a problematic husband. When I questioned her about why she was staying with her alcoholic, abusive husband, she said she had not suffered enough. She further stated that if her suffering was great enough and acknowledged by her family and friends they would understand and support her when she finally did leave. She was unable to tell me how much suffering was enough and when she could actually leave. She has been married to this man for 15 years! And for 15 years he had been an active alcoholic. Her core issue was her desire to be a good Christian and honor Christ's suffering by emulating Him.

She and I had many conversations about the changing ages and how suffering was not what Christ expected of her. After much introspection, emotional changes and attitudinal shifts, she is giving her husband one year to seek help for his alcoholism. If he cannot take charge of his life she has told him and her family she will leave him in a year. She is not suffering anymore, and her friends and family acknowledge her courage.

I believe that depression occurs when we turn our anger, conflicts and grief into and against ourselves. When this happens our connection to our

Soul becomes weakened and often terminated. Can you emotionally relate to Piscean beliefs? Considering that your Soul has reincarnated many times during the Age of Pisces, can you imagine how angry you have likely been over 2,000 years of being taught that you can never honor or take care of yourself? Can you tap into the anger associated with having been treated for thousands of years as an inadequate, powerless child? Can you feel old frustrations that are now manifesting as ground glass in your body because spiritual authority figures have told you that you should be guilty and ashamed for not being perfect? Have you ever felt helpless because you have been trained to believe in extremes? This unconscious level of anger leads to what I call spiritual depression because it is eroding our sense of peace and well-being.

I recommend that you have the courage to feel these old, contaminated, angry feelings. The next step is to engage in a process that draws these old emotional toxins out of your bodies. My favorite anger exercise is to sit with your root chakra (located at the base of your spine) against a tree. Ground yourself by feeling the deep earth energy of the tree. Feel the tree's energy and draw it into your body at the base of your spine. As you are feeling it move into your body, change the energy into the color red. Allow the energy to circle your root chakra, remembering those Piscean beliefs that have made you angry over the years. Imagine that red turning into a dirty, toxic red. Then bring that color with all of its old anger up through your body, out of your right hand into the earth. You will begin to feel lighter and less depressed. Do this exercise once a week, and you will be amazed at how much better you feel.

Let's do another little exercise together. Think of a situation in your life that seems to have an either/or solution. Pay attention to your body: how are you feeling? Tense? Watch your hands: do they feel like making a fist? Go with that feeling and pay attention to how tight those fists can be. This is your body's reaction to an old Piscean belief that there are only two solutions to any problem. Lodged deep in our unconscious is a set of binary beliefs that has us viewing our lives through the limiting lens of good or evil, heaven or hell, black or white, right or wrong. I have spent many years coaching and teaching people to find their own unique path to independence from these outdated and imprisoning beliefs, hallmarks of the Age of Pisces. In all of my years of experience, I have seen that living a life of extremism seems to be the most difficult belief to change.

You have lived for two thousand years being brainwashed to believe in a simplistic, childish view that can lead to feeling tense, scared and often immobilized. How often do you believe that if you take an action it must be done "right" if not "perfect"? I would bet that this extreme attitude often stops you in your tracks toward accomplishing what's important to you and you end up doing nothing at all. So many clients tell me that they are chronic procrastinators and even lazy in their approach to life. I do not believe that procrastination is the culprit, and I certainly would not judge you as lazy. I would tell you that you are most likely afraid that you will not achieve the perfect results that you want and so you stop trying. Perfectionism is the culprit, not procrastination or laziness. If this sounds familiar to you, you are likely living in the throes of old Piscean beliefs.

TRANSFORMING PISCEAN BELIEFS

I wrote for five years for an online website called Spirit Crossing.org. One of my Spirit Crossing readers wrote: "I think it would be a good idea for you to rewrite your old Pisces beliefs as positive Pisces beliefs. These new beliefs can then be entered into our psyche." I think that is a good idea because I do not want any of you to think that we must scrub everything that we have learned in the Age of Pisces. I had another reader upset because she loves the energy of Pisces and doesn't want to lose it. She said, "I love the compassion and empathy of Pisces. Why would I want to lose that?" I agreed. We certainly do not want to do anything extreme, which is what we in fact need to avoid doing, based on our learning during the Pisces era! Clearly all of us want to hold onto the Piscean consciousness of love, compassion and forgiveness. We need, however, to let go of the beliefs that have caused us to feel weak, vulnerable, inadequate, and guilt ridden.

We are, at the onset of the Aquarian Age, coming away with the refined gold of Pisces, bringing with us its faith, compassion, goodness, and power. In my quest to integrate the Age of Pisces into the Age of Aquarius, I developed a transformed version of my table of old Pisces beliefs, which can be useful in guiding us to embrace the best of the Age of Pisces and to leave its destructive elements in the past.

Old Piscean Beliefs	Transformed Piscean Beliefs
Christ is the archetype of sacrifice and redemption	Christ is the archetype of love, forgiveness, and compassion
We must emulate Christ; therefore we must be martyrs and victims	We are free to emulate Christ and to live a life of love and grace
Christ is perfect; therefore we must strive for perfection	Christ symbolizes the perfection of God and has told us that the kingdom of God lies within us; therefore that piece of us is already perfect
We are sinful and should be filled with guilt; our journey is to be redeemed through penance and sacrifice	We have committed actions that have caused others pain, and we have the ability to ask for and receive forgiveness*
God exists outside of us. We are basically inadequate and child-like and need an external God to guide us and take care of us	God lives inside of us and we are empowered

The spiritual plane is more desirable than the material plane, so earthly pleasures are to be renounced for more spiritual pursuits	My spirit dwells within my earthly body and walks the earth that I honor and love; therefore I need to integrate spiritual and earthly values
Heaven (good) and Hell (evil) are the only choices of our earthly experience; therefore all important decisions also exist in an extreme right/wrong paradigm	The other side or Heaven welcomes all souls to learn, grow and find karmic balance in future lives; therefore we have many creative opportunities
Love conquers all so we must never be self-centered or love ourselves first	Loving our heart and soul is akin to loving God and provides us with the compassion to help others
Humility and compassion are morally correct so we must always turn the other cheek	Loving ourselves means that we honor and respect ourselves and maintain good boundaries that others may not cross
Religious authorities represent God's word on earth and must never be challenged	God's words come through our Souls into our hearts, and if we listen it will become our truth

*I believe, as Nelson Mandala said, that forgiveness is an act of self-love and freedom. It is my opinion that the most important spiritual quality that we needed to learn in the 2,000 years of the Age of Pisces is the power of Forgiveness.

And so, I call on us all to keep the treasures of the Age of Pisces while being open to embodying the new values of the Age of Aquarius, which represents the next phase of spiritual and emotional evolution that is awaiting us. Are we ready to be open with curiosity and wonder at the new possibilities of what the future can bring? As Albert Einstein noted in "The Merging of Spirit and Science" in 1954,

"The most beautiful and most profound experience is the sensation of the mystical. It is the source of all true science. He to whom this emotion is a stranger, who can no longer wonder, and stand rapt in, is as good as dead."

Here are some practice points for those of us ready to become transformed Piscean citizens. Be willing to:

- engage in love for experimentation, creativity, and inventiveness
- free ourselves from old, self-destructive, and sacrificial Piscean beliefs such as guilt, shame, suffering, and martyrdom
- manifest the art of forgiveness
- connect to the mind of God and to our Soul
- discover our inner dreamer and manifest our vision
- surrender ourselves to universal love
- develop our imagination and create magic in our lives
- use our night dreams to connect with our unconscious power
- make our unconscious minds our best friends
- seek personal independence with emotional and spiritual strength
- balance merging with the Universe with the individuation of self-boundaries
- embrace change and take actions to manifest transformed beliefs.

The Age of Pisces is now behind us. It serves as the ultimate prologue to the new age we are entering. *Discovering Your Soul Mission: How to Use Karmic Astrology to Create the Life You Want* was written at the end of the Age of Pisces. It has been revised and upgraded in the Age of Aquarius to help you navigate this new era, thus the book has been retitled as *Discovering Your Soul Mission: New Rules for a New Age.* Now let's get started!

—Linda and Michael Brady
November 2015

INTRODUCTION

You Have a Soul Mission

When people come to me for a counseling session, they usually want answers to their life questions: "Should I change my career? Why can't I find the right relationship? Why am I unhappy? What is my purpose in life?" It doesn't take me long to help them realize the fundamental reason they've sought my help: to discover their soul's direction and align their personality with it in order to create harmony in their lives.

Through my use of karmic astrology, I serve as a soul translator, to remind them about what their soul has created for them in their life and why. I am not a predictive astrologer; I will not tell anyone's future. I will, however, use an astrological chart to gain information about their past, their relationships, and their soul mission. As a practicing astrologer for almost forty years, I am constantly amazed at how perfectly an astrological chart captures the feelings, concerns, memories, hopes, and desires of the people I serve. As a commentator, I make no judgments and offer no advice that isn't already present in their chart.

For thousands of years astrologers have read charts, determined planetary positions, and analyzed how the alignment of the stars affects people's lives. In fact, astrology's origins can be traced as far back as 2000 B.C. to Babylonia, in what is now the southeastern portion of Iraq. To this day, people continue to go to astrologers in the hope of regaining some control over their lives by hearing how their life will be played out: to brace themselves for a malady or to prime themselves for incipient good fortune. Implicit in those meetings is the immutability of that future. Their fate is only to anticipate what will befall them. That the power of predictive astrology originated from some external force in the heavens above fits neatly into our fundamental religious belief that God was an external power separate and apart from us.

Traditional astrology's value to us lies in its ability to help us understand ourselves. But the practice implies that our life choices are made by someone or something else. Traditional astrology maintains that our chart—with its houses, planets, and aspects—is the determining factor in our lives. This deterministic claim has led to astrology being mocked in recent times. But astrology—as a symbolic language—helps cultivate a deeper understanding of the connection between the inner and outer worlds—nature and the heavens. As Will Keepin, Ph.D., says, "Astrology [is ridiculed] because it bridges the implicate and explicate orders more clearly than any other esoteric science that I know of."

Karmic astrology is about making informed and expanded choices, on the assumption that our soul is the primary force behind us forging our destiny and is never-ending. While traditional astrology implies that we abdicate responsibility for what befalls us to the cosmos, karmic astrology equips us with the understanding to shape our life the way we want it to be.

On her audiotape series "Inner and Outer Space," Caroline W. Casey explains that astrology is a language of self-possession, revitalizing and connecting us to all creation. She says astrology can help us unleash our own distinct energies so we can be creative agents for positive change in the world.

"Men at some time are masters of their fates:
The fault, dear Brutus, is not in our stars But
in ourselves, that we are underlings."

—**William Shakespeare,** *Julius Caesar*

Traditional Astrology	Karmic Astrology
1. Planet centered	Person centered
2. Predictive	Creative
3. Event oriented	Process oriented
4. Fate	Free will
5. Implies external power	Implies self-empowerment
6. Scientific	Multisensory
7. Old Age/representing an external God	New Age/representing the God in all of us

Perhaps the best metaphor for comparing traditional astrology with karmic astrology comes from Casey's citation of the late quantum physicist and Albert Einstein colleague David Bohm. An airplane, Bohm said, uses radio waves to guide it, but the radio waves do not cause the plane to turn. The radio waves simply supply the pilot with information upon which he or she must act. Similarly in karmic astrology, unlike the common perception of traditional astrology, the planet and stars in the firmament don't force fate upon us, causing us to behave in certain, deterministic ways. On the contrary, they provide us with symbols that feed our intuition, helping to connect us to our soul path.

ALIGNING YOUR PERSONALITY WITH YOUR SOUL

Each of us has a personality with a corresponding road to travel and a destination to reach within our given lifetime. The journey will be filled with relationships, work, challenges and obstacles, trials and triumphs. Each of us also has a soul with its own destination and a road to follow, a road that began in the distant past and will continue forever. However, the soul has a plan, a purpose for our personality in this life. The soul's intention is to assist the personality in its life journey, to help it reach the destination that the soul intends for it.

Too often these roads are divergent. The experiences of our lives— enacted with our families, our relationships, and sometimes our jobs— often influence our personality's direction, sometimes causing it to stray or simply veer off altogether from the path our soul intends for it. Most of us, in fact, are beset with inner conflicts arising from a clash between our soul and our personality, a phenomenon that can manifest itself as sorrow, depression, anger, a gnawing lack of fulfillment or deep emptiness. The challenge for us, as budding spiritual adults, is to find the soul road on which our personality can prosper. I call this process soul/personality integration, and I have dedicated my life to understanding it.

My own personality path, for instance, is to be a loner, a recluse, venturing out only to teach astrology. My personality would be very content if I were a traveling astrologer: doing a quick session here and there with no lasting relationships would be just fine. But my soul path is quite different. Its mission is to create and commit to long-term relationships, and to inspire my students to deal with their spiritual and emotional lives. For my soul, there is no being a recluse, no being alone.

My evolution into spiritual adulthood began when I starting learning astrology. I was trained in experimental psychology and behavior modification. I have a bachelor's degree in psychology and a master's in educational administration. I believed in what could be measured, analyzed, and charted. I also believed in Christ, the Episcopal church, and its mysteries in a childlike, naive way. I did not question; I had faith. But life has a way of intruding on faith, and my faith did not stand the test.

I began my study of astrology in an earnest quest to disprove it, but I found instead that it gave me answers. Even more important, it gave me questions. The idea that the stars wielded the energy to create the perfect chart for me had always made me uncomfortable: it meant that I was not in control of my life and that I could blame the stars for my problems, including my struggles with my weight. (I have a moon in Pisces—it loves rich foods.) As my understanding of astrology grew, however, the answer became quite clear: my soul had created my astrological chart. My soul knew the symbolic meanings of all the astrological signs and planets and the relationships between them. It had created an astrological mandala to provide me with the tools I needed to experience my life.

My soul knew my past; it had been there. My soul knew what this life needed to be as a continuation of what was left from other lives. My soul, in other words, understood my karma. Although this word has been maligned, ridiculed, and misunderstood, karma has a relatively simple meaning for me. It means if I take an action, I set up a reaction. We have all heard this rephrased in the axioms "What goes around, comes around" and "We reap what we sow." It is an energetic, universal, and physical law. Karma continues from one life to another. If I betray you in a past life, I can expect that you will betray me in our next one.

Karma is complete only when we have balanced our previous actions through consciousness, commitment, and new actions. Our soul knows these situations and relationships and will create opportunities for us to resolve them. Our astrological chart, created by our soul, provides us with information about these karmic experiences as a spiritual reminder, a road map to understanding.

Even with all of these philosophical insights, I remember the conflicts I had when I first began to entertain the real possibility that all my life experiences were perfect and for my ultimate good. My personality and ego ranted and raved for days. I was a litany of "what about this" and "what about that." I thought about the scores of hardships and tragedies, the rampant pain and injustice in our world. Why would a loving God and compassionate soul put us through such trauma? The answer becomes more apparent when we see our lives as part of a larger whole.

Sometimes, in order to create a karmic balance and to rectify a past life injustice, we "create" experiencing pain. I have often thought of the childhood and life that Adolf Hitler would have to create to begin his process of karmic retribution. Without karmic understanding, the tragedies of life—pain, disease, accidents, violence, loss, and betrayal—appear arbitrary. With it, life is fair. Always. We can't whitewash an agonizing experience, but if we are aware that it will yield us a better understanding, a better sense of why, it doesn't seem as arbitrary.

My soul was in the process of teaching me something that my ego did not want to understand. I had spent forty years believing that I was basically imperfect—a belief fostered by my family and society at large—and that the only way to change that was to strive for perfection. It never occurred to me that perfection could exist at any given moment. I had spent eighteen years in schools that had measured me by a strict criterion. I knew the ecstasy of straight A's and the agony of a D in high school chemistry. Now my beliefs were in serious conflict. How would I motivate myself to excellence with a conviction that I was imperfect?

Becoming bored with the same conflict, I decided to review what striving for perfection had really done in my life. What I learned shocked me: striving for perfection had taught me procrastination and feelings of inadequacy, failure, and fear. It had put me on a treadmill, always searching and never finding. It had taught me to value the end product and disregard the process. I made a decision to let the old belief die. Perfection goals are not so perfect! I transformed this old belief into a commitment to being the best that I could be, valuing the process of life, and entrusting my soul to create my life perfectly.

What is the perfection that my soul wants me to see in its many creations? How would that experience serve me? When I was 31, I decided to go back to school and earn a doctorate in psychology. I was accepted at a fine university and held a great evening position at a local hospital. I was poised to advance my career. Two months before I was to begin my Ph.D., however, I was involved in a head-on automobile collision. The accident left me with a back injury and vision problems. I was unable to start school in the fall.

During that time my surrogate father died, I separated from my second husband, and I sank into a severe depression—it was not a "perfect" three months. The truth is it was the most crucial, most important turning point of my life. After I recovered from both my mental and my physical wounds, my soul led me back to an institution for the mentally handicapped where I had worked several years before. I became a diagnostic specialist and later vice principal. I saw my first aura there. I began my process of understanding reincarnation there. I met my third husband and soul mate there. I became an astrologer while I was there. My soul created that automobile accident to change my life's direction and to put me on the path to my soul mission.

Think about your own life. Try to recall one particularly painful experience. Feel the emotions that the memory evokes. Now ask yourself the following questions: Why did I bring this experience into my life? What opportunity for growth and awareness did it provide me? What did it teach me about myself or someone else? How did it change my life for the better? By asking yourself these sensitive questions, note how your perspective changes, and think about some of the new insights you may have developed.

YOUR SOUL

Your soul is the common thread that weaves all of your personalities from your past and present lives together, the multidimensional part of you that transcends this life, that exceeds the here and now. Your soul is your continuity expert, ensuring that each of the personalities from various lifetimes performs its essential role in your grand drama. It supplies you with the past life link you need in order to understand your karmic responsibilities in this life, and it helps you carry them out.

"The soul is the captain and ruler of the life of mortals."

—**Sallust**

Your soul provides you with a plan, revealing it to you through dreams, symbols, your unconscious mind, your relationships, and your experiences. The soul holds the reason for your personality to exist and grow. It is the essence of your spiritual core, the energy of truth and love unfettered by the external stimuli that affect your personality.

"Now I lay me down to sleep,
I pray the Lord my soul to keep;
If I should die before I wake,
I pray the Lord my soul to take."

—**Prayer from *The New England Primer*, 1784**

While we have become inured to reciting the words soul and spirit in our prayers seemingly by rote, their meanings continue to be misunderstood. The two words mean the same thing, but religions tend to use the word spirit in the context of the afterlife, while soul has a more secular usage in the context of living a fulfilling and meaningful life. Soul/personality integration is about improving the quality of your life now by embracing and nurturing your soul on a daily basis.

"Either death is a state of nothingness and utter unconsciousness, or as men say, there is a change and migration of the soul from this world to another. . . . Now if death be of such a nature, I say that to die is to gain; for eternity is then only a single night."

—**Plato**

WHAT WE KNOW ABOUT THE SOUL

Generally, the soul is:

- *Immortal*: It is energy that cannot be created or destroyed.
- *Perfect*: It is our gift from God and is intrinsically connected to the Universal Order.
- *Love*: It is the opportunity during our lifetime to change fear to love.
- *Our spiritual creator*: It provides perfect experiences for our karmic growth.
- *A filter*: Through it information comes from the higher realms.
- *Transcendent*: It is transcendent both before and after this lifetime.

Personally, the soul is:

- Your spiritual companion and best friend.
- Your creator of your soul mission.
- Your guide to directing you to your soul's mission.
- Your continuity expert, keeping track of your past and creating your future.

YOUR PERSONALITY

Your personality is the specific lens through which you see your current lifetime. Its lucidity and focus are constantly being adjusted almost instantaneously by your vast and varied experiences. Through this lens you react to the world and make judgments about it. It is the part of you that responds, often impulsively, to the ebbs and flows of life, at various turns fortified and scarred by the ups and downs of your emotions. Your personality is your social and emotional template, helping you distinguish who you are. It encompasses your thoughts, morality, feelings, senses, motivations, and dreams, and it carries the indelible stamp of your family history.

On an unconscious level, your personality links you to your seminal belief system learned from your parents; the hidden child within you; memories and pain not dealt with in your conscious life; and your night dreams, fears, and phobias. At this deep level, it also remembers personalities you've had from other lives and important information about who and what you have been. These memories of the thoughts, actions, and feelings of previous personalities share a common thread with you now, and they become the source of much of your unconscious motivation, impulse, angst, and relationship challenges. Unlike your soul, your personality does not transcend this life.

"Your personality is that part of you that was born into, lives within, and will die within time. To be a human and have a personality are the same thing. Your personality, like your body, is the vehicle of your evolution."

—**Gary Zukav**, *Seat of the Soul*

COSMIC TWO-BY-FOURS

Suppose you lose your job. Your spouse or partner leaves. You get sick. Your journey on the personality road winds to a crawl. You get scared, stuck, and stressed out. You get depressed. The skills that delivered you to the roadblock in the first place don't help. Nothing works. Your personality doesn't know what your soul requires—it only knows that it doesn't want you to change, which leaves you mired in a powerful soul/personality conflict. You should view this turbulence, rattling you to the core, as a signal that you've arrived at a junction. Now you can discover solutions to issues that have long vexed you, by using an approach that differs drastically from the one that delivered you to the roadblock in the first place.

It is usually at this crisis point that people show up at my office for the first time. Imagine their surprise when I smile and say, "Congratulations." I am, in fact, reframing conflict into opportunity. Their souls have adroitly created the necessary roadblocks, with perfect timing. These obstacles are their souls' way of providing them with a deeper awareness of the other road they need to travel.

I frequently refer to these roadblocks as cosmic two-by-fours, which are meant to get our attention and prepare us for a major karmic insight. A cosmic two-by-four is actually an experience created for us by our soul to stop us in our tracks and draw our attention to a behavior or habit we were unable to detect previously.

According to Swiss psychologist Carl Jung, the more we repress a behavior, the more likely we will be to create the behavior outside ourselves as chaos or conflict. A cosmic two-by-four is my name for the chaos and conflict to which Jung referred. It is our soul's way of giving us a new perspective on our life, enabling us to see what heretofore had been invisible. The impact of a cosmic two-by-four varies in severity from a reminding tap on the shoulder to what feels like a mind-splitting whack across the head. Since most of us are not conditioned to notice the smaller, less pronounced taps, cosmic two-by-fours become increasingly powerful until one finally gets our attention. Experiencing a cosmic two-by-four affords us the opportunity to stop, collect ourselves, and hopefully alter our behavior. My husband Michael describes the more extreme instances we encounter as "getting our worlds stopped."

When you become cognizant of how untenable your current path is, and when you realize there might be a more fulfilling road to travel, you are ready to discover your soul's purpose on a conscious level. As you read on, you will not only discover that road to fulfillment—your raison d'être—but you'll learn how to embrace it and live it every day.

PART I
SOUL CREATION: TAKING CONTROL OF YOUR LIFE

CHAPTER 1

CREATING OUR OWN LIVES

D o you believe that you possess some measure of responsibility for the way the experiences and events in your life unfold? When I ask my clients if they "create their own lives," more often than not they say yes. After all, personal accountability is a spiritually correct philosophy currently on the rise. However, when they experience a specific tragedy in their own lives—a divorce, the death of a loved one, the loss of a job—many of the same clients respond by saying, "But I didn't create that."

A general misperception exists about the theory of creation. Many believe it is a conscious and intellectual experience: creating goals and committing to them, as well as planning proactive stratagems for organizing and affirming them. Some of us believe—and many recent books reinforce the point—that if we visualize a positive outcome, create a mantra and

3

concentrate on it consistently, and take actions that support the creation, we will get what we want.

Others believe that life creation is an unconscious process whose rudiments lie in our psychology. Jung, for instance, believed that we tend to repress and store in our unconscious the emotions and beliefs with which we are the most uncomfortable. Later, at a time it deems appropriate, our unconscious mind brings those averse feelings to the fore of our conscious mind and creates them externally. In other words, Jung said, we project an unconscious part of ourselves onto the people in our lives. For instance, if you've repressed all of your aggressive anger, then you would project that aggressive anger onto one of your close friends or a family member, whom you would see as having those same aggressive qualities, so that you could learn from them. While our unconscious, intellect, and emotions all play important roles in creating our lives, I believe they are complements to the fundamental role that our soul plays in life creation. Why do we create our lives to be the way they are, with their distinct experiences and relationships? Because our soul yearns for us to have that life in order to learn new lessons and evolve to a higher spiritual order. Soul creation is the practice of taking ultimate responsibility for the way our lives transpire. Our souls create exactly the lives we need.

The difference between our intellect, our emotions, and our soul, however, is that our intellect and emotions are related only to our personality and its current life experiences. The task of creating our life comes from our soul, a dimension that transcends this life and its permutations.

"Welcome, O life! I go to encounter for the millionth time the reality of experience and to forge in the smithy of my soul the uncreated conscience of my race."

—**James Joyce**, *Portrait of the Artist as a Young Man*

I know how difficult it can be to distinguish the domain of our souls from the orientations and motivations of our minds and bodies; I see this challenge almost every day in my work with my clients and interns. A workshop I conducted for an AIDS support group in Washington, D.C. made me painfully aware of how difficult it can be to discern the role of the soul in creation. Ironically, the surge in interest in the mind/body connection has somehow made this process even more confusing.

The AIDS support group consisted of nine men—all infected with HIV—who had been using a holistic orientation to treat their illness. They had adopted macrobiotic diets and used visualization and meditative techniques as part of their belief and exploration into the mind/body connection and its healing potential. They met on a weekly basis to discuss and review the progress being made in alternative treatments.

In my workshop I explained to them that what was missing in their mind/body philosophy was the understanding of their souls' creation of reality. Our soul creates our life with a certain purpose, I said, and thus there were reasons why they had "created" their illness. In other words, I continued, our soul presents us with life possibilities, and sometimes illness is one of those possibilities. I posited that having AIDS was an event that each of their respective souls had needed them to experience. Having AIDS enabled each of them to meet new people that their souls wanted them to meet and to follow a path that they wouldn't have taken otherwise.

They reacted angrily, taking my brief explanation to mean that they had "created" AIDS consciously, a notion that would only add to their guilt and shame and further damage their already fragile physical and emotional well-being. They thought I was implying they had deliberately brought on their own illnesses. They could not tolerate that belief, which they found demeaning and offensive. I understood why these young men were so upset—and justifiably so. The medical community, and to a greater degree the media, have perpetuated the notion that AIDS is a behavioral by-product of promiscuous gay male sex and/or intravenous drug use.

Since contracting the disease is sometimes tied to behavior, they were deeply offended at what they thought was my inference that they had purposely gone out and contracted AIDS.

It was not their fault, I told them. They shouldn't feel guilty about having AIDS, and they shouldn't judge their previous behaviors that might have led to their contracting the disease. I spoke about the soul and the reasons why it might create illness. As soon as they were able to detach themselves from their shame and guilt and understand their souls' respective motivations from a karmic standpoint—that their souls were perhaps balancing past life experiences with their encounter with AIDS in this life—they were able to see the bigger picture and were more receptive to my message.

"If our souls are loving and compassionate, why would they do such a terrible thing?" they wanted to know, a question all my clients ask when confronted with tragedy. I explained that as soon as we are better able to comprehend our lives in the context of a grander scheme, we begin to see our experiences not as good or bad but as inordinately fair lessons that our souls need in order to evolve to a higher order. I wasn't seeking to diminish the emotional and physical ramifications of AIDS. Rather, I was explaining how they could make some spiritual sense of their disease: how to learn and grow from the experience, to consider what impact it has had on others, and what has happened in their lives as a result. Difficult lives are not punishments, but rather opportunities for astonishingly spiritual growth.

"We're here to participate joyfully
in the sorrows of the world."

—Joseph Campbell

A few of the men began relaying stories of powerful transformational experiences that they had encountered since finding out they were infected with the disease. One of the men, Tim, 27, said that getting AIDS was "the most significant thing that ever happened" to him. He offered this observation after discovering that his soul had "so many things in mind for me." He was a vice president of a Washington, D.C., bank and he hated being a banker. After contracting AIDS, he left his job to become an artist.

Most important, the disease allowed Tim to become more honest and open with his family. Prior to becoming HIV positive, his relationship with his family had been serviceable at best. It's not that they didn't know he was gay; they just didn't readily acknowledge it. His relationship with them was safe and anesthetized: his parents buffered themselves from the pain and disappointment of having a gay son. Once he got sick and his mother and father realized they might lose him, their attitude changed. Their burdensome judgments over who Tim had become and the choices he had made dissipated, and they began to cherish him for what he was: their "only boy." Now he is more emotionally connected to his parents than ever before. They discuss treatments with him and are curious to know more about AIDS. His father makes periodic trips to the nearby college's medical library to research the disease. Tim talked about how the disease had liberated him: he and the other men began to see how getting AIDS was leading them to their respective soul missions. Considering their future with this new philosophical outlook gave the men power, hope, and a sense of completion.

Another man from the AIDS support group, John, had subsequent sessions with me; he recounts the progress he has made and how his life has been different since participating in the workshop:

Shortly before I began working with Linda, I learned I was HIV positive. I was twenty-eight, single, and working in a job that neither challenged me nor helped me realize my potential. I was depressed and generally feeling defeated and fatalistic toward life. My doctor had me convinced that I should wrap things up and prepare to die in less than two years (a common diagnosis for someone with HIV in 1987).

By learning and adopting the fundamentals of soul creation, of taking responsibility for all the misfortune in my life—including AIDS—I was able to see that I held the choices I needed to turn these things around. I had to make changes in my personal and family relationships, own my sexuality, redesign my finances and career thinking, and in general adopt a thought process and life philosophy that, at the time, scared the hell out of me. I had to learn to jump off cliffs that were higher than I could possibly imagine. I had to take the risk of revealing myself not only to those I encountered, but to myself as well, and that was the most difficult part. "Creating my own reality" meant learning to love this new image of myself.

In time I learned how to let my intuition guide me to people and situations that I never guessed were out there. I found new work, new relationships, and new ways to manifest my creativity as well as a profound understanding of how my world worked. I am now thirty-six. I haven't died of AIDS. In fact I have empowered myself and many others to live far beyond our medical deadlines. My immune system is stronger than ever due to my growth and understanding of alternative therapies and self-healing techniques. I have been in a relationship for more than six years. I live in Tucson and look out of my home to mountain views and magnificent sunsets. I do the kind of work I want and don't limit my options. I had spent most of my life trapped inside myself not knowing if I was crazy or not, unclear about who I was and what I had to offer. Not anymore.

I had to allow myself to act intuitively and fully trust that the risk of speaking to anyone from the soul and heart was worth taking in order to find the joy that is available to all of us. The healing from this is a great reward, the prosperity endless. However, this journey is a great challenge, and it isn't over yet. I am just over the first big hill; and with any luck I will find many more. I have created a splendorous and expansive reality. I didn't give up and surrender to the great weakness or spirit that sabotages us. I didn't die from AIDS.

"You want to live your longest healthiest life? Find your way, your path. Be in touch with your soul."

—**Bernie Siegel**, M.D.

We often become discouraged in the pursuit of our goals and dreams when we fail to exact the results we had envisioned. When things don't go our way, we stop striving, unceremoniously cutting short what could have been a fulfilling and meaningful journey. We turn a deaf ear to the realm of possibility.

Unless we accept serendipity as an invaluable link to our potential, we are hard pressed to live with verve, to celebrate and revel in our soul missions. Good things seem to happen to some people, while we sit on the sidelines. But who are those people who land the big job that we can't seem to get, who have the intensely passionate relationship that we envy? They are the ones who have faith that something good will come from serendipitous events, whether it be a learning experience or a positive twist of fate. But when we are paralyzed by our own fear of failure, limited by our own internal rules, we exude negative energy and obsess over why things didn't turn out the way we planned.

Serendipity is an unexpected outcome that stems from taking an action. The only way we can adopt serendipity as a personal creed is to let go of committing ourselves emotionally to a single desired outcome. The outcome we expect comes from our intellect, our conscious mind. Too often we are restricted by the myopia of our intellect, by its willingness to accept only one anticipated scenario. Looking at the spectrum of choices with our soul allows us to diversify our expectations, to realize that the possibility of the unexpected—with some adjustments—can be better than anything we imagined.

I agree with today's cadre of self-help experts who say we need to set goals and take decisive action through vision and commitment. The key to ensuring success, however, hinges not on the exact result itself but on our ability to learn from and stay pliant during the process, no matter what the outcome. Successful people gain by rebuilding, revamping, and reconfiguring. We may see them as lucky, but they've been busy building on their own serendipity, embracing it as a springboard to accomplishment. So remember: stay receptive to other possibilities.

By enhancing the communication between your personality and soul, you are creating a conversation that gives you an expanded positive view of the meaning of your life's experiences. Here's an example. Your boss calls you into his office. His face has a look of urgency that you haven't seen before. You sense this isn't going to be a pleasant chat. You sit down, and he adjusts his tie, and without looking directly at you, he tells you that he's "letting you go." You're fired. You've heard him, but you deny it inside. You feel scared. Your mind races. You think about the new house you just bought. How will you pay the mortgage and the kids' bills? Now you're angry. How dare he fire you! You've always been a very conscientious worker, totally committed to the company. Then you begin to feel guilty and ashamed: *What could I have done wrong to deserve this?*

The range of emotions—anger, fear, shame, guilt, embarrassment—that flow forth is typical of your personality's response to a traumatic event, in this case, the news you've been fired. Now imagine you are practiced at bringing your soul's perspective to your experiences. Here's how your soul might orchestrate a conversation with your personality:

I know you're really upset about this, as well you should be. It's okay that you're intensely emotional about being fired. But let's start to work on finding the meaning, purpose, and serendipity of the situation. Try to answer these questions. It's all right if you're too upset to answer all of them now. Just try to ask yourself these questions, and you can figure out the answers later:

- Why have I (your soul) created this situation for you, and what can you learn from it?
- How will this experience ultimately help you achieve your soul mission?
- What is the possible serendipity of this challenge?

WHY WE HAVE TROUBLE BELIEVING IN SOUL CREATION

Like the men in the AIDS support group, most of us have difficulty coming to terms with the fact that the spiritual part of us has a role in creating an event or relationship that knocks the wind out of us. However, our souls play just as essential a role in our encounters with the fantastic and the enchanting. Again, to reiterate: our souls base an experience not on whether it is good or bad, but on what lessons we can learn from it.

"I only believe what I can see.
Or what I know is true.
Argument against what I can see:
Electricity, emotions."
—**Linda Brady**, 1997

Soul creation is an effective process that helps us eliminate feelings of victimization. Yet many of us still experience those feelings on a daily basis.

I have been engaging in soul creation conversations with myself every day for the last fifteen years, but on occasion, even I can't help feeling like a victim—one of the most basic and reflexive of human emotions—when I feel I've been misunderstood or disrespected.

That's why you must practice being aware of soul creation every minute of every hour of every day. As you ingrain it into your belief system as a prevailing philosophy, you will minimize your tendency to react like a victim. While I acknowledge that it can be tiring to maintain such an intense self-awareness, it's important for you to keep practicing soul creation. You will stumble, and like all of us, you will have bad days when you can't help but feel victimized.

However, the end product—the quality of your life and the degree to which you are happy and fulfilled—will take care of itself.

Darlene went through a period when she figured that the calamities in her life entitled her to feel like a victim. However, her ability to adopt a belief in soul creation helped her embrace a different, more liberating path:

> *In 1975 at the age of twenty-five, I felt like a victim of the world, powerless to alter my life circumstances. On some level, I was waiting for the money pressures, heart trouble, lung trouble, lower back trouble, diabetes, negativity, depression, and boredom that were part of my family history to be mine. In October of that year, my mother hung herself in our back yard. She was forty-eight. Later that same year my fiancé ended our five-year relationship, and my grandmother had passed on the year before on New Year's Day. Now I had even more ammunition for believing the world was out to get me. I had some great excuses for self-pity. Who could blame me?*
>
> *For a number of years I was resistant to the belief that we create what happens to us, because it meant I would have to change. This*

new philosophy asked that I find my soul's direction and purpose, commit to it, and live life in that direction. When I finally began to adopt creation theory, these changes were quite scary and often confusing. It meant a change in my identity and the way that I had lived my life until then. No more excuses! No more blame! It wasn't easy. During that confusing and transitional time, it was easy to accept the creation of the "good" things—not so easy to "own" my creations of the painful. Now my life would be my personal responsibility.

Two months after I had begun working with Linda, I was in an automobile accident. I called her from my hospital bed, expecting, I suppose, to be told that this would be an exception to the creation "rule." After a few minutes of making sure I was okay, she asked me the big question: "Why do you think your soul created this, Darlene?" I didn't know the answer then. It took weeks of reflection and struggle. Finally I came to understand that the accident represented a turning point for me. It was an opportunity to truly practice what I had been learning. I created that accident to learn in a powerful way that my soul did, in fact, create my life. It was a chance to leap out of my personality and ego and leap into the unknown abyss of what was best for my soul. Staying in old patterns, although familiar and comfortable, would have been even more painful. I took the risk and accepted my soul's creation of the accident. I healed very quickly, did not blame the elderly gentleman who was driving the car that hit my car, and learned a valuable lesson.

From there, events in my life flowed more easily, and I felt a tremendous sense of freedom. I was no longer stuck. It has been fifteen years since I came to realize that I have the power to create exactly what I want from life. It required only that I decide what I wanted. I finally learned to see obstacles as challenges. I embrace even the most painful experiences, because it means I am alive and doing my soul's work. I see my relationships, my work, and my health as conscious choices. I approach life from a more aware and empowered perspective. I am no longer a victim. I have inner peace.

YOUR SOUL'S IMPACT

Answering some of these questions will help you to see the more obvious instances in your life where your soul has made a palpable impact.

- Have you ever had an experience that was so weird that you couldn't explain it?
- Have you ever felt déjà vu?
- Have you ever known someone was going to call you and they did?
- Have you ever felt watched over or protected?
- Have you ever felt the presence of someone who has died?
- Have you ever heard a little voice inside you say something that you had never contemplated before?
- Have you ever felt a gentle caress when no one was there?
- Have you ever taken a wrong turn that led you to an unexpected experience?
- Have you ever felt energy from a person, a plant, or an animal?
- Have you ever felt strongly attracted or repulsed by a person you just met for no logical reason?
- Have you ever felt strongly attracted or repulsed by a color, a gem, or a flower?
- Have you ever felt irresistibly drawn to a country, or a time in history, for no reason?
- Did you have any childhood experiences that were unusual?
- Have you ever just known that a situation or a person was "right" for you and acted on it?

- Have you ever felt deep emotions about something without a reason?
- Have you ever been stopped from doing something that you later discovered would have been harmful to you?

Cliff, 38, had been referred to me by a longtime client of mine, Wendy. She had told me he would see me but warned me he would be "tough." He didn't believe in religion, astrology, or anything else. But Wendy was worried about him: he was at the tail end of a painful separation from his girlfriend, Sylvia, and was not handling it well. He had seen a psychiatrist for a few weeks, but he felt the therapy wasn't working. He was depressed, hopeless, and angry.

Cliff made an appointment with me a few days later. As he sat down on the sofa in my office, he smiled wanly and said: "I'm really doing this under protest, you know. Wendy wouldn't stop nagging me until I had at least one session with you." I retorted, "So I have one shot to convince you of something. Okay, Cliff, I'll take that challenge. Tell me how you felt when you met Sylvia. Your first impression, your first thoughts."

Cliff paused a moment and then said. "You know, I felt like I had met her before. I felt so strongly about her. I can't believe it's over. I felt like I had finally found the woman I would live with forever."

When I asked him about his parents, he said that his mother had died when he was 21. "Have you felt her presence since she died?" I asked.

"Not really," he answered, "but I always wear her wedding ring on my small finger. Sometimes I swear I can feel a gentle wind gliding over it. I'm sure it's my imagination, but it happens sometimes."

"Cliff, this may sound like a strange question for me to ask, but is your favorite color lavender?" I knew from his chart that lavender was his soul color.

Cliff was befuddled and agitated. I thought he was going to get up and walk out.

I reached over and touched his arm. "Lavender is your soul color, Cliff, and judging from the way you look right now, it has some significance to you, doesn't it?"

Cliff poised himself, straightened his body, and answered, "It was my mother's favorite color. I made sure the flowers at her funeral were predominantly lavender. I planted lilacs in my backyard to remind me of her. This is getting very weird. I really don't know how to feel about any of this."

"Cliff, you said when you walked in that you only believed in what you could see. I'm trying to help you realize that there are other things in your life that have been very powerful and important that have nothing to do with physical reality. The experiences that you recounted have to do with an energetic or spiritual reality. They are just as significant, just as real as anything that you can see or touch. We could hypothesize that they were all orchestrated by your soul, couldn't we?" I asked.

Cliff answered a little haltingly. "Okay, so let's say I agree that it's a possibility. How could it help me?" he asked.

"Well, for one thing it could help you understand why the color lavender is so important," I said. "Understanding your soul could provide you with inner peace. It could help you deal with your depression, lessen your conflicts, and make sense of what has happened in your life. It could also help you make sense of your relationship with Sylvia. Why it felt so familiar and why it ended. You might even find out what other karmic experiences you've had with Sylvia that led to this breakup. Wouldn't that help you right now?"

Cliff nodded. "I am in so much pain that anything you can do to help would be appreciated. I can tell you that for some reason I do feel better. I'm willing to give this a try."

We scheduled our next meeting, and Cliff left a little happier and more at ease than when he arrived. In the ensuing sessions we concentrated on his painful breakup with Sylvia. We worked together for more than a year on a regular basis. Three years later I met his new love and did her chart. Now I counsel them together as clients. They are committed to each other and their soul missions.

SOUL CREATION AND CHANGE

Belief in soul creation challenges not only two thousand years of history but even, to some extent, our principles and morality. Many of us will consider migrating from the status quo only when our circumstances have become so horrible that anything would be better. Having nothing to lose sometimes gives us everything to gain, because at that point our fear of change has diminished and change is the only thing that will transform the situation.

I have clients whom I've sent home, requesting they not call me again until their lives are unbearable. As heartless as this may sound, many of us won't even entertain the notion of making changes in our lives until we reach such a point. How often have you heard about a smoker who passionately adheres to his right to smoke, until he almost dies of a heart attack? Most of us have the same unhealthy tendency to cling to what is familiar until it almost ruins us. Yet to achieve our soul mission, we must embrace change—and to understand soul creation, we must practice it.

One new client, Ann, was referred to me by her sister. Ann was 40 years old and continued to live with her mother in the same house she was born in. Her most distinguishing characteristic was her reticence. She was so nervous to be in our first session alone that her sister had to stay with us. Through her sister I learned that she was still living at home, caring for her elderly mother. Her mother was relatively healthy for a woman of 70 but endured occasional spells of vertigo. In fact, about ten years earlier Ann had been offered a promising job in a neighboring state. She had wanted to take the job but turned it down when her mother complained that her vertigo was worsening.

Ann took an office job near her home instead. She spent her free time watching television with her mother. Her sister was worried that she was wasting away her life, but Ann said she was perfectly content. In fact, Ann was comfortable and felt safe. She admitted to hating anything that disrupted her routine. She listened politely when I described her soul mission but had no response. Surprisingly, however, she made another appointment. At the third session I suggested to her that she not come back. I finally elicited a minor response: she was surprised by my comment. I told her that her life was not difficult enough for her to want to alter anything, and that her greatest fear was of change. When she was better prepared to take action, I would love to see her, I said.

It took Ann two years to return. Her mother had met a man, and they were going to be married. They had asked Ann, in so many words, to move out. She was devastated and scared—and furious with her mother. Now we could make some progress. She listened to what I said about her soul mission and began to create her own freedom by leaving her comfort zones and moving into the world. She planned her first real vacation, a critical step in gaining the courage to finally embrace her own experiences and independence. She soon overcame her fear of leaving home, unshackling herself from the only life she knew. Her progress helped her overcome her anger toward her mother. She was brighter, more vibrant than I had ever seen her. She received a promotion at work.

In my own life my fledgling belief in soul creation was put to the test in 1980. My boyfriend Michael and I had been living together for two years and had just moved into our first house. Then one night Michael told me he had had an affair. I felt as if I had been thrown from a horse. Michael was my soul mate. For twelve hours I cried and screamed at him for doing this to me. The pain that I felt was unbearable: I was angry, scared, and confused.

I remember sitting in our backyard, staring at an old oak tree, silently screaming at my soul. The whole concept of soul creation was new to me then; I was just beginning to understand it, and now my soul had done this. It was so unfair, I couldn't stand it. The next morning Michael reluctantly went to work. I was alone with my pain. I sat for a long time trying to make sense of it all. In the end I finally understood that my soul had created this crisis so I could prove to myself that I truly believed what I said about soul creation. I profoundly changed that day, my new practice safe from my own doubt.

I canceled my evening appointments, grabbed my dog Ti, and drove to the hospital where Michael worked. We met in the picnic area. I told him that I knew my soul had created this situation and that although it would take a while, I would figure out all the details of that creation. Our relationship survived, and we were married six months later. Our marriage is strong today because of that moment. We both live in our relationship now, knowing that we are soul mates and confident that our souls will continue to provide us with experiences to strengthen it.

My belief in my soul as the creator of my reality and as my spiritual companion got me through that experience with Michael, and it will get me through others. Change and new experiences are what our souls require to help us migrate to the exciting, powerful, and joyful lives we want. One of the emotions we feel when we are confronted with change is fear. But being afraid to do something yet doing it anyway is called courage.

Despite our inert tendencies, change is the ultimate reality. Every day we change, internally and externally. Cells die, hair grows. We think or feel something we haven't thought or felt before. The change may seem negligible, but it's dynamic nonetheless. Weather changes, the earth changes, seasons change, our scenery changes. The tree in our backyard changes, politics change, the news changes. We witness change on a daily basis, yet most of us are unaware of it. Our souls know the truth, and each day they seek to teach us that basic principle.

TAKING RESPONSIBILITY

Many of us would agree that life doesn't seem fair. In my case, it was the sheer randomness of the world's inequities that moved me to study reincarnation as a viable possibility. I had had a notion of God as being fair and just, like a loving, wise father. I believed in a perfect universal order and a benign God. But as a logical person, I couldn't understand why God would allow so many people to be subjected to such rampant tragedy and misery. It didn't make sense to me that this loving father would give his children only one chance to learn and to right their lives. Providing them with many chances, many opportunities, made more sense to me. This conclusion helped me come to terms with the theory that there is a uniform fairness and justice in all our experiences, whether we perceive them as good or bad. We have many lives in which to practice, many lives in which to rebalance, many lives in which to become more God-like.

Those who dismiss soul creation and discount the possibility of reincarnation often exhibit an either/or mentality. Some believe in heaven or hell as the ultimate reward or punishment. Others have martyristic leanings, believing that fulfilling certain honorable duties in life affords one a higher standing in death. Fairness, to followers of this mutually exclusive philosophy, is measured by the barometer of how much good fortune comes to those who do good things. When bad things happen to good people, these people often become disillusioned. Their beliefs are broadsided, and they become confused, jaded, and angry. Many others adopt a fatalistic approach: they take life as it comes, believing that you live, you die, and that's it. They may not even entertain the abstract concepts of justice; they are too busy surviving their daily adversities. I know that when I was a young adult, struggling to get through school and pay my bills, I had no time or energy to be philosophical about the meaning of life and to deal with the more abstract theories of justice. I met life every day on a pedestrian level, because it was what I had been taught to do. Many of the people I see are angry at God for allowing "bad things to happen."

"Only when we realize that there is no eternal, unchanging truth or absolute truth can we arouse in ourselves a sense of intellectual responsibility."

—Hu Shih

I'm sure that you would tell me that you do take responsibility. You could probably list a hundred things for which you are responsible. But think about the last time you blamed someone else for something that happened to you. Perhaps it was earlier today, or yesterday. I did it five minutes before I sat down to work on this chapter. I have worked for years to stop blaming others, and yet I still find myself doing it.

"We do not do what we want and yet we are responsible for what we are—that is the fact."

—Jean-Paul Sartre

If we're blaming others, we aren't taking personal responsibility. Write down your account of the last time you blamed someone, and your thoughts about it now. If you feel justified, beware. We love feeling justified—in fact we need to—and so we continue to assign blame. But only when we let go of blaming others can we examine what else stands in the way of our inability to accept responsibility. But taking responsibility doesn't mean simply shifting blame for everyone else to yourself, either. It doesn't mean beating yourself up and second-guessing yourself over every incident and relationship in your life that doesn't play out exactly the way you had planned. The primary reasons we take responsibility are so we can identify and learn from our experiences.

I acknowledge that taking responsibility requires work—a discouraging prospect. We work at our jobs, we work on our relationships, we work on our physical health, we devote time to our children, and on and on. Now I'm proposing that you do even more: that you take a leap of faith and commit to being responsible for your actions, reactions, and life experiences for one month. Write about the difficult circumstances in your journal. Reframe your reactions by asking the following questions:

- Why did my soul create that situation?
- What can I learn from it?
- What actions do I take to rectify it?

Write down what you've learned. At the end of the month, take a hard look at your work, relationships, children, and health. I bet they've improved. This exercise probably won't give you the same level of short-term gratification that you derive from blaming, but it will give you insights that will help you alter your behavior. In time, your relationships will show some subtle changes, and you'll feel better.

Judy knew she had the capabilities to fashion a successful career: she was well educated, intelligent, and creative. But by her early forties, she had failed to produce anything more than a string of short-lived and unsatisfying jobs and several failed entrepreneurial ventures. Soul creation helped her redefine what career success really meant to her and helped her thrive in the process:

I love my work. I feel privileged, gratified, challenged, and inspired by the opportunity it gives me to express myself, and to make a difference in people's lives. Looking back over the years, I can see how all the pieces came together perfectly to propel me forward into this glorious future. Of course, I can see that now in hindsight. I wasn't always so visionary. Ten years ago, I walked into Linda's office feeling defeated, victimized, and badly in need of foresight.

Linda helped me to understand my career as a "calling," to consider it my "life's work" or "soul mission"—a possibility I hardly considered in my pursuit of money and reputation. My astrological chart identified key elements to the success of my mission: a commitment to service, communication skills, and the promotion of avant-garde ideas. We addressed my fear of failure. Like many "late bloomers," I had needed time to gain wisdom and maturity. I easily grasped the concept of self-creation because I had already seen evidence of the relationship between past crises and opportunities for self-awareness. However, taking responsibility for creating my whole life was a larger leap: one that proved very cathartic. Trusting the wisdom of my soul allowed me to release old anger, blame, and regret. I left my first session with Linda pointed in the right direction, and hopeful.

My test of faith continued. Could I own all of my experiences? Could I remain patient and optimistic in the space between the appearance of a problem and its resolution? Could I create my future consciously? By living in these questions, I gradually shifted my values. Activities I had once regarded as "unproductive," including personal growth and volunteer work, moved up from footnotes into the main text of my experience. A sense of purpose replaced my former angst. I more quickly recognized the gifts in adversity. I treasured the journey and surrendered the results.

DEALING WITH GRIEF AND LOSS

Many clients come to me grieving the loss of a loved one. They tell me heart-wrenching stories involving the tragic death of a child, father, mother, brother or sister, or friend. My goal is to help those who are grieving overcome their sense of guilt, by imbuing them with a spiritual perspective.

Death in and of itself often seems distressingly arbitrary: only when we explore its meaning through soul creation can a sense of its fairness begin to take shape. On a mundane level, we can't explain why, for example, a 3-year-old girl would be gunned down during a drive-by shooting. But on a spiritual level, we can begin to understand why the little girl's soul needed her to have that violent experience. Since our souls are the continuity experts for our lives, they know everything that has come before and what experiences we need to create in this lifetime in order to continue to evolve and learn. If we could understand the soul contracts (discussed in Chapter 2) that this child had with her parents, and the past lives she brought to this short life, perhaps we could make some sense of the tragedy.

The soul gives me this information through the language of karmic astrology. The astrological chart provides us with the insights we need to understand such things.

We all are confronted by choices that are based on what our soul knows we need to learn. And while our souls create certain choices for us, we make the final creative decision at the critical point when the path needs to be chosen.

CHAPTER 2

SOUL MATES AND
SOUL CONTRACTS

The contemporary surge in spirituality and New Age philosophy has ushered the term soul mate into our culture's lexicon primarily as a term of endearment. Some of us consider our soul mate to be a partner to whom we are bound by a love and understanding that transcends our material world: our ultimate relationship. I have a more in-depth explanation of what a soul mate is.

All the relationships we enter into—including those involving soul mates—are karmic. By initiating a relationship, we set in motion a soul contract with that soul to learn a lesson and resolve an issue from a previous life. A soul mate represents a karmic relationship that we have resolved: a deep conflict that has been settled, an obligation that has been fulfilled, and love that has replaced fear and anger. We recognize a soul mate by the supreme level of comfort and security we feel with that person. That doesn't mean that there aren't issues that remain to be ironed out. Rather, it means we know intuitively that we can resolve issues with our soul mate without losing his or her love and respect. When feelings of abandonment and betrayal arise with a soul mate, they do not last. Once soul mates achieve an ultimate level of symbiosis and serenity with each other, it remains forever.

"We should help people discover their vocation in life, their calling, fate or destiny. This is especially focused on finding the right career and the right mate."

—Abraham Maslow

Having a soul mate is not necessarily a rare occurrence. It's just that few of us have the understanding or the tools to recognize whether the significant person in our life is indeed a soul mate. One must be evolving spiritually to have this awareness: cognizant of love as the basic fabric of life. Soul mates tend to find each other during their respective pursuits of their soul missions. Creating a soul mate could be seen as a spiritual reward that we give ourselves, after pursuing many soul contracts rife with discord.

A soul contract is an agreement we make with souls whom we've known previously from other lifetimes to work through situations in this life that need special attention. Soul contracts occur between all of us, all the time. We incarnate with a certain group of people, who represent different things to us, from one life to the next. They are companion souls off whom we can "bounce" our life's experiences. They agree to "play" with us to help make us aware of the lessons we need to learn. As part of the contract, we agree to do the same for them. Some of these people are closer to us than others, but all are important in helping us discover who we've been and how to learn our next major lesson.

Edgar Cayce, renowned in spiritual circles for creating a better understanding of reincarnation and psychic healing during the post-Depression era, said souls reincarnate with others to whom they are closely related for three reasons:

- to overcome conflict
- to repay an obligation
- to perpetuate love

Lee came to see me as a last resort. She had undergone a lot of psychotherapy but still could not overcome her guilt over her brother's death. She was jaded by the counseling process, having been to more than her share of therapists and psychologists. She told me matter-of-factly that her brother Dan had committed suicide ten years before, at the age of 17. It had come as a complete shock to Lee and the rest of her family. Each member of the family, in his or her own way, had assumed blame for his death, preventing them from resolving the issue and moving on with their lives.

Lee, who had been 14 at the time, had loved her older brother but was very jealous of him. Dan had been active in sports and had won the admiration of her father in a way Lee could not. She remembers hating Dan for "taking her father away" from her. The day before he died, he had won a state-level tennis competition. Lee had left Dan's celebration party upset and angry because of the attention he received from her mother and father. The next day Dan shot himself in the head. He left no note, gave no explanation. Lee blamed herself for it. She felt that her jealousy and anger had driven him to take his own life.

When Lee was finished telling me this story, I asked her why she would create a soul contract with a brother prone to suicide. My question visibly jolted her. I explained that through the contracts that our souls forge with each other, we create the experiences and relationships from which we need to learn. Lee, who was just getting started in social work, was already adept at controlling her emotions, but I could sense her anger and disbelief as she pulled a couple of pillows up to her stomach, barricading herself.

"Why would my soul do such a thing to me or my brother?" she asked. "That would be so unfair—worse, it would mean that I really did kill him," she said, tears now streaming down her face.

I explained to Lee that on a personality level, she had nothing to do with her brother's suicide. Making a contract with someone else's soul to learn a lesson—even if it included an aspect of death—did not make her or her soul an accomplice in a criminal act. On a soul level, she knew even before she and Dan incarnated in this life that he could choose to end his life. She had decided to be his sister for her own reasons. In essence, they had agreed to go through this tragedy together.

As Lee listened, she started to calm down. "Do you mean that my brother knew that he was going to kill himself when he came into this world?" Lee asked. I answered carefully, telling her that her brother's personality had not known. His soul, however, knew that suicide was a possibility and his soul also knew the reasons why it might happen.

Although aspects of Lee's and Dan's story have the trappings of fatalism, the truth is their souls did give them choices. Soul creation and fatalism diverge at one of the fundamental tenets of soul creation: that ultimately, the choice of which path to follow lies with us. The older we get, in fact, the more choices we have. Dan had choices, and suicide was one of them. Perhaps he was too young to see the other possibilities that his soul was showing him.

Many souls deliver people into this world, aware that suicide may be a potential event from which they will need to learn. But plenty of them choose a different path perhaps because their soul determined that they had already learned the desired lesson from another experience or relationship.

Lee and I reviewed Dan's astrological chart and found some possible reasons why he might have chosen to leave the earth plane early. His chart was dominated by female energy. He was sensitive, creative, emotional, and spiritual. Even though he was a natural athlete and a competitor on the tennis court, he was gentle and compassionate. He would often agonize over how his opponents might feel after losing to him. After a tennis match he would go to his room and stay there for hours, refusing to eat or talk to anyone. He had wanted to quit sports and concentrate on writing but was terrified to confront his father, who strongly supported his tennis career.

After his death, his mother found a journal of poems he had written. In several of them he wrote of a palace that was white and crystal, with fountains surrounded by white marble courtyards. Beautiful music and tinkling bells made this palace truly magical. The family saw these poems as a manifestation of a side of Dan that he had kept hidden. I saw them as a description of the other side beyond death and as evidence of Dan's yearning to go home. I believe—and I shared this with Lee—that Dan longed for the other side and never felt comfortable with his life. Before I even knew of the content of these poems, I had described the other side similarly to Lee, so she was able to truly believe that her brother had chosen to return to his spiritual home.

Lee now began to look at death in a more secure, thoughtful way. As a small child, she had been terrified of death. She had always hated the nightly prayer she was required to say: "If I should die, before I wake..." conjured up dreams of dark places with eerie monsters. At 14, Dan's death had brought back the fear and the nightmares. Her religious training was spotty, and she did not have a spiritual base to help her deal with death or offer her an afterlife. The only thing she could relate to was the darkness and the monsters.

One of her first thoughts after Dan died was that he had gone into "that black hole and was living with those terrible monsters." Talking to me about the soul, the other side, and soul contracts helped diminish her terrible fear of dying. She began to see the real possibility that her brother had gone to a peaceful and beautiful place.

For the first time in ten years, Lee could have a conversation about her brother's death without feeling guilty. Guilt no longer interfered with her grieving process. Now she is able to help her family deal with it on a different level. In fact, Lee now volunteers at a hospice and helps other families deal with the death of their loved ones. She is able to love Dan and honor him for helping her to transform her own fear of death. His death, Lee learned, enabled her to discover and utilize her ability to help others learn about the dying process and share her own life experience, the essence of her soul mission. That experience, for Lee, was the basis of the soul contract she had made with her brother's soul.

One day Jill, a woman in her early forties, called me from Seattle in tears. Carl, her husband of fourteen years, had just told her he was leaving. There was no other woman, and he said he still loved her. He told her that he "needed to be free," to relieve himself of the collective burden of all the responsibilities they had accumulated during their marriage. As Jill and I worked together on her problem, I found information in her astrological chart that indicated that in another life she had been very commitment-phobic.

By doing a chart comparison (in which I analyze one person's chart against another), I discovered that in another life she had been in a relationship with a man (probably a previous incarnation of her present husband) but felt she could not marry him. She had left him abruptly and never given the relationship the closure that it deserved. In fact, she hadn't even said good-bye.

Because Jill had an unresolved issue with Carl left over from that previous existence, her soul brought them back together in marriage in this life so she could experience him leaving her and learn from it. She was able to see that she needed to repay this old obligation by dealing with Carl's needs. After a few sessions she decided to "let him go," to allow him to find the freedom he craved with impunity. This decision helped her eschew anger and blame, our most common reflexive tendencies. She refused to consider herself a victim. A few months later Carl came back, Jill's old karmic obligation having been paid in full. The two of them were now free to explore the next level of their relationship.

Cayce's law about needing to resolve left-over conflict sounds similar to his law of needing to meet a remaining obligation, but there is an important distinction: a conflict need not create obligation and demand repayment; rather, it may require some form of resolution. The conflict can be anything from a personality conflict where two people simply do not like each other, to a couple of colleagues vying for the same promotion.

Tom knew the moment his son David was born that something was wrong. The unadulterated joy that most fathers experience upon witnessing the birth of a child, the sheer euphoria, was absent. It wasn't the prospect of impending parental responsibilities and commitments that overwhelmed him, nor was he worried about what kind of father he'd be. Instead, Tom felt a deep, visceral, free-floating paranoia.

Too ashamed to tell his wife, Tom tried for several months to deal with his ambivalence toward David on his own. Finally, as a last resort, he came to me. An investigation of both Tom's and David's charts illuminated a past life conflict between the two of them. David had been in a position of great power and had had control over Tom's very existence. Tom had lost the only security he had, his land, which had taken him years of hard work to acquire. The culprit had been David. In that past life Tom had died an angry, frustrated man, never recovering the land that he felt was rightfully his and blaming David for his misfortune.

Thus Tom's conflict in this life centered on his inability to control his fate, his sense of feeling victimized—and his real desire to love his child. But now, in this life, through his newborn, he would have an opportunity to resolve the conflict by loving and caring for him. By being in control of his relationship with his son in this life, he was resolving that past life experience of powerlessness and, in effect, creating a karmic symmetry: just as Tom's fate had previously been in David's hands, David's fate was now in Tom's hands.

How did Tom and I know this past life experience was legitimate? The only way we ever know is by sensing how it feels. When we began talking of his possible karma with his son, Tom began to cry. The information felt right, and his body was responding to the truth. The most powerful part of the session was its result: Tom left no longer feeling conflicted, no longer afraid of the feelings that his little boy had catalyzed within him. Once he understood the soul contract he and his son had made—to overcome his feeling victimized by resolving the conflict and creating a life of love—he was free to be the open, generous, loving father he had always wanted to be.

Resolving major conflicts and fulfilling obligations leaves us with unconditional love, a hallmark of a soul-mated relationship. Discord will continue to surface periodically—our soul ensures it—but love and commitment become the prevailing tools of resolution.

KARMIC WARNING BELLS

While we enjoy karmic relationships with all the various souls with whom we share soul contracts, they are not necessarily our soul mates. However, just because two people in a relationship aren't soul mates doesn't render their soul contract any less important.

Most of us have experienced the heady emotions, the passionate rush, that accompany our initial foray with someone special. All the signs are there: the energy, the sexual electricity, the infatuation. While these symptoms are commonly known as emotions of the heart, I refer to them as karmic warning bells. Upon meeting someone to whom you are attracted, you may really be falling in love—or you may be getting a wakeup call.

What feels like love in many cases is really a cosmic two-by-four meant to get our attention and prepare us for a major karmic insight. In such cases we create the intensely amorous feelings in order to keep the relationship going long enough for us to discover the past life connection, alter it, and change ourselves. The relationship ends once we have the reflections we need. Sometimes it's difficult to draw a distinction between love and a karmic warning bell. Usually, with the latter, one feels a vague sense of familiarity and a strong "here-I-go-again" dread.

When Olivia came to see me, she was totally stressed out. At 42, she was happily married and had two young children, but she had fallen in love with another man—despite knowing that the relationship imperiled her marriage. While she loved and respected her husband, Olivia found the appeal of a younger, good-looking man intoxicating. He was arrogant and indiscreet—and to make matters worse, he worked with her husband. Olivia was putting her whole life on the line, and she couldn't figure out why. She said she "couldn't help it." She felt like she was "addicted" to this person, a rare emotion for her, considering that she exhibited not even the slightest indication of addictive tendencies. Her lust for George allowed her to overlook the fact that he was a heavy drinker.

We needed to find out the karmic implications between her and George, and we needed to do it quickly: Olivia was terrified that George, in a drunken stupor, would tell her husband what was going on. When I explained to Olivia that she was in this bizarre relationship with George in order to learn something important about herself and that these intense feelings were her soul's way of keeping her in the relationship, it made sense to her. As a matter of fact, it was the only thing that did make sense. From looking at Olivia's and George's astrological charts, we learned that in a previous life George had been in Olivia's employ. Her arrogance had demeaned and threatened him, but as a subordinate, he had felt powerless to confront her. As a result, Olivia now had an obligation to repay, and George had a conflict to resolve. They had come together in this life to balance their karma. As soon as Olivia recognized her previous ties to George and the need to balance their karma, she was able to talk to him, and end their relationship. She even convinced him to go to Alcoholics Anonymous. Her karmic warning bells stopped ringing, and the intense feelings dissipated. This obsessive kind of falling in love is particularly intense, yet its intensity can be altered just as quickly when it is understood. Olivia was able to preserve her family and move on with her life.

We spent a few sessions figuring out why her soul had needed her to understand her arrogant behavior from the past. We discovered more about who she had been in that life: she had been autocratic and had misused her power. She also felt that her life had been ended rather abruptly either by accident or murder at the hands of someone she had abused. A deep-seated fear had plagued Olivia for years: she had always been afraid of being center stage, had dreams of being assassinated, and on several occasions had a paranoia about someone being "out to get" her. Understanding this past life helped her make some sense of those fears. Her karmic relationship with George had given her the opportunity to discover herself at another level. At my suggestion, Olivia wrote George a thank-you note explaining all she had learned.

Too often our friends and family members, we ourselves—even society's most notable and accomplished people—engage in behavior that seems unexplainable. They make seemingly bizarre choices that defy their better judgment. Even the most emotionally grounded, commonsensical person you know could be drawn into a relationship completely incongruent with their sapience. But although this behavior is incomprehensible to our personalities, our souls understand it. Olivia knew George acted like a "jerk" but was able to stop seeing him when she realized that the relationship was showing her issues about herself.

KARMIC VERSUS SOUL-MATED RELATIONSHIPS

The distinction between soul mates and other people with whom our souls have contracted relationships is that the issues between ourselves and our soul mates have come to some form of resolution, while issues in karmic relationships have yet to be resolved. Soul mates tend to cooperate, while those in karmic relationships tend to compete. Still, we can learn just as much from our experiences in both types of relationship.

Conflicts among soul mates are more stimulating and creative because there is an attitude of expansion and a knowing that the conflict will be resolved. Often a soul-mated relationship serves a spiritual purpose. As soul mates, we sometimes help each other explore and find our own spiritual missions. Sometimes we work together to accomplish important life goals.

I know that if I had not been spiritually prepared, I wouldn't have attracted my husband into my life. Michael's support and unfailing generosity have aided me to become the person that I am and given me the time to dedicate myself to my work, even time taken away from our relationship. Years ago I was caught in an emotional quagmire. I knew that I had old anger festering within me. I knew it was unhealthy to bury it, but I couldn't find a way to express it. The morning after Michael told me about his affair, we were in the kitchen arguing. For one instant I literally saw red. For the first time in my life, I lashed out. I shoved him up against the refrigerator. When I finally stopped my raging tirade, I looked at him, and he was smiling. It was so incongruent: I was angry; I was close to being abusive; and he was smiling. I didn't know whether to laugh or cry. At that moment I knew I had broken through my inability to vent—I had actually gotten angry. Only a soul mate would have smiled.

SOUL CIRCLES OF LIFE

Some people are disappointed to learn that our soul mates are not the only people with whom we have shared our past. In fact, we each have a very large group of people, hundreds or more, who are linked to us from one life to the next. Some relationships are closer than others, and their type may vary from life to life. You could be married to the person who was your mother-in-law in a previous life; your child could have been your father in another life—the combinations are endless. The homeless person now asking you for some change may have been your boss in a previous incarnation.

CIRCLES OF RELATIONSHIPS

Imagine yourself in the middle of three concentric circles. The first circle contains the people whose karmic relationships with you are most important for your growth in this life: your parents, children, lovers, soul mate, husband, wife, beloved pet, counselor, spiritual teacher, or any other family member or intimate who has played an important role in your life experience. These circle-one relationships are intense, passionate, powerful, and sometimes disruptive because they are formative.

The second circle, one step removed from the intimacy and intensity of the first circle, comprises people whose karmic relationships with you have provided some interaction but are less significant. They could include an important teacher who helped you realize your career, a teenage romance that began an important relational pattern, a boss who challenged you, or possibly a friend who left your life after several years of an enriching relationship.

The third circle comprises people whose karmic relationships with you have been punctuated with some poignant moments but lack the sustained potency and vitality of the first two. Circle three-type relationships could involve a sales clerk with whom you shared a profound, intimate moment; the man who ran into your car; the doctor who operated on your gall bladder. One of my circle-three relationships was with a postal clerk. I was at the post office last spring talking with her, and she helped me decide what mode of delivery would be best to deliver my book contract to my agent as quickly as possible. As she was stamping the mailing envelope, she looked at me and said, smiling, "Now I'm a part of your book too." People in circles two and three can have a very powerful impact on you in the midst of an experience with them.

Circle 1 Relationships	Circle 2 Relationships	Circle 3 Relationships
Spouse	Roommates	Passing acquaintances
Child	Friends	Cab drivers
Parent	Coworkers	Store clerks
Sibling	Teachers	Person on the street
Aunt/uncle	Club members	
Close Friend	Neighbors	
Grandparent	Cousins	

The concept of group karma explains why certain people are linked together to experience poignant life situations together. You may have ended up in one history class rather than another, or been stuck in an elevator with certain people. Maybe you, or someone you know or read about, missed that doomed plane, while several other passengers went down. Or perhaps you were stranded at a diner in a snow storm and had a meaningful interaction with a stranger. Try to recall an event in your life when you ended up with a group of people, even strangers, who seemed vaguely familiar to you. Try to envision it as a group karmic experience. Think about what you learned from it and how it affected your life.

I will never forget getting caught in a terrific hailstorm on the Southern Illinois University campus in Edwardsville, Illinois, in the summer of 1973. I was close to finishing my master's degree and was in the process of deciding whether to join my husband, who had been transferred to the Philippines, or return home to Baltimore. About ten of us were waiting out the storm, making idle chatter. I mentioned that my husband was serving a two-year tour in the Philippines. One person in the group related a story about a friend in the Philippines whose dog had been stolen and was later found skinned in a marketplace in Manila. That was all I needed to hear. My dog's safety had always been an obsession with me. I did not go to the Philippines but came back to Baltimore—and began the most significant transformational period of my life.

DETECTING SOUL MATES

Soul-mated relationships are distinguished by their deep feelings of permanence and comfort. Soul mates are secure in their knowledge that there will never be a situation they can't handle. Another indicator is how soul mates feel when they initially meet. Instead of karmic warning bells, they feel a low-level hum. The new person in their life seems familiar; they feel that they have "known" each other before. In essence, they are saying hello again.

My interest in the distinction between soul-mated and other karmic relationships grew as a result of my clients' fervent inquiries about soul mates. They wanted to know when they would find their own and how they could make it happen soon. As I explored dozens upon dozens of my clients' existing relationships, I came to the conclusion that many of them already had soul mates but didn't know it.

A story I often tell my clients is that our soul mates are waiting on our soul path. The more committed we are to what is in our soul's best interest, the more likely we are to find them. I had known my soul mission for several years before Michael appeared. His soul path was the same as mine. Although we are socialized to idealize soul mates as the stuff of storybook romance, soul-mated relationships come in many forms.

Many years ago, when I taught school, the administrator for whom I worked was also my mentor and my friend. In retrospect, I "knew" John from the moment we met. He left the school, but he never left my memory. I haven't talked to him in twenty years, and I probably never will again—at least, not in this life. Yet he fits the criteria of a soul mate. We were comfortable and at ease with each other. We could argue and know that we would resolve the conflict. We were constantly exploring a win-win model. He and I never had a social relationship outside the school; we were not lovers. We were two people who worked together for a common purpose, and we had a bond that I will always cherish. He was one of my soul mates.

As you think about your relationships, try to broaden your concept of what a soul mate is. You may be surprised and thrilled to find you already have one or several in your life. To clarify the difference, look at the following chart and review a few important relationships in your life.

Soul Mates: Win-Win	Other Karmic Relationships: Win-Lose
Cooperative	Competitive
Peer relationship	Hierarchical relationship
Comfort	Agitation
Expansive	Constrictive
Inspirational	Antagonistic
Stimulating	Challenging
Creative	Draining
Integrated	Isolative
Ease of flow	Disruptive
Secure	Exposed

Karmic relationships are challenging and therefore offer us opportunities to ascend to new heights in our spiritual growth. We have the potential to change their inherent difficulties by understanding and being aware of the gifts they bring. Soul-mated relationships have their own share of conflicts and arguments. The differences lie in the attitude of cooperation and in the deep inner knowledge that we will resolve the problems. Soul-mated and karmic relationships are synthesized at exactly the right time to enable us to learn about those sacred truths at our emotional core. Since our soul coordinates all our relationships, it presents these situations to us when the timing is right. What we do with these situations is our choice.

Imagine yourself as a soul on the other side. You are preparing to incarnate back to the earth plane. You meet with other souls to plan the relationships you need to fulfill your life's purpose. You talk to your circle-one karmic relationships first. Circle two and circle three come next. You speak to the soul, for instance, who is to be your father in your next earthly existence. Together you recall your previous life experiences, as well as the conflicts that will need to be resolved and the obligations that will need to be met. You acknowledge the love that has endured throughout time. You decide on the context of the relationship you will share to help both of you evolve. Your souls cocreate a soul contract. You have many meetings like this one, to consummate all the contracts you need to evolve and grow spiritually in your next life.

Your soul then integrates your soul contracts into your astrological chart. Information in the chart reminds you of the contracts and the souls with whom you've contracted. That vague sense of "knowing" or familiarity we experience when we meet new people can be attributed to the fact that we usually don't recognize the personalities behind our soul agreements, but we always recognize their souls. Our soul knows the people we're going to bring into our lives. Our astrological chart only serves as a blueprint of what our soul intends for us to help us evolve. We might not recognize someone immediately, but if we have some notion of what our soul needs us to learn in this life, the reasons for their presence in our life will become more readily apparent. This rationale also explains the common experience of meeting under the flukiest of circumstances—while asking for directions, at a school or job orientation, on the plane while traveling, in a doctor's office—someone who becomes a central influence in your life. These "chance" meetings are not at all random.

Many people have asked me why we do not remember our past lives. The reason is that our soul has all those experiences record and brings them forth when they are needed. Many karmic experiences create poignant emotions that we have difficulty confronting because we do not understand where they come from. Until we have a philosophic context in which to deal with these feelings, they stay repressed.

All karmic relationships are familiar to some degree. We have known the person for whom we've developed strong feelings many times before. That's how we know we are entering into a relationship to complete what we failed to complete before.

It is important to distinguish between comfort and familiarity. The comfort of a soul-mated relationship is different from the familiarity of a karmic relationship. Familiarity could involve myriad types of relating. For instance, if in previous lifetimes you created abusive relationships, then an abusive relationship will seem familiar to you now. Falling back into the well of familiarity is the easiest thing for us to do. Being in a relationship created by old behavior characteristics is like being on automatic pilot.

Unfortunately, many people repeat the same behavioral patterns countless times without alteration. I've seen it over and over again in my practice, and it truly saddens me. Ultimately our souls do give us opportunities to alter our lives. If we ignore these opportunities, we end up taking these unresolved issues into our next life. We will learn sooner or later—our souls are infinitely patient.

THE GIFT OF REFLECTION

Knowing this truth has helped my clients—as well as myself—make tremendous inroads into learning more about themselves. Yet we all have painful memories that we consciously do not want to unearth. Scores of my clients have undergone extensive past life therapy and remember lives where they were persecuted, victimized, and betrayed. But few remember lives where they were the persecutor, the abuser, or the betrayer. We wish to bury these memories, and we do.

Some of my clients create major cosmic two-by-fours over and over again. They get increasingly stronger until sooner or later we can no longer ignore them. The more blocked we are, the stronger the two-by-fours. Consider the statements you make repeatedly: they reflect an unconscious memory, waiting for you to interpret and understand it.

All significant relationships provide us with information about our blind spots. Jung thought that the more deeply we repress our thoughts and feelings about ourselves, the more intensely we create them outside ourselves as conflict and chaos. We will attract another person to show us precisely what we don't consciously know about ourselves. Once we understand that we bring all our relationships to ourselves for learning and balance, we can alter and transform the behaviors that need changing.

Take a moment to think about an important person in your life. Now isolate a behavior from that person that irritates you, scares you, or causes you pain. That person's action may cause irritation or fear in you, but it may hardly bother another colleague, family member, or friend. If this is the case, could it be that you actually behave in that irritating or painful way yourself? If so, my guess is that you've experienced an extreme reaction to that behavior before. Try claiming that behavior as your own, and make a commitment to change. Suddenly you may find that it alters the reaction you have toward that other person. That person may not change what he or she does; what has changed is your perception of that person's behavior by changing your own.

BIG SOULS AND LITTLE SOULS

God and the universe have a perfect order, and that perfect order filters down through us. We don't have to strive for perfection, because we share the energy of God. Most people scurry about trying to prove that they're perfect, but they don't see that they are part of God, and that God has already given us the greatest gift he can give us: our soul.

When we are in communication with our soul, our relationship with it exemplifies growth and healing. But people who are not in sync with their soul are more often sick, tired, angry, frustrated, frayed, and jaded than those who are. We've all encountered people who are jaded; they seemingly have everything but sound as if they have nothing. They don't have spirit, they don't have joy, they don't have drama, and they don't have the zeal to celebrate life. Above all, they don't believe in their soul. I'm better today than I've ever been because I'm in concert with my soul, and this sacred connection is bringing me to personal and professional heights I never thought possible twenty years ago. My soul helps me do more important things, endeavors that have significant meaning not only for me but for countless others.

I believe we all have a big soul and a little soul. Our big soul is connected to God. In fact, God and the big soul are one. The big soul is our container for the total human condition, our orchestrator of life's events, our continuity expert from one life to the next, our total awareness and knowledge as a people. For those who believe that God "keeps track" of our lives, the big soul is his reference point. The big soul knows everything about us, everything we have done, and what we will need to do in the future to learn and evolve. It creates our experiences here on this material plane.

The big soul, in its infinite wisdom and love, gives to each of us a little piece of itself, which I call the little soul. The little soul is our spiritual companion, a function of our daily existence. It is the essence of God that is within each of us, as if he were holding each of our hands. It aids our personality, pushing us to fulfill our potential, and helps us evolve by confronting us with the encounters and relationships from which we need to learn. Our little soul is the impetus behind our realizing our soul mission and our purpose in life. It is our deepest strength and our greatest joy, and with it we are never alone. The little soul and the big soul are always connected, and the big soul is always connected to God.

The big soul guides the little soul in its respective relationship with us. It deals with issues of a larger scope, like choosing a particular generation with a specific path to significance and a large group karmic track. Each generation is different, but a common thread runs through it, a similarity of karmic lessons and a major need to transform them. Each generation has a larger purpose to fulfill that will advance its evolution and awareness. The big soul also coordinates the massive number of soul contracts into which each of us has entered. For instance, my interns are part of my own karmic group, each for their own individual reasons. Some come to learn from me and stay connected; others decide to separate from me. I know that I have created meeting all of them to push me toward a better understanding of my soul's work. The big soul is more connected to the bigger picture.

KARMIC AMALGAMS: YOUR KARMIC JIGSAW PUZZLE

Karmic amalgams are aggregate images of the people who are most meaningful to us. Drawing a karmic amalgam is a dynamic process that helps us figure out how to learn from the new, interpersonal situations we are constantly creating in our lives. They are effective because we've already known the people we attract from other lives, having entered into soul contracts with them. A karmic amalgam gives us the opportunity to see ourselves through the people we create. For instance, if I had been a dogmatic father in another life and my soul needed for me to understand the devastating effects that being dogmatic had on my family, I would likely ask my son in that life to be that kind of father to me in my next. If my "son" takes on that contract, he is helping me by being dogmatic and unrelenting. Then we can resolve the conflict we had in our last life.

Whenever we experience a new, important relationship, we must adjust and revise our karmic amalgam. Adding each new, essential relationship as it evolves enables us to understand what that relationship symbolizes and provides us with insights to learn from it. Once we understand that our souls seek to confront us with all our own relationships as a learning experience, we can alter and transform the behaviors that need changing.

In the workshops I conduct to help people glean powerful information from their relationships, I use an exercise based on a theory that we enter this life with a jigsaw puzzle without pieces. Every karmic relationship we create becomes a pertinent piece of the jigsaw puzzle. The completed puzzle shows us in a very profound way who we have been and what memories we may have hidden from our conscious understanding of ourselves.

Circle-one relationships are our biggest jigsaw pieces. Your mother and father may encompass as much as one-third of your puzzle. Your soul has chosen them to provide you with very significant karmic information. Understanding how your parents serve you through their reflections back to you is the first step in cobbling together your karmic amalgam. The power and importance of a reflection is judged by the emotional impact it has on us. I always admired my mother for her compassion, her deep desire to serve humanity, her charm and graciousness, her love of books, and her writing skills. She was a career woman who worked her way up the career ladder. Having had a major influence on the evolution of volunteerism in this country, my mother was an inspiration for me. She was open-minded and totally supported my need to leave the traditional world of education and become the holistic teacher that I am today.

Still, as a young girl, it used to frustrate me when my mother was committed to her work responsibilities at my expense. I felt abandoned and scared. As a teenager, my frustration and fear turned to anger. It upset me that she could so easily sacrifice herself and her role as my mother for her career. But as I got older, I saw that I was doing the same thing. I was a workaholic. I sacrificed myself for my work. I had chosen my mother to show me myself.

Our parents' interactions with us help us to remember the soul contracts we have made with them. This Parents Exercise will highlight the important role your parents played in helping you learn more about yourself and the "perfection" of their service to you.

PARENTS EXERCISE

- Think about your mother. Write down in your journal five things that you admire about her.
- Now write down five things about her that frustrate you.
- Do the same thing with your father.

Often in our previous incarnations, we were much more extreme versions of our parents. In essence, we make our parents bigger than life so that we can get in touch with that karmic part of us. We create a soul contract with them to show us that part of ourselves.

Nadine, a 43-year-old writer from Hercules, California, was able to come to terms with her mother only after realizing that their volatile, angst-ridden relationship was providing her with a life-altering lesson.

"You picked your parents." Linda's words ricocheted off my ears, only to boomerang back later. Instinctively and almost defensively, I felt a chill and thought to myself: "No way in hell." And then I thought, "Maybe that accounts for all of my previous poor judgments and decisions."

Sometime after the humor wore off, I finally understood. Ironically, what has taken me almost my entire adult life to understand has left me feeling grateful that I finally "got" it. Now I can spend the rest of my life making a real difference. This coming to terms—or maybe better, coming of age—happened after three years of living with my mother in a volatile relationship, then not speaking to her for another three years after that. After more than six years of external and internal turmoil, I finally came to terms with...me.

First I realized that a gift is not only what we have been given but what we ultimately do with it. Since the gifts my mother gave me were not conscious and certainly did not come from a loving place, it took me a while to validate them. The gift became my own growth out of a fiery place.

I have not only reconciled her back into my life, I have clearly gained more respect for her journey. The added benefit is that my compassion for others is now more evident in my daily life.

We all have a profound need to look deeply inside—to go beyond the conventional rhetoric and teaching, to find our own truth and accept our appointed tasks, our purpose for living. But before that, it's really only about love. Once you give yourself compassion, you see the world through loving eyes. That moment of understanding transformed the course of my life forever.

Traits we display in our significant relationships show us not only the behaviors we tend to repress but the jigsaw puzzle pieces of ourselves as we were in other times. The following exercise will walk you through the process of finding the personality pieces that will allow you to learn about the puzzle that is you.

EXERCISE: KARMIC AMALGAM FOR FEMALE ENERGY

This exercise will provide information on characteristics you have had in the past as a woman. If you are a woman in this life, it will supply you with more information about your past. If you are a man, it will inform you about your female side as well as provide you with insights about what qualities you are attracted to in women. The female amalgams you "create" will give you important insights into your hidden female side.

STEP 1

Choose and list in your journal five women with whom you have had an important relationship. (Always use your mother as the first one, since she is a circle-one soul contract.) If you don't have five, list as many as you can. Here are five examples: your mother, a childhood friend, a supervisor, a professor, and your grandmother.

STEP 2

Examine the personalities of the five women you've chosen. Look for their attributes that have deeply affected you. Identify and journalize roughly half a dozen strong and weak or challenging characteristics for each of the women you've chosen. Your selection of attributes as positive or negative should not imply a judgment about them. What is significant is how you view them and the effect that their behavior has had on you.

STEP 3

List the strengths that most of the five women have in common. These strengths now can become pieces of your jigsaw puzzle: they are characteristics that you may not have realized that you have yourself.

STEP 4

List the weaknesses that most of the five women have in common. As with your strengths, you can now add your aggregate weaknesses to your karmic jigsaw puzzle. Chances are these weaknesses are aspects of yourself that you've chosen not to identify. They could offer a glimmer of information about who you've been in past lives.

EXERCISE: KARMIC AMALGAM FOR MALE ENERGY

This exercise will provide information on characteristics you have had in the past as a man. If you are a man in this life, it will supply you more information about your past. If you are a woman, it will inform you about your male side as well as provide you with insights about what qualities you are attracted to in men. The male amalgams you "create" will give you important insights into your hidden male side.

STEP 1

Choose and list five men with whom you have had an important relationship. (Always use your father as the first one, since he is a circle-one soul contract.) If you don't have five, list as many as you can. Some examples: your father, your uncle, a first love, your husband, a married lover.

STEP 2

Examine the personalities of the men you've chosen. Look for their attributes that have deeply affected you. Identify roughly half a dozen strong and weak characteristics for each of the men you have chosen. Your selection of attributes as positive or negative should not imply a judgment about them. What is significant is how you view them and the effect that their behavior has had on you.

STEP 3

List the strengths that most of the five men have in common. These strengths can become pieces of your jigsaw puzzle: they are characteristics you may not have realized you possess yourself.

STEP 4

List the weaknesses that most of the five men have in common. You now have six more characteristics to add to your karmic jigsaw puzzle. Again, the weak or challenging traits you've elicited may indicate parts of yourself that you've chosen to repress. They could also offer you some insight into the type of person you were in previous incarnations.

Your karmic jigsaw puzzle will ease your heart, expand your consciousness, and give you a sense of continuity that you have never before experienced. It will give you vital information on why you've chosen your soul contracts. You will be free to love and honor your parents and all the others who have joined with you on a soul level to teach you what you have needed to know. You will feel more empowered because you will no longer need to create others to show you what you already know. You will be able to put karmic memories in perspective and discriminate their value. You will be less vulnerable to the chaos created by unconsciousness. Finally, you will be operating in partnership with your soul.

PART II
JOURNEY TO YOUR SOUL MISSION

CHAPTER 3

FROM WHO YOU ARE TO WHO YOU WANT TO BE

H aving a fundamental working knowledge of your soul and your personality and being aware of their spiritual dynamic will help you align them in such a way that you can experience living your soul mission. You gain access to your personality through your intellect, your sensations, and your feelings. You gain access to your soul through your intuition.

"When the personality comes fully to serve the energy of the soul, that is authentic empowerment. This is the goal of the evolutionary process and the reason for your being.

Every experience that you have and will have upon the Earth encourages the alignment of your personality with your soul."

—**Gary Zukav**, *The Seat of the Soul*

When your soul and personality are aligned, you will finally be able to devote yourself to your soul's mission, your life's work. You will experience an unparalleled level of satisfaction and purpose, leading to a fundamental inner peace. In Seat of the Soul, Zukav discusses the relationship between personality and soul: "When a personality is in full balance you cannot see where it ends and the soul begins. That is a whole human being."

Your soul mission is always that which you say you cannot do. It is your growth path—the singular, distinctive purpose that represents your fulfillment. Your soul mission becomes your journey to reaching your fullest potential, to become something you haven't been before. It is diametrically opposite to your comfort zone.

YOUR NORTH/SOUTH NODES

The North/South Node process is fundamental to learning and living your soul mission. Through your North and South Nodes, you uncover words and symbols that you will use to bridge the gap between past lives and this one. You don't have to believe in reincarnation or past lives to benefit from the North/South Node process, but if you believe life has some purpose and meaning, it's easier to grasp the concept.

The nodes are points in the heavens where the moon intercepts the earth's orbit around the sun. Your North and South Nodes are thus represented by astrological signs that diametrically oppose each other in the cosmos. If your North Node is Cancer, your South Node would be

Capricorn; if your North Node is Taurus, your South Node would be Scorpio, and so on.

The South Node, which we will refer to as your Soul Pattern, embodies the type of person you are when you exhibit your old, predictable habits and behaviors. It represents your most familiar thoughts, feelings, and beliefs. It tells you the past lives you need to remember, karmic debts you need to repay, and relationships that will support your vision. (A karmic debt is an unresolved issue from a previous life.) It shows you your unresolved themes from the past that are causing you pain and frustration in this life.

Martin Schulman, author of *Karmic Astrology*, describes the Soul Pattern (South Node)

> as symbolic of man's past. [The South Node] is not symbolic of one incarnation, but [rather] a combination of events, ideas, attitudes and thoughts from every incarnation whose accumulated unresolved effects have created the current life. For some the South Node can be limiting, while for others whose past foundations are firm and large it can be just the factor which brings the present life to fruition and achievement.

You must evolve from the habits and tendencies confirmed by your Soul Pattern to reach the possibilities signified by your North Node, which we will refer to as your Soul Potential. In the simplest terms, your Soul Pattern represents your past, while your Soul Potential represents your future, your soul mission.

Each of us brings specific tendencies or issues from one life to the next because they are unresolved. Once you learn the lessons your soul wants you to learn, you need not carry that "karmic baggage" into your next incarnation. Your Soul Potential offers you a road map of words and concepts helping you to understand who you need to be to achieve your soul mission. It could be described, fundamentally, as what scares you the most, eliciting feelings of insecurity or fear, because it seeks to take you into new, unfamiliar terrain. We are all drawn to our Soul Potential, as a moth to a flame, yet we are terrified of it at the same time.

Once you embrace it, your Soul Potential will provide you with a clear path to a life of profound joy, purpose, and congruence. Schulman explains one's Soul Potential (North Node) as

> the symbol of the future. It represents a new experience as yet untried. For the individual this is the new cycle to which he is looking forward, carrying with it all the apprehensions of the unknown and as yet untried experiences. This nodal position nevertheless has a curious, magnetic allure, pulling the soul to its future growth. . . . It symbolizes the highest area of expression to be reached in the current life and therefore must be interpreted by the highest qualities of the sign and house in which it is placed.

The best way to begin to learn about your soul journey is to consult your Soul Pattern. Like your Sun sign, your Soul Pattern sign is determined by your date of birth, providing you with information about your past lives and showing you how you've manifested certain past life tendencies in this life (see the charts in Chapter 4). Your Soul Potential, on the other hand, represents your soul mission, and symbolizes your future. It gives you a conscious understanding of your life issues that have—up until now—been dormant. By confronting certain life issues via your Soul Pattern and extracting the negative habits and behaviors that have held you back from pursuing your dreams and goals, you can focus on traveling the road to your Soul Potential, to live the kind of life endeavored by your soul.

WHY BREAKING OLD HABITS IS SPIRITUALLY THERAPEUTIC

"To fall into a habit is to begin to cease to be."

—**Miguel de Unamuno**

Your soul is on a perpetual growth path. It wants you to evolve to a higher order, learning lessons cumulatively from one lifetime to the next. It wants you to encounter new experiences. Remaining stuck in an old and familiar Soul Pattern hinders your evolution. Your life circumstances may feel familiar for now, but your Soul Pattern will eventually arouse you by creating an unpleasant or life-jarring experience.

Most people, when they are content with the status quo, do not make wholesale life changes. They change only by having to confront a problem—specifically, one they created themselves via their Soul Pattern. At some point in each of our lives, our soul says to us, "You've got to do something different now." But leaving your Soul Pattern behind for the good of your soul mission is at best uncomfortable and at worst downright terrifying.

*"Ill habits gather by unseen degrees—
As brooks make rivers, rivers run to seas."*

—**John Dryden**

Unlike your personality, your soul is not judgmental. It assesses your experiences not in terms of whether they are positive or negative but rather if they are new or old. Your soul is interested in exposing you to discovery, in plying you with new experiences and insights that will lead you to your next incarnation.

WHY WE FEAR CHANGE

The fundamental reason we fear change is that, consciously or unconsciously, we equate it with death. Our mortality is the ultimate transformation, but most of us see it as a finality rather than as a new beginning.

"The sun...

In dim eclipse, disastrous twilight sheds
On half the nations, and with fear of change
Perplexes monarchs."

—John Milton

Those who fear change often say they feel as though they have lost touch with their spiritual center. But being in touch with our spiritual energy is part of our soul journey of discovery, change, and novelty. If we don't allow ourselves to continue on that journey, we get stuck. A journey implies movement, and those who refuse to take action are paralyzed by their fear of change, of finding themselves in territory that is unfamiliar.

In order to follow our Soul Potential, we need to trust our soul and take a leap of faith. Many of us, as youngsters, were fearful before we took that first dive into the pool, and we see the same terrifying feeling in our own children as they take their first dives. The same apprehension prevents us from seizing new, promising business opportunities, making dramatically different career moves, or cultivating meaningful and fulfilling relationships. Nothing could reduce our fear of entering the water headfirst but the actual first dive itself. Our Soul Potential is about not knowing, but trusting our soul that it's right. Invariably it is.

> *"In spite of illness, in spite even of the archenemy of sorrow, one can remain alive long past the usual date of disintegration if one is unafraid of change, insatiable in intellectual curiosity, interested in big things, and happy in small ways."*
>
> **—Edith Wharton**

Influenced by the misguided adage "Don't rock the boat," many people have been conditioned to believe that dramatic change is not worth affecting. Most of us were raised by parents in a society that valued security. In the history of the world, the individuals who are now considered agents of change—from Plato and Galileo to Susan B. Anthony and Martin Luther King—were often condemned and ridiculed for their visionary beliefs in their respective times.

Greek officials shut down Plato's learning academy because he was teaching innovative aspects of physics that they determined to be "dangerous." Galileo was arrested and ostracized for his adoption of the Copernican belief that the sun, not the earth, was the center of the solar system. Because of their ground-breaking efforts in furthering the causes of women's suffrage and birth control, respectively, Anthony and Sanger both suffered at the hands of society's mainstream: Anthony paid with her life and Sanger was jailed. At a time when blacks did not share the basic inalienable rights that America's forefathers had mandated for its citizens, King emerged as a voice of love and reason and, most of all, change. His efforts cost him his life.

Three Reasons Why We Fear/Loathe Change
1. Most of us equate it with fear of dying.
2. We've been taught not to rock the boat.
3. It is not a logical process but an emotional one.

WHY INTUITION IS ESSENTIAL TO YOUR SOUL MISSION

In our culture we are taught to value and trust logic in making decisions. We look askance at our intuition, considering it "weird" when we receive a major revelation. Logic is based on what we already know, but intuition defies what we already know. A stop-the-world moment, intuition itself can drastically alter our lives. Insight creates change, and insight that comes from intuition yields the greatest change.

According to Jung, we see our environment through four filters: intellect, emotion, sensation, and intuition. While intellect, emotion, and sensation are the filters related to our personality, intuition is the filter to our soul. It transcends the other three filters, allowing us to interpret and understand life's events with more clarity and a deeper perspective. I call it a divine spark, a moment in time when a thought you've never had before helps you see things differently. A passel of growth workshops and self-help seminars can help yield you some insights—or "ahas," as I sometimes refer to them—but insight that is not developed and acted upon fades away.

SOUL PATTERN: OLD PREDILECTIONS

From your Soul Pattern you can glean information about the areas in your life where you persistently hold on to your past. Your Soul Pattern may be so familiar, you've become inured to the fact it even exists. Your behavior, intentions, attitude, and perspective—traits of your personality—are as much a part of you as the color of your eyes, the sound of your voice, and the way you walk, personal aspects you hardly consider in daily life. Mining these habitual characteristics through Soul Pattern exercises can yield a rare introspective look at yourself. Investigating your Soul Pattern allows you to peel back the layers of your psyche, to help you identify qualities about yourself that could be keeping you from achieving your soul mission. In fact, you'd be hard pressed to achieve the soul mission that your Soul Potential has laid out for you without discovering the personal mysteries of your Soul Pattern.

Those with a Soul Pattern (South Node) in the sign of Capricorn, for example, tend toward rigidity and perfectionism. Having their South Node in Capricorn signals their strong need to be responsible, as well as their penchant for rules. Their bias toward order may hamper their ability to achieve their soul mission, which often is about taking a less restrained approach to life. But unless they become consciously aware of their rigid inclinations, they will continue to repeat the same behavior, fueled by the same obstinacy.

Four Things You Should Know About Your Soul Pattern

1. It provides you with your spiritual starting point, and tells you where and what you've been before, alerting you to your toxic tendencies.
2. It identifies what is safe, predictable, and familiar to you.
3. If you are not aware of your Soul Pattern, you will tend to create problematic relationships based on it.
4. If you don't tend to your Soul Pattern, it will, at some point, rear itself as a major crisis.

SOUL POTENTIAL: WHAT YOU CAN BE

Our soul mission terrifies us, like a hair-raising roller-coaster ride, because our soul takes us into unfamiliar terrain, full of unknown twists and turns we couldn't possibly anticipate. Your soul reveals itself through your Soul Potential, evincing its personality, color, passion, energy, and essence. Those with a Soul Potential in the sign of Cancer, for example, would aspire toward understanding their emotions and learning how to be nurturing. Having one's Soul Potential in Cancer signals the need to become the consummate mother, who expresses her creativity through caring for others with sensitivity and compassion. Needing to be needed by those they love is vital to their self-esteem.

Four Things You Should Know About Your Soul Potential
1. On a spiritual level, your Soul Potential represents the light at the end of the tunnel.
2. It provides you with information about the type of energy, characteristics, and traits your soul wants you to manifest.
3. It represents a "stretch" in ambition, pulling you to do things that you are not inherently comfortable or confident doing but that will be fulfilling once you overcome your anxiety and "take the leap."
4. Your Soul Potential is not a destination to reach, not a static end product, but the journey your soul wants you to take, a dynamic ongoing process.

Embracing Your Soul Potential

When you aspire to live your soul mission, you commit to becoming more than you think you are. You glean happiness and fulfillment not only from realizing your soul mission, but from the process of striving for it. Life itself is a process, not an end product. Thus, we are always in the process of becoming what our soul wants us to become. The more we are able to stay on our soul road, the happier and more content we are, regardless of whether we ever definitively reach our soul mission. Staying on our soul road keeps us motivated and connected to our life's possibilities. Pursuing your soul mission and striving to live your Soul Potential take work and commitment. But the process doesn't end when you reach your perceived destination; in fact, as you try to refine your soul mission and attain its highest levels, it takes on a different type of spiritual obligation. Once you identify your soul mission,you should try to do things that mesh with it but that you don't think you can do.

> *"Most people live, whether physically, intellectually or morally, in a very restricted circle of their potential being. They make use of a very small portion of their possible consciousness, and of their soul's resources in general, much like a man who ... should get in a habit of using and moving only his little finger. Great emergencies and crises show us how much greater our vital resources are than we had supposed."*
>
> **—William James**

Once you have discovered its path, maintaining your soul mission becomes easier over time. As you grow older, you become increasingly conscious of eschewing your Soul Pattern and are more committed to embracing the life endeavors articulated by your Soul Potential. Achieving your soul mission can be elusive; the key is to continue to strive for it so that you never lose track of what it is.

When you are aware of your Soul Pattern and what it represents, your soul no longer needs to create obstructions to clue you in to your problem areas. Your daily life will look a lot different: more peaceful, less chaotic, happier, healthier, and more prosperous. The cosmic two-by-fours will dissipate, and when you do encounter a problem, you'll be able to negotiate it with greater ease, channeling it into an opportunity for personal growth. Remember, realizing your soul mission is all about the quest for it.

Committing to Your Soul Potential

It's essential that you make a meaningful commitment to reaching your Soul Potential, a commitment that will be reflected in a more positive way of life with a greater sense of purpose. Whether you succeed is predicated not just on making the commitment but on evaluating the actions that stem from that commitment—actions that your soul wants you to take. You have to ask yourself:

Do your actions represent your Soul Potential (your soul path) or your Soul Pattern (the path from your past)? You know you're committed to your Soul Potential when you find yourself asking how you would utilize the energies surrounding your Soul Potential to handle an opportunity or problem.

Achieving your Soul Potential is the result of a conscious choice, but it is also comparable to the experience of buying a new leather coat: each time you wear it, it feels more comfortable and looks better. Similarly, the more you commit to and practice the soul mission symbolized by your Soul Potential, the better it feels. Your Soul Pattern, on the other hand, is comparable to your skin: it is ever-present, and wearing it involves no conscious choice.

Jim, whose Soul Pattern is in Pisces and whose Soul Potential is in Virgo, is a recovering alcoholic who hadn't had a drink in ten years. When alcohol was part of his life, he remained in darkness and pain, unable to escape his spiritual agony. Although he had a college degree in music, he was employed as a janitor. A very talented musician, he couldn't perform in public because he was so withdrawn.

Devastated and suicidal, Jim came to see me after his girlfriend left him for another man. I suggested he see a psychiatrist, but he refused. He wanted nothing to do with therapists and medication. I learned that most of his relationships had turned out the same way this one had: he would wear down his partners with his needful and codependent tendencies, and they would leave. In this latest affair, he had lost himself, having given up all personal boundaries.

We talked about Jim's Soul Pattern in Pisces, about his being extraordinarily sensitive and vulnerable to the energies of those who entered his life. We talked about how fragile and pure of spirit he had been in his past lives. I told him that his previous personalities had cowered from arguments, that he had been repulsed by expressions of anger and hatred. In one life he had lived deep in the woods, far from people and the savagery of his culture. He had been so empathic that he absorbed the energy from others and could not separate himself from them. However, his musical talent was a common theme, an emotional outlet for him in many lives, a means of expression by which he could honor himself. In previous lives he had been a healer, a priest, a nun, and a physician: all lives of self-denial and martyrdom. In this life, instead of living in the woods, he had sealed himself off from having to interact with people by abusing alcohol and working as a janitor at night.

Spiritually Jim remembered the beauty, harmony, and peace of the other side and had not been able to feel secure on the earth without his addictions. He had to learn the lesson of his Soul Potential in Virgo: to value the earthly plane and not try to escape from it. We talked a lot about the beauty of the earth, and soon he began to feel a little more secure in it. He was amazed when I was able to show him how judgmental he had been of the earth and the people on it. As he learned to value the earth, he learned to develop more physical structures in his own life, and to create boundaries by being more discriminating. He worked on other skills relating to having his Soul Potential in Virgo, including prioritizing and organizing his life.

Jim was thrilled to discover that he did have a logical mind. Soon, his emotional paralysis gave way to long-denied emotions. His shyness began to dissipate when he committed himself to helping people without totally losing himself in the process. He decided to return to school and become a music teacher. Teaching music enabled him to use his creative talent as well as be a healer again, this time with more solid personal boundaries and stronger priorities.

Bob, whose Soul Pattern is in Taurus and whose Soul Potential is in Scorpio, worked in a bank for fifteen years—his whole adult life. He came to me when he was 37, unhappy, stuck, and resistant to any form of change. His wife had given him a gift certificate to see me one year before he actually made his appointment. He admitted that he was afraid that I might induce him to change, which was anathema to him.

Bob's life at the bank, however, was becoming increasingly restrictive and depressing. He came to me as a last resort, and I noticed immediately that he had come from many lives as a personality that valued the earth and all that it represented. Security and safety were old foundations that he believed would protect him. I mentioned that Taurus is the sign of the builder on the earth plane: before Bob chose to study finance in college, he had almost become an architect in this life. I shared with him Taurus's fear of change, its need for stability. We talked about money as a symbol for that security. He admitted that he derived great comfort from going into the bank's vault and just looking at the rows of money. He didn't need to have it; he just liked knowing it was there. Taurus collects things as a form of protection.

Bob began to realize how frightened he was of anything that was transitional. He had even hated the interval between leaving college and finding his job because he loathed uncertainty. He would connect with people, showing a great deal of loyalty to them. He still communicated with a childhood friend, even though he really didn't like him.

We zeroed in on a past life where he had been a housewife to a farmer in the Midwest. She had loved her uncomplicated pastoral life and had been a wonderful gardener and cook. Her life was good, Bob remembered, because it was predictable, unchangeable, and secure. His Taurean belief was that life had to continue unchanged if he were to be secure and safe. He recalled another past life as a settler whose farm had been burned and destroyed by a tribe of marauding Indians. That memory impressed upon him how quickly security can be destroyed by sudden, momentous change. In this life, familiarity and a need for predictability became his foundations, and the bank served as a symbol of that security. But now the old ways were becoming problematic for him. He was in the throes of a significant conflict.

Bob's karmic issue around fear of change is very consistent with the energy of Taurus. Taurus needs the earth under its feet, and it values steadfastness and other endurable qualities. Many people with a Soul Pattern in Taurus have had lives as builders, bankers, farmers, potters, and architects. They are comfortable working within the boundaries of the material plane. But sometimes they get caught when the earth turns into mud. Taurus is symbolized by the bull, in its strength and in its stubbornness. It is the farmer who has the patience and the wisdom to know the growing seasons. And it is the banker who is obsessed with the money accruing in his vault. Bob's career was the perfect symbol for his Soul Pattern. He stayed in the bank for years, even when he felt unhappy and stuck.

When I told Bob that he needed to become more Scorpian, to emulate his Soul Potential, he was appalled. His father had been a Scorpio—and was a violent and vengeful man who had done irreparable harm to his family. The last thing Bob ever wanted was to be like his father. However, I helped him understand another side of Scorpio: a gentler, more sensitive, more emotional, trans-formative side.

This new side of Scorpio made more sense to Bob. His wife had complained for years that he held back his feelings, both emotionally and sexually. Once Bob learned more about his Soul Potential in Scorpio, he soon realized that becoming more Scorpian would be in his best interest. I explained to him that Scorpio stands for having the courage to confront issues and probe one's emotions. For Bob, that meant forgiving his father.

I describe those with Soul Potential in Scorpio as "the Sherlock Holmeses of the universe," because they are very interested in probing their own unconscious, to learn more about their emotions, desires, and needs. They also have a propensity for helping others transform and regenerate themselves passionately. Interestingly, Bob followed along this path, seeking not only to uncover layers of himself but to help others do the same. He has been studying psychology for some time now and is close to completing his Ph.D.

Bob's journey to realizing his Soul Potential took him from a mundane existence to investigating the full range of emotions, both in himself and in others. Scorpio is about what "I want" and what "I need" and is unafraid to pursue its aspirations. From a person who was terrified of change with his Soul Pattern in Taurus, Bob evolved to a person who recognized that change is the only reality, a promising indicator of his Soul Potential in Scorpio.

CHAPTER 4

Learning About Your Soul Pattern and Soul Potential

As we have mentioned, your Soul Pattern and Soul Potential signs are diametrically opposite each other. Thus, if your Soul Pattern is in Gemini, your Soul Potential is in Sagittarius, or vice versa. The other five pairs are: Taurus/Scorpio, Aries/Libra, Pisces/Virgo, Aquarius/Leo, and Capricorn/Cancer. In order to determine which signs correspond to your Soul Pattern and your Soul Potential, consult Chart 1, referring to the day, month, and year you were born.

Chart 1: Soul Pattern and Soul Potential Signs

Date Interval	Soul Pattern	Soul Potential
Jan. 1, 1900–Dec. 28, 1900	Gemini	Sagittarius
Dec. 29, 1900–July 17, 1902	Taurus	Scorpio
July 18, 1902–Feb. 4, 1904	Aries	Libra
Feb. 5, 1904–Aug. 23, 1905	Pisces	Virgo
Aug. 24, 1905–Mar. 13, 1907	Aquarius	Leo
Mar. 14, 1907–Sept. 29, 1908	Capricorn	Cancer
Sept. 30, 1908–April 18, 1910	Sagittarius	Gemini
April 19, 1910–Nov. 7, 1911	Scorpio	Taurus
Nov. 8, 1911–May 26, 1913	Libra	Aries
May 27, 1913–Dec. 13, 1914	Virgo	Pisces
Dec. 14, 1914–July 2, 1916	Leo	Aquarius
July 3, 1916–Jan. 19, 1918	Cancer	Capricorn
Jan. 20, 1918–Aug. 9, 1919	Gemini	Sagittarius
Aug. 10, 1919–Feb. 26, 1921	Taurus	Scorpio
Feb. 27, 1921–Sept. 15, 1922	Aries	Libra
Sept. 16, 1922–April 4, 1924	Pisces	Virgo
April 5, 1924–Oct. 22, 1925	Aquarius	Leo
Oct. 23, 1925–May 12, 1927	Capricorn	Cancer
May 13, 1927–Nov. 28, 1928	Sagittarius	Gemini
Nov. 29, 1928–June 18, 1930	Scorpio	Taurus
June 19, 1930–Jan. 6, 1932	Libra	Aries
Jan. 7, 1932–July 25, 1933	Virgo	Pisces
July 26, 1933–Feb. 12, 1935	Leo	Aquarius
Feb. 13, 1935–Sept. 1, 1936	Cancer	Capricorn
Sept. 2, 1936–Mar. 21, 1938	Gemini	Sagittarius
Mar. 22, 1938–Oct. 9, 1939	Taurus	Scorpio
Oct. 10, 1939–April 27, 1941	Aries	Libra
April 28, 1941–Nov. 15, 1942	Pisces	Virgo
Nov. 16, 1942–June 3, 1944	Aquarius	Leo
June 4, 1944–Dec. 23, 1945	Capricorn	Cancer
Dec. 24, 1945–July 11, 1947	Sagittarius	Gemini
July 12, 1947–Jan. 28, 1949	Scorpio	Taurus

Jan. 29, 1949–Aug. 17, 1950	Libra	Aries
Aug. 18, 1950–Mar. 7, 1952	Virgo	Pisces
Mar. 8, 1952–Oct. 2, 1953	Leo	Aquarius
Oct. 3, 1953–April 12, 1955	Cancer	Capricorn
April 13, 1955–Nov. 4, 1956	Gemini	Sagittarius
Nov. 5, 1956–May 21, 1958	Taurus	Scorpio
May 22, 1958–Dec 8. 1959	Aries	Libra
Dec. 9, 1959–July 3, 1961	Pisces	Virgo
July 4, 1961–Jan. 13, 1963	Aquarius	Leo
Jan. 14, 1963–Aug. 5, 1964	Capricorn	Cancer
Aug. 6, 1964–Feb. 21, 1966	Sagittarius	Gemini
Feb. 22, 1966–Sept. 10, 1967	Scorpio	Taurus
Sept. 11, 1967–April 3, 1969	Libra	Aries
April 4, 1969–Oct. 15, 1970	Virgo	Pisces
Oct. 16, 1970–May 5, 1972	Leo	Aquarius
May 6, 1972–Nov. 22, 1973	Cancer	Capricorn
Nov. 23, 1973–June 12, 1975	Gemini	Sagittarius
June 13, 1975–Dec. 29, 1976	Taurus	Scorpio
Dec. 30, 1976–July 19, 1978	Aries	Libra
July 20, 1978–Feb. 5, 1980	Pisces	Virgo
Feb. 6, 1980–Aug. 25, 1981	Aquarius	Leo
Aug. 26, 1981–Mar. 14, 1983	Capricorn	Cancer
Mar. 15, 1983–Oct. 1, 1984	Sagittarius	Gemini
Oct. 2, 1984–April 20, 1986	Scorpio	Taurus
April 21, 1986–Nov. 8, 1987	Libra	Aries
Nov. 9, 1987–May 28, 1989	Virgo	Pisces
May 29, 1989–Dec. 15, 1990	Leo	Aquarius
Dec. 16, 1990–July 4, 1992	Cancer	Capricorn
July 5, 1992–Jan. 21, 1994	Gemini	Sagittarius
Jan. 22, 1994–Aug. 11, 1995	Taurus	Scorpio
Aug. 12, 1995–Feb. 27, 1997	Aries	Libra
Feb. 28, 1997–Sept. 17, 1998	Pisces	Virgo
Sept. 18, 1998–April 9, 2000	Aquarius	Leo
April 10, 2000–Oct. 13, 2001	Capricorn	Cancer
Oct. 14, 2001–April 13, 2003	Sagittarius	Gemini
April 14, 2003–Dec. 26, 2004	Scorpio	Taurus

Dec 27, 2004–June 22, 2006	Libra	Aries
June 23, 2006–Dec. 18, 2007	Virgo	Pisces
Dec. 19, 2007–Aug. 21, 2009	Leo	Aquarius
Aug. 22, 2009–Mar. 3, 2011	Cancer	Capricorn
Mar. 4, 2011–Aug. 30, 2012	Gemini	Sagittarius
Aug. 31, 2012–Feb.18, 2014	Taurus	Scorpio
Feb. 19, 2014–Nov. 12, 2016	Aries	Libra
Nov. 13, 2016–May 9, 2017	Pisces	Virgo
May 10, 2017–Nov. 6, 2018	Aquarius	Leo
Nov. 7, 2018–May 5, 2020	Capricorn	Cancer
May 6, 2020–Jan. 18, 2022	Sagittarius	Gemini
Jan. 19, 2022–July 17, 2023	Scorpio	Taurus
July 18, 2023–Jan. 11, 2025	Libra	Aries
Jan.12, 2025–July 27, 2026	Virgo	Pisces
July 28, 2026–Mar. 26, 2028	Leo	Aquarius
Mar. 27, 2028–Sept. 23, 2029	Cancer	Capricorn
Sept. 24, 2029–Mar. 21, 2031	Gemini	Sagittarius
Mar. 22, 2031–Dec. 2, 2032	Taurus	Scorpio
Dec.3, 2032–June 3, 2034	Aries	Libra
June 4, 2034–Nov. 30, 2035	Pisces	Virgo

After you find your Soul Pattern and Soul Potential signs, consult Chart 2 to learn more about the energies and characteristics associated with them.

Chart 2: Soul Pattern Energetics Model

Aries	Taurus	Gemini
Defiant	Opinionated	Deceptive
Dominating	Greedy	Nervous
Brash	Fearful	Always tense
Tactless	Retentive	Unreliable
Arrogant	Lazy	Inconsistent
Uncooperative	Materialistic	Moody
Combative	Indulgent	Distracted

Self-absorbed	Jealous	Gossipy
Selfish	Stubborn	Easily bored
Accident prone	Fearful of change	Unfocused
Angry	Slow	Manipulative
Impetuous	Overvalues self	Scattered
Hot-headed	Undervalues self	Lost in present
Unreliable	Stingy	High-strung
Cancer	*Leo*	*Virgo*
Too sensitive	Fearful of aging	Tends to blame
Crabby	Needs attention	Judgmental
Manipulative	Requires applause	Obsessive
Obsessed with past	Demands respect	Too logical
Clingy	Melodramatic	Perfectionistic
Too reserved	Dictating	Sometimes petty
Childish	Self-centered	Melancholy
Passive	Vain	Martyristic
Needs being needed	Needs center stage	Too analytical
Smothering	Pretentious	Fussy
Insecure	Autocratic	Fears disease
Negative	Conceited	Work-obsessed
Easily hurt	Patronizing	Dissecting
Timid	Disdainful	Needs to be right
Libra	*Scorpio*	*Sagittarius*
Ambivalent	Raging	Preachy
Wishy-washy	Fanatical	Academic
Superficial	Manipulative	Outspoken
Fears conflict	Withholding	Claustrophobic
Avoids anger	Secretive	Hot-headed
Overly compromising	Too intense	Restless
Too relational	Loves chaos	Too abstract
Passive	Jealous	Too generous
Peace at any price	Possessive	Impatient
Status conscious	Revengeful	Afraid of commitment
Apathetic	Judgmental	Unrealistic

Dishonest	Caustic	Too futuristic
Vain	Distrustful	Overly expansive
Procrastinating	Paranoid	Irresponsible
Fickle	Intimidating	Impractical
Capricorn	*Aquarius*	*Pisces*
Materialistic	Overly logical	Timid
Rigid	Too detached	Feels inadequate
Overly ambitious	Oblivious	Martyristic
Obsessed with past	Intolerant	Escapist
Pessimistic	Meddlesome	Addictive
Unresponsive	Cold	Easily deceived
Stern	Remote	Illusionary
Disciplinarian	Repressed	Codependent
Always needs rules	Impersonal	Fearful
Overly cautious	Radical	Introvert
Arrogant	Opinionated	Indolent
Stubborn	Too predictable	Impractical
Brooding	Erratic	Sacrificing
Insensitive	Aloof	Wounded healer

These characteristics are the tendencies that each Soul Pattern may repress and then project into the world. Most of our past life themes are unconscious, and therefore we project them outside ourselves. These words give you an opportunity to bring your memories to light and deal with them on a conscious level.

SOUL PATTERN: PUTTING WORDS
AND SYMBOLS INTO CONTEXT

When you look at the Energetics Model for the words concerning your Soul Pattern sign, they may well elicit in you an emotional response ranging from anger to ambivalence. The emotional reaction you're experiencing tells you that an unconscious theme has just been catalyzed. The stronger your reaction, the more significant is the past life memory.

Soul Pattern Exercise
This five-step exercise gives you an opportunity to access your past life memories, bring them to light, and deal with them on a conscious level. Once you are conscious of your past, you can value the emotions you feel and utilize them to more clearly understand your past lives.

STEP 1
Identify the words in your Soul Pattern sign in Chart 2 that elicit in you the most negative emotions, that make you feel uneasy, uncomfortable, or annoyed.

STEP 2
Take the words you've just selected, and create a short story from them. Using these words will help you provide a structure for the story and kindle your memory. The karmic story you write will come from your reservoir of past memories. Don't be concerned that you're only "making it up" and that it won't be valid. Do not discount the information because you feel it came from your imagination. Of all the thousands of stories you could have written, there is an important reason why you created that particular one. It could explain why you are stuck in patterns that keep you from creating the love you want and pursuing your soul mission.

STEP 3
Using your imagination, set your story in a specific time and place. Think about a historical period you've been interested in, and place your story in that time. Using the words you have chosen, decide if you were a man or a woman. Keep true to the words, and develop a story.

Years ago when I did this exercise, I chose July 3, 1863, in Gettysburg, Pennsylvania, because as a small child I had been fascinated by Pickett's Charge. I would go to a special place, a hundred yards from the bloody angle near the stone wall that was held by the Union, and play there. When I got older, I felt drawn to Gettysburg for a different reason: that day and place held an important past life memory. Because of the words I had chosen from my Soul Pattern (rebel, revolutionary, individualistic, out of sync), coupled with my past life memory, I concluded that I had been a male, a rebel, and a Confederate soldier.

STEP 4

If this story you just scripted was an actual past life of yours, would it explain issues with which you are experiencing difficulty in this life? My memory of being a Confederate soldier began my search for a past life that finally cleared many of my current life phobias and guilts. I have always been reluctant to be a leader, preferring to stay behind the scenes, to such a degree that I created a speech problem so that I would have to stay reclusive. But this reclusiveness was explained by the fact that I had been a commander in Pickett's Charge, leading my men into a battle that left most of them dead or wounded. It also explained my current terror that my dogs would die because of some imagined carelessness of mine. I learned that, in that battle from a past life, my prized horse had also died. Knowing these past life stories helped me work through my fears in this life. Think about an unexplained anxiety or fear that you have had, and see if it dovetails with your story.

STEP 5

If you could, how would you change one aspect of the story you just wrote? To make that change, write down a commitment you are willing to make now. Take action on that commitment for three weeks, and see what happens. I have made many such commitments based on my past life story.

SOUL POTENTIAL: ENERGIES YOU NEED TO BRING INTO YOUR LIFE

After finding your Soul Potential sign in Chart 1, consult the Soul Potential Energetics Model in Chart 3 to learn more about the energies and characteristics associated with that sign.

Chart 3: Soul Potential Energetics Model

Aries	Taurus	Gemini
Assertive	Values self	Curious
Values the physical	Creative	Present to the now
Independent	A builder	Self-expressive
Self-aware	Resolute	Literary
Initiating	Patient	Open-minded
Likes novelty	A finisher	Gathers information
Risk-taking	Loves the earth	Social
Spontaneous	Sensual	Reflective
Prefers actions	Warm-hearted	Versatile
Eager	Reliable	Intelligent
Competitive	Loyal	Shares information
Self-motivated	Creates security	Articulate
Courageous	Serene	Quick
Explorer	Loves home	Clever
Cancer	Leo	Virgo
Nurturing	Whimsical	Service-oriented
Sensitive	Self-confident	Analytical
Intuitive	Leader	Health-aware
Emotional	Dramatic	Ordered
Focuses on home	Generous	Conscientious

Maternal	Fun-loving	Practical healer
Empathetic	Courageous	Efficient
Devoted	Commanding	Methodical
Values family	Exuberant	Discriminating
Faithful	Heart-centered	Industrious
Supportive	Inspiring	Productive
Tenacious	Dignified	Organized
Protective	Influential	Practical
Romantic	Willing to act	Studious
Libra	*Scorpio*	*Sagittarius*
Loves beauty	Seeks to transform	Honest
Needs balance	Sexual	Philosophical
Mediating	Understands power	Globe-trotter
Touts honesty	Magnetic	Loves freedom
Just	Self-controlled	Values nature
Diplomatic	Intense	Loves animals
Refined	Passionate	Futuristic
Cooperative	Strong-willed	Goal-directed
Harmonious	Piercing	Optimistic
Fair-minded	Investigative	Straightforward
Social	Ingenious	Seeks truth
Charming	Deals with death	Loves physicality
Desires peace	Loves mysteries	Teacher
Capricorn	*Aquarius*	*Pisces*
Self-sufficient	Humanistic	Adapting
Responsible	Individualistic	Psychic
Paternal	Values equality	Romantic
Wise	Inventive	Intuitional
Ambitious	Social activist	Devoted
Hardworking	Intellectual	Musical
Conservative	Tolerant	Forgiving
Traditional	Friendly	Spiritual
Meticulous	Broad-minded	Generous

Enterprising	Imaginative	Emotional
Economical	Objective	Introspective
Disciplined	Altruistic	Poetic
Committed	Idealistic	Visionary
Goal directed	Progressive	Charitable

Examine the words in the Energetics Model under your Soul Potential sign. Do any of them elicit in you an emotional reaction? The words that cause the most fear or anxiety are usually the most important, because they are the characteristics that you probably feel unable to integrate into your life. Ironically, many of my clients have said that those words describe their friends, lovers, or family members. The truth is that we have attracted those people to ourselves to show us what we can become. You can "fake it until you make it," or alter your external behavior until you finally realize that it is right for you. Certain words represent new experiences and energies for you. Have faith in your soul's direction that you can become something that you think you can't be. Keep practicing until it becomes more natural to you.

Living your Soul Potential is not much different from learning to hit a backhand in tennis. Initially it doesn't feel right, and the first few experiences are frustrating. But as you practice and become increasingly comfortable with the new stroke, your confidence will build, and you will hit the ball more consistently and with more authority.

WHY ASPECTS OF YOUR SOUL POTENTIAL MIGHT RANKLE YOU

At first glance, the words associated with your Soul Potential may not seem entirely appealing to you. Although we are loath to admit it, we often don't like what we can't emulate; we often become resentful. In fact, you might look at your Soul Potential characteristics and say, "That's not who I am."

Remember, your Soul Potential is not about who you are but rather who your soul wants you to aspire to be. Thus the words that you say "aren't you" actually refer to the type of energy your soul wants you to bring into your life. For instance, you may be a supremely ambitious person who has drawn a lot of satisfaction out of succeeding in a career or in a business. Now your Soul Potential tells you that you need to be more nurturing, more devoted to home life. At first glance, the notion of "domestication" may make you wince in discontent. In actuality, that initial aversion is your soul's way of telling you it wants you to experience an aspect of life that has heretofore been unfamiliar to you.

The evolution of the soul from one life to the next is all about learning and discovery, about taking on new experiences. Your soul, unlike your personality, does not judge experiences based upon whether they are negative or positive, but upon whether there is a lesson to be learned from your exposure to a new or unfamiliar experience.

Soul Potential Exercise

STEP 1

The words in the Soul Potential Energetics Model are positive aspects of the astrological sign that bespeak your potential. They are words that your soul wishes to bring into your life as part of your soul mission. Choose several words that inspire and excite you. Emphasize the words that refer to what you would like to become but feel you cannot. These are directions you need to take in order to follow your soul path.

STEP 2

Choose one of the words, and create a goal around it. Write it down in your journal to confirm your commitment. Take action on the commitment for three weeks, until it becomes more of a habit. Many of my clients have noticed that the more they take action on a goal, the easier it becomes, because it is aligned with their soul's intention. Being on the path means your soul goes with you.

STEP 3

Educate yourself about your Soul Potential and the astrological sign that symbolizes it. Learning everything you can about it is extremely important. Many of my clients have done extensive research on their Soul Potential sign, making it easier to live it. The more you know about your Soul Potential, the easier it is to fulfill. Use the Internet, the library, bookstores. Become well versed in your Soul Potential sign.

STEP 4

Pay attention to people whose Sun sign is the same as your Soul Potential sign. They are invaluable. Ask them how they would handle various life situations. You will be amazed at how different their responses are from what yours would be. Since my Soul Potential sign is Leo, I've made it a point to learn everything I can from my Leo friends. They have taught me more about Leo than anything I've read.

STEP 5

Each astrological sign has a color, a stone, a metal, an herb, an animal, and much more that symbolizes its energy. Become aware of the symbols that remind you of your Soul Potential. Since my Soul Potential is Leo, I wear gold, and a lion ring. I have a collection of lions that constantly remind me of the lion's courage, power, and regal qualities.

STEP 6

Evaluate the results. Keeping a journal is very important. It will make you more aware of your progress.

WINDOW TO YOUR SOUL

Think of your Soul Potential as a window through which you can see your soul. Through its attributes, you can understand your soul better. It's as if your soul were saying to you, "This is who I am in this life for you, and I am making it easier for you to understand that by assuming these characteristics." The following information for each of the twelve signs will give you a good head start toward learning more about your Soul Potential and considering how to integrate it to improve the quality of your life. Remember, you may not identify immediately with the description of your sign because it does not correspond to what's familiar to you. Rather, it signifies who you need to be and the energies your soul wants you to bring into your life to make it more fulfilling. Your Sun sign contains characteristics that are more familiar to you and more aptly describe who you are now. After you read about these energies, consider incorporating them into your life and then see how you feel about it.

CHAPTER 5

MERCURY: YOUR ORIENTATION TO THE WORLD

The way we view the world is colored by all the obvious components of our identity: race, religion, economic strata, gender, geography, and culture. For examples, we need look no farther than the deep fissure in the United States between blacks and whites, the tortuous struggle for peace between Israelis and Palestinians, the age-old hatred between Catholics and Protestants in Northern Ireland, the continued savagery between Hutus and Tutsis in Rwanda, and unrest that continues to plague the fractionalized states of the former Yugoslavia. John Gray's *Men Are from Mars, Women Are from Venus* has sold millions of copies predicated on one premise: that men and women are different and perceive things from entirely different vantage points.

But our perceptions are also greatly influenced by a less obvious factor that has nothing to do with our ethnicity, our genitalia, the color of our skin, or our religion. The impact of our personal filter—our Mercury placement—transcends all of the effects manifested in us by our nationality, race, gender, and so on. Mercury is about who we are, how we receive and perceive information, what we do with it, and how we express ourselves once we have it.

Mercury symbolizes the way each of us indigenously comprehends the world at large within the context of our own lives. Children of the same parents, raised in the same home, attending the same school, trained in the same religious and social environment, can be extraordinarily different in how they filter their world.

Mercury helps us understand our intellectual and emotional orientations to life, showing us how we communicate our innate talents and connect with others. It defines how we wish to align ourselves with others by sharing our ideas, thoughts, and ideals. It represents our desire to express our needs, perceptions, and ideas through speech, as well as our need to be understood.

I divide Mercury traits into two categories:

1. Receptive—receiving information
2. Expressive—giving information

One of the first things I tell my new interns is that it is our responsibility to hear, understand, and communicate effectively with our clients. In order to do that, I tell them, they must learn and master the symbols, meanings, and energies of all twelve astrological signs. You can imagine their reaction upon learning that they must master twelve languages! But acknowledging that there are twelve different ways to perceive and process information is the philosophical underpinning on which the study of Mercury is based.

Considering that people's views of the world are influenced by twelve different spiritual filters, compounded by their religious, racial, and ethnic contexts, the enduring conflagrations across the globe become easier to comprehend, if no less distressing. Communicating effectively is one of our highest priorities, paramount to the success of all our relationships, yet few people understand that there are twelve different ways to do it. Learning about your personal filter—your Mercury's traits—and the filters of those people with whom you interact undoubtedly will be one of the most essential lessons you glean from this book.

Mercury differs from the other planets in that it is not a karmic planet. It deals only with issues relating to our personality in this life. Your Mercury filter was chosen for you by your soul, for your personality's intellectual evolution.

> *"Since the measuring device has been constructed by the observer …we have to remember that what we observe is not nature in itself but nature exposed to our method of questioning."*
>
> **—Werner Heisenberg**

MERCURY TRAITS: HOW WE PROCESS INFORMATION

Each of us has a sign into which the planet Mercury is located at the time of our birth. The following chart provides you with your personal Mercury placement.

Mercury Placements

If you were born:	Your Mercury is in:	If you were born:	Your Mercury is in:
Jan. 1–Jan. 15, 1915	Capricorn	Mar. 26–April 9, 1917	Aries
Jan. 16–Feb. 2, 1915	Aquarius	April 10–June 14, 1917	Taurus
Feb. 3–Feb. 23, 1915	Pisces	June 15–July 3, 1917	Gemini
Feb. 24–Mar. 19, 1915	Aquarius	July 4–July 17, 1917	Cancer
Mar. 20–April 10, 1915	Pisces	July 18–Aug. 2, 1917	Leo
April 11–April 26, 1915	Aries	Aug. 3–Aug. 26, 1917	Virgo
April 27–May 10, 1915	Taurus	Aug. 27–Sept. 14, 1917	Libra
May 11–May 29, 1915	Gemini	Sept. 15–Oct. 10, 1917	Virgo
May 30–Aug. 4, 1915	Cancer	Oct. 11–Oct. 28, 1917	Libra
Aug. 5–Aug. 19, 1915	Leo	Oct. 29–Nov. 15, 1917	Scorpio
Aug. 20–Sept. 5, 1915	Virgo	Nov. 16–Dec. 5, 1917	Sagittarius
Sept. 6–Sept. 28, 1915	Libra	Dec. 6–Feb. 10, 1918	Capricorn
Sept. 29–Oct. 21, 1915	Scorpio	Feb. 11–Mar. 1, 1918	Aquarius
Oct. 22–Nov. 11, 1915	Libra	Mar. 2–Mar. 17, 1918	Pisces
Nov. 12–Dec. 1, 1915	Scorpio	Mar. 18–April 2, 1918	Aries
Dec. 2–Dec. 20, 1915	Sagittarius	April 3–June 10, 1918	Taurus
Dec. 21–Jan. 8, 1916	Capricorn	June 11–June 24, 1918	Gemini
Jan. 9–Mar. 15, 1916	Aquarius	June 25–July 9, 1918	Cancer
Mar. 16–April 2, 1916	Pisces	July 10–July 28, 1918	Leo
April 3–April 17, 1916	Aries	July 29–Oct. 3, 1918	Virgo
April 18–May 2, 1916	Taurus	Oct. 4–Oct. 20, 1918	Libra
May 3–July 10, 1916	Gemini	Oct. 21–Nov. 8, 1918	Scorpio
July 11–July 26, 1916	Cancer	Nov. 9–Dec. 1, 1918	Sagittarius
July 27–Aug. 10, 1916	Leo	Dec. 2–Dec. 15, 1918	Capricorn
Aug. 11–Aug. 29, 1916	Virgo	Dec. 16–Jan. 13, 1919	Sagittarius
Aug. 30–Nov. 4, 1916	Libra	Jan. 14–Feb. 3, 1919	Capricorn
Nov. 5–Nov. 23, 1916	Scorpio	Feb. 4–Feb. 21, 1919	Aquarius
Nov. 24–Dec. 12, 1916	Sagittarius	Feb. 22–Mar. 9, 1919	Pisces
Dec. 13–Jan. 1, 1917	Capricorn	Mar. 10–May 16, 1919	Aries
Jan. 2–Jan. 18, 1917	Aquarius	May 17–June 2, 1919	Taurus
Jan. 19–Feb. 15, 1917	Capricorn	June 3–June 16, 1919	Gemini
Feb. 16–Mar. 8, 1917	Aquarius	June 17–July 2, 1919	Cancer
Mar. 9–Mar. 25, 1917	Pisces	July 3–Sept. 9, 1919	Leo

If you were born:	Your Mercury is in:	If you were born:	Your Mercury is in:
Sept. 10–Sept. 25, 1919	Virgo	Jan. 12–Feb. 1, 1922	Aquarius
Sept. 26–Oct. 13, 1919	Libra	Feb. 2–Feb. 9, 1922	Pisces
Oct. 14–Nov. 2, 1919	Scorpio	Feb. 10–Mar. 18, 1922	Aquarius
Nov. 3–Jan. 8, 1920	Sagittarius	Mar. 19–April 7, 1922	Pisces
Jan. 9–Jan. 27, 1920	Capricorn	April 8–April 22, 1922	Aries
Jan. 28–Feb. 13, 1920	Aquarius	April 23–May 7, 1922	Taurus
Feb. 14–Mar. 2, 1920	Pisces	May 8–June 1, 1922	Gemini
Mar. 3–Mar. 19, 1920	Aries	June 2–June 10, 1922	Cancer
Mar. 20–April 17, 1920	Pisces	June 11–July 13, 1922	Gemini
April 18–May 8, 1920	Aries	July 14–July 31, 1922	Cancer
May 9–May 24, 1920	Taurus	Aug. 1–Aug. 15, 1922	Leo
May 25–June 7, 1920	Gemini	Aug. 16–Sept. 2, 1922	Virgo
June 8–June 26, 1920	Cancer	Sept. 3–Oct. 1, 1922	Libra
June 27–Aug. 2, 1920	Leo	Oct. 2–Oct. 5, 1922	Scorpio
Aug. 3–Aug. 10, 1920	Cancer	Oct. 6–Nov. 8, 1922	Libra
Aug. 11–Aug. 31, 1920	Leo	Nov. 9–Nov. 27, 1922	Scorpio
Sept. 1–Sept. 16, 1920	Virgo	Nov. 28–Dec. 17, 1922	Sagittarius
Sept. 17–Oct. 5, 1920	Libra	Dec. 18–Jan. 4, 1923	Capricorn
Oct. 6–Oct. 30, 1920	Scorpio	Jan. 5–Feb. 6, 1923	Aquarius
Oct. 31–Nov. 10, 1920	Sagittarius	Feb. 7–Feb. 13, 1923	Capricorn
Nov. 11–Dec. 11, 1920	Scorpio	Feb. 14–Mar. 13, 1923	Aquarius
Dec. 12–Dec. 31, 1920	Sagittarius	Mar. 14–Mar. 30, 1923	Pisces
Jan. 1–Jan. 19, 1921	Capricorn	Mar. 31–April 14, 1923	Aries
Jan. 20–Feb. 5, 1921	Aquarius	April 15–May 1, 1923	Taurus
Feb. 6–April 14, 1921	Pisces	May 2–July 8, 1923	Gemini
April 15–May 1, 1921	Aries	July 9–July 23, 1923	Cancer
May 2–May 15, 1921	Taurus	July 24–Aug. 7, 1923	Leo
May 16–May 31, 1921	Gemini	Aug. 8–Aug. 27, 1923	Virgo
June 1–Aug. 8, 1921	Cancer	Aug. 28–Oct. 4, 1923	Libra
Aug. 9–Aug. 23, 1921	Leo	Oct. 5–Oct. 11, 1923	Virgo
Aug. 24–Sept. 9, 1921	Virgo	Oct. 12–Nov. 2, 1923	Libra
Sept. 10–Sept. 29, 1921	Libra	Nov. 3–Nov. 20, 1923	Scorpio
Sept. 30–Dec. 5, 1921	Scorpio	Nov. 21–Dec. 9, 1923	Sagittarius
Dec. 6–Dec. 24, 1921	Sagittarius	Dec. 10–Feb. 14, 1924	Capricorn
Dec. 25–Jan. 11, 1922	Capricorn	Feb. 15–Mar. 5, 1924	Aquarius

If you were born:	Your Mercury is in:	If you were born:	Your Mercury is in:
Mar. 6–Mar. 21, 1924	Pisces	June 30–Sept. 5, 1926	Leo
Mar. 22–April 5, 1924	Aries	Sept. 6–Sept. 21, 1926	Virgo
April 6–June 13, 1924	Taurus	Sept. 22–Oct. 9, 1926	Libra
June 14–June 29, 1924	Gemini	Oct. 10–Oct. 31, 1926	Scorpio
June 30–July 13, 1924	Cancer	Nov. 1–Nov. 28, 1926	Sagittarius
July 14–July 30, 1924	Leo	Nov. 29–Dec. 13, 1926	Scorpio
July 31–Oct. 7, 1924	Virgo	Dec. 14–Jan. 5, 1927	Sagittarius
Oct. 8–Oct. 24, 1924	Libra	Jan. 6–Jan. 24, 1927	Capricorn
Oct. 25–Nov. 12, 1924	Scorpio	Jan. 25–Feb. 10, 1927	Aquarius
Nov. 13–Dec. 2, 1924	Sagittarius	Feb. 11–April 17, 1927	Pisces
Dec. 3–Dec. 31, 1924	Capricorn	April 18–May 6, 1927	Aries
Jan. 1–Jan. 14, 1925	Sagittarius	May 7–May 20, 1927	Taurus
Jan. 15–Feb. 7, 1925	Capricorn	May 21–June 4, 1927	Gemini
Feb. 8–Feb. 25, 1925	Aquarius	June 5–June 28, 1927	Cancer
Feb. 26–Mar. 13, 1925	Pisces	June 29–July 14, 1927	Leo
Mar. 14–April 1, 1925	Aries	July 15–Aug. 12, 1927	Cancer
April 2–April 15, 1925	Taurus	Aug. 13–Aug. 28, 1927	Leo
April 16–May 17, 1925	Aries	Aug. 29–Sept. 14, 1927	Virgo
May 18–June 6, 1925	Taurus	Sept. 15–Oct. 3, 1927	Libra
June 7–June 20, 1925	Gemini	Oct. 4–Dec. 9, 1927	Scorpio
June 21–July 5, 1925	Cancer	Dec. 10–Dec. 29, 1927	Sagittarius
July 6–July 26, 1925	Leo	Dec. 30–Jan. 16, 1928	Capricorn
July 27–Aug. 27, 1925	Virgo	Jan. 17–Feb. 3, 1928	Aquarius
Aug. 28–Sept. 11, 1925	Leo	Feb. 4–Feb. 29, 1928	Pisces
Sept. 12–Sept. 29, 1925	Virgo	Mar. 1–Mar. 18, 1928	Aquarius
Sept. 30–Oct. 17, 1925	Libra	Mar. 19–April 11, 1928	Pisces
Oct. 18–Nov. 5, 1925	Scorpio	April 12–April 27, 1928	Aries
Nov. 6–Jan. 11, 1926	Sagittarius	April 28–May 11, 1928	Taurus
Jan. 12–Jan. 31, 1926	Capricorn	May 12–May 28, 1928	Gemini
Feb. 1–Feb. 17, 1926	Aquarius	May 29–Aug. 4, 1928	Cancer
Feb. 18–Mar. 6, 1926	Pisces	Aug. 5–Aug. 19, 1928	Leo
Mar. 7–May 13, 1926	Aries	Aug. 20–Sept. 5, 1928	Virgo
May 14–May 29, 1926	Taurus	Sept. 6–Sept. 27, 1928	Libra
May 30–June 12, 1926	Gemini	Sept. 28–Oct. 24, 1928	Scorpio
June 13–June 29, 1926	Cancer	Oct. 25–Nov. 11, 1928	Libra

If you were born:	Your Mercury is in:	If you were born:	Your Mercury is in:
Nov. 12–Dec. 1, 1928	Scorpio	Mar. 19–April 3, 1931	Aries
Dec. 2–Dec. 20, 1928	Sagittarius	April 4–June 11, 1931	Taurus
Dec. 21–Jan. 8, 1929	Capricorn	June 12–June 26, 1931	Gemini
Jan. 9–Mar. 16, 1929	Aquarius	June 27–July 10, 1931	Cancer
Mar. 17–April 3, 1929	Pisces	July 11–July 28, 1931	Leo
April 4–April 19, 1929	Aries	July 29–Oct. 4, 1931	Virgo
April 20–May 3, 1929	Taurus	Oct. 5–Oct. 22, 1931	Libra
May 4–July 11, 1929	Gemini	Oct. 23–Nov. 10, 1931	Scorpio
July 12–July 27, 1929	Cancer	Nov. 11–Dec. 1, 1931	Sagittarius
July 28–Aug. 11, 1929	Leo	Dec. 2–Dec. 20, 1931	Capricorn
Aug. 12–Aug. 30, 1929	Virgo	Dec. 21–Jan. 14, 1932	Sagittarius
Sept. 1–Nov. 5, 1929	Libra	Jan. 15–Feb. 5, 1932	Capricorn
Nov. 6–Nov. 24, 1929	Scorpio	Feb. 6–Feb. 23, 1932	Aquarius
Nov. 25–Dec. 13, 1929	Sagittarius	Feb. 24–Mar. 9, 1932	Pisces
Dec. 14–Jan. 2, 1930	Capricorn	Mar. 10–May 15, 1932	Aries
Jan. 3–Jan. 23, 1930	Aquarius	May 16–June 2, 1932	Taurus
Jan. 24–Feb. 15, 1930	Capricorn	June 3–June 16, 1932	Gemini
Feb. 16–Mar. 9, 1930	Aquarius	June 17–July 2, 1932	Cancer
Mar. 10–Mar. 26, 1930	Pisces	July 3–July 27, 1932	Leo
Mar. 27–April 10, 1930	Aries	July 28–Aug. 10, 1932	Virgo
April 11–May 1, 1930	Taurus	Aug. 11–Sept. 9, 1932	Leo
May 2–May 17, 1930	Gemini	Sept. 10–Sept. 26, 1932	Virgo
May 18–June 14, 1930	Taurus	Sept. 27–Oct. 13, 1932	Libra
June 15–July 4, 1930	Gemini	Oct. 14–Nov. 2, 1932	Scorpio
July 5–July 19, 1930	Cancer	Nov. 3–Jan. 8, 1933	Sagittarius
July 20–Aug. 4, 1930	Leo	Jan. 9–Jan. 27, 1933	Capricorn
Aug. 5–Aug. 26, 1930	Virgo	Jan. 28–Feb. 14, 1933	Aquarius
Aug. 27–Sept. 20, 1930	Libra	Feb. 15–Mar. 3, 1933	Pisces
Sept. 21–Oct. 11, 1930	Virgo	Mar. 4–Mar. 25, 1933	Aries
Oct. 12–Oct. 29, 1930	Libra	Mar. 26–April 17, 1933	Pisces
Oct. 30–Nov. 17, 1930	Scorpio	April 18–May 10, 1933	Aries
Nov. 18–Dec. 6, 1930	Sagittarius	May 11–May 25, 1933	Taurus
Dec. 7–Feb. 11, 1931	Capricorn	May 26–June 8, 1933	Gemini
Feb. 12–Mar. 2, 1931	Aquarius	June 9–June 27, 1933	Cancer
Mar. 3–Mar. 18, 1921	Pisces	June 28–Sept. 2, 1933	Leo

If you were born:	Your Mercury is in:	If you were born:	Your Mercury is in:
Sept. 3–Sept. 18, 1933	Virgo	Nov. 30–Dec. 18, 1935	Sagittarius
Sept. 19–Oct. 6, 1933	Libra	Dec. 19–Jan. 6, 1936	Capricorn
Oct. 7–Oct. 30, 1933	Scorpio	Jan. 7–Mar. 13, 1936	Aquarius
Oct. 31–Nov. 16, 1933	Sagittarius	Mar. 14–Mar. 31, 1936	Pisces
Nov. 17–Dec. 12, 1933	Scorpio	April 1–April 15, 1936	Aries
Dec. 13–Jan. 1, 1934	Sagittarius	April 16–May 1, 1936	Taurus
Jan. 2–Jan. 20, 1934	Capricorn	May 2–July 8, 1936	Gemini
Jan. 21–Feb. 6, 1934	Aquarius	July 9–July 23, 1936	Cancer
Feb. 7–April 15, 1934	Pisces	July 24–Aug. 7, 1936	Leo
April 16–May 2, 1934	Aries	Aug. 8–Aug. 27, 1936	Virgo
May 3–May 16, 1934	Taurus	Aug. 28–Nov. 2, 1936	Libra
May 17–June 1, 1934	Gemini	Nov. 3–Nov. 21, 1936	Scorpio
June 2–Aug. 9, 1934	Cancer	Nov. 22–Dec. 10, 1936	Sagittarius
Aug. 10–Aug. 25, 1934	Leo	Dec. 11–Jan. 1, 1937	Capricorn
Aug. 26–Sept. 10, 1934	Virgo	Jan. 2–Jan. 9, 1937	Aquarius
Sept. 11–Sept. 30, 1934	Libra	Jan. 10–Feb. 14, 1937	Capricorn
Oct. 1–Dec. 6, 1934	Scorpio	Feb. 15–Mar. 6, 1937	Aquarius
Dec. 7–Dec. 25, 1934	Sagittarius	Mar. 7–Mar. 23, 1937	Pisces
Dec. 26–Jan. 13, 1935	Capricorn	Mar. 24–April 7, 1937	Aries
Jan. 14–Feb. 1, 1935	Aquarius	April 8–June 13, 1937	Taurus
Feb. 2–Feb. 15, 1935	Pisces	June 14–July 1, 1937	Gemini
Feb. 15–Mar. 18, 1935	Aquarius	July 2–July 15, 1937	Cancer
Mar. 19–April 8, 1935	Pisces	July 16–July 31, 1937	Leo
April 9–April 24, 1935	Aries	Aug. 1–Oct. 8, 1937	Virgo
April 25–May 8, 1935	Taurus	Oct. 9–Oct. 26, 1937	Libra
May 9–May 29, 1935	Gemini	Oct. 27–Nov. 13, 1937	Scorpio
May 30–June 20, 1935	Cancer	Nov. 14–Dec. 3, 1937	Sagittarius
June 21–July 13, 1935	Gemini	Dec. 4–Jan. 6, 1938	Capricorn
July 14–Aug. 2, 1935	Cancer	Jan. 7–Jan. 12, 1938	Sagittarius
Aug. 3–Aug. 16, 1935	Leo	Jan. 13–Feb. 8, 1938	Capricorn
Aug. 17–Sept. 3, 1935	Virgo	Feb. 9–Feb. 27, 1938	Aquarius
Sept. 4–Sept. 28, 1935	Libra	Feb. 28–Mar. 14, 1938	Pisces
Sept. 29–Oct. 12, 1935	Scorpio	Mar. 15–April 1, 1938	Aries
Oct. 13–Nov. 10, 1935	Libra	April 2–April 23, 1938	Taurus
Nov. 11–Nov. 29, 1935	Scorpio	April 24–May 16, 1938	Aries

If you were born:	Your Mercury is in:	If you were born:	Your Mercury is in:
May 17–June 8, 1938	Taurus	Aug. 12–Aug. 29, 1940	Leo
June 9–June 22, 1938	Gemini	Aug. 30–Sept. 14, 1940	Virgo
June 23–July 7, 1938	Cancer	Sept. 15–Oct. 3, 1940	Libra
July 8–July 26, 1938	Leo	Oct. 4–Dec. 9, 1940	Scorpio
July 27–Sept. 3, 1938	Virgo	Dec. 10–Dec. 29, 1940	Sagittarius
Sept. 4–Sept. 10, 1938	Leo	Dec. 30–Jan. 16, 1941	Capricorn
Sept. 11–Oct. 1, 1938	Virgo	Jan. 17–Feb. 3, 1941	Aquarius
Oct. 2–Oct. 18, 1938	Libra	Feb. 4–Mar. 7, 1941	Pisces
Oct. 19–Nov. 6, 1938	Scorpio	Mar. 8–Mar. 16, 1941	Aquarius
Nov. 7–Jan. 12, 1939	Sagittarius	Mar. 17–April 12, 1941	Pisces
Jan. 13–Feb. 1, 1939	Capricorn	April 13–April 28, 1941	Aries
Feb. 2–Feb. 19, 1939	Aquarius	April 29–May 13, 1941	Taurus
Feb. 20–Mar. 7, 1939	Pisces	May 14–May 29, 1941	Gemini
Mar. 8–May 14, 1939	Aries	May 30–Aug. 6, 1941	Cancer
May 15–May 31, 1939	Taurus	Aug. 7–Aug. 21, 1941	Leo
June 1–June 13, 1939	Gemini	Aug. 22–Sept. 6, 1941	Virgo
June 14–June 30, 1939	Cancer	Sept. 7–Sept. 28, 1941	Libra
July 1–Sept. 7, 1939	Leo	Sept. 29–Oct. 29, 1941	Scorpio
Sept. 8–Sept. 23, 1939	Virgo	Oct. 30–Nov. 11, 1941	Libra
Sept. 24–Oct. 11, 1939	Libra	Nov. 12–Dec. 2, 1941	Scorpio
Oct. 12–Nov. 1, 1939	Scorpio	Dec. 3–Dec. 22, 1941	Sagittarius
Nov. 2–Dec. 3, 1939	Sagittarius	Dec. 23–Jan. 9, 1942	Capricorn
Dec. 4–Dec. 13, 1939	Scorpio	Jan. 10–Mar. 16, 1942	Aquarius
Dec. 14–Jan. 6, 1940	Sagittarius	Mar. 17–April 5, 1942	Pisces
Jan. 7–Jan. 25, 1940	Capricorn	April 6–April 20, 1942	Aries
Jan. 26–Feb. 11, 1940	Aquarius	April 21–May 5, 1942	Taurus
Feb. 12–Mar. 4, 1940	Pisces	May 6–July 12, 1942	Gemini
Mar. 5–Mar. 8, 1940	Aries	July 13–July 29, 1942	Cancer
Mar. 9–April 17, 1940	Pisces	July 30–Aug. 13, 1942	Leo
April 18–May 6, 1940	Aries	Aug. 14–Aug. 31, 1942	Virgo
May 7–May 21, 1940	Taurus	Sept. 1–Nov. 7, 1942	Libra
May 22–June 4, 1940	Gemini	Nov. 8–Nov. 25, 1942	Scorpio
June 5–June 26, 1940	Cancer	Nov. 26–Dec. 14, 1942	Sagittarius
June 27–July 21, 1940	Leo	Dec. 15–Jan. 3, 1943	Capricorn
July 22–Aug. 11, 1940	Cancer	Jan. 4–Jan. 27, 1943	Aquarius

If you were born:	Your Mercury is in:	If you were born:	Your Mercury is in:
Jan. 28–Feb. 15, 1943	Capricorn	June 5–June 18, 1945	Gemini
Feb. 16–Mar. 11, 1943	Aquarius	June 19–July 3, 1945	Cancer
Mar. 12–Mar. 28, 1943	Pisces	July 4–July 26, 1945	Leo
Mar. 29–April 12, 1943	Aries	July 27–Aug. 17, 1945	Virgo
April 13–April 30, 1943	Taurus	Aug. 18–Sept. 10, 1945	Leo
May 1–May 26, 1943	Gemini	Sept. 11–Sept. 27, 1945	Virgo
May 27–June 14, 1943	Taurus	Sept. 28–Oct. 14, 1945	Libra
June 15–July 6, 1943	Gemini	Oct. 15–Nov. 3, 1945	Scorpio
July 7–July 20, 1943	Cancer	Nov. 4–Jan. 9, 1946	Sagittarius
July 21–Aug. 5, 1943	Leo	Jan. 10–Jan. 29, 1946	Capricorn
Aug. 6–Aug. 27, 1943	Virgo	Jan. 30–Feb. 15, 1946	Aquarius
Aug. 28–Sept. 25, 1943	Libra	Feb. 16–April 16, 1946	Pisces
Sept. 26–Oct. 11, 1943	Virgo	April 17–May 11, 1946	Aries
Oct. 12–Oct. 30, 1943	Libra	May 12–May 27, 1946	Taurus
Oct. 31–Nov. 18, 1943	Scorpio	May 28–June 10, 1946	Gemini
Nov. 19–Dec. 8, 1943	Sagittarius	June 11–June 27, 1946	Cancer
Dec. 9–Feb. 12, 1944	Capricorn	June 28–Sept. 3, 1946	Leo
Feb. 13–Mar. 3, 1944	Aquarius	Sept. 4–Sept. 19, 1946	Virgo
Mar. 4–Mar. 19, 1944	Pisces	Sept. 20–Oct. 7, 1946	Libra
Mar. 20–April 3, 1944	Aries	Oct. 8–Oct. 30, 1946	Scorpio
April 4–June 11, 1944	Taurus	Oct. 31–Nov. 20, 1946	Sagittarius
June 12–June 27, 1944	Gemini	Nov. 21–Dec. 12, 1946	Scorpio
June 28–July 11, 1944	Cancer	Dec. 13–Jan. 3, 1947	Sagittarius
July 12–July 28, 1944	Leo	Jan. 4–Jan. 21, 1947	Capricorn
July 29–Oct. 5, 1944	Virgo	Jan. 22–Feb. 8, 1947	Aquarius
Oct. 6–Oct. 22, 1944	Libra	Feb. 9–April 16, 1947	Pisces
Oct. 23–Nov. 10, 1944	Scorpio	April 17–May 4, 1947	Aries
Nov. 11–Dec. 1, 1944	Sagittarius	May 5–May 18, 1947	Taurus
Dec. 2–Dec. 23, 1944	Capricorn	May 19–June 2, 1947	Gemini
Dec. 24–Jan. 14, 1945	Sagittarius	June 3–Aug. 10, 1947	Cancer
Jan. 15–Feb. 5, 1945	Capricorn	Aug. 11–Aug. 26, 1947	Leo
Feb. 6–Feb. 23, 1945	Aquarius	Aug. 27–Sept. 11, 1947	Virgo
Feb. 24–Mar. 11, 1945	Pisces	Sept. 12–Oct. 1, 1947	Libra
Mar. 12–May 16, 1945	Aries	Oct. 2–Dec. 7, 1947	Scorpio
May 17–June 4, 1945	Taurus	Dec. 8–Dec. 26, 1947	Sagittarius

If you were born:	Your Mercury is in:	If you were born:	Your Mercury is in:
Dec. 27–Jan. 14, 1948	Capricorn	Mar. 25–April 8, 1950	Aries
Jan. 15–Feb. 2, 1948	Aquarius	April 9–June 14, 1950	Taurus
Feb. 3–Feb. 20, 1948	Pisces	June 15–July 2, 1950	Gemini
Feb. 21–Mar. 18, 1948	Aquarius	July 3–July 16, 1950	Cancer
Mar. 19–April 9, 1948	Pisces	July 17–Aug. 2, 1950	Leo
April 10–April 25, 1948	Aries	Aug. 3–Aug. 27, 1950	Virgo
April 26–May 9, 1948	Taurus	Aug. 28–Sept. 10, 1950	Libra
May 10–May 28, 1948	Gemini	Sept. 11–Oct. 9, 1950	Virgo
May 29–June 28, 1948	Cancer	Oct. 10–Oct. 27, 1950	Libra
June 29–July 11, 1948	Gemini	Oct. 28–Nov. 15, 1950	Scorpio
July 12–Aug. 2, 1948	Cancer	Nov. 16–Dec. 5, 1950	Sagittarius
Aug. 3–Aug. 17, 1948	Leo	Dec. 6–Feb. 9, 1951	Capricorn
Aug. 18–Sept. 3, 1948	Virgo	Feb. 10–Feb. 29, 1951	Aquarius
Sept. 4–Sept. 27, 1948	Libra	Mar. 1–Mar. 16, 1951	Pisces
Sept. 28–Oct. 17, 1948	Scorpio	Mar. 17–April 2 , 1951	Aries
Oct. 18–Nov. 10, 1948	Libra	April 3–May 1, 1951	Taurus
Nov. 11–Nov. 29, 1948	Scorpio	May 2–May 15, 1951	Aries
Nov. 30–Dec. 18, 1948	Sagittarius	May 16–June 9, 1951	Taurus
Dec. 19–Jan. 6, 1949	Capricorn	June 10–June 24, 1951	Gemini
Jan. 7–Mar. 14, 1949	Aquarius	June 25–July 8, 1951	Cancer
Mar. 15–April 1, 1949	Pisces	July 9–July 27, 1951	Leo
April 2–April 16, 1949	Aries	July 28–Oct. 2, 1951	Virgo
April 17–May 2, 1949	Taurus	Oct. 3–Oct. 19, 1951	Libra
May 3–July 10, 1949	Gemini	Oct. 20–Nov. 8, 1951	Scorpio
July 11–July 25, 1949	Cancer	Nov. 9–Dec. 1, 1951	Sagittarius
July 26–Aug. 9, 1949	Leo	Dec. 2–Dec. 12, 1951	Capricorn
Aug. 10–Aug. 28, 1949	Virgo	Dec. 13–Jan. 13, 1952	Sagittarius
Aug. 29–Nov. 3, 1949	Libra	Jan. 14–Feb. 3, 1952	Capricorn
Nov. 4–Nov. 22, 1949	Scorpio	Feb. 4–Feb. 20, 1952	Aquarius
Nov. 23–Dec. 11, 1949	Sagittarius	Feb. 21–Mar. 7, 1952	Pisces
Dec. 12–Jan. 1, 1950	Capricorn	Mar. 8–May 14, 1952	Aries
Jan. 2–Jan. 15, 1950	Aquarius	May 15–May 31, 1952	Taurus
Jan. 16–Feb. 14, 1950	Capricorn	June 1–June 14, 1952	Gemini
Feb. 15–Mar. 7, 1950	Aquarius	June 15–June 30, 1952	Cancer
Mar. 8–Mar. 24, 1950	Pisces	July 1–Sept. 7, 1952	Leo

If you were born:	Your Mercury is in:	If you were born:	Your Mercury is in:
Sept. 8–Sept. 23, 1952	Virgo	Dec. 5–Dec. 23, 1954	Sagittarius
Sept. 24–Oct. 11, 1952	Libra	Dec. 24–Jan. 10, 1955	Capricorn
Oct. 12–Nov. 1, 1952	Scorpio	Jan. 11–Mar. 17, 1955	Aquarius
Nov. 2–Jan. 6, 1953	Sagittarius	Mar. 18–April 6, 1955	Pisces
Jan. 7–Jan. 25, 1953	Capricorn	April 7–April 22, 1955	Aries
Jan. 26–Feb. 11, 1953	Aquarius	April 23–May 6, 1955	Taurus
Feb. 12–Mar. 2, 1953	Pisces	May 7–July 13, 1955	Gemini
Mar. 3–Mar. 15, 1953	Aries	July 14–July 30, 1955	Cancer
Mar. 16–April 17, 1953	Pisces	July 31–Aug. 14, 1955	Leo
April 18–May 8, 1953	Aries	Aug. 15–Sept. 30, 1955	Virgo
May 9–May 23, 1953	Taurus	Oct. 1–Nov. 8, 1955	Libra
May 24–June 6, 1953	Gemini	Nov. 9–Nov. 27, 1955	Scorpio
June 7–June 26, 1953	Cancer	Nov. 28–Dec. 16, 1955	Sagittarius
June 27–July 28, 1953	Leo	Dec. 17–Jan. 4, 1956	Capricorn
July 29–Aug. 11, 1953	Cancer	Jan. 5–Mar. 11, 1956	Aquarius
Aug. 12–Aug. 30, 1953	Leo	Mar. 12–Mar. 31, 1956	Pisces
Aug. 31–Sept. 15, 1953	Virgo	April 1–April 12, 1956	Aries
Sept. 16–Oct. 4, 1953	Libra	April 13–April 29, 1956	Taurus
Oct. 5–Oct. 31, 1953	Scorpio	April 30–July 6, 1956	Gemini
Nov. 1–Nov. 6, 1953	Sagittarius	July 7–July 21, 1956	Cancer
Nov. 7–Dec. 10, 1953	Scorpio	July 22–Aug. 5, 1956	Leo
Dec. 11–Dec. 30, 1953	Sagittarius	Aug. 6–Aug. 26, 1956	Virgo
Dec. 31–Jan. 18, 1954	Capricorn	Aug. 27–Sept. 30, 1956	Libra
Jan. 19–Feb. 4, 1954	Aquarius	Oct. 1–Oct. 11, 1956	Virgo
Feb. 5–April 13, 1954	Pisces	Oct. 12–Oct. 31, 1956	Libra
April 14–April 30, 1954	Aries	Nov. 1–Nov. 18, 1956	Scorpio
May 1–May 14, 1954	Taurus	Nov. 19–Dec. 8, 1956	Sagittarius
May 15–May 30, 1954	Gemini	Dec. 9–Feb. 12, 1957	Capricorn
May 31–Aug. 7, 1954	Cancer	Feb. 13–Mar. 4, 1957	Aquarius
Aug. 8–Aug. 22, 1954	Leo	Mar. 5–Mar. 20, 1957	Pisces
Aug. 23–Sept. 8, 1954	Virgo	Mar. 21–April 4, 1957	Aries
Sept. 9–Sept. 29, 1954	Libra	April 5–June 12, 1957	Taurus
Sept. 30–Nov. 4, 1954	Scorpio	June 13–June 27, 1957	Gemini
Nov. 5–Nov. 11, 1954	Libra	June 28–July 12, 1957	Cancer
Nov. 12–Dec. 4, 1954	Scorpio	July 13–July 30, 1957	Leo

If you were born:	Your Mercury is in:	If you were born:	Your Mercury is in:
July 31–Oct. 6, 1957	Virgo	April 17–May 4, 1960	Aries
Oct. 7–Oct. 23, 1957	Libra	May 5–May 19, 1960	Taurus
Oct. 24–Nov. 11, 1957	Scorpio	May 20–June 2, 1960	Gemini
Nov. 12–Jan. 14, 1958	Sagittarius	June 3–June 30, 1960	Cancer
Jan. 15–Feb. 6, 1958	Capricorn	July 1–July 6, 1960	Leo
Feb. 7–Feb. 24, 1958	Aquarius	July 7–Aug. 10, 1960	Cancer
Feb. 25–Mar. 12, 1958	Pisces	Aug. 11–Aug. 27, 1960	Leo
Mar. 13–May 17, 1958	Aries	Aug. 28–Sept. 12, 1960	Virgo
May 18–June 5, 1958	Taurus	Sept. 13–Oct. 1, 1960	Libra
June 6–June 20, 1958	Gemini	Oct. 2–Dec. 7, 1960	Scorpio
June 21–July 4, 1958	Cancer	Dec. 8–Dec. 27, 1960	Sagittarius
July 5–July 26, 1958	Leo	Dec. 28–Jan. 14, 1961	Capricorn
July 27–Aug. 23, 1958	Virgo	Jan. 15–Feb. 1, 1961	Aquarius
Aug. 24–Sept. 11, 1958	Leo	Feb. 2–Feb. 24, 1961	Pisces
Sept. 12–Sept. 28, 1958	Virgo	Feb. 25–Mar. 18, 1961	Aquarius
Sept. 29–Oct. 16, 1958	Libra	Mar. 19–April 10, 1961	Pisces
Oct. 17–Nov. 5, 1958	Scorpio	April 11–April 26, 1961	Aries
Nov. 6–Jan. 10, 1959	Sagittarius	April 27–May 10, 1961	Taurus
Jan. 11–Jan. 30, 1959	Capricorn	May 11–May 28, 1961	Gemini
Jan. 31–Feb. 17, 1959	Aquarius	May 28–Aug. 4, 1961	Cancer
Feb. 18–Mar. 5, 1959	Pisces	Aug. 5–Aug. 18, 1961	Leo
Mar. 6–May 12, 1959	Aries	Aug. 19–Sept. 4, 1961	Virgo
May 13–May 28, 1959	Taurus	Sept. 5–Sept. 27, 1961	Libra
May 29–June 11, 1959	Gemini	Sept. 28–Oct. 22, 1961	Scorpio
June 12–June 28, 1959	Cancer	Oct. 23–Nov. 10, 1961	Libra
June 29–Sept. 5, 1959	Leo	Nov. 11–Nov. 30, 1961	Scorpio
Sept. 6–Sept. 21, 1959	Virgo	Dec. 1–Dec. 20, 1961	Sagittarius
Sept. 22–Oct. 9, 1959	Libra	Dec. 21–Jan. 7, 1962	Capricorn
Oct. 10–Oct. 31, 1959	Scorpio	Jan. 8–Mar. 15, 1962	Aquarius
Nov. 1–Nov. 25, 1959	Sagittarius	Mar. 16–April 3, 1962	Pisces
Nov. 26–Dec. 13, 1959	Scorpio	April 4–April 18, 1962	Aries
Dec. 14–Jan. 4, 1960	Sagittarius	April 19–May 3, 1962	Taurus
Jan. 5–Jan. 23, 1960	Capricorn	May 4–July 11, 1962	Gemini
Jan. 24–Feb. 9, 1960	Aquarius	July 12–July 26, 1962	Cancer
Feb. 10–April 16, 1960	Pisces	July 27–Aug. 10, 1962	Leo

If you were born:	Your Mercury is in:	If you were born:	Your Mercury is in:
Aug. 11–Aug. 29, 1962	Virgo	Dec. 17–Jan. 13, 1965	Sagittarius
Aug. 30–Nov. 5, 1962	Libra	Jan. 14–Feb. 3, 1965	Capricorn
Nov. 6–Nov. 23, 1962	Scorpio	Feb. 4–Feb. 21, 1965	Aquarius
Nov. 24–Dec. 12, 1962	Sagittarius	Feb. 22–Mar. 9, 1965	Pisces
Dec. 13–Jan. 2, 1963	Capricorn	Mar. 10–May 15, 1965	Aries
Jan. 3–Jan. 20, 1963	Aquarius	May 16–June 2, 1965	Taurus
Jan. 21–Feb. 15, 1963	Capricorn	June 3–June 16, 1965	Gemini
Feb. 16–Mar. 9, 1963	Aquarius	June 17–July 1, 1965	Cancer
Mar. 10–Mar. 26, 1963	Pisces	July 2–July 31, 1965	Leo
Mar. 27–April 9, 1963	Aries	Aug. 1–Aug. 3, 1965	Virgo
April 10–May 3, 1963	Taurus	Aug. 4–Sept. 8, 1965	Leo
May 4–May 10, 1963	Gemini	Sept. 9–Sept. 25, 1965	Virgo
May 11–June 14, 1963	Taurus	Sept. 26–Oct. 12, 1965	Libra
June 15–July 4, 1963	Gemini	Oct. 13–Nov. 2, 1965	Scorpio
July 5–July 18, 1963	Cancer	Nov. 3–Jan. 7, 1966	Sagittarius
July 19–Aug. 3, 1963	Leo	Jan. 8–Jan. 27, 1966	Capricorn
Aug. 4–Aug. 26, 1963	Virgo	Jan. 28–Feb. 13, 1966	Aquarius
Aug. 27–Sept. 16, 1963	Libra	Feb. 14–Mar. 3, 1966	Pisces
Sept. 17–Oct. 10, 1963	Virgo	Mar. 4–Mar. 22, 1966	Aries
Oct. 11–Oct. 28, 1963	Libra	Mar. 23–April 17, 1966	Pisces
Oct. 29–Nov. 16, 1963	Scorpio	April 18–May 9, 1966	Aries
Nov. 17–Dec. 6, 1963	Sagittarius	May 10–May 24, 1966	Taurus
Dec. 7–Feb. 10, 1964	Capricorn	May 25–June 7, 1966	Gemini
Feb. 11–Feb. 29, 1964	Aquarius	June 8–June 26, 1966	Cancer
Mar. 1–Mar. 16, 1964	Pisces	June 27–Sept. 1, 1966	Leo
Mar. 17–April 2, 1964	Aries	Sept. 2–Sept. 17, 1966	Virgo
April 3–June 9, 1964	Taurus	Sept. 18–Oct. 5, 1966	Libra
June 10–June 24, 1964	Gemini	Oct. 6–Oct. 30, 1966	Scorpio
June 25–July 9, 1964	Cancer	Oct. 31–Nov. 13, 1966	Sagittarius
July 10–July 27, 1964	Leo	Nov. 14–Dec. 11, 1966	Scorpio
July 28–Oct. 2, 1964	Virgo	Dec. 12–Jan. 1, 1967	Sagittarius
Oct. 3–Oct. 20, 1964	Libra	Jan. 2–Jan. 19, 1967	Capricorn
Oct. 21–Nov. 8, 1964	Scorpio	Jan. 20–Feb. 6, 1967	Aquarius
Nov. 9–Nov. 30, 1964	Sagittarius	Feb. 7–April 14, 1967	Pisces
Dec. 1–Dec. 16, 1964	Capricorn	April 15–May 1, 1967	Aries

If you were born:	Your Mercury is in:	If you were born:	Your Mercury is in:
May 2–May 16, 1967	Taurus	Oct. 8–Oct. 9, 1969	Virgo
May 17–May 31, 1967	Gemini	Oct. 10–Nov. 1, 1969	Libra
June 1–Aug. 8, 1967	Cancer	Nov. 2–Nov. 20, 1969	Scorpio
Aug. 9–Aug. 24, 1967	Leo	Nov. 21–Dec. 9, 1969	Sagittarius
Aug. 25–Sept. 9, 1967	Virgo	Dec. 10–Feb. 13, 1970	Capricorn
Sept. 10–Sept. 30, 1967	Libra	Feb. 14–Mar. 5, 1970	Aquarius
Oct. 1–Dec. 5, 1967	Scorpio	Mar. 6–Mar. 22, 1970	Pisces
Dec. 6–Dec. 24, 1967	Sagittarius	Mar. 23–April 6, 1970	Aries
Dec. 25–Jan. 12, 1968	Capricorn	April 7–June 13, 1970	Taurus
Jan. 13–Feb. 1, 1968	Aquarius	June 14–June 30, 1970	Gemini
Feb. 2–Feb. 11, 1968	Pisces	July 1–July 14, 1970	Cancer
Feb. 12–Mar. 17, 1968	Aquarius	July 15–July 31, 1970	Leo
Mar. 18–April 7, 1968	Pisces	Aug. 1–Oct. 7, 1970	Virgo
April 8–April 22, 1968	Aries	Oct. 8–Oct. 25, 1970	Libra
April 23–May 6, 1968	Taurus	Oct. 26–Nov. 13, 1970	Scorpio
May 7–May 29, 1968	Gemini	Nov. 14–Dec. 3, 1970	Sagittarius
May 30–June 13, 1968	Cancer	Dec. 4–Jan. 2, 1971	Capricorn
July 14–July 31, 1968	Cancer	Jan. 3–Jan. 14, 1971	Sagittarius
Aug. 1–Aug. 15, 1968	Leo	Jan. 15–Feb. 7, 1971	Capricorn
Aug. 16–Sept. 1, 1968	Virgo	Feb. 8–Feb. 26, 1971	Aquarius
Sept. 2–Sept. 28, 1968	Libra	Feb. 27–Mar. 14, 1971	Pisces
Sept. 29–Oct. 7, 1968	Scorpio	Mar. 15–April 1, 1971	Aries
Oct. 8–Nov. 8, 1968	Libra	April 2–April 18, 1971	Taurus
Nov. 9–Nov. 27, 1968	Scorpio	April 19–May 17, 1971	Aries
Nov. 28–Dec. 16, 1968	Sagittarius	May 18–June 7, 1971	Taurus
Dec. 17–Jan. 4, 1969	Capricorn	June 8–June 21, 1971	Gemini
Jan. 5–Mar. 12, 1969	Aquarius	June 22–July 6, 1971	Cancer
Mar. 13–Mar. 30, 1969	Pisces	July 7–July 26, 1971	Leo
Mar. 31–April 14, 1969	Aries	July 27–Aug. 29, 1971	Virgo
April 15–April 30, 1969	Taurus	Aug. 30–Sept. 11, 1971	Leo
May 1–July 8, 1969	Gemini	June 14–July 13, 1968	Gemini
July 9–July 22, 1969	Cancer	Sept. 12–Sept. 30, 1971	Virgo
July 23–Aug. 7, 1969	Leo	Oct. 1–Oct. 17, 1971	Libra
Aug. 8–Aug. 27, 1969	Virgo	Oct. 18–Nov. 6, 1971	Scorpio
Aug. 28–Oct. 7, 1969	Libra	Nov. 7–Jan. 11, 1972	Sagittarius

If you were born:	Your Mercury is in:	If you were born:	Your Mercury is in:
Jan. 12–Jan. 31, 1972	Capricorn	May 13–May 29, 1974	Gemini
Feb. 1–Feb. 18, 1972	Aquarius	May 30–Aug. 5, 1974	Cancer
Feb. 19–Mar. 5, 1972	Pisces	Aug. 6–Aug. 20, 1974	Leo
Mar. 6–May 12, 1972	Aries	Aug. 21–Sept. 6, 1974	Virgo
May 13–May 30, 1972	Taurus	Sept. 7–Sept. 28, 1974	Libra
May 31–June 12, 1972	Gemini	Sept. 29–Oct. 26, 1974	Scorpio
June 13–June 28, 1972	Cancer	Oct. 27–Nov. 11, 1974	Libra
June 29–Sept. 5, 1972	Leo	Nov. 12–Dec. 2, 1974	Scorpio
Sept. 6–Sept. 21, 1972	Virgo	Dec. 3–Dec. 21, 1974	Sagittarius
Sept. 22–Oct. 9, 1972	Libra	Dec. 22–Jan. 8, 1975	Capricorn
Oct. 10–Oct. 30, 1972	Scorpio	Jan. 9–Mar. 16, 1975	Aquarius
Oct. 31–Nov. 29, 1972	Sagittarius	Mar. 17–April 4, 1975	Pisces
Nov. 30–Dec. 12, 1972	Scorpio	April 5–April 19, 1975	Aries
Dec. 13–Jan. 4, 1973	Sagittarius	April 20–May 4, 1975	Taurus
Jan. 5–Jan. 23, 1973	Capricorn	May 5–July 12, 1975	Gemini
Jan. 24–Feb. 9, 1973	Aquarius	July 13–July 28, 1975	Cancer
Feb. 10–April 16, 1973	Pisces	July 29–Aug. 12, 1975	Leo
April 17–May 6 , 1973	Aries	Aug. 13–Aug. 30, 1975	Virgo
May 7–May 20, 1973	Taurus	Aug. 31–Nov. 6, 1975	Libra
May 21–June 4, 1973	Gemini	Nov. 7–Nov. 25, 1975	Scorpio
June 5–June 27, 1973	Cancer	Nov. 26–Dec. 14, 1975	Sagittarius
June 28–July 16, 1973	Leo	Dec. 15–Jan. 2, 1976	Capricorn
July 17–Aug. 11, 1973	Cancer	Jan. 3–Jan. 25, 1976	Aquarius
Aug. 12–Aug. 28, 1973	Leo	Jan. 26–Feb. 15, 1976	Capricorn
Aug. 29–Sept. 13, 1973	Virgo	Feb. 16–Mar. 9, 1976	Aquarius
Sept. 14–Oct. 2, 1973	Libra	Mar. 10–Mar. 26, 1976	Pisces
Oct. 3–Dec. 8, 1973	Scorpio	Mar. 27–April 10, 1976	Aries
Dec. 9–Dec. 28, 1973	Sagittarius	April 11–April 29, 1976	Taurus
Dec. 29–Jan. 16, 1974	Capricorn	April 30–May 19, 1976	Gemini
Jan. 17–Feb. 2, 1974	Aquarius	May 20–June 13, 1976	Taurus
Feb. 3–Mar. 2, 1974	Pisces	June 14–July 4, 1976	Gemini
Mar. 3–Mar. 17, 1974	Aquarius	July 5–July 18, 1976	Cancer
Mar. 18–April 11, 1974	Pisces	July 19–Aug. 3, 1976	Leo
April 12–April 28, 1974	Aries	Aug. 4–Aug. 25, 1976	Virgo
April 29–May 12, 1974	Taurus	Aug. 26–Sept. 21, 1976	Libra

If you were born:	Your Mercury is in:	If you were born:	Your Mercury is in:
Sept. 22–Oct. 10, 1976	Virgo	Mar. 4–Mar. 28, 1979	Aries
Oct. 11–Oct. 29, 1976	Libra	Mar. 29–April 17, 1979	Pisces
Oct. 30–Nov. 16, 1976	Scorpio	April 18–May 10, 1979	Aries
Nov. 17–Dec. 6, 1976	Sagittarius	May 11–May 26, 1979	Taurus
Dec. 7–Feb. 10, 1976	Capricorn	May 27–June 9, 1979	Gemini
Feb. 11–Mar. 2, 1977	Aquarius	June 10–June 27, 1979	Cancer
Mar. 3–Mar. 18, 1977	Pisces	June 28–Sept. 2, 1979	Leo
Mar. 19–April 3, 1977	Aries	Sept. 3–Sept. 18, 1979	Virgo
April 4–June 10, 1977	Taurus	Sept. 19–Oct. 7, 1979	Libra
June 11–June 26, 1977	Gemini	Oct. 8–Oct. 30, 1979	Scorpio
June 27–July 10, 1977	Cancer	Oct. 31–Nov. 18, 1979	Sagittarius
July 11–July 28, 1977	Leo	Nov. 19–Dec. 12, 1979	Scorpio
July 29–Oct. 4, 1977	Virgo	Dec. 13–Jan. 2, 1980	Sagittarius
Oct. 5–Oct. 21, 1977	Libra	Jan. 3–Jan. 21, 1980	Capricorn
Oct. 22–Nov. 9, 1977	Scorpio	Jan. 22–Feb. 7, 1980	Aquarius
Nov. 10–Dec. 1, 1977	Sagittarius	Feb. 8–April 14, 1980	Pisces
Dec. 2–Dec. 21, 1977	Capricorn	April 15–May 2, 1980	Aries
Dec. 22–Jan. 13, 1978	Sagittarius	May 3–May 16, 1980	Taurus
Jan. 14–Feb. 4, 1978	Capricorn	May 17–May 31, 1980	Gemini
Feb. 5–Feb. 22, 1978	Aquarius	June 1–Aug. 8, 1980	Cancer
Feb. 23–Mar. 10, 1978	Pisces	Aug. 9–Aug. 24, 1980	Leo
Mar. 11–May 16, 1978	Aries	Aug. 25–Sept. 9, 1980	Virgo
May 17–June 3, 1978	Taurus	Sept. 10–Sept. 29, 1980	Libra
June 4–June 17, 1978	Gemini	Sept. 30–Dec. 5, 1980	Scorpio
June 18–July 2, 1978	Cancer	Dec. 6–Dec. 24, 1980	Sagittarius
July 3–July 27, 1978	Leo	Dec. 25–Jan. 12, 1981	Capricorn
July 28–Aug. 13, 1978	Virgo	Jan. 13–Jan. 31, 1981	Aquarius
Aug. 14–Sept. 9, 1978	Leo	Feb. 1–Feb. 16, 1981	Pisces
Sept. 10–Sept. 26, 1978	Virgo	Feb. 17–Mar. 17, 1981	Aquarius
Sept. 27–Oct. 14, 1978	Libra	Mar. 18–April 8, 1981	Pisces
Oct. 15–Nov. 3, 1978	Scorpio	April 9–April 24, 1981	Aries
Nov. 4–Jan. 8, 1979	Sagittarius	April 25–May 8, 1981	Taurus
Jan. 9–Jan. 28, 1979	Capricorn	May 9–May 28, 1981	Gemini
Jan. 29–Feb. 14, 1979	Aquarius	May 29–June 22, 1981	Cancer
Feb. 15–Mar. 3, 1979	Pisces	June 23–July 12, 1981	Gemini

If you were born:	Your Mercury is in:	If you were born:	Your Mercury is in:
July 13–Aug. 1, 1981	Cancer	Nov. 15–Dec. 4, 1983	Sagittarius
Aug. 2–Aug. 16, 1981	Leo	Dec. 5–Feb. 9, 1984	Capricorn
Aug. 17–Sept. 2, 1981	Virgo	Feb. 10–Feb. 27, 1984	Aquarius
Sept. 3–Sept. 27, 1981	Libra	Feb. 28–Mar. 14, 1984	Pisces
Sept. 28–Oct. 13, 1981	Scorpio	Mar. 15–Mar. 31, 1984	Aries
Oct. 14–Nov. 9, 1981	Libra	April 1–April 25, 1984	Taurus
Nov. 10–Nov. 28, 1981	Scorpio	April 26–May 15, 1984	Aries
Nov. 29–Dec. 17, 1981	Sagittarius	May 16–June 7, 1984	Taurus
Dec. 18–Jan. 5, 1982	Capricorn	June 8–June 22, 1984	Gemini
Jan. 6–Mar. 13, 1982	Aquarius	June 23–July 6, 1984	Cancer
Mar. 14–Mar. 31, 1982	Pisces	July 7–July 26, 1984	Leo
April 1–April 15, 1982	Aries	July 27–Sept. 30, 1984	Virgo
April 16–May 1, 1982	Taurus	Oct. 1–Oct. 17, 1984	Libra
May 2–July 9, 1982	Gemini	Oct. 18–Nov. 6, 1984	Scorpio
July 10–July 24, 1982	Cancer	Nov. 7–Dec. 1, 1984	Sagittarius
July 25–Aug. 8, 1982	Leo	Dec. 2–Dec. 7, 1984	Capricorn
Aug. 9–Aug. 27, 1982	Virgo	Dec. 8–Jan. 11, 1985	Sagittarius
Aug. 28–Nov. 2, 1982	Libra	Jan. 12–Feb. 1, 1985	Capricorn
Nov. 3–Nov. 21, 1982	Scorpio	Feb. 2–Feb. 18, 1985	Aquarius
Nov. 22–Dec. 10, 1982	Sagittarius	Feb. 19–Mar. 6, 1985	Pisces
Dec. 11–Jan. 1, 1983	Capricorn	Mar. 7–May 13, 1985	Aries
Jan. 2–Jan. 12, 1983	Aquarius	May 14–May 30, 1985	Taurus
Jan. 13–Feb. 14, 1983	Capricorn	May 31–June 13, 1985	Gemini
Feb. 15–Mar. 6, 1983	Aquarius	June 14–June 29, 1985	Cancer
Mar. 7–Mar. 23, 1983	Pisces	June 30–Sept. 6, 1985	Leo
Mar. 24–April 7, 1983	Aries	Sept. 7–Sept. 22, 1985	Virgo
April 8–June 14, 1983	Taurus	Sept. 23–Oct. 10 1985	Libra
June 15–July 1, 1983	Gemini	Oct. 11–Oct. 31, 1985	Libra
July 2–July 15, 1983	Cancer	Nov. 1–Dec. 4, 1985	Scorpio
July 16–Aug. 1, 1983	Leo	Dec. 5–Dec. 12, 1985	Sagittarius
Aug. 2–Aug. 29, 1983	Virgo	Dec. 13–Jan. 5, 1986	Scorpio
Aug. 30–Sept. 5, 1983	Libra	Jan. 6–Jan. 24, 1986	Sagittarius
Sept. 6–Oct. 8, 1983	Virgo	Jan. 25–Feb. 11, 1986	Capricorn
Oct. 9–Oct. 26, 1983	Libra	Feb. 12–April 17, 1986	Aquarius
Oct. 27–Nov. 14, 1983	Scorpio	April 18–May 7, 1986	Pisces

If you were born:	Your Mercury is in:	If you were born:	Your Mercury is in:
May 8–May 22, 1986	Aries	Aug. 31–Nov. 6, 1988	Libra
May 23–June 5, 1986	Taurus	Nov. 7–Nov. 25, 1988	Scorpio
June 6–June 26, 1986	Gemini	Nov. 26–Dec. 14, 1988	Sagittarius
June 27–July 23, 1986	Cancer	Dec. 15–Jan. 2, 1989	Capricorn
July 24–Aug. 11, 1986	Leo	Jan. 3–Jan. 28, 1989	Aquarius
Aug. 12–Aug. 29, 1986	Cancer	Jan. 29–Feb. 14, 1989	Capricorn
Aug. 30–Sept. 14, 1986	Leo	Feb. 15–Mar. 10, 1989	Aquarius
Sept. 15–Oct. 3, 1986	Virgo	Mar. 11–Mar. 27, 1989	Pisces
Oct. 4–Dec. 9, 1986	Libra	Mar. 28–April 11, 1989	Aries
Dec. 10–Dec. 29, 1986	Scorpio	April 12–April 29, 1989	Taurus
Dec. 30–Jan. 17, 1987	Sagittarius	April 30–May 28, 1989	Gemini
Jan. 18–Feb. 4, 1987	Capricorn	May 29–June 12, 1989	Taurus
Feb. 5–Mar. 11, 1987	Aquarius	June 13–July 5, 1989	Gemini
Mar. 12–Mar. 13, 1987	Pisces	July 6–July 20, 1989	Cancer
Mar. 14–April 12, 1987	Aquarius	July 21–Aug. 4, 1989	Leo
April 13–April 29, 1987	Pisces	Aug. 5–Aug. 26, 1989	Virgo
April 30–May 13, 1987	Aries	Aug. 27–Sept. 26, 1989	Libra
May 14–May 29, 1987	Taurus	Sept. 27–Oct. 11, 1989	Virgo
May 30–Aug. 6, 1987	Cancer	Oct. 12–Oct. 30, 1989	Libra
Aug. 7–Aug. 21, 1987	Leo	Oct. 31–Nov. 17, 1989	Scorpio
Aug. 22–Sept. 7, 1987	Virgo	Nov. 18–Dec. 7, 1989	Sagittarius
Sept. 8–Sept. 28, 1987	Libra	Dec. 8–Feb. 12, 1990	Capricorn
Sept. 29–Oct. 31, 1987	Scorpio	Feb. 13–Mar. 3, 1990	Aquarius
Nov. 1–Nov. 11, 1987	Libra	Mar. 4–Mar. 19, 1990	Pisces
Nov. 12–Dec. 3, 1987	Scorpio	Mar. 20–April 4, 1990	Aries
Dec. 4–Dec. 22, 1987	Sagittarius	April 5–June 12, 1990	Taurus
Dec. 23–Jan. 10, 1988	Capricorn	June 13–June 27, 1990	Gemini
Jan. 11–Mar. 16, 1988	Aquarius	June 28–July 11, 1990	Cancer
Mar. 17–April 4, 1988	Pisces	July 12–July 29, 1990	Leo
April 5–April 20, 1988	Aries	July 30–Oct. 5, 1990	Virgo
April 21–May 4, 1988	Taurus	Oct. 6–Oct. 23, 1990	Libra
May 5–July 12, 1988	Gemini	Oct. 24–Nov. 10, 1990	Scorpio
July 13–July 28, 1988	Cancer	Nov. 11–Dec. 1, 1990	Sagittarius
July 29–Aug. 12, 1988	Leo	Dec. 2–Dec. 25, 1990	Capricorn
Aug. 13–Aug. 30, 1988	Virgo	Dec. 26–Jan. 14, 1991	Sagittarius

If you were born:	Your Mercury is in:	If you were born:	Your Mercury is in:
Jan. 15–Feb. 5, 1991	Capricorn	June 3–Aug. 10, 1993	Cancer
Feb. 6–Feb. 24, 1991	Aquarius	Aug. 11–Aug. 26, 1993	Leo
Feb. 25–Mar. 11, 1991	Pisces	Aug. 27–Sept. 11, 1993	Virgo
Mar. 12–May 16, 1991	Aries	Sept. 12–Oct. 1, 1993	Libra
May 17–June 5, 1991	Taurus	Oct. 2–Dec. 7, 1993	Scorpio
June 6–June 19, 1991	Gemini	Dec. 8–Dec. 26, 1993	Sagittarius
June 20–July 4, 1991	Cancer	Dec. 27–Jan. 14, 1994	Capricorn
July 5–July 26, 1991	Leo	Jan. 15–Feb. 1, 1994	Aquarius
July 27–Aug. 19, 1991	Virgo	Feb. 2–Feb. 21, 1994	Pisces
Aug. 20–Sept. 10, 1991	Leo	Feb. 22–Mar. 18, 1994	Aquarius
Sept. 11–Sept. 28, 1991	Virgo	Mar. 19–April 9, 1994	Pisces
Sept. 29–Oct. 15, 1991	Libra	April 10–April 25, 1994	Aries
Oct. 16–Nov. 4, 1991	Scorpio	April 26–May 9, 1994	Taurus
Nov. 5–Jan. 10, 1992	Sagittarius	May 10–May 28, 1994	Gemini
Jan. 11–Jan. 29, 1992	Capricorn	May 29–Aug. 3, 1994	Cancer
Jan. 30–Feb. 16, 1992	Aquarius	Aug. 4–Aug. 18, 1994	Leo
Feb. 17–Mar. 3, 1992	Pisces	Aug. 19–Sept. 4, 1994	Virgo
Mar. 4–April 14, 1992	Aries	Sept. 5–Sept. 27, 1994	Libra
April 15–May 11, 1992	Aries	Sept. 28–Oct. 19, 1994	Scorpio
May 12–May 26, 1992	Taurus	Oct. 20–Nov. 10, 1994	Libra
May 27–June 9, 1992	Gemini	Nov. 11–Nov. 30, 1994	Scorpio
June 10–June 27, 1992	Cancer	Dec. 1–Dec. 19, 1994	Sagittarius
June 28–Sept. 3, 1992	Leo	Dec. 20–Jan. 6, 1995	Capricorn
Sept. 4–Sept. 19, 1992	Virgo	Jan. 7–Mar. 14, 1995	Aquarius
Sept. 20–Oct. 7, 1992	Libra	Mar. 15–April 2, 1995	Pisces
Oct. 8–Oct. 29, 1992	Scorpio	April 3–April 17, 1995	Aries
Oct. 30–Nov. 21, 1992	Sagittarius	April 18–May 2, 1995	Taurus
Nov. 22–Dec. 12, 1992	Scorpio	May 3–July 10, 1995	Gemini
Dec. 13–Jan. 2, 1993	Sagittarius	July 11–July 25, 1995	Cancer
Jan. 3–Jan. 21, 1993	Capricorn	July 26–Aug. 10, 1995	Leo
Jan. 22–Feb. 7, 1993	Aquarius	Aug. 11–Aug. 29, 1995	Virgo
Feb. 8–April 15, 1993	Pisces	Aug. 30–Nov. 4, 1995	Libra
April 16–May 3, 1993	Aries	Nov. 5–Nov. 22, 1995	Scorpio
May 4–May 18, 1993	Taurus	Nov. 23–Dec. 12, 1995	Sagittarius
May 19–June 2, 1993	Gemini	Dec. 13–Jan. 1, 1996	Capricorn

If you were born:	Your Mercury is in:	If you were born:	Your Mercury is in:
Jan. 2–Jan. 17, 1996	Aquarius	May 16–June 1, 1998	Taurus
Jan. 18–Feb. 15, 1996	Capricorn	June 2–June 15, 1998	Gemini
Feb. 16–Mar. 7, 1996	Aquarius	June 16–June 30, 1998	Cancer
Mar. 8–Mar. 24, 1996	Pisces	July 1–Sept. 8, 1998	Leo
Mar. 25–April 8, 1996	Aries	Sept. 9–Sept. 24, 1998	Virgo
April 9–June 13, 1996	Taurus	Sept. 25–Oct. 12, 1998	Libra
June 14–July 2, 1996	Gemini	Oct. 13–Nov. 1, 1998	Scorpio
July 3–July 16, 1996	Cancer	Nov. 2–Jan. 7, 1999	Sagittarius
July 17–Aug. 1, 1996	Leo	Jan. 8–Jan. 26, 1999	Capricorn
Aug. 2–Aug. 26, 1996	Virgo	Jan. 27–Feb. 12, 1999	Aquarius
Aug. 27–Sept. 12, 1996	Libra	Feb. 13–Mar. 2, 1999	Pisces
Sept. 13–Oct. 9, 1996	Virgo	Mar. 3–Mar. 18, 1999	Aries
Oct. 10–Oct. 27, 1996	Libra	Mar. 19–April 17, 1999	Pisces
Oct. 28–Nov. 14, 1996	Scorpio	April 18–May 8, 1999	Aries
Nov. 15–Dec. 4, 1996	Sagittarius	May 9–May 23, 1999	Taurus
Dec. 5–Feb. 9, 1997	Capricorn	May 24–June 7, 1999	Gemini
Feb. 10–Feb. 28, 1997	Aquarius	June 8–June 26, 1999	Cancer
Mar. 1–Mar. 16, 1997	Pisces	June 27–July 31, 1999	Leo
Mar. 17–April 1, 1997	Aries	Aug. 1–Aug. 11, 1999	Cancer
April 2–May 5, 1997	Taurus	Aug. 12–Aug. 31, 1999	Leo
May 6–May 12, 1997	Aries	Sept. 1–Sept. 16, 1999	Virgo
May 13–June 8, 1997	Taurus	Sept. 17–Oct. 5, 1999	Libra
June 9–June 23, 1997	Gemini	Oct. 6–Oct. 31, 1999	Scorpio
June 24–July 8, 1997	Cancer	Nov. 1–Nov. 9, 1999	Sagittarius
July 9–July 27, 1997	Leo	Nov. 10–Dec. 11, 1999	Scorpio
July 28–Oct. 2, 1997	Virgo	Dec. 12–Dec. 31, 1999	Sagittarius
Oct. 3–Oct. 19, 1997	Libra	Jan. 1, 2000–Jan. 18, 2000	Capricorn
Oct. 20–Nov. 7, 1997	Scorpio	Jan. 19, 2000–Feb. 5, 2000	Aquarius
Nov. 8–Nov. 30, 1997	Sagittarius	Feb. 6, 2000–April 13, 2000	Pisces
Dec. 1–Dec. 13, 1997	Capricorn	April 14, 2000–April 30, 2000	Aries
Dec. 14–Jan. 12, 1998	Sagittarius	May 1, 2000–May 14, 2000	Taurus
Jan. 13–Feb. 2, 1998	Capricorn	May 15, 2000–May 30, 2000	Gemini
Feb. 3–Feb. 20, 1998	Aquarius	May 31, 2000–August 7, 2000	Cancer
Feb. 21–Mar. 8, 1998	Pisces	August 8, 2000–August 22, 2000	Leo
Mar. 9–May 15, 1998	Aries	August 23, 2000–Sept. 7, 2000	Virgo

If you were born:	Your Mercury is in:	If you were born:	Your Mercury is in:
Sept. 8, 2000–Sept. 28, 2000	Libra	Feb. 14, 2003 –March 5, 2003	Aquarius
Sept. 29, 2000–Nov. 7, 2000	Scorpio	March 6, 2003–March 21, 2003	Pisces
Nov. 8, 2000–Nov. 8, 2000	Libra	March 22, 2003–April 5, 2003	Aries
Nov. 9, 2000–Dec. 3, 2000	Scorpio	April 6, 2003–June 13, 2003	Taurus
Dec. 4, 2000–Dec. 23, 2000	Sagittarius	June 14, 2003–June 29, 2003	Gemini
Dec. 24, 2000–Jan. 10, 2001	Capricorn	June 30, 2003–July 13, 2003	Cancer
Jan. 11, 2001–Feb. 1, 2001	Aquarius	July 14, 2003–July 30, 2003	Leo
Feb. 2, 2001–Feb. 6, 2001	Pisces	July 31, 2003–Oct. 7, 2003	Virgo
Feb. 7, 2001–March 17, 2001	Aquarius	Oct. 8, 2003–Oct. 24, 2003	Libra
March 18, 2001–April 6, 2001	Pisces	Oct. 25, 2003–Nov. 12, 2003	Scorpio
April 7, 2001–April 21, 2001	Aries	Nov. 13, 2003–Dec. 2, 2003	Sagittarius
April 22, 2001–May 6, 2001	Taurus	Dec. 3, 2003–Dec. 30, 2003	Capricorn
May 7, 2001–July 12, 2001	Gemini	Dec. 31, 2003–Jan. 14, 2004	Sagittarius
July 13, 2001–July 30, 2001	Cancer	Jan. 15, 2004–Feb. 7, 2004	Capricorn
July 31, 2001–August 14, 2001	Leo	Feb. 8, 2004–Feb. 25, 2004	Aquarius
August 15, 2001–Sept. 1, 2001	Virgo	Feb. 26, 2004–March 12, 2004	Pisces
Sept. 2, 2001–Nov. 7, 2001	Libra	March 13, 2004–April 1, 2004	Aries
Nov. 8, 2001–Nov. 26, 2001	Scorpio	April 2, 2004–April 13, 2004	Taurus
Nov. 27, 2001–Dec. 15, 2001	Sagittarius	April 14, 2004–May 16, 2004	Aries
Jan. 4, 2002–Feb. 4, 2002	Aquarius	May 17, 2004–June 5, 2004	Taurus
Feb. 5, 2002–Feb. 13, 2002	Capricorn	June 6, 2004–June 19, 2004	Gemini
February 14, 2002–March 11, 2002	Aquarius	June 20, 2004–July 4, 2004	Cancer
March 12, 2002–March 29, 2002	Pisces	July 5, 2004–July 25, 2004	Leo
March 30, 2002–April 13, 2002	Aries	July 26, 2004–August 25, 2004	Virgo
April 14, 2002–April 30, 2002	Taurus	August 26, 2004–Sept. 10, 2004	Leo
May 1, 2002–July 7, 2002	Gemini	Sept. 11, 2004–Sept. 28, 2004	Virgo
July 8, 2002–July 21, 2002	Cancer	Sept. 29, 2004–Oct. 15, 2004	Libra
July 22, 2002–August 6, 2002	Leo	Oct. 16, 2004–Nov. 4, 2004	Scorpio
August 7, 2002–August 26, 2002	Virgo	Nov. 5, 2004–Jan. 10, 2005	Sagittarius
August 27, 2002–Oct. 2, 2002	Libra	Jan. 11, 2005–Jan. 30, 2005	Capricorn
Oct. 3, 2002–Oct. 11, 2002	Virgo	Jan. 31, 2005–Feb. 16, 2005	Aquarius
Oct. 12, 2002–Oct. 31, 2002	Libra	Feb. 17, 2005–March 5, 2005	Pisces
Nov. 1, 2002–Nov. 19, 2002	Scorpio	March 6, 2005–May 12, 2005	Aries
Nov. 20, 2002–Dec. 8, 2002	Sagittarius	May 13, 2005–May 28, 2005	Taurus
Dec. 9, 2002–Feb. 13, 2003	Capricorn	May 29, 2005–June 11, 2005	Gemini

If you were born:	Your Mercury is in:	If you were born:	Your Mercury is in:
June 12, 2005–June 28, 2005	Cancer	Oct. 25, 2007–Nov. 11, 2007	Libra
June 29, 2005–Sept. 4, 2005	Leo	Nov. 12, 2007–Dec. 1, 2007	Scorpio
Sept. 5, 2005–Sept. 20, 2005	Virgo	Dec. 2, 2007–Dec. 20, 2007	Sagittarius
Sept. 21, 2005–Oct. 8, 2005	Libra	Dec. 21, 2007–Jan. 8, 2008	Capricorn
Oct. 9, 2005–Oct. 30, 2005	Scorpio	Jan. 9, 2008–March 14, 2008	Aquarius
Oct. 31, 2005–Nov. 26, 2005	Sagittarius	March 15, 2008–April 2, 2008	Pisces
Nov. 27, 2005–Dec. 12, 2005	Scorpio	April 3, 2008–April 17, 2008	Aries
Dec. 13, 2005–Jan. 3, 2006	Sagittarius	April 18, 2008–May 2, 2008	Taurus
Jan. 4, 2006–Jan. 22, 2006	Capricorn	May 3, 2008–July 10, 2008	Gemini
Jan. 23, 2006–Feb. 9, 2006	Aquarius	July 11, 2008–July 26, 2008	Cancer
Feb. 10, 2006–April 16, 2006	Pisces	July 27, 2008–August 10, 2008	Leo
April 17, 2006–May 5, 2006	Aries	August 11, 2008–August 29, 2008	Virgo
May 6, 2006–May 19, 2006	Taurus	August 30, 2008–Nov. 4, 2008	Libra
May 20, 2006–June 3, 2006	Gemini	Nov. 5, 2008–Nov. 23, 2008	Scorpio
June 4, 2006–June 28, 2006	Cancer	Nov. 24, 2008–Dec. 12, 2008	Sagittarius
June 29, 2006–July 10, 2006	Leo	Dec. 13, 2008–Jan. 1, 2009	Capricorn
July 11, 2006–August 11, 2006	Cancer	Jan. 2, 2009–Jan. 21, 2009	Aquarius
August 12, 2006–August 27, 2006	Leo	Jan. 22, 2009–Feb. 14, 2009	Capricorn
August 28, 2006–Sept. 12, 2006	Virgo	Feb. 15, 2009–March 8, 2009	Aquarius
Sept. 13, 2006–Oct. 2, 2006	Libra	March 9, 2009–March 25, 2009	Pisces
Oct. 3, 2006–Dec. 8, 2006	Scorpio	March 26, 2009–April 9, 2009	Aries
Dec. 9, 2006–Dec. 27, 2006	Sagittarius	April 10, 2009–April 30, 2009	Taurus
Dec. 28, 2006–Jan. 15, 2007	Capricorn	May 1, 2009–May 13, 2009	Gemini
Jan. 16, 2007–Feb. 2, 2007	Aquarius	May 14, 2009–June 14, 2009	Taurus
Feb. 3, 2007–Feb. 27, 2007	Pisces	June 15, 2009–July 3, 2009	Gemini
Feb. 28, 2007–March 18, 2007	Aquarius	July 4, 2009–July 17, 2009	Cancer
March 19, 2007–April 10, 2007	Pisces	July 18, 2009–August 2, 2009	Leo
April 11, 2007–April 27, 2007	Aries	August 3, 2009–August 25, 2009	Virgo
April 28, 2007–May 11, 2007	Taurus	August 26, 2009–Sept. 18, 2009	Libra
May 12, 2007–May 29, 2007	Gemini	Sept. 19, 2009–Oct. 10, 2009	Virgo
May 30, 2007–August 4, 2007	Cancer	Oct. 11, 2009–Oct. 28, 2009	Libra
August 5, 2007–August 19, 2007	Leo	Oct. 29, 2009–Nov. 16, 2009	Scorpio
August 20, 2007–Sept. 5, 2007	Virgo	Nov. 17, 2009–Dec. 5, 2009	Sagittarius
Sept. 6, 2007–Sept. 27, 2007	Libra	Dec. 6, 2009–Feb. 10, 2010	Capricorn
Sept. 28, 2007–Oct. 24, 2007	Scorpio	Feb. 11, 2010–March 1, 2010	Aquarius

If you were born:	Your Mercury is in:	If you were born:	Your Mercury is in:
March 2, 2010–March 17, 2010	Pisces	June 27, 2012–Sept. 1, 2012	Leo
March 18, 2010–April 2, 2010	Aries	Sept. 2, 2012–Sept. 16, 2012	Virgo
April 3, 2010–June 10, 2010	Taurus	Sept. 17, 2012–Oct. 5, 2012	Libra
June 11, 2010–June 25, 2010	Gemini	Oct. 6, 2012–Oct. 29, 2012	Scorpio
June 26, 2010–July 9, 2010	Cancer	Oct. 30, 2012–Nov. 14, 2012	Sagittarius
July 10, 2010–July 27, 2010	Leo	Nov. 15, 2012–Dec. 11, 2012	Scorpio
July 28, 2010–Oct. 3, 2010	Virgo	Dec. 12, 2012–Dec. 31, 2012	Sagittarius
Oct. 4, 2010–Oct. 20, 2010	Libra	Jan. 1, 2013–Jan. 19, 2013	Capricorn
Oct. 21, 2010–Nov. 8, 2010	Scorpio	Jan. 20, 2013–Feb. 5, 2013	Aquarius
Nov. 9, 2010–Dec. 1, 2010	Sagittarius	Feb. 6, 2013–April 14, 2013	Pisces
Dec. 2, 2010–Dec. 18, 2010	Capricorn	April 15, 2013–May 1, 2013	Aries
Dec. 19, 2010–Jan. 13, 2011	Sagittarius	May 2, 2013–May 15, 2013	Taurus
Jan. 14, 2011–Feb. 3, 2011	Capricorn	May 16, 2013–May 31, 2013	Gemini
Feb. 4, 2011–Feb. 21, 2011	Aquarius	June 1, 2013 –Aug. 8, 2013	Cancer
Feb. 22. 2011–March 9, 2011	Pisces	Aug. 9, 2013–Aug. 23, 2013	Leo
March 10, 2011–May 15, 2011	Aries	Aug. 24, 2013–Sept. 9, 2013	Virgo
May 16, 2011–June 2, 2011	Taurus	Sept. 10, 2013–Sept. 29, 2013	Libra
June 3, 2011–June 16, 2011	Gemini	Sept. 30, 2013–Dec. 5, 2013	Scorpio
June 17, 2011–July 2, 2011	Cancer	Dec. 6, 2013–Dec. 24, 2013	Sagittarius
July 3, 2011–July 28, 2011	Leo	Dec. 25, 2013–Jan. 11, 2014	Capricorn
July 29, 2011–Aug. 8, 2011	Virgo	Jan. 12, 2014–Jan. 31, 2014	Aquarius
Aug. 9, 2011–Sept. 9, 2011	Libra	Feb. 1, 2014–Feb. 13, 2014	Pisces
Sept. 10, 2011–Sept. 25, 2011	Virgo	Feb. 14, 2014–March 17, 2014	Aquarius
Sept. 26, 2011–Oct. 13, 2011	Libra	March 18, 2014–April 7, 2014	Pisces
Oct. 14, 2011–Nov. 2, 2011	Scorpio	April 8, 2014–April 23, 2014	Aries
Nov. 3, 2011–Jan. 8, 2012	Sagittarius	April 24, 2014–May 7, 2014	Taurus
Jan. 9, 2012–Jan. 27, 2012	Capricorn	May 8, 2014–May 29, 2014	Gemini
Jan. 28, 2012–Feb. 14, 2012	Aquarius	May 30, 2014–June 17, 2014	Cancer
Feb. 15, 2012–March 2, 2012	Pisces	June 18, 2014–July 13, 2014	Gemini
March 3, 2012–March 23, 2012	Aries	July 14, 2014–July 31, 2014	Cancer
March 24, 2012–April 16, 2012	Pisces	Aug. 1, 2014–Aug. 15, 2014	Leo
April 17, 2012–May 9, 2012	Aries	Aug. 16, 2014–Sept. 2, 2014	Virgo
May 10, 2012–May 24, 2012	Taurus	Sept. 3, 2014–Sept. 27, 2014	Libra
May 25, 2012–June 7, 2012	Gemini	Sept. 28, 2014–Oct. 10, 2014	Scorpio
June 8, 2012–June 26, 2012	Cancer	Oct. 11, 2014–Nov. 8, 2014	Libra

If you were born:	Your Mercury is in:	If you were born:	Your Mercury is in:
Nov. 9, 2014–Nov. 28, 2014	Scorpio	April 21, 2017–May 16, 2017	Aries
Nov. 29, 2014–Dec. 17, 2014	Sagittarius	May 17, 2017–June 6, 2017	Taurus
Dec. 18, 2014–Jan. 5, 2015	Capricorn	June 7, 2017–June 21, 2017	Gemini
Jan. 6, 2015–March 13, 2015	Aquarius	June 22, 2017–July 6, 2017	Cancer
March 14, 2015–March 31, 2015	Pisces	July 7, 2017–July 25, 2017	Leo
April 1, 2015–April 14, 2015	Aries	July 26, 2017–August 31, 2017	Virgo
April 15, 2015–May 1, 2015	Taurus	Sept. 1, 2017–Sept. 10, 2017	Leo
May 2, 2015–July 8, 2015	Gemini	Sept. 11, 2017–Sept. 30, 2017	Virgo
July 9, 2015–July 23, 2015	Cancer	Oct. 1, 2017–Oct. 17, 2017	Libra
July 24, 2015–Aug. 7, 2015	Leo	Oct. 18, 2017–Nov. 5, 2017	Scorpio
Aug. 8, 2015–Aug. 27, 2015	Virgo	Nov. 6, 2017–Jan. 11, 2018	Sagittarius
Aug. 28, 2015–Nov. 2, 2015	Libra	Jan. 12, 2018–Jan. 31, 2018	Capricorn
Nov. 3, 2015–Nov. 20, 2015	Scorpio	Feb. 1, 2018–Feb. 18, 2018	Aquarius
Nov. 21, 2015–Dec. 10, 2015	Sagittarius	Feb. 19, 2008–March 6, 2018	Pisces
Dec. 11, 2015–Jan. 2, 2016	Capricorn	March 7, 2018–May 13, 2018	Aries
Jan. 3, 2016–Jan. 8, 2016	Aquarius	May 14, 2018–May 29, 2018	Taurus
Jan. 9, 2016–Feb. 13, 2016	Capricorn	May 30, 2018–June 12, 2018	Gemini
Feb. 14, 2016–March 5, 2016	Aquarius	June 13, 2018–Sept. 6, 2018	Leo
March 6, 2015–March 22, 2016	Pisces	Sept. 7, 2018–Sept. 22, 2018	Virgo
March 23, 2016–April 5, 2016	Aries	Sept. 23, 2018–Oct. 10, 2018	Libra
April 6, 2016–June 12, 2016	Taurus	Oct. 11, 2018–Oct. 31, 2018	Scorpio
June 13, 2016–June 29, 2016	Gemini	Nov. 1, 2018–Dec. 1, 2018	Sagittarius
June 30, 2016–July 14, 2016	Cancer	Dec. 2, 2018–Dec. 12, 2018	Scorpio
July 15, 2016–July 30, 2016	Leo	Dec. 13, 2018–Jan. 5, 2019	Sagittarius
July 31, 2016–Oct. 7, 2016	Virgo	Jan. 6, 2019–Jan. 24, 2019	Capricorn
Oct. 8, 2016–Oct. 24, 2016	Libra	Jan. 25, 2019–Feb. 10, 2019	Aquarius
Oct. 25, 2016–Nov. 12, 2016	Scorpio	Feb. 11, 2019–April 17, 2019	Pisces
Nov. 13, 2016–Dec. 2, 2016	Sagittarius	April 18, 2019–May 6, 2019	Aries
Dec. 3, 2016–Jan. 4, 2017	Capricorn	May 7, 2019–May 21, 2019	Taurus
Jan. 5, 2017–Jan. 12, 2017	Sagittarius	May 22, 2019–June 4, 2019	Gemini
Jan. 13, 2017–Feb. 7, 2017	Capricorn	June 5, 2019–June 27, 2019	Cancer
Feb. 8, 2017–Feb. 25, 2017	Aquarius	June 28, 2019–July 19, 2019	Leo
Feb. 26, 2017–March 13, 2017	Pisces	July 20, 2019–Aug. 11, 2019	Cancer
March 14, 2017–March 31, 2017	Aries	Aug. 12, 2019–Aug. 29, 2019	Leo
April 1, 2017–April 20, 2017	Taurus	Aug. 30, 2019–Sept. 14, 2019	Virgo

If you were born:	Your Mercury is in:	If you were born:	Your Mercury is in:
Sept. 15, 2019–Oct. 3, 2019	Libra	March 11, 2022–March 27, 2022	Pisces
Oct. 4, 2019–Dec. 9, 2019	Scorpio	March 28, 2022–April 11, 2022	Aries
Dec. 10, 2019–Dec. 29, 2019	Sagittarius	April 12, 2022–April 29, 2022	Taurus
Dec. 30, 2019–Jan. 16, 2020	Capricorn	April 30, 2022–May 23, 2022	Gemini
Jan. 17, 2020–Feb. 3, 2020	Aquarius	May 24, 2022–June 13, 2022	Taurus
Feb. 4, 2020–March 4, 2020	Pisces	June 14, 2022–July 5, 2022	Gemini
March 5, 2020–March 16, 2020	Aquarius	July 6, 2022–July 19, 2022	Cancer
March 17, 2020–April 11, 2020	Pisces	July 20, 2022–Aug. 4, 2022	Leo
April 12, 2020–April 27, 2020	Aries	Aug. 5, 2022–Aug. 26, 2022	Virgo
April 28, 2020–May 11, 2020	Taurus	Aug. 27, 2022–Sept. 23, 2022	Libra
May 12, 2020–May 28, 2020	Gemini	Sept. 24, 2022–Oct. 10, 2022	Virgo
May 29, 2020–Aug. 5, 2020	Cancer	Oct. 11, 2022–Oct. 29, 2022	Libra
Aug. 6, 2020–Aug. 20, 2020	Leo	Oct. 30, 2022–Nov. 17, 2022	Scorpio
Aug. 21, 2020 – Sept. 5, 2020	Virgo	Nov. 18, 2022–Dec. 6, 2022	Sagittarius
Sept. 6, 2020–Sept. 27, 2020	Libra	Dec. 7, 2022–Feb. 11, 2023	Capricorn
Sept. 28, 2020–Oct. 28, 2020	Scorpio	Feb. 12, 2023–March 2, 2023	Aquarius
Oct. 29, 2020–Nov. 10, 2020	Libra	March 3, 2023–March 19, 2023	Pisces
Nov. 11, 2020–Dec. 1, 2020	Scorpio	March 20, 2023–April 3, 2023	Aries
Dec. 2, 2020–Dec. 20, 2020	Sagittarius	April 4, 2023–June 11, 2023	Taurus
Dec. 21, 2020–Jan. 8, 2021	Capricorn	June 12, 2023–June 27, 2023	Gemini
Jan. 9, 2021–March 15, 2021	Aquarius	June 28, 2023–July 11, 2023	Cancer
March 16, 2021–April 4, 2021	Pisces	July 12, 2023–July 28, 2023	Leo
April 5, 2021–April 19, 2021	Aries	July 29, 2023–Oct. 5, 2023	Virgo
April 20, 2021–May 4, 2021	Taurus	Oct. 6, 2023–Oct. 22, 2023	Libra
May 5, 2021–July 11, 2021	Gemini	Oct. 23, 2023–Nov. 10, 2023	Scorpio
July 12, 2021–July 28, 2021	Cancer	Nov. 11, 2023–Dec. 1, 2023	Sagittarius
July 29, 2021–Aug. 11, 2021	Leo	Dec. 2, 2023–Dec. 23, 2023	Capricorn
Aug. 12, 2021–Aug. 30, 2021	Virgo	Dec. 24, 2023–Jan. 14, 2024	Sagittarius
Aug. 31, 2021–Nov. 5, 2021	Libra	Jan. 15, 2024–Feb. 5, 2024	Capricorn
Nov. 6, 2021–Nov. 24, 2021	Scorpio	Feb. 6, 2024–Feb. 23, 2024	Aquarius
Nov. 25, 2021–Dec. 13, 2021	Sagittarius	Feb. 24, 2024–March 10, 2024	Pisces
Dec. 14, 2021–Jan. 2, 2022	Capricorn	March 11, 2024–May 15, 2024	Aries
Jan. 3, 2022–Jan. 26, 2022	Aquarius	May 16, 2024–June 3, 2024	Taurus
Jan. 27, 2022–Feb. 14, 2022	Capricorn	June 4, 2024–June 17, 2024	Gemini
Feb. 15, 2022–March 10, 2022	Aquarius	June 18, 2024–July 2, 2024	Cancer

If you were born:	Your Mercury is in:	If you were born:	Your Mercury is in:
July 3, 2024–July 25, 2024	Leo	Dec. 26, 2026–Jan. 13, 2027	Capricorn
July 26, 2024–Aug. 15, 2024	Virgo	Jan. 14, 2027–Feb. 1, 2027	Aquarius
Aug. 16, 2024–Sept. 9, 2024	Libra	Feb. 2, 2027–Feb. 18, 2027	Pisces
Sept. 10, 2024–Sept. 26, 2024	Virgo	Feb. 19, 2027–March 18, 2027	Aquarius
Sept. 27, 2024–Oct. 13, 2024	Libra	March 19, 2027–April 8, 2027	Pisces
Oct. 14, 2024–Nov. 2, 2024	Scorpio	April 9, 2027–April 24, 2027	Aries
Nov. 3, 2024–Jan. 8, 2025	Sagittarius	April 25, 2027–May 9, 2027	Taurus
Jan. 9, 2025–Jan. 28, 2025	Capricorn	May 10, 2027–May 28, 2027	Gemini
Jan. 29, 2025–Feb. 14, 2025	Aquarius	May 29, 2027–June 26, 2027	Cancer
Feb. 15, 2025–March 3, 2025	Pisces	June 27, 2027–July 12, 2027	Gemini
March 4, 2025–March 30, 2025	Aries	July 13, 2027–Aug. 2, 2027	Cancer
March 31, 2025–April 16, 2025	Pisces	Aug. 3, 2027–Aug. 17, 2027	Leo
April 17, 2025–May 10, 2025	Aries	Aug. 18, 2027–Sept. 3, 2027	Virgo
May 11, 2025–May 26, 2025	Taurus	Sept. 4, 2027–Sept. 27, 2027	Libra
May 27, 2025–June 8, 2025	Gemini	Sept. 28, 2027–Oct. 16, 2027	Scorpio
June 9, 2025–June 26, 2025	Cancer	Oct. 17, 2027–Nov. 10, 2027	Libra
June 27, 2025–Sept. 2, 2025	Leo	Nov. 11, 2027–Nov. 29, 2027	Scorpio
Sept. 3, 2025–Sept. 18, 2025	Virgo	Nov. 30, 2027–Dec. 18, 2027	Sagittarius
Sept. 19, 2025–Oct. 6, 2025	Libra	Dec. 19, 2027–Jan. 6, 2028	Capricorn
Oct. 7, 2025–Oct. 29, 2025	Scorpio	Jan. 7, 2028–March 13, 2028	Aquarius
Oct. 30, 2025–Nov. 19, 2025	Sagittarius	March 14, 2028–March 31, 2028	Pisces
Nov. 20, 2025–Dec. 11, 2025	Scorpio	April 1, 2028–April 15, 2028	Aries
Dec. 12, 2025–Jan. 1, 2026	Sagittarius	April 16, 2028–May 1, 2028	Taurus
Jan. 2, 2026–Jan. 20, 2026	Capricorn	May 2, 2028–July 9, 2028	Gemini
Jan. 21, 2026–Feb. 6, 2026	Aquarius	July 10, 2028–July 24, 2028	Cancer
Feb. 7, 2026–April 15, 2026	Pisces	July 25, 2028–Aug. 8, 2028	Leo
April 16, 2026–May 3, 2026	Aries	Aug. 9, 2028–Aug. 27, 2028	Virgo
May 4, 2026–May 17, 2026	Taurus	Aug. 28, 2028–Nov. 2, 2028	Libra
May 18, 2026–June 1, 2026	Gemini	Nov. 3, 2028–Nov. 21, 2028	Scorpio
June 2, 2026–Aug. 9, 2026	Cancer	April 17, 2032–May 7, 2032	Aries
Aug. 10, 2026–Aug. 25, 2026	Leo	Nov. 22, 2028–Dec. 10, 2028	Sagittarius
Aug. 26, 2026–Sept. 10, 2026	Virgo	Dec. 11, 2028–Dec. 31, 2028	Capricorn
Sept. 11, 2026–Sept. 30, 2026	Libra	Jan. 1, 2029–Jan. 13, 2029	Aquarius
Oct. 1, 2026–Dec. 6, 2026	Scorpio	Jan. 14, 2029–Feb. 13, 2029	Capricorn
Dec. 7, 2026–Dec. 25, 2026	Sagittarius	Feb. 14, 2029–March 6, 2029	Aquarius

If you were born:	Your Mercury is in:	If you were born:	Your Mercury is in:
March 7, 2029–March 23, 2029	Pisces	July 1, 2031–Sept. 7, 2031	Leo
March 24, 2029–April 7, 2029	Aries	Sept. 8, 2031–Sept. 23, 2031	Virgo
April 8, 2029–June 13, 2029	Taurus	Sept. 24, 2031–Oct. 11, 2031	Libra
June 14, 2029–July 1, 2029	Gemini	Oct. 12, 2031–Nov. 1, 2031	Scorpio
July 2, 2029–July 15, 2029	Cancer	Nov. 2, 2031–Dec. 8, 2031	Sagittarius
July 16, 2029–July 31, 2029	Leo	Dec. 9, 2031–Dec. 11, 2031	Scorpio
Aug. 1, 2029–Aug. 27, 2029	Virgo	Dec. 12, 2031–Jan. 6, 2032	Sagittarius
Aug. 28, 2029–Sept. 8, 2029	Libra	Jan. 7, 2032–Jan. 25, 2032	Capricorn
Sept. 9, 2029–Oct. 8, 2029	Virgo	Jan. 26, 2032–Feb. 11, 2032	Aquarius
Oct. 9, 2029–Oct. 26, 2029	Libra	Feb. 12, 2032–March 2, 2032	Pisces
Oct. 27, 2029–Nov. 13, 2029	Scorpio	March 3, 2032–March 13, 2032	Aries
Nov. 14, 2029–Dec. 3, 2029	Sagittarius	March 14, 2032–April 16, 2032	Pisces
Dec. 4, 2029–Feb. 8, 2030	Capricorn	May 8, 2032–May 22, 2032	Taurus
Feb. 9, 2030–Feb. 27, 2030	Aquarius	May 23, 2032–June 5, 2032	Gemini
Feb. 28, 2030–March 15, 2030	Pisces	June 6, 2032–June 25, 2032	Cancer
March 16, 2030–April 1, 2030	Aries	July 26, 2032–Aug. 10, 2032	Cancer
April 2, 2030–April 28, 2030	Taurus	Aug. 30, 2032–Sept. 14, 2032	Virgo
April 29, 2030–May 15, 2030	Aries	Aug. 11, 2032–Aug. 29, 2032	Leo
May 16, 2030–June 8, 2030	Taurus	June 26, 2032–July 25, 2032	Leo
June 9, 2030–June 22, 2030	Gemini	Sept. 15, 2032–Oct. 3, 2032	Libra
June 23, 2030–July 7, 2030	Cancer	Oct. 4, 2032–Oct. 31, 2032	Scorpio
July 8, 2030–July 26, 2030	Leo	Nov. 1, 2032–Nov. 4, 2032	Sagittarius
July 27, 2030–Oct. 1, 2030	Virgo	Nov. 5, 2032–Dec. 9, 2032	Scorpio
Oct. 2, 2030–Oct. 18, 2030	Libra	Dec. 10, 2032–Dec. 29, 2032	Sagittarius
Oct. 19, 2030–Nov. 7, 2030	Scorpio	Dec. 30, 2032–Jan. 17, 2033	Capricorn
Nov. 8, 2030–Dec. 1, 2030	Sagittarius	Jan. 18, 2033–Feb. 3, 2033	Aquarius
Dec. 2, 2030–Dec. 10, 2030	Capricorn	Feb. 4, 2033–April 12, 2033	Pisces
Dec. 11, 2030–Jan. 12, 2031	Sagittarius	April 13, 2033–April 29, 2033	Aries
Jan. 13, 2031–Feb. 1, 2031	Capricorn	April 30, 2033–May 13, 2033	Taurus
Feb. 2, 2031–Feb. 19, 2031	Aquarius	May 14, 2033–May 29, 2033	Gemini
Feb. 20, 2031–March 7, 2031	Pisces	May 30, 2033–Aug. 6, 2033	Cancer
March 8, 2031–May 14, 2031	Aries	Aug. 7, 2033–Aug. 21, 2033	Leo
May 15, 2031–May 31, 2031	Taurus	Aug. 22, 2033–Sept. 7, 2033	Virgo
June 1, 2031–June 14, 2031	Gemini	Sept. 8, 2033–Sept. 28, 2033	Libra
June 15, 2031–June 30, 2031	Cancer	Sept. 29, 2033–Nov. 2, 2033	Scorpio

If you were born:	Your Mercury is in:	If you were born:	Your Mercury is in:
Nov. 11, 2033–Dec. 3, 2033	Scorpio	May 6, 2034–July 12, 2034	Gemini
Nov. 3, 2033–Nov. 10, 2033	Libra	July 13, 2034–July 29, 2034	Cancer
Dec. 4, 2033–Dec. 22, 2033	Sagittarius	July 30, 2034–Aug. 13, 2034	Leo
Dec. 23, 2033–Jan. 9, 2034	Capricorn	Aug. 14, 2034–Aug. 31, 2034	Virgo
Jan. 10, 2034–March 16, 2034	Aquarius	Sept. 1, 2034–Nov. 7, 2034	Libra
March 17, 2034–April 5, 2034	Pisces	Nov. 8, 2034–Nov. 25, 2034	Scorpio
April 6, 2034–April 20, 3034	Aries	Nov. 26, 2034–Dec. 15, 2034	Sagittarius
April 21, 2034–May 5, 2034	Taurus	Dec. 16, 2034–Jan. 3, 2035	Capricorn

Although the characteristics of the twelve signs are widely disparate, they can be classified into four general groups based on some shared similarities: Earth, Fire, Air, and Water. Since the four elements are the foundations of the natural, they manifest in the heavens through the astrological signs. For example, the Earth element reflects Earth energy in the heavens through the constellations of Taurus, Virgo, and Capricorn; Water reflects Cancer, Scorpio, and Pisces; Air reflects Gemini, Libra, and Aquarius; and Fire reflects Aries, Leo, and Sagittarius. Each of the elements symbolizes a general temperament. For instance, Earth signs are concrete, practical, material, and sensation-oriented. Water signs are emotional, intuitive, sensitive, and creative. Air signs are intellectual, communicative, and relational. Fire signs are action-oriented, willful, inspirational, and spontaneous. The totality of the four groups is the human personality. Mercury takes on the basic temperament of the element in which it is placed.

Once you've looked up the sign of your Mercury placement, consult the elements chart below to determine the type of filter you possess and how it influences the way you receive, process, and express information.

The Elements

Mercury in Earth: Taurus, Virgo, Capricorn
- Ideas and thoughts are practical, determined, visual, and concrete.
- Learning is best accomplished through the five senses: visual, auditory, tactile, kinesthetic, and olfactory.

- Filter is earthy and sensational, focused on the senses.
- Communication is persistent, specific, cautious, and patient.
- Thought processes are shaped by practical realities and traditional material concerns.

Mercury in Water: Cancer, Scorpio, Pisces
- Ideas and thoughts are influenced by deeply felt emotions.
- Learning is best accomplished by being creative, intuitional, and sensitive.
- Filter is the feeling and desire for emotional connectedness.
- Communication is emotional, empathic, intuitional, sometimes psychic, and withheld and evasive if strong emotions are present.
- Thought processes are shaped by emotional and intuitional concerns.

Mercury in Air: Gemini, Libra, Aquarius
- Ideas and thoughts are important in and of themselves.
- Learning is best accomplished by gathering information about many different ideals, and social and environmental situations.
- Filter is based on curiosity and versatility.
- Communication is versatile, socially adept, articulate, innovative, and objective.
- Thought processes are shaped by a love of sharing ideas.

Mercury in Fire: Aries, Leo, Sagittarius
- Ideas and thoughts are influenced by future visions, philosophy, beliefs, and hopes.
- Learning is best accomplished through understanding abstract concepts or the bigger picture, as well as by taking action assertively.
- Filter is the need to have insight, to understand the gestalts of life.

- Communication is powerful, inspirational, assertive, quick, spontaneous, and enthusiastic.
- Thought processes are shaped by sharing inspired philosophical beliefs.

AWARENESS OF FILTERS

As a former administrator in education, I remain fascinated with the way children communicate. I strongly believe that if we would approach teaching by trying to reach children based on their respective orientations to the world, they would learn more quickly and encounter less frustration. More recently, I was very fortunate to be introduced to the teachers and administrators of two fine private schools. One teacher invited me to come to her third-grade class for Career Day. I used it as an opportunity to introduce the children to their Mercury placements. It was the first time that I had grouped children by Mercuries. I divided them into groups according to the four elements. Soon they began to develop relationships between themselves and their elemental filter. They talked about "their" element as if it were their best friend. They laughed and discussed how the members of their own group were so alike. Then I did some role-playing, using a stuffed dog as a prop. I had a child with Mercury in Air discuss the dog with a child who had Mercury in Water. The Air child, because of her orientation toward wanting to share ideas, told the Water child she wanted to name the dog. The Water child, with her filter skewed toward emotion, wanted to love the dog, hug the dog, and pet it. The Air child became a little annoyed and started listing possible names. The Water child shrugged and continued to hug the stuffed animal. There was virtually no communication between the two children.

What happened? The Air child's filter to the world was to think about it and label it. That's what Air Mercuries do: they're interested in words, in labeling, articulating, and classifying things by description. Naming the dog was important to her, but expressing her opinion to the Water child was equally important. She wanted an intellectual exchange to find the right name. By contrast, the Water child's filter was to perceive the world through feelings and to express herself emotionally. She wanted to connect with the stuffed animal and did. She was unable to identify with the Air child on an emotional level, so she put her feelings where she could: on the dog.

I then had two more children do the same role-playing with the dog, except this time one little girl had a Fire Mercury, the other an Earth Mercury. The Fire child took the dog from me, put it on the floor, and pretended to walk it. She wanted the Earth Mercury to walk it with her. The Earth child did not respond. Getting bored, the Fire child began to play catch with it. Consistent with the characteristics of Fire in Mercury, the Fire child's first two impulses upon seeing the dog were to take action in some way. The Earth child reached down and took the dog and began to pet it. She needed to have the dog in her possession. She was interested in the dog's coat and its texture. She told the Fire child how soft the dog's fur was. The Fire child took the dog and again played catch with it. This bothered the Earth child, who wanted to pet it. Once again, there was no communication between the children.

Before resuming the role-playing, I talked to all four girls about their experience and their inherent differences. Then I coached them to help them create alignment in their interaction. I reminded the Air child that her friend, "Water," was more interested in feelings than thoughts. I asked her to think about and share her emotions about the dog, even though that wasn't her first reaction. I told the Air child that if she wanted to talk to her friend, she would have to use words her friend could understand. So "Air" told "Water" she "felt happy" when she held the dog and then asked "Water" how she felt. "Water" responded by agreeing that she also felt happy when she held the dog. Then I asked the Water child to pay attention to her feelings after talking with "Air." She told me she was happy because "Air" was "interested" in her feelings. After I reminded her, the Water child was able to cooperate with the Air child about what she needed.

I used the same coaching technique to reach the Fire and Earth children. All I had to do was to remind each one of the other's needs. I told the Fire child how important touching was to the Earth child, and she suggested that the Earth child "hold the dog." In turn, I reminded the Earth child that doing something was important to "Fire." Because the Earth child was secure with having the dog in her possession, she was able to participate in "Fire's" game. In turn, the Fire child was happy because she was able to create some new action—an imaginary three-way game of catch—for both of them to enjoy. "Earth" happily complied. "Fire" threw a make-believe ball to the dog, and "Earth" caught the "ball" from the dog and threw it back to "Fire."

YOUR PERSONAL FILTER TO THE WORLD

This section chronicles the twelve filters, the communication style associated with each, the challenges inherent in each, and ways to overcome those challenges. To maximize this information, research the Mercuries of the most important people in your life in addition to consulting your own Mercury filter. Having an awareness of your own filter is significant, but ultimately you can create harmony with the people closest to you only by grasping the philosophical underpinnings of the way they see the world.

Remember, your Mercury sign represents your orientation, some of which may be embedded in your unconscious. Thus, some of the qualities listed here may seem more familiar to you than others. Karmic astrology embodies symmetry and balance. For additional guidance in how to overcome the challenges inherent in each filter, consult the sign of the Mercury filter that opposes yours: Taurus/Scorpio, Gemini/Sagittarius, Aries/Libra, Pisces/ Virgo, Aquarius/Leo, and Capricorn/Cancer.

Mercury in Aries

You see the world through the eyes of an explorer, always seeking to discover uncharted territory. The world is an exciting reality to be explored and conquered. You are confident that you can impact any situation by being strong, assertive, and independent. You believe that through your self-awareness and creativity, you can make anything happen. You welcome physical challenges and usually rise to the top because of your physical strength, will, and agility.

The way you communicate You are a dynamic, fiery, optimistic, and talkative communicator. You will fight for your ideals. You can be enthusiastic in your eagerness to share new ideas. You are willing to take risks with your communication style and can be quite creative and pioneering. Albert Einstein is a wonderful example of this energy. You can sometimes be sarcastic, combative, and brusque when angry. Others may be afraid of your impulsive and aggressive style. You can be self-absorbed, and your insistence on making yourself the center of your communication may turn off others.

Challenges to your filter You can be impatient if things go too slowly. You want life to be a series of new beginnings and can be easily distracted and bored if it is not.

Overcoming your challenges When you are bored, remember how creative you are and that you are in charge of creating new beginnings. Then take an action. Curb your impulsiveness by choosing to think before you speak. Deal with anger as a self process; don't use it against someone else. Transform aggression into physical challenges. Constantly be cognizant of ways to mediate and be diplomatic. Practice seeing both sides of a conflict and listening.

Mercury in Taurus

You see the world through the eyes of a creative gardener to be seeded and tended. You desire material security and creating physical bonds with the earth on many different levels. Because you value consistency, you build your earthy life cautiously, carefully, and conservatively. You seed your garden one step at a time so that it will flourish forever. You are patient and determined to finish the projects you begin. Quality and practical value are vital in all things you create and possess. You seek serenity and calm in your responses to the world. You are ultimately interested in the integration of earthly and spiritual concerns. The Buddha is a wonderful example of this energy.

The way you communicate You speak in a slow, methodical fashion to make sure that your ideas will be understood. You tend to create pictures with your words because of your desire to use all the physical senses in your communication. Many of you are singers who do exactly that. The communication of your ideas and thoughts is practical and conservative in orientation. You do not waste words. When challenged, you can be argumentative and fixed in your opinions. Your tendency toward indolence keeps you from communicating effectively.

Challenges to your filter You can be stubborn and fixed in your beliefs. You are resistant to change. You can be indulgent and lazy.

Overcoming your challenges When you are fixed and stubborn in communicating your beliefs, work on being probing and curious about someone else's beliefs. Agree to disagree when you're feeling argumentative, and find your comfort zone of serenity. Think about being passionate and intense when you have an inclination to be lazy.

Mercury in Gemini

You see the world through the eyes of an information gatherer. Life is a library filled with new ideas, thoughts, and experiences to satisfy your insatiable curiosity. Because you are mentally alert, you are quick to grasp a new idea. You love words and language, and you are an avid reader and writer. You respond to the world with mental agility, brightness, and cleverness.

The way you communicate You are a messenger: Gemini is always about talking, sharing, and communicating. You speak eloquently with flair and excitement. You cleverly put different words together and are known for your creative use of language. President Harry Truman's colloquial, down-home communication style is an excellent example of this Mercury. You often do more than one thing at a time: watching TV, reading a book, and talking on the phone. You make an excellent reporter because you wish to share ideas as quickly as you can. Sometimes you become distracted and speak in vague and confusing patterns. Being gossipy and deceptive are potential problems for you. You are more interested in the trees than the forest.

Challenges to your filter You can become too intellectually stimulated and confused. You may be restless and distracted.

Overcoming your challenges When you are too intellectually stimulated, go to a favorite spot outdoors. Ground yourself by hugging a tree or sitting on the grass. Allow your mind energy to connect to the earth. Write down goals instead of keeping everything in your mind. Transmute your restlessness into philosophic exploration. Choose inspirational, broader concept words instead of mundane, gossipy ones. This will help you include the forest (abstraction) as well as the trees (specific details) in your communication.

Mercury in Cancer

You see the world through the eyes of an emotionally sensitive cosmic nurturer and mother. You would like the world to be an extended home to provide you with emotional foundations, support, and security. You are a sensitive listener, always paying close attention to your emotional environment. If the words you hear don't mesh with your emotions, you often ignore them. Emotions color all your perceptions and thoughts. There are moments when you may lose your emotional identity because of your highly developed empathy to others. Princess Diana is a poignant example of this Mercury.

The way you communicate Your speech is emotional, caring, and nurturing. You are sympathetic and supportive in your relationships. You frequently refer to your love of home, family, children, and the past. Much of your communication is not through words but through actions, like cooking, finding a sentimental greeting card, or being emotionally present when someone is in pain. You are emotionally expressive by being affectionate and physical. You are highly creative, especially in the area of the home. Because of your gentle nature, you can be intimidated easily by others and feel a need to close down emotionally for protection, at which time communicating with you becomes very difficult.

Challenges to your filter You can lack objectivity because you are so sensitive. You can be moody and too self-pitying. You continually bring past memories into the present.

Overcoming your challenges You need to learn how to protect yourself from your own emotional sensitivity. Learning personal boundaries, like when to say no, or when not to need being needed, will help. When you're too caught up in your emotions, looking at situations from a practical and earthy perspective will also help. Being organized and structured will keep you more centered in reality and less emotional. Be realistic and discriminating about how much you need to bring past experiences into the present.

Mercury in Leo

You see the world through the eyes of an actor. The world then becomes a stage on which you dramatically perform your life. You watch for opportunities to be on center stage and obtain the applause you feel is necessary for your happiness. You perceive the world from your heart, needing relationships that will enhance your sense of dignity and acknowledgment. You find fun, excitement, and childlike wonder in the world. You love luxuries and have a strong sense of style. Jacqueline Kennedy Onassis exemplifies this Mercury.

The way you communicate Your speech has a strong dramatic, self-confident flair. You are commanding and self-assured in your communication. You have pride and dignity, and much of your speech resonates with the power of royalty. Much of your need for powerful expression comes from your heart's desire to explore fun, childlike wonder, and heart-to-heart connection. Much of what you say is calculated to receive admiration, praise, and approval, making your words appear to some as boastful, insincere, and theatrical.

Challenges to your filter You can be self-indulgent and too self-absorbed. Because you may believe you are the ruler of your domain, you can be dominating and overbearing. Vulnerable to others' approval, you can be too vulnerable to needing their love and respect.

Overcoming your challenges Being able to refocus your authoritarian tendencies into leadership qualities will help when you are feeling too self-centered. Think about how you can inspire and become more attuned to humanitarian concerns. Learning how to become benignly detached and more objective will help you when you are feeling susceptible to your own internal demands. Learning to love, honor, and approve of yourself will keep you from communicating this vulnerability to others.

Mercury in Virgo

You perceive the world through the eyes of an organizer. The world, then, is a complex system of thought, work, and service needing structure and order. Because you consider yourself the right person to create this systematic environment, you become its efficient, concerned promoter. You believe in its intrinsic, earthly perfection. You want to maintain high standards through your methodical, logical, analytical style. You look for ways to create healthy physical systems for yourself and others. You use your powers of discrimination to find ways to be of service to those who request it. You are exacting, and you seek to bring coherence to the world. Labor leader Walter Reuther embodies this Mercury filter.

The way you communicate Your speech is clear, analytical, discriminating, and exact. You are devoted to organizing your speech to be practical, efficient, and precise. Your propensity for inductive reasoning shows through your words and expressed thoughts. Much of your language involves health issues, work habits and environment, and a need for order. You are interested in fixing situations you consider broken. You can be judgmental, critical, and extreme in your speech. Because your standards are so high, you can appear as a worried, anxious communicator.

Challenges to your filter You can be obsessed with very small details, putting your life in boxes. You can be too analytical and perfectionistic.

Overcoming your challenges Changing your orientation to perfection is critical to overcoming your challenges. Realizing the intrinsic perfection of your deep self will keep you from worrying about external perfection. Strive for excellence, not perfection. Be gentle and compassionate with yourself when you are inclined to be anxious about doing things right. Be cognizant of your extreme expectations, and be more creative.

Mercury in Libra

You see the world through the eyes of a benevolent judge with the world as your cosmic courtroom. You abhor injustice and unfairness. You seek refinement, beauty, balance, and harmony in the world. Your world is a web of social relationships that need mediation and arbitration, through your skills of cooperation and need for justice. You perceive both sides of all arguments and endeavor to find the balanced center and middle ground. You want to see a socially refined and charming world. President Dwight Eisenhower is a good example of this Mercury.

The way you communicate Your speech is diplomatic, cultured, and socially oriented. You can be charming, affectionate, and persuasive in your words. You express thoughts that produce compromise and negotiation in social situations. Your actions, as much a part of your communication as words, seek to please, to avoid conflict, and to create beautiful surroundings. You can be too flattering of others because you do not wish to hurt anyone's feelings. You compromise so much that at times you compromise yourself and are more interested in others' needs than your own.

Challenges to your filter You can be superficial and too interested in what other people think of you. Your desperate need for finding balance and harmony can mire you in indecision and ambivalence. You care about pleasing others, at the expense of yourself.

Overcoming your challenges Learning to think about yourself as an important relationship in addition to all your external relationships is vital. Create the same level of compromise for you as you do for them. Learn how to say no on occasion. Learn how to be present to a conflict, if it is important to you. An assertiveness training course would help. Take an action on an issue on which you would otherwise straddle the fence.

Mercury in Scorpio

You perceive the world through the eyes of the phoenix, seeing the transformational potential in all things. You are an emotional investigator seeking intensity and passion—even emotional chaos—in order to find the deep understanding you desire. Your thoughts and ideas are colored by your emotional needs to probe the human psyche. You seek the transformation of material desires into spiritual values. You respect and attract all forms of courage. You see the world as exciting, intriguing, and somewhat dangerous. You seek to understand the darker side of the human condition. Gandhi is a wonderful example of this Mercury.

The way you communicate Your speech is tinged with emotional intensity and a need for internal power. You are extreme; your all-or-nothing attitude is evident in your words as well as your expressed ideas and thoughts. You are passionate about your beliefs and are not afraid to articulate them to others. Your speech can be intimidating and frightening to those less intense than you. You can be relentless in your quest to sort out the mysteries of life—especially death and sexuality—and you seek to communicate your ideas frequently. Because you can be extreme, you can also withhold communication and appear to be cold and emotionally withdrawn.

Challenges to your filter You can be controlling, wanting power for its own sake. You can be relentless and judgmental. You may never know how much is enough.

Overcoming your challenges Learn patience and serenity. Gardening can help because it will modulate your intensity. Read *Desiderata*, and observe how its words resonate with you. Use your deep understanding of emotions to read others' feelings, and act accordingly. Find creative outlets for your passion. Be aware of your tendency toward extremes; find third options and discover how being creative relieves your need to withdraw.

Mercury in Sagittarius

You perceive the world through the eyes of a philosopher. Your environment is a giant cornucopia of boundless opportunities and knowledge. Nature becomes the symbol for freedom, expansion, the natural order, and experience. You learn, through the explicate order of nature, how things work. Through it you see and learn about serendipity, prosperity, joy, and survival. You learn best by experiencing life, not just thinking or talking about it. You see the highest potential in all people through your filter of faith, hope, and optimism. You perceive the world as something to be experienced, without boundary or restriction. All things are possible as long as you have enough faith. You wish to discover the truth so you can share it and teach it to others. You are the spiritual visionary and teacher, creating goals that are idealistic and devotional. Anthropologist Margaret Mead is a vivid example of this Mercury.

The way you communicate You express your thoughts and ideas with optimism and enthusiasm. You are continually searching for the truth in all of life's situations. You speak as a teacher and a philosopher exploring abstract ideas. You are more interested in the forest than the trees. Honesty and openness are vital to your communication style. You are an enthusiastic traveler searching for enlightenment with every step you take. You easily communicate with nature and animals. Teaching others is your way of learning more. Sometimes you can be too honest and too direct, hurting others. You can be so involved with your philosophy that you speak it dogmatically.

Challenges to your filter Your truth is the only truth. You can be pedantic and preachy and too brutally honest. Your bias is to philosophize and not listen to others' communication.

Overcoming your challenges Paying attention to the trees as well as the forest is essential. Gathering more information to support your philosophies will help you be less dogmatic. Learning to listen as well as talk will help you be better understood by those with whom you wish to communicate. Thinking before you speak is vital to curbing the directness that can get you in trouble.

Mercury in Capricorn

You perceive the world through the eyes of the wise man. You want the world to be a place of practical, traditional wisdom. You seek reality in thought and action and are methodical in how you view the world. You are disciplined and reserved, careful and cautious in your judgment of how things work. You want to impose your responsible organizational nature on life's inconsistencies. You look at the ladder of life and want to climb to the top. You value the world's material bounty and want to claim it. Ronald Reagan is a good example of this Mercury placement.

The way you communicate Your speech is conservative and reserved. You think long and hard before you speak. Your words are practical, realistic, and mature. You have excellent common sense. You incorporate your respect for history and traditions into your thoughts and words. You prepare for any verbal presentation thoroughly, because you take your communication seriously. You have an avuncular way, and you tend to speak about self-reliance, honor, and respect. You are an excellent disciplinarian and leader. However, you may be inflexible and intolerant of views that seem too far-fetched for you. Your rigidity may make you judgmental of others' views.

Challenges to your filter You can be stern and rigid. You can be pessimistic and see life's failures rather than its successes.

Overcoming your challenges Work on accessing your emotions as well as your beliefs. Work on becoming more relaxed and optimistic. Be cognizant of your tendency toward rigidity; figure out what it represents and alter it. Try to be more whimsical, carefree, and enthusiastic. Make an effort to do something fun when you feel pressured to do something more weighty.

Mercury in Aquarius

You perceive the world through the eyes of a reformer. For you, the world is a place filled with innovation and invention, with a rational divine order to the universe. You think that all things that occur in life have a reason, although you may not always understand them. Accepting others' differences, you value individuals for their innovation and uniqueness. You search for global tolerance, cooperation, and humanitarianism. You see future possibilities and invent new technologies to improve the human condition. With a broad philosophical outlook, you understand the New Age triangle of mind, body, and soul. You seek equality and gravitate toward like-minded groups that share your reformer's vision. Inventor Thomas Edison is a wonderful example of this Mercury placement.

The way you communicate You are a highly innovative thinker and communicator. You are intuitional in what you say and how you say it. You value and speak about equality. Wishing to share your ideas with the world, you are a progressive, cause-oriented thinker. You have a predilection toward high tech, computers, science, and New Age philosophy, and you express your ideas unabashedly. You are humanistic and talk about how one person can make a difference. However, you can be erratic and eccentric at times, occasionally losing your audience. Your speech hints at your rebellious and radical side.

Challenges to your filter You can be so detached that you appear as if your mind is somewhere else. You can be very internal and impersonal.

Overcoming your challenges Learning to connect with other people is important. This will help you get into the game of life, instead of being so emotionally unavailable. Find activities that will help you appreciate more practical, mundane realities. Be aware of your radical tendencies; work on being inspirational instead.

Mercury in Pisces

You perceive the world through the eyes of a spiritual romantic. You want the world to be beautiful, sensitive, and loving. You seek the creative, the poetic, the lyrical. Your psychic, intuitive self seeks ways to make the world a more spiritual place. Your thoughts and ideas are colored by your deep emotional desire for compassion and love. You are sensitive to the emotional pain of the world. You absorb environmental energies because you are so empathetic. Mystic Edgar Cayce is a good example of this Mercury.

The way you communicate You are a sensitive, intuitional communicator. Your language is gentle, loving, spiritual, and creative. You express your ideas and thoughts carefully, so as not to hurt anyone's feelings. And because you are so perceptive and intuitional, you know what to say and how to say it. However, this may mean that you're not entirely honest in how you express your own wants and needs. You express your poetic and romantic feelings when you feel safe. Otherwise you can be very quiet and shy. Because you are so sensitive to others' feelings, you can alter your own emotions very quickly to match theirs and therefore appear moody and inconsistent.

Challenges to your filter You sometimes sacrifice your own needs in order to satisfy the needs of others. You have set no boundaries between yourself and the rest of the world. You are so sensitive that sometimes you have trouble dealing with harsh realities.

Overcoming your challenges Because you are so intuitional and empathetic, you need to learn how to create personal boundaries so you know where you and your emotions stop and someone else's begin. Learn to be as gentle and compassionate with yourself as you are with others. Be more assertive: say no occasionally. Express what you want. You'll become more comfortable expressing your creative self by working on feeling more secure within yourself.

Exercise: Mercury Filter
This brief exercise will help you confirm and better understand your Mercury filter.

My Mercury is in:

My Mercury is ruled by the element of:

My filter to the world is:

I am most comfortable expressing myself in the following ways:

I learn best by (consult the "Elements" chart and your personal Mercury filter):

MERCURY IN RELATIONSHIPS

The notion that men are strong and silent and tend to eschew communication while women are emotional and needful of interaction is a parochial attempt to oversimplify the way we relate to one another. Our societal expectations require that a man communicate like a man, a woman like a woman, further perpetuating these rules and the myths they embody. When we cross the line and express ourselves in a way considered gender atypical, we're criticized and discouraged.

Despite their obvious flaws, on some level we feel we need the reinforcement of our predictable, age-old concepts. They make our lives simpler and easier to understand. Still, this narrow, all-or-nothing approach has limited us by producing expectations that are unrealistic and damaging to our relatedness. With twelve different orientations and four elemental categories, a person's sex makes little difference.

Let's take a look at the importance of Mercury in relationships. Mercury can be further divided into masculine and feminine energy, but clearly the distinction is energetic rather than sexual. Masculine energy represents focused externalized action or expressed energy. Female energy, conversely, represents enveloping, internal reaction or receptive energy. Masculine Mercuries are Aries, Leo, Scorpio, Sagittarius, and Capricorn; those classified as feminine are Taurus, Cancer, Virgo, Libra, and Pisces. Two signs, Gemini and Aquarius, represent the integration of male and female energy and are therefore androgynous.

We need to be clear: men can have Mercuries that have feminine energy and women can have Mercuries that are masculine. Thus a man's filter to the world can be emotional, intuitional, sensitive, and receptive, and his expressive communication style can be emotional, shy, and intuitional. A woman's filter can be assertive, aggressive, action oriented, and dynamic, and her expressive communication style can be strong, powerful, and dominating. This incongruence complicates relationships quite a bit, because we often feel uncomfortable with it.

Mark and Denise's relationship embodies this basic role reversal. Both in their late twenties, they were having serious communication problems and sought me out based on a relative's recommendation. Mark explained that he felt shell-shocked when trying to talk to Denise. He described her communication style as too aggressive, too direct, too hostile, and too impulsive. Her Mercury was in the sign of Aries, a masculine sign. Whenever they had a confrontation or a disagreement, he would become intimidated and defensive; he would feel himself "closing down" emotionally, unable to speak. His Mercury was in the sign of Pisces, a female sign, which he understood to mean that he was highly intuitive, emotional, spiritual, creative, and compassionate. Denise's complaint about Mark was that he was too sensitive, too insecure, too vulnerable and weak. These judgments devastated him, a reaction that further perpetuated her beliefs about him. She said that she basically agreed with his assessment of her communication style, although she would have described herself as assertive rather than aggressive; honest instead of direct; healthily angry, not hostile; and spontaneous, not impulsive.

This couple is a classic example of how a man can have a strong feminine orientation in thinking and speaking and a woman can express herself with a more masculine energy. Until Mark and Denise met me and learned about their particular Mercury placements, all they had were judgments about each other. Mark also shared his confusion and fear that he was "weird" because he knew how sensitive he was and felt that it wasn't "manly." He had been teased as a child for crying a lot and being emotional. Denise, on the other hand, had always been proud of her powerful and aggressive communication abilities.

For this couple, understanding each other's differences was the first step in untangling their communication conflicts. The second step was to ask each of them to honor and respect each other's individuality and to curb their judgments and criticisms of one another. They wanted to, and they did. Step three was to convince them to respect their soul contract and to learn from each other. For example, Mark needed to learn how to be more assertive instead of closing down and being quiet. Denise needed to learn how to become less self-oriented and more sensitive to her partner's needs.

Mark and Denise are happily married and continue to work on their relationship. Their opposite-sex Mercuries are now a gift, not a problem, because they understand what each of them has to learn from the other. This philosophical shift has enhanced the lives of both of them. They now have a child, whose Mercury is in the sign of Aquarius. Mark and Denise both know the potential challenges they will have with their son, since he is different from both of them. They are becoming experts in understanding how Aquarians communicate, so they will be better able to align with him.

Marcy's marriage was fine; it was her son she had had trouble connecting with, almost since he was born. But once she learned more about his filter, she was able to improve her relationship with him.

I have a child named Billy, who is now ten years old. Almost from the moment Billy could talk, we had terrible conflicts, the source of which was inexplicable. I was either angry at him, or feeling guilty because I was angry at him. It didn't take long before I had become very jealous of my husband's relationship with him. They never argued, always had fun together, and laughed a lot. I know this sounds terribly selfish, but it broke my heart every time I heard them giggling. I would walk into the room, say something to my son, and immediately sparks would fly. I never could say anything to him that worked. Mostly he wouldn't listen to me.

So when a friend told me about a workshop that she had attended that had helped her understand her child, I knew that I had to do it too. The workshop changed everything for me. I discovered that my Mercury is in Leo (Fire) and my son's is in Scorpio (Water). I learned that my communication style was a little overbearing and that I could be dominating. I also learned how truly vulnerable I was to other people's approval and appreciation. My pride would get wounded if I was ignored or not listened to. Before we had Billy, my vision of having a child had been that he would show me constant love and adoration. But Billy never did. My heart ached each time he would look at me as if I were the child and he the adult.

Because Billy's Mercury is in Scorpio, part of the Water element, he could read my insecurity, fear, and vulnerability, because of his sensitivity to emotions. He didn't even hear my words most of the time, and when he did they seemed not to make sense to him. My words were powerful, but my feelings were childlike. His Mercury in Scorpio was probing, intense, and controlling. He intimidated me, and I didn't know it. The bottom line was that my little boy was inherently more self-possessed than I was, and I hated him for that.

I took that workshop three years ago. Billy and I have made great strides in our communication. I have learned to be okay with his intense style and share my feelings with him openly. He responds to that and is less intimidating to me. I have learned not to expect his adoration. He has learned to be less intense and to communicate with me gently and with compassion, because I have shared my vulnerability with him. I also learned that my husband has Mercury in Scorpio too. That could explain why he and Billy understood each other's communication styles so well. That made me feel a lot better.

MERCURY AND YOUR SOUL MISSION

How is understanding our filter through Mercury connected to obtaining and living our soul mission? If we are aware of our own orientation toward life's experiences, then we can see that our filter is either congruent or in conflict with the way we need to see life in order to achieve our soul mission. Just by being cognizant that the way you actually see things may diverge widely from the way you need to see things, you are beginning to alter your prevailing filter for the approach embodied by your Soul Potential sign.

The only way to understand and distinguish between your actual orientation and the orientation you need to undertake is to learn about your personal filter, as well as the filter represented by your Soul Potential sign in Mercury. As mentioned earlier, some of us have trouble contemplating living our soul mission, or the type of life articulated by our Soul Potential. The reason is that we are viewing that soul mission through the same Mercury filter, rather than through the Mercury filter of our Soul Potential.

Only when we are able to envision life through the filter represented by our Soul Potential will we be able to overcome the challenges inherent in reaching our Soul Potential. For example, if I have a client whose Mercury is in Taurus, she will have a Taurean outlook on life, meaning she will desire material security and may create physical bonds with the earth on many different levels. She will value consistency, building her life with caution and care. She may be argumentative and fixed in her opinions. According to the Energetics Model in Chapter 4, her Soul Potential is in Cancer. She needs to access Mercury in her Soul Potential sign—Cancer—to see things from that vantage point and achieve and live her soul mission. Having an outlook influenced by Cancer means seeing life through the eyes of a nurturer, wanting to be supportive and an influence in all one's relationships. She would have to explore how that felt, and continue to think about what life would be like from that vantage point.

Some people's Mercury is located in the same sign as their Soul Potential, making it easier for them to grasp the traits, characteristics, and energy of their Soul Potential; since their filter already aligns with their soul mission, less reframing is needed. Conversely, those whose Mercuries are located in the same sign as their Soul Pattern face a more difficult challenge in gaining the perspective needed to achieve their soul mission. For example, if both your Mercury and your Soul Pattern are in Cancer, then your filter to the world is emotional and you will have a propensity to be emotional. Conversely, your Soul Potential sign is in Capricorn, requiring more practical, realistic, and rational behavior from you. You have a great challenge in altering your orientation before you can make that leap of faith to your spiritual mission.

Regardless of what sign your Mercury is in, the filter through which you perceive the world will affect how you perceive your spiritual mission. It will also add a specific flavor to your spiritual experience, which could either support or detract from it. An example of how it can support: suppose you have Mercury in Sagittarius and your Soul Potential is in Leo (both Fire signs). The inspirational leader quality of Leo will be expressed and manifested through the philosophy, optimism, and teaching talents of Sagittarius. An example of how the filter can detract: suppose your Mercury filter is in Capricorn and your Soul Potential is in Pisces. Your filter makes you earthy, structured, reality-based, and practical, while your Soul Potential sign requires you to work on being intuitional, faith-based, spiritual, and adaptive. You can see the potential difficulties with these two energies. Yet in all situations, whether supportive or not, there is an important reason why our souls would create these challenges. Refer to your Soul Potential and your Mercury placement, and see how they could support or detract from achieving your spiritual mission. Being consciously aware of the relationship between your Mercury filter and your Soul Potential could help you reframe your orientation and communication style, which would assist you in achieving your soul mission.

Exercise: Linking Your Mercury Filter to Your Soul Mission

Below is an example of the correlation between someone's Mercury filter and Soul Potential.

Sample Worksheet

My Soul Potential is in the sign of: Leo

My Mercury is in the sign of: Sagittarius

Soul Potential Characteristics (Leo)	Mercury Characteristics (Sagittarius)
charismatic, inspired leader	teacher, philosopher
self-confident, powerful	expansive, experiential
fun-loving, dramatic	seeker of truth, too honest
connected to others, joyful	preachy, insatiable
freedom, understanding	

Here's how you might use this information, to answer the following questions:

1. How can my Mercury aid me in achieving my soul potential?

    My Sagittarius Mercury can provide me with philosophical truths so that I can fulfill my Leo potential to teach and inspire others. It can seek the personal experiences I need so that I gain Leo's confidence. It helps me teach others in an expansive manner so that I can be powerful and charismatic.

2. How can my Mercury challenge me in achieving my soul potential?

    My Sagittarius Mercury can be too preachy, which would turn people off and interfere with my leadership. Its need for so much freedom would keep me from being committed to the people who need me. Speaking before I think and being too brutally honest could keep me from connecting on a heart-centered level to the people I teach.

3. How can I transform my Mercury challenges so that they will aid me in achievement of my soul potential?

I can transform my preachiness into speaking about my truth as only my truth, not someone else's. I can understand freedom as an internal experience so that I don't need so much on an external level. I can commit to relationships, and I can learn how to think before I talk, to make sure I don't hurt someone with words that I can't take back.

Your Worksheet

My Soul Potential is in the sign of:

My Mercury filter is in the sign of:

List your Soul Potential characteristics:

List your Mercury characteristics:

Using this information, answer the following questions in your journal.

1. How can my Mercury aid me in achieving my soul potential?
2. How can my Mercury challenge me in achieving my soul potential?
3. How can I transform my Mercury challenges so that they will aid me in achievement of my soul potential?

CHAPTER 6

SYMBOLISM AND THE UNCONSCIOUS

Through the unconscious mind, the soul provides us with answers to all of life's questions, by deluging us with hundreds of symbols. Jung defines the unconscious, in The Structure and Dynamics of the Psyche, as: "Everything of which I know, but of which I am not at the moment thinking; everything of which I was once conscious, but have now forgotten; everything perceived by my senses, but not noted by my conscious mind; everything which, involuntarily and without paying attention to it, I feel, think, remember, want and do; all the future things that are taking shape in me and will sometime come to consciousness; all this is the content of the unconscious." To Jung's definition I would add that the unconscious contains memories not only from this life but from other lives as well. Our unconscious minds project all of the wisdom gleaned from previous incarnations through the language of symbology.

The unconscious part of our personality also contains many of the undesirable traits we consciously reject and therefore repress. This is also referred by Jung as the Shadow. Afraid of the dark, unseemly memories we might unearth and the havoc they might wreak, many of us fear our unconscious mind. However, it is the converse that is true: what we don't know *can* hurt us.

Your unconscious mind can be your best friend, a warehouse of information that you want to bring to consciousness. The challenge is how to access that information. The source of the difficulty is that our unconscious mind has no direct communication with our conscious mind, which means we can explore its knowledge only indirectly. Moreover, while our conscious mind provides us with information more literally, the language of our unconscious mind is largely symbolic. Thus to pursue our unconscious mind's vast information, we must use processes that include astrology, dream interpretation, and various forms of symbology.

CULLING PERSONAL DATA THROUGH DREAMS

"The dream is the small hidden door in the deepest and most intimate sanctum of the soul, which opens into that primeval cosmic night that was soul long before there was conscious ego and will be soul far beyond what a conscious ego could ever reach."

—Carl Jung

Analyzing our dreams can be an illuminating and insightful experience, as long as we know how to interpret the symbols provided by our unconscious mind. Numerous theories and books on the subject of dream analysis abound, but my view is simple: like Jung, I believe that everything in your dream is a reflection of you. I also believe that there is a correlation between your dream symbology and your astrological symbols. Using both provides an enormous amount of relevant data. Before I show you how it works, let's consider a few symbolic structures.

Sex

What role does sex play in a dream? Usually, whichever sex you dream about is the part of you that you need to explore. If you're female and have a dream about a man, then he is a manifestation of your male side. If you're male dreaming about a woman, the converse is true. If the man in your dream is angry, it could mean that you need to look at the anger that you've been hiding from yourself. This approach can be somewhat unsettling since our dreams can portray the players as nightmarish. You may find it difficult to believe that that garish person could represent any part of yourself. If, however, you are experiencing the same types of conflicts in your waking life, you need to be able to claim those behaviors and take responsibility for them.

Suppose, for example, that you're a man and have been having periodic dreams about your Aunt Bianca. Aunt Bianca is now a representation of your female side. You wish to discover more about that hidden side, so you analyze Aunt Bianca's behaviors in your dreams. In your list of her characteristics, you notice that one in particular causes you some discomfort: her tendency to be somewhat clingy and dependent. Perhaps the hidden female in you has a tendency to be clingy and dependent. And maybe in your waking life, you attract women who are clingy and dependent, a tendency that you find deplorable but unalterable. Dreaming about Aunt Bianca has given you a phenomenal gift: you are now aware of the female part of you that you can explore and change, to help create a resolution.

Houses are a common dream symbol. They are separated into floors: the basement can represent what is not known to us—our unconscious; the first floor can be our ego or personality; and the attic, our spiritual side. Houses also can be seen as an opportunity to put the dream in the context of time: old houses often symbolize past life memories, as do houses that we perceive as ours in our dream but in actuality aren't. Various parts of a house and its surroundings are also significant and correspond to specific astrological characteristics. The following list will give you an idea of the correspondence between the parts of a house and the astrological signs:

Aries: doorway, any entrance like an anteroom, reception rooms
Taurus: garden, furniture
Gemini: hallway, telephone, garage
Cancer: kitchen, family room, water faucet
Leo: children's room, game room, television room
Virgo: bathroom, shower, laundry
Libra: art and decorations, living room
Scorpio: septic system, toilet
Sagittarius: balcony, deck, library, attic
Capricorn: formal dining room, roof, home office
Aquarius: electrical wiring and appliances, computers
Pisces: drainage system

Many of my clients have difficulty remembering their dreams. Here are a few tips that can help. First and foremost, make a commitment to recalling your dreams by keeping a dream journal. Have it available by your bed. As soon as you wake up, jot down any remembrance, no matter how small. If you dislike writing in a journal, have a tape recorder there and record yourself describing the dream. Give yourself time in the morning to remember. Before you go to sleep each night, ask your soul to aid you in remembering your dreams. Let it know that you are ready to know what memories are stored in your unconscious mind—that you are not afraid.

Another helpful hint is to spend a few minutes thinking about your day before you sleep. This way your dreams will be more than just a mundane review of your day. People who have difficulty remembering their dreams usually are reluctant to deal with their unconscious on other levels. They may be afraid of the information stored there, preferring the "what-I-don't-know-won't-hurt-me" approach. But by having the courage to listen to their unconscious, they would live happier, more fulfilling lives. Thomas Edison, just one of a score of notable personalities who believed that answers could be mined from our unconscious, would "sleep" on a problem involving one of his inventions. Below are some examples of the type of information we can glean from our dreams:

- skills we've had in past lives
- details about our shadow self
- information on past life personalities
- karmic events that have shaped us
- explanations about our present fears and phobias
- aspects of our soul mission
- ways to communicate with our soul
- how we've been victimized
- how we've abused others
- past life relationships
- the meaning of our soul contracts

Nightmares are also important because of the potential insights they represent. We've all had them; some of us have had the same ones repeatedly. I often ask my clients to tell me about their bad dreams, especially the recurring ones. The clues to past life conflicts may manifest through the terrifying imagery of a nightmare. Singling out those symbols and pairing them with karmic astrological symbology is an effective way to find their meaning.

For instance, suppose you dream you are running. It is night and very foggy. You know that you are being followed. You find yourself at the top of a cliff, trapped. You panic. A noise, and then a large man is in front of you. He has flaming red hair and is wearing a dark cape. He's angry. He shouts words that you cannot understand. He draws a knife and lunges at you.

You wake up, physically shaken and scared. You've had this dream before. But this time you decide you're going to interpret the dream as a manifestation of yourself. You have Saturn in Aries (see Chapter 7), which you know is a symbol of yourself in a past life. The man in your dream has red hair (an Aries symbol), he is angry (another Aries symbol), and he is lunging at you with a knife (a major Aries symbol).

If you have fears of knives and blood in this life, you may have found the source of those fears in the nightmare—not as a victim, but as an aggressor. In a past life you were a large angry man who probably injured someone. Your unconscious mind has given you these nightmares so that you can become aware of this life, get rid of your guilt, and be free. Chances are very good that you will not have this nightmare again. Once we figure out what our dreams symbolize, they need not return.

"The major task of the twentieth century will be to explore the unconscious, to investigate the subsoil of the mind."

—Henri Bergson

Let's interpret the meaning of a fairly typical dream, by combining what we now know about astrology, house symbology, and colors. You dream that you are in an old house that is yours but does not look like your current home. Walking into a red kitchen that is located in the basement of that house, you are very upset.

This dream is telling you that an unconscious memory (the basement) involving something from the past (the old house), involving nurturing and emotions (the kitchen as an astrological Cancer symbol), has made you angry (red). Your unconscious mind has allowed an old memory from the past to resurface in this dream. Now that you are conscious of it, you can explore it further.

Dreams can provide us with unifying cultural themes. In the 1970s and 1980s many people were having tidal wave dreams, which, I believe, were symbolic of the coming of the Age of Aquarius. One cold, wintry January evening in 1983, I had a tidal wave dream that has proven to be one of the most important transformational experiences of my life.

In this dream a white, expansive beach was filled with hundreds of people. Telephone lines crisscrossed the beach, with men dangling from the telephone poles. People were milling about in small groups, with a view of a very calm ocean. Yet there was an ominous sense of foreboding. Children were even caught up in the anxiety. No one was in the water; no one was playing in the sand. I was standing apart, on a higher dune of sand. I could see the entire beach and the men perched high on the telephone poles. I was terrified! My husband Michael appeared and took my hand to calm me, but to no avail. I was sure something terrible was going to happen. But what?

My attention was drawn to the telephone wires. Somehow they had the answer. A voice said: "You will have a warning from the wires. It will tell you when it will begin. The wave is coming. You will soon know how many will survive. What you have done is all that you had time to do. Wait and relax. It is soon to come." I ran down to the beach, leaving Michael. I was now the leader of the group. I had a moment of panic that Michael and I would be lost to each other. The people gathered around me in a circle. I shared the voice's message. We sat on the sand

and waited for the wires to hum. Holding hands, we passed blue energy around the circle.

I began to relax and then felt incredible peace within me. I looked at the people and knew that they were feeling the same energy. I was relieved when Michael appeared in the circle, sitting directly across from me. Seconds later, the wires vibrated. The men got the message, scurried down the poles, and joined the circle. "Five minutes!" they shouted. The minutes crept by, giving way to a deafeningly thunderous sound unrivaled by anything I had ever heard before. As we looked out to sea, a mountain of water began to rise higher and higher, until the whole scene in front of us was filled with this crushing sight. The wave moved in closer and closer. And then it was on the beach—and then I woke up.

This dream was an enigma to me for several weeks. However, the fact that several other people in my life were having a similar dream gave me the clue I needed. I concluded that this dream was my unconscious mind's way, by dint of my soul, of providing me with information about my role in the transition from the Age of Pisces to the Age of Aquarius.

Synchronicity, according to Jung, is the coincidence in time of two or more causally unrelated events that have the same or similar meaning. Suppose you haven't seen your best friend from college in ten years. One day you come across a picture of her, while cleaning your attic. You remember a conflict that was left unresolved between the two of you, and you feel regret. A few hours later she calls. Most of us would call that a coincidence. Jung would call it synchronicity, citing the relationship between the two events. He distinguishes synchronicity from coincidence according to whether the situation has inherent meaning. The situation with the college friend has that meaning. Jung said that meaningful coincidences are unthinkable as pure chance; they have to be thought of as meaningful arrangements. And meaning is what we are looking for in the symbols we create each day.

One client, Faye, who had just turned 40, had seen me a few times intermittently, dropped out, then returned a year later. In her first session after her hiatus, we talked about her problematic relationship with her mother. Faye was actively working on healing some of her conflicts with her mother and had visited her in Florida. While visiting, she noticed that her mother had begun collecting elephants: mainly pictures and a few statues. Shortly after she returned home, she came across an unusual necklace with elephants on it and sent it to her mother. Her mother loved it. Faye was amazed: it was the first gift she had given her mother that she had really appreciated. Mother's Day was approaching, and Faye, who could paint, decided to do a watercolor of a mother elephant and its baby for her mother.

During one of our sessions, I asked Faye to pick a card from a deck portraying different nature scenes. I asked her to ask a question and pick a card. The question she asked was whether she and her mother would continue to reconcile their differences. The card she picked was an elephant and its baby—just the picture that she was planning to paint for her mother. I asked Faye what the card symbolized to her. "Elephants represent home, tradition, and loyalty. This card is clearly about a mother's love for its child." In that moment of synchronicity, Faye knew that something beyond her own personality was at work.

THE SYMBOLISM OF THE BODY

Our physical body represents one of the most ample means through which our unconscious mind expresses itself. Our physiology serves as a clear barometer of how we are faring, emotionally and physically. More than twenty years ago, when I began my practice, few people understood the mind/body/spirit connection. Physical problems were just that, physical. We ignored what was happening on an emotional and spiritual plane. Today a holistic approach is widely accepted. In order to understand basic body symbology, imagine each body part has a connection to an astrological sign. The following chart will give you an idea of how it works.

Astrological Energy of the Physical Body

Astrological Sign	Body Part
Aries	Head, brain, eyes, face
Taurus	Neck, throat, ears
Gemini	Hands, arms, shoulders, lungs, nervous system
Cancer	Breast, stomach
Leo	Heart, upper back, sides
Virgo	Gall bladder, liver, intestines, pancreas
Libra	Kidneys, lower back
Scorpio	Reproductive organs, genitals, rectum, bladder
Sagittarius	Upper leg, thigh, hips
Capricorn	Knees and lower leg
Aquarius	Ankles, circulatory system
Pisces	Feet

The right side of the body symbolizes the masculine principle: external, directed, action-oriented, assertive, and conscious. As an agent of time, it represents the present and the future. The left side of the body symbolizes the feminine principle: receptive, emotional, intuitional, passive, and unconscious. In time it represents the past and can help us understand karmic illnesses or accidents. The left side of the body can also be a valuable asset in helping us understand past life memories.

Let's say that while running up a stairway to catch a train, you trip and hurt your left knee. Knees are a Capricorn symbol, and Capricorn is about rules, responsibility, structure, discipline, commitment, reality, caution, rigidity, arrogance, inflexibility, and more. You now know that your unconscious has created your painful knee to take a look at these symbols. Maybe you've been carrying the burden of too much responsibility at work lately and need to rest. Maybe you've been too inflexible with your husband and need to change your behavior. Or maybe you need to become more committed or disciplined in a particular area of your life. Using Capricorn words can help you ferret out your unconscious mind's symbolic communication.

Now let's add to the equation the fact that it was your left knee. That ties the injury to emotions of the past, maybe even a past life.

Use your imagination, and seek out a possible past life using Capricorn words. As with every other story that you have written from exercises in this book, use the astrological words as a guide, relax, and have fun with it. Writing is another conduit from which your unconscious mind and soul can ply you with information. Use the astrological words as catalysts to discover past life possibilities. Pay attention to how you feel when the possibilities take form. You'll know when it feels "right."

Bradley, 45, a house painter, suffered from the worst psoriasis I have ever seen. Both of his hands would become dry, then crack and bleed when he used them. He tried everything—creams, ointments, herbs—and nothing worked. In an act of desperation, he made an appointment with me. Hands are ruled by Gemini, which gave me a place to start.

I asked him if he had any difficulty with communication. "Y-Yes," he stammered. Bradley had begun to stutter when he was 10 years old, although since then he had learned to control it. Prior to that, he been a very fast talker, but he had gotten himself in trouble with his acerbic tongue. Stuttering had slowed him down and taught him to listen more to what other people were saying. He still had moments when he would stutter under stress.

But that did not explain the psoriasis. I asked him if communication or the inability to communicate was causing him any pain in his life now. He hesitated for a moment, then answered, "People are always saying that I talk over them. They feel intimidated by what I say and feel that I am too powerful in how I speak. I cuss a lot and will admit that I can be pretty intense. I love to have deep conversations with people, and sometimes I feel that they shy away from me. It makes me angry when I see that and it hurts my feelings."

"Has it occurred to you that your hands might be trying to tell you something about this conflict?" I asked.

"Well, not until you told me that hands can symbolize communication," he answered ruefully. "So what should I do?"

"Remember how you learned to slow down and listen after you started to stutter? Do you think that would work now? Gemini, at its best, is a great listener and knows the best way to articulate its message so that others will understand. Maybe if you work on that your hands will get better."

Bradley said he'd give it a try. A few sessions later he reported that he was, in fact, more conscious of his communication style and had seen a marked improvement in his dialogue with others. His psoriasis, however, was no better.

A short while later Bradley mentioned offhandedly an occasional conversation that he would have with himself while he was doing physical work. He said that was also when the outbreaks happened.

"What are you saying to yourself when you're doing this physical work?" I asked.

"I say to myself how much I hate doing it. I don't like working on house stuff. I feel it's beneath me. I guess I'm angry that I have to do it," said Bradley, visibly annoyed.

"Well, Bradley, I think we've uncovered your problem. Your hands are an obvious manifestation of the anger that you have in working with them.

I would like you to spend a month honoring the physical work you do, and not railing against it. Will you pledge to do that?" I asked.

Bradley said that he would, but clearly he was not happy. It took months to reframe his aversion to what he referred to as "menial work."

Six months ago, Bradley came to his session bragging that he was repainting his old Victorian home, and the great news was that he was loving the work. His hands, although not without some cracks, were much improved.

Exercise: Body Parts

Take a moment, and try to recall an illness or injury that you've had recently. After isolating the part of the body involved, find the corresponding astrological sign. Then check the challenging qualities of the sign found in the Soul Pattern Energetics Model (Chart 2 in Chapter 4). Ask yourself about the sign's most challenging characteristics.

Now factor in the side of the body. If your left side was involved in the problem, put your imagination to work, use the appropriate astrological words, and create a possible past life scenario. By conjuring that scenario, you are learning about a past issue that your soul wants you to resolve. If the illness or injury was on the right side of your body, there is a current action you need to perform.

My illness or injury was:

The part of my body affected was:

It corresponds to the astrological sign of:

Keywords of that sign that could be appropriate to this issue are:

Reasons for this illness or injury are:

The illness or injury was on the ___ side of my body.

The timing that this illness or injury symbolizes is:

Betty is a very committed client. At 47, she has seen me almost every week for more than three years, during which time she's learned a great deal about her soul mission and her Soul Potential. A very cautious, shy woman, Betty still talks about a river of darkness that lurks deeply within her. It terrifies her. She feels that if she is not totally "vigilant" and very careful, this dark side will "become a tidal wave" that will destroy her. If she lives her life within certain tight parameters, takes no risks, does not draw attention to herself, and stays in the shadows, maybe it won't "get" her. After years of work she knew that this darkness had nothing to do with this life; it was a karmic memory. Yet she was still reluctant to explore it. "It is bigger than I am," she said, and if she acknowledged it, it would take control of her and she would cease to "exist." Nothing I said could convince her otherwise. She could not bring herself to put a halt to this dark obsession.

But shortly after her mother had major surgery and was put on a respirator, Betty experienced a turning point. She could not stay in her mother's hospital room without panicking: her throat constricted and she felt as though she needed to scream. The next day her mother was taken off the respirator, and Betty was able to visit her and was fine. She related this incident to me in our next session. She knew it was important but didn't know why. We spent most of the session investigating other issues surrounding her throat. We found two very significant experiences. The first one had happened as a child, after a tonsillectomy. Betty had awakened from the surgery to another child's screams. For an instant, disoriented, she thought that the child was "having his skin ripped off," and she believed that she was in a torture chamber. It made her so sick that she threw up. The second incident occurred when she worked in a hospital X-ray unit during her college years. A young man had broken his neck and was brought into radiology for X-rays. Betty became unnerved and had to call on someone to complete the X-rays.

We set about correlating Betty's traumatic experiences centering on her throat and neck, with her obsessive fear of her dark side. The throat symbolizes creativity and the power of communication. Ruled by the sign of Taurus, it is the vehicle through which we express ourselves creatively and communicate what is true to ourselves and others. We encounter problems with our throat and neck when we are unduly reticent. When we are not living up to our creative potential, our throat center closes to remind us that we are not being creatively expressive—a point that made perfect sense to Betty. She admitted always being hesitant to speak her mind, ever mindful of what she said and how she said it. Through these experiences Betty's unconscious was trying to get her attention in a powerful way. Her body wanted to help her see that she needed to open up and investigate this darkness, to find the truth, express it, and be free. At that point she would be able to fully express her creativity and begin to love her life.

THE MEANING OF COLORS

Our universe comprises energy that emits a brilliant spectrum of color. Each color vibrates at a level that corresponds to a part of the body and the emotion that dwells there, and thus to an astrological sign. Colors can effect a change in our emotions, provide us with peace and serenity, warm our soul, or jolt us into action. Colors stimulate, galvanize, relax, relieve, and even heal us. Given our own subjective associations, colors can shape our experience. In meditation color is a powerful vehicle to enhance and heal our internal world, while in our external environment it helps us create surroundings that feel energetically correct to us.

The following colors have specific emotional potential as well as symbolic importance. This chart lists their corresponding astrological signs and emotional properties.

Red: Aries

Symbolizes: will, assertiveness, power, anger

Characteristics:
stimulates, warms, excites, and cheers
provides quick energy
counteracts feeling depressed
encourages constructive anger
increases physical strength

Green: Taurus

Symbolizes: growth, springtime, love, prosperity

Characteristics:
promotes serenity
enhances desire to evolve
provides inner balance and harmony
encourages prosperity
increases fertility

Yellow: Gemini

Symbolizes: intellectual stimulation, clarity

Characteristics:
stimulates creative potential
encourages a cerebral approach
promotes communication
advances understanding
fosters educational enrichment
enhances ability to be open-minded

Silver Blue: Cancer

Symbolizes: deep feeling, calm, serenity

Characteristics:

promotes relaxation

encourages creative expression

aids in accessing emotion

calms anger and agitation

shields against negative emotional influences

Gold: Leo

Symbolizes: authentic connections from the heart

Characteristics:

creates self-confidence

builds self-love and self-respect

provides warm connections to others

promotes courage

Orange: Virgo

Symbolizes: healing, energizing

Characteristics:

manifests feeling of well-being

decreases depression

decreases fears

increases physical healing when emotions have created pain

creates self-confidence

Rose Pink: Libra

Symbolizes: balance, harmony, and cooperation

Characteristics:

encourages cooperation

enhances understanding in relationships

promotes creativity

creates air of refinement

increases harmony and balance

Dark Red: Scorpio

Symbolizes: power, sexuality, and passion

Characteristics:

releases old karmic anger

encourages intensity

enhances sexual passion

increases determination and drive

provides an increase in enduring energy

Purple: Sagittarius

Symbolizes: transcendental experience

Characteristics:

increases philosophical expansion

enhances spiritual awareness

promotes enhanced intuition

advances communication with the soul

encourages optimism

Brown: Capricorn

Symbolizes: being earthy, reliable

Characteristics:

concentrates on reality

encourages discipline and responsibility

maintains focus on goals

promotes connection to body for all healing to occur

Electric Blue: Aquarius

Symbolizes: individuality and originality

Characteristics:

encourages uniqueness

stimulates need for humanism

creates innovation

enhances ability to be open-minded

promotes being rational

Lavender: Pisces

Symbolizes: spirit, connection to God

Characteristics:

increases spiritual awareness

promotes attunement with higher consciousness

cleanses psychic channels

encourages self-forgiveness

promotes communication with the soul

creates meditative states that encourage rest and healing

Color can provide us with symbols that we can then correlate to our astrological energy. Madeline, who was in her early fifties, called me in a panic because she had almost been run over by a very large red truck. It was the latest in a series of encounters with red vehicles that she had had in the last few weeks. According to Madeline, "Red cars were coming out of the woodwork." She called me because she was afraid that she would get into an accident.

Red symbolizes anger and assertion; Madeline had a history of avoiding confrontations and anger. We had already talked repeatedly about her need to deal with anger on a more realistic level. It terrified her, and she had avoided the work, but the red truck was the last straw. She decided to start working on anger. She knew the color red symbolized her problems with Aries energy. Her soul had created that near-miss with the red truck to push her to making that decision. She can now work to transform red to gain the courage, confidence, and energy to use her anger constructively.

Bill, while he was in the middle of a session with me, mentioned that he had decided to change his image and buy some new clothes. "Any special color?" I asked. "You know I've always hated the color brown, but now it's all that I seem to be attracted to. Does that mean anything?" I smiled. "Bill, you know me better than that. Of course it means something." Brown symbolizes Capricorn, which is practical, earthy, goal-directed, reliable, stable, and success-oriented. Bill, at 42, was in the running for a promotion at work, and his attraction to brown began soon after he found out about it. This casual aside from Bill about a color turned into several sessions of learning more about his Capricorn energy. His soul had drawn the color brown to him so that he could have this transformational experience.

Colors are all around us; their symbols abound. Pay attention to what colors attract you, and tinker with what each one means to you. See if you can find a pattern. Look at your wardrobe. What colors do you prefer? What color makes you feel powerful? What color makes you feel sexy? Intellectual? Spiritual? Keep the color chart available to check the corresponding meanings. Are you getting ready to redecorate your home? Choose colors that are not only visually pleasing but symbolically evocative. For instance, if you need to experience more self-confidence at work, try adding a bit of orange to your office decor. Every day spend a moment meditating on the color to increase your sense of inner power. Do you have an important presentation to give at a meeting? You need to be sharp and clear to communicate your ideas effectively. Take a few minutes beforehand to channel the color yellow into your body. It will stimulate your intellectual creativity. Wear a yellow tie or scarf to remind you of the color's power. Do you need to create more money in your life? Buy a green plant; then watch it grow and expand. Your affirmation is that as the plant grows, so does your financial picture.

Pay close attention to the color that relates to your Soul Potential. Many of my clients, when I tell them their soul color, say that it is the one color they truly dislike. I remember my chagrin when I learned that the soul color that symbolized my Soul Potential sign, Leo, was gold. I hated gold. I had a beautiful jewelry wardrobe of silver—and a whole series of judgments against gold. I found it ostentatious, gaudy, and flashy. In essence, I made the same judgments about Leo people: that they were pretentious, self-centered, and melodramatic. The truth was, I didn't want my Soul Potential sign in Leo because I didn't like what I couldn't emulate. My aversion to gold was a poignant symbol in helping me understand that. Needless to say, I now have a wonderful collection of gold jewelry. Wearing gold now reminds me of the highest attributes of Leo. I even wear a little gold lion ring that symbolizes my commitment to my soul mission: to be courageous, inspirational, commanding, and confident.

Your soul color vibrates to the same level as your Soul Potential and will help you connect to your soul's energy. When you want to connect and communicate with your soul, imagine your soul color gently flowing through your body, warming you, loving you, and giving you peace. You will be amazed at how easy it is to talk to your soul when you are at its vibrational level. When you wish to live in your soul's love, wear its color and feel its love every minute of the day. Make sure that you have your soul color in your home, car, and office.

SYMBOLS IN YOUR EVERYDAY LIFE

So far in this chapter, we have discussed the symbols that our soul and unconscious mind give us to interpret. But we can also choose symbols that have conscious meaning to us. For example, I have chosen a symbol that I use for serendipity. As you know from previous chapters, I am a devout believer in serendipity, in understanding and appreciating that unexpected outcomes are just as viable to our evolution and happiness as expected ones. This philosophy is very important to my serenity and optimism, but I've had moments when I forgot about the power and peace of serendipity. I wanted to have an external symbol to remind me of it, so I chose a symbol: a red cardinal. Since then, I've found that this beautiful bird crosses my path at all the right moments. When I catch a glimpse of it, I know my soul is saying, "Serendipity is alive, Linda. Remember." And no matter what is going on, regardless of how painful the moment, it reminds me that a wonderful, unexpected surprise is waiting to be discovered.

All of my students have serendipity symbols, and I would like you to have one too. But I can't tell you which one to choose. Open your mind to finding one that is pleasing to you, that will bring out your innate optimism, hope, and faith. One of my friends chose a golden crown; another, a rose; another, a pearl. My students have chosen blue jays, windmills, diamonds, oak trees, archways, wheat fields, oriental rugs, waterfalls, willow trees, pinafores, and baby grand pianos. After you've chosen your serendipity symbol, your unconscious mind will attract you to it when you need to be reminded of serendipity. It will lighten your heart and spark your mind to see the positive surprises awaiting you by expecting the unexpected.

Everyday symbols can also answer specific routine questions. I often ask my soul to provide me with symbolic answers to current problems. I ask a question—perhaps why I'm feeling sad today— and pay attention to the symbols that my soul creates for me. How do I know which object out of hundreds I encounter represents the answer? I know by how I feel about the things I see. Suppose a blue car is parked outside my house.

It is parked there often, but on the particular day that I've queried my soul, perhaps about my sullenness, I not only notice it, but I really hone in on it. I see a dent in the left fender. I have an emotional reaction to the bumper sticker that reads "One Day at a Time." This car is a symbol to help me with my question. For me, cars symbolize movement in the world, while blue represents the ability to access emotion. A dent in the left side represents something in the past that is "dented" or maybe damaged. And the bumper sticker is self-explanatory. Based on this information, I have my answer: I am remembering something painful from my past that is interfering with my ability to move on, and my soul wants me to understand that living today's experiences is more important than reveling in yesterday's memories.

Paying attention to your emotional reactions to normal, everyday symbols will tell you that your soul has given you these clues to help answer a question. You then can interpret the symbols based on your experience with them. A car represents movement to me, but may not symbolize the same thing to you. Find your own personal symbolic language, and practice it. Not only will it help you answer questions, it will help you become more aware of the abundance of information awaiting you from your unconscious mind. Astrology is a language, and as such it has many words. The following chart lists a few common objects that you may encounter in the course of your day or in your dreams, and the astrological sign that symbolizes them. I am sure you will see the correlation as you review them. As you look at your world through this astrological filter, you will find an increasing number of symbols. When you find a symbol, find its related astrological sign here; then refer to the Energetics Models (Charts 2 and 3 in Chapter 4) to see which characteristics your soul wants you to confront.

Astrological Signs and the Common Objects They Symbolize

Sign	Objects
Aries	Knives and other sharp objects, the desert, the ram, firemen, soldiers, daybreak, battles, Moses, fire, matches, lighters, karate and other martial arts, the direction east, spring, the number 1
Taurus	Gardens, the Buddha, the bull, sculptors, bankers, money, earth, leaves, singers, songwriters, investments, a wallet, bank deposits, easy chairs, any soft material like velvet or silk, the number 2
Gemini	The wind, cars, newspapers, journalists, books, birds, traffic signs, twins, watches, writing materials, libraries, con men, respiratory therapists, speech therapists, writers, the number 3
Cancer	Lakes, mothers, containers that hold liquid, home, milk products, boats, cooks, food, historians, sailors, restaurants, farmers, the direction north, pools, summer, the number 4
Leo	Actors, theaters, crowns, television, games, children, sun, vacations, parties, movies, kings, a throne, gifts, fun, the lottery, all things glamorous, holidays, the number 5
Virgo	Health foods, doctors, nurses, nutritionists, lists, any program that creates order, organized labor, soap, virgins, wheat, cleaning supplies, prescriptions, small animals, homework, chores, tests, the number 6
Libra	Judges, court, the direction west, partners, contracts, fall fashion designers, color, harmony, scales, stylish clothes, art dealers, weddings, all things beautiful and refined, mediation and mediators, objects that are in balance, the number 7
Scorpio	Hidden things, dark places, secrets, researchers, tornadoes, death, funerals, insurance, nuclear weapons, ice, Niagara Falls, psychiatrists, loans, investigators, garbage, sexual affairs, the Mafia, pathologists, dark alleys, occult matters, the number 8
Sagittarius	Horses, gambling, mountains, travel, travel agents, sports, college professors, clergy, law, lawyers, legal affairs, colleges, publications, arrows, religious rituals, space, anything that deals with expansion, luck, the future, the number 9
Capricorn	Father, authority figures, elders, wise people, grandfather clocks, the direction south, winter, licenses, government and government officials, CEOs, calendars, boundaries, foundations, big business, the rewards of recognition, antiques, the number 10
Aquarius	Airplanes, computers, astrology, politics, volunteerism, the Internet, causes, revolutionary ideas, new technology, genius, inventors, rebellion, a team approach, gay population, like-minded groups, holistic practitioners, space technology, the number 11
Pisces	Oceans, whales and dolphins, anesthesia, alcohol, drugs, dreams, psychics, psychic experiences, prisons, hospitals, martyrs, musicians, the ballet and ballet dancers, alcoholics and drug addicts, places of retreat, illusions, secret enemies, the number 12

My role as a karmic astrologer and teacher is to listen. Most of my new clients arrive expecting me to "read" their chart, which would mean that I would talk to them for most of the hour while they listen. Imagine their surprise when the session becomes a conversation in which they talk more than I do. While they talk, I listen for the symbols their souls provide as answers to their important life issues. These symbols lead me to specific areas of their astrological information.

Mindy, 36, walked into her first session very upset. But she was able, with my help, to transform her trauma into a symbol that helped her realize her soul mission.

I was actually crying when Linda answered the door. Concerned, she asked me what was wrong. I told her that a deer had just been killed by a car directly in front of me. Once I sat down in her office and she made me some herbal tea, I felt a little better. I could tell that my story had had an effect on Linda too. I told her I had never seen anything like it before and that it wouldn't have happened if I hadn't been coming to see her, because I never traveled that road.

Linda asked me what deer symbolize to me. I didn't know what she meant; I didn't think of life symbolically. But when I thought about it, it occurred to me that deer had always been special to me. My parents had a summer home in New Hampshire when I was a little girl. Deer were everywhere. The feeling that I had when I saw them was happiness. They were symbolic of nature and freedom.

When I told Linda that, she nodded. "That's what they are for me, too," she said. Linda also told me that death represents transformation and change. She then looked at my astrological chart and smiled. "Nature and freedom are symbols of Sagittarius. And your Soul Potential sign is Sagittarius! It's important for you to become more involved in nature, the country, freedom, and expansion," she added. I was amazed. I am a loyal city dweller, and except for occasional trips to New Hampshire, I had never considered moving to the country. Yet the reason I had come to see her in the first place was to discuss a possible job move to Northern California. Linda told me that the deer had given me the answer twenty minutes before I got to her office. "You could have saved yourself some money," she laughed, "if you'd known how to read the deer's symbol." She told me that I needed to transform my attitude about moving to the country as a symbol of doing more of my soul's mission. She told me to thank the deer for what it had given

California three months later. That deer had answered so many questions. After the move, Linda and I talked regularly, so when she explained about the necessity of a serendipity symbol, I of course chose a deer! It is the symbol of my soul mission.

We must listen to ourselves when we talk to others. We often use essential words that our soul has given us to answer our own questions, especially in important conversations with the people who mean the most to us. How often do you say something to someone else that is exactly what you need to hear yourself? For me, quite often. When I hear myself providing specific advice to a client that rings especially true to me, I file it away to mull over later, to ask, "Is my soul saying this to me too?" Think about the words that you tend to use to talk to friends, family, and children. Write them down. We all have favorite truisms or sayings that we tend to use over and over. They mean something! They are words your soul wishes you to understand.

PART III

KARMIC TRUTH: THE KEY TO FULFILLING YOUR SOUL MISSION

CHAPTER 7

SATURN: YOUR JOURNEY
TO PERSONAL TRUTH

n his book *Revelations: The Birth of a New Age*, David Spangler outlines seven laws detailing how we can enhance our spiritual energy and use it more creatively. Two of those laws—one involving love, the other truth—are essential to helping us learn more about ourselves.

The Law of Love "Through love we expand our vision beyond our own seeming limitations and live in awareness of the whole of which we are a part. Hence, we must love ourselves as well, not as a private, selfish entity, but as a unique and meaningful expression and part of the whole."

The Law of Truth "Truth does not accept all things to itself: it accepts only what is right and true for that time and place, but it does this without needing to judge the ultimate rightness or wrongness of the person, thing or concept under its discrimination."

Love and truth must be expressed together, writes Spangler. Love enables truth to grow and expand its discriminatory powers without allowing them to settle into a crystallized pattern of judgment and organization. "Truth protects love and gives the power of appropriateness to the energy of love," he explains. "Truth tempers love's acceptance with a keen perception of what is right in the moment and prevents the energy of love from being dissipated over too wide a field or from being taken advantage of."

"Truth is one forever absolute, but opinion is truth filtered through the moods, the blood, the disposition of the spectator."

—Wendell Phillips

How many of us can really say that we are "in love" with ourselves, much less "in truth" with ourselves? Although being "in truth" with oneself sounds misplaced, it is just as important as loving oneself. When we are deceiving ourselves and perpetuating illusions, we are limiting our reality, which saps our ability to be happy. Living with illusions requires us to maintain a misshapen belief system to support the falsehoods. Often these misperceptions are based on guilt. Thus we don't create happiness or prosperity, because we don't believe we deserve it. Without inner truth, we create distorted images not only of ourselves but of those around us, because we have a "need" to see them in a certain light in order to feed our illusion. Understanding the truth about ourselves, past and present, and having the courage to delve into the vast recesses of our unconscious to confront our karmic demons, will lead to personal awareness and freedom.

"No one is such a liar as the indignant man."
—**Friedrich Nietzsche**

After centuries of a culture in which we deny who we are and what we've done and why, we head into the next millennium with a deep desire to undertake a personal journey where truth is the final destination. As evidenced by the proliferation of self-help and inspirational offerings now available in every medium, we want to do it better, as well as to learn more about who we are as individuals. What we're really doing is expressing a pent-up need to transform our deepest blind spots into awareness, understanding, and empowerment. We've all repressed into our unconscious issues that are too terrible to bear on a conscious level. I describe these deeply guarded secrets we are hesitant to confront as karmic memories. Until we become conscious of them, they feel foreboding, foreign, and unexplainable, to be feared and tucked away more safely.

Repressing feelings of fear, shame, and anger constricts the way we live and prevents us from expanding our creative abilities. Ironically, the more determined we are to repress our deepest fears and weaknesses, the more they will emerge in our relationships and experiences. Shining the light of understanding on our karmic memories will help us discriminate the truth about ourselves from all of our old, predictable beliefs and feelings.

Gwenn, 50, used to be "stuck, very uncertain about what to do," and was "unclear" about her choices. However, "things began clicking" for her, she says, when she learned the truth about herself and made a conscious effort not to view her experiences through the filters of her past.

For the first time in a long time, I'm really showing up for myself in creative and unexpected ways. I have clarity and direction and new life goals. I have a newfound appreciation for my relationships and how I express myself within them. I'm letting go of old patterns that never made sense to me anyway, but I felt stuck with them. I'm getting more and more free to live this life in the way that my true self—my soul—longs for.

I chose to see the possibility in this work. I suspended disbelief and judgment about astrology, karma, past lives, and the idea of a soul mission. I chose to act as if it all held potential for me, even truth. By opening myself to the possibility and experience of this approach, I am being rewarded with the richness of my own discoveries.

I found it particularly wrenching to explore and accept my own darkness—the shadow part, the stuff I secretly "knew" and hated about myself. Linda suggested I start watching the sun rise, to become an observer of the new dawn each day. "Okay," I thought, "I'll give it a try," even though the winter sky seemed so unwelcoming.

The first morning, I noticed how chilly and still it was, and how long it actually took the sun to rise above the horizon.

The second day, I noticed how beautiful the light was as it came into being, how long a "warning" the sun gives us before showing up.

By the third day, I had a deep appreciation for the subtleties of the whole thing: how the edges of darkness keep giving way to the pinky glow in a slow and sensuous unfolding.

By the fourth and fifth days, it started to make sense for me: the darkness is a natural part of the cycle of life. As I pondered that, I found it increasingly easy to acknowledge my own darkness, as a natural part of my being, just like the light.

Each day I looked forward to the coming of the light more and more, especially the gentle way it "took over" the darkness, and its power once the sun emerged. And day by day I became more comfortable with the idea of darkness—the night's and my own—as I watched the power and beauty and triumph of light.

As I accepted my darkness, I found it increasingly easy to accept and embrace my light. I became more peaceful with the totality of my being—a wonderful gift. I've been able to discover my own metaphors and recapture my own passion, vision, power, voice—my own life.

YOUR KARMIC CONDUCTOR

Saturn is our karmic teacher. It teaches us the truth about ourselves and helps us create order and structure in our lives. Without it, we could not accomplish our soul mission. Saturn presents to us the personal karmic reality each of us needs to face in order to progress toward our soul mission. Saturn tells us the truth about what we need to do rather than what we want to hear.

Imagine that the North Node, your Soul Potential, is the final destination on a train's route. Let's say you board the train at its first stop, which happens to be your South Node, or Soul Pattern. The train signifies the journey to achieving your soul mission. And Saturn is the symbolic conductor of the train. His job is to keep the train and us on the track to ensure we reach our destination. Consult the "Saturn Placements" chart to find the astrological sign your individual Saturn is in. Then use its information to help structure and organize your life to achieve your soul mission.

Saturn Placements

If you were born:	Your Saturn is in:	If you were born:	Your Saturn is in:
Jan. 22, 1900–July 18, 1900	Capricorn	April 26, 1937–Oct. 18, 1937	Aries
July 19, 1900–Oct. 17, 1900	Sagittarius	Oct. 19, 1937–Jan. 14, 1938	Pisces
Oct. 18, 1900–Jan. 19, 1903	Capricorn	Jan. 15, 1938–Mar. 20, 1940	Aries
Jan. 20, 1903–April 13, 1905	Aquarius	Mar. 21, 1940–May 9, 1942	Taurus
April 14, 1905–Aug. 17, 1905	Pisces	May 10, 1942–June 20, 1944	Gemini
Aug. 18, 1905–Jan. 8, 1906	Aquarius	June 21, 1944–Aug. 2, 1946	Cancer
Jan. 9, 1906–Mar. 19, 1908	Pisces	Aug. 3, 1946–Sept. 19, 1948	Leo
Mar. 20, 1908–May 17, 1910	Aries	Sept. 20, 1948–April 3, 1949	Virgo
May 18, 1910–Dec. 15, 1910	Taurus	April 4, 1949–May 29, 1949	Leo
Dec. 16, 1910–Jan. 19, 1911	Aries	May 30, 1949–Nov. 20, 1950	Virgo
Jan. 20, 1911–July 7, 1912	Taurus	Nov. 21, 1950–Mar. 7, 1951	Libra
July 8, 1912–Nov. 30, 1912	Gemini	Mar. 8, 1951–Aug. 13, 1951	Virgo
Dec. 1, 1912–Mar. 26, 1913	Taurus	Aug. 14, 1951–Oct. 22, 1953	Libra
Mar. 27, 1913–Aug. 24, 1914	Gemini	Oct. 23, 1953–Jan. 12, 1956	Scorpio
Aug. 25, 1914–Dec. 7, 1914	Cancer	Jan. 13, 1956–May 14, 1956	Sagittarius
Dec. 8, 1914–May 11, 1915	Gemini	May 15, 1956–Oct. 10, 1956	Scorpio
May 12, 1915–Oct. 17, 1916	Cancer	Oct. 11, 1956–Jan. 5, 1959	Sagittarius
Oct. 18, 1916–Dec. 7, 1916	Leo	Jan. 6, 1959–Jan. 3, 1962	Capricorn
Dec. 8, 1916–June 24, 1917	Cancer	Jan. 4, 1962–Mar. 24, 1964	Aquarius
June 25, 1917–Aug. 12, 1919	Leo	Mar. 25, 1964–Sept. 17, 1964	Pisces
Aug. 13, 1919–Oct. 7, 1921	Virgo	Sept. 18, 1964–Dec. 16, 1964	Aquarius
Oct. 8, 1921–Dec. 20, 1923	Libra	Dec. 17, 1964–Mar. 3, 1967	Pisces
Dec. 21, 1923–April 6, 1924	Scorpio	Mar. 4, 1967–April 29, 1969	Aries
April 7, 1924–Sept. 13, 1924	Libra	April 30, 1969–June 18, 1971	Taurus
Sept. 14, 1924–Dec. 2, 1926	Scorpio	June 19, 1971–Jan. 10, 1972	Gemini
Dec. 3, 1926–Mar. 15, 1929	Sagittarius	Jan. 11, 1972–Feb. 21, 1972	Taurus
Mar. 16, 1929–May 5, 1929	Capricorn	Feb. 22, 1972–Aug. 1, 1973	Gemini
May 6, 1929–Nov. 30, 1929	Sagittarius	Aug. 2, 1973–Jan. 7, 1974	Cancer
Dec. 1, 1929–Feb. 24, 1932	Capricorn	Jan. 8, 1974–April 18, 1974	Gemini
Feb. 25, 1932–Aug. 13, 1932	Aquarius	April 19, 1974–June 5, 1976	Cancer
Aug. 14, 1932–Nov. 19, 1932	Capricorn	June 6, 1976–Nov. 16, 1977	Leo
Nov. 20, 1932–Feb. 14, 1935	Aquarius	Nov. 17, 1977–Jan. 5, 1978	Virgo
Feb. 15, 1935–April 25, 1937	Pisces	Jan. 6, 1978–July 26, 1978	Leo

If you were born:	Your Saturn is in:	If you were born:	Your Saturn is in:
July 27, 1978–Sept. 21, 1980	Virgo	June 5, 2003–July 16, 2005	Cancer
Sept. 22, 1980–Nov. 29, 1982	Libra	July 17, 2005–Sept. 2, 2007	Leo
Nov. 30, 1982–May 6, 1983	Scorpio	Sept. 3, 2007–Oct. 29, 2009	Virgo
May 7, 1983–Aug. 24, 1983	Libra	Oct. 30, 2009–April 7, 2010	Libra
Aug. 25, 1983–Nov. 16, 1985	Scorpio	April 8, 2010–July 21, 2010	Virgo
Nov. 17, 1985–Feb. 13, 1988	Sagittarius	July 22, 2010–Oct. 5, 2012	Libra
Feb. 14, 1988–June 10, 1988	Capricorn	Oct. 6, 2012–Dec. 23, 2012	Scorpio
June 11, 1988–Nov. 12, 1988	Sagittarius	Dec. 24, 2014–June 15, 2015	Sagittarius
Nov. 13, 1988–Feb. 6, 1991	Capricorn	June 16, 2015–Sept. 18, 201	Scorpio
Feb. 7, 1991–May 20, 1993	Aquarius	Sept. 19, 2015–Dec. 20, 2017	Sagittarius
May 21, 1993–June 30, 1993	Pisces	Dec. 21, 2017–March 22, 2020	Capricorn
July 1, 1993–Jan. 28, 1994	Aquarius	March 23, 2020–July 1, 2020	Aquarius
July 1, 1993–Jan. 28, 1994	Aquarius	July 2, 2020–Dec. 17, 2020	Capricorn
Jan. 29, 1994–April 7, 1996	Pisces	Dec. 18, 2020–March 7, 2023	Aquarius
April 8, 1996–June 9, 1998	Aries	March 8, 2023–May 25, 2025	Pisces
June 10, 1998–Oct. 25, 1998	Taurus	May 26, 2025–Sept. 1, 2025	Aries
Oct. 26, 1998–Feb. 28, 1999	Aries	Sept. 2, 2025–Feb. 14, 2026	Pisces
Mar. 1, 1999–Aug. 10, 2000	Taurus	Feb. 15, 2026–April 13, 2028	Aries
Jan. 1, 2000 –Aug. 10, 2000	Taurus	April 14, 2028–June 1, 2030	Taurus
Aug. 11, 2000–Oct. 16, 2000	Gemini	June 2, 2030–July 14, 2032	Gemini
Oct. 17, 2000–April 20, 2001	Taurus	July 15, 2032–Aug. 27, 2034	Cancer
April 21, 2001–June 4, 2003	Gemini	Aug. 28, 2034–Feb. 15, 2035	Leo

When faced with the unknowns of how to go about achieving our soul mission, we all ask a number of practical questions: How do I reorganize my life to do what I have not done before? How do I set priorities? What specific commitments do I make to achieve success? To what areas should I apply repeated efforts to make my soul mission happen? What responsibilities do I need to claim to realize my Soul Potential? The answers to all these questions may be found in the astrological sign in which your Saturn, your personal conductor, falls. Suppose you have Saturn in Aquarius and your Soul Potential lies in Cancer. Your soul mission is to develop your feminine nature, explore your emotions, and develop a home base for yourself and your family. You would look to your

Saturn in Aquarius to provide guidance. What follows is a brief summary of how Saturn in Aquarius, as well as in the eleven other signs, can help us achieve our soul mission.

SATURN IN THE ASTROLOGICAL SIGNS

Saturn in Aries

You have possible past life experiences as a warrior, a pioneer, an adventurer, or a Native American. Your possible karmic fears are of being alone, taking risks and/or actions, being independent, violence, and anger. You need to take considered risks and spring into action when necessary. Create the strength of will to become more self-assertive in order to take the initiative. You have a strong karmic need to discover true independence on all levels. Committed to having physical energy and to being physically strong and fit, you have a need to be personally competitive and a desire to win for yourself. Know when to forge a new beginning. The path to your soul mission is to become self-aware, self-assured, and self-motivated. Take personal stands when necessary.

Saturn in Taurus

You have possible past lives as a farmer, a banker, and a builder. Your possible karmic fears are of poverty, possessions being taken away, change, and insecurity. Learn how to integrate material and spiritual values, and to create a practical reality in order to increase your self-esteem and self-value. Your need to foster security within yourself and in your environment is strong. Committed to exploring and manifesting your creative talents, you have the wisdom to create a firm "earthy" foundation and build on it with patience and determination. Building a home, honoring the land, and having comfort and happiness there are important to you. The path to your soul mission is to have a strong sense of personal values that create comfort, security, and serenity.

Saturn in Gemini

You have possible past lives as a writer, a lecturer, and a salesperson. Your possible karmic fears are of being talked about, lied to, and manipulated with words. You must structure and organize a practical and secure intellectual foundation. Constantly needing to gather information and share it, you must become a strong, trustful, and versatile communicator to share your ideas, thoughts, and philosophies. Become a communication chameleon, with the ability to talk to a variety of people with different needs. Commit yourself to being present in the moment and to exploring the possibilities of that moment to their fullest. The path to your soul mission is to intellectually create wise, challenging, and productive thoughts and communicate them with all people.

Saturn in Cancer

You have possible past lives as a mother, a cook, an abandoned child, an emotional woman. Your possible karmic fears are of being too emotional and vulnerable, not feeling love, losing a child, having not been nurtured, and failing to assess someone's emotions. Learn to understand and express emotions, and to have the strength to be vulnerable and sensitive to others' emotional needs. You need to become nurturing and mothering and female. At the same time you must break out of a gloomy frame of mind and become more youthful and childlike. Commit yourself to creating and building an emotionally secure and happy home environment for family. The path to your soul mission is to become more female, more emotional, and more connected to nurturing others by understanding their feelings.

Saturn in Leo

You have possible past lives as a king, an actor, a perennial child, a gambler. Your possible karmic fears are of assassination, not being applauded, getting old, having fun, and being disregarded. You need to learn about inspired leadership instead of rulership: about being a role model of power and love. Learn to love, honor, and respect yourself instead of requiring it from others. Become an inspired teacher. Find the strength of heart and will to take risks that will ultimately lead to self-confidence and self-empowerment. Try to understand the joyful, spontaneous child within: be creative with fun and activity. Commit yourself to connecting with people heart to heart. The path to your soul mission is to become a self-confident, courageous, inspired leader to those who seek it from you.

Saturn in Virgo

You have possible past lives as a doctor, a nurse, a labor leader, a servant, an animal activist. Your possible karmic fears are of doctors and nurses who cause injury to patients, making mistakes, not being perfect, being too organized, not being organized enough, not understanding, getting ill. You are responsible for understanding the true meaning of perfection (internal, not external). Commit yourself to being of service to others, especially in physical and emotional health. Be organized and efficient, but do not be obsessed with the extremes of what is right or wrong, good or bad. Learn to be highly discriminating by using your analytical and logical strengths. Instead of being overwhelmed by details, incorporate them into a system that encourages productivity. The path to your soul mission is to be a voice of discernment and logic, to encourage health and congruence in yourself and others.

Saturn in Libra

You have possible past lives as a judge, an interior designer, a mediator, a social climber, an artist, and a relationship junkie. Your possible karmic fears are of imbalance, disharmony, confrontation, loss of relationship, loss of identity (being merged with another), injustice, and unfairness. You are responsible for finding the true balance and harmony between yourself and others. Consider sharing ideas that will create negotiation and mediation. Put yourself in another's shoes to foster understanding and communication. Search for fairness and justice, and share these attitudes with others. Be creative in your use of color and symmetry to produce beauty and peace in your environment. The path to your soul mission is to be a calm, mediating force to create more understanding between people.

Saturn in Scorpio

You have possible past lives as an investigator, a CEO, a psychiatrist, a magician, a financial consultant, a mortician. Your possible karmic fears are of loss of power, too much power, loss of control, being controlled, death, sex, rage, secrets, betrayal, and loss of money. You are responsible for turning chaos into intensity, and fear into drive. Pursue success with great determination and vigor. Reframe your anger and resentment into a passion for more creative pursuits such as philosophy or emotional and sexual intimacy. Commit yourself to probing the mysteries of life and finding personal answers to significant questions. The path to your soul mission is to use your desire and will to understand and connect with another's values.

Saturn in Sagittarius

You have possible past lives as a teacher, a philosopher, a lawyer, a cowboy, a wandering minister, and a traveler. Your possible karmic fears are of commitment, loss of freedom and open spaces, traveling, loss of independence, not being believed, and being controlled by religion. You are responsible for structuring your philosophy so it can be shared and taught to others without preachiness. Travel and explore other cultures and religions. Commit yourself to learning how to organize your life based on optimism, truth, and personal freedom. Use your penetrating mind to search for depth and meaning in life. The path to your soul mission is to honestly and enthusiastically share your life experiences to help others find their life's purpose.

Saturn in Capricorn

You have possible past lives as a business manager, an architect, a strict father, a land baron, and an industry leader. Your possible karmic fears are of financial success or failure, emotions, lack of structure, and controlling men in authority. You are responsible for finding your road to success, organizing and following it with persistence and determination. Claim your authority and ambition and patiently climb your personal mountain to achievement. Commit yourself to self-discipline, self-responsibility, and self-actualization by deliberately ordering your internal and external life. Hone your wisdom and love through your protection of and loyalty to your family and friends. The path to your soul mission is to create an ordered, structured, responsible approach to appropriate goals that will manifest as a mature and wise life.

Saturn in Aquarius

You have possible past lives as an astrologer, an inventor, a rebel, a revolutionary, a humanitarian, and an astronomer. Your possible karmic fears are of being misunderstood, becoming too emotionally involved, being ostracized, being radical, and mistrust of friends. You have the responsibility to claim your originality and individuality. Find your humanity and translate it into a political and spiritual cause; then join with others who feel the same way. Understand your rational, logical, and observing nature, but also the holistic model (mind, body, and spirit), and integrate it into your approach to life. Maintain an equal, humanistic view in the groups you join and the friends you keep. The path to your soul mission requires that you be avant-garde, visionary, and uniquely different in your objectives.

Saturn in Pisces

You have possible past lives as a psychic healer, a dancer, a musician, a martyr, and an addict. Your possible karmic fears are of addiction, sacrificing yourself, being subservient, being used, escapism, and being emotionally obsessed. You have a responsibility for understanding your feelings and expressing them through a strong sense of self. Commit yourself to using your psychic and intuitional gifts to help others claim their spiritual and creative talents and to experience life as an imaginative, magical, and spiritual adventure. Provide gentle service to self and others. Be compassionate and sensitive to others without giving yourself away. The path to your soul mission is to be emotionally and creatively strong, to experience a life of spiritual awareness and interaction with others.

LEARNING MORE ABOUT YOUR SATURN TRAITS

In order to make sense of the continuum of our existence over lifetimes, we must understand who we have been in the past, and how we were trained and programmed by the beliefs and value systems of the past. Since we often make the mistake of assigning today's values and social mores to previous incarnations, we are left with the residue of guilt. Guilt left unresolved (which we will discuss in Chapter 9) can play a major role in undermining our ability to discover and achieve our soul mission.

The exercises that follow will help you uncover which karmic experiences—critical issues from the past—you've been afraid to confront and have been hiding from yourself. Dealing with a higher level of truth will imbue you with more positive energy and give your relationships more conscious meaning. Although each of you will find different experiences based on your karmic journey, many of us have several recurring themes or life issues in common. We all tend to abhor the misuse of power, greed, disregard of others, selfishness, abuse, dogmatism, ignorance, and self-serving manipulation, to name a few. All of us, in our journey in this lifetime, have experienced all that we abhor. It has been an intrinsic part of the human condition.

Putting your past life experiences into a historical context will help you distinguish the truth about yourself from what you want to believe. Have you ever wondered why so many of the males you draw into your life are so similar in character and temperament? Our souls choose our Saturn placement—the astrological constellation that Saturn was moving through on the day we were born— to remind us of important past lives as men.

Your soul is interested in you having the full panoply of life's experiences from every vantage point imaginable: both genders, all races, all religions, all cultures, and all economic strata. Besides helping you learn more about your male qualities, this exercise will help you understand why you created your father to be the way he is. Learning more about your "Saturn energy" or your "male energy" will also help you focus on the areas in your life where you need to improve by committing yourself to being more responsible, as well as on what you need to do in order to be successful in your endeavors and fulfill your soul mission.

First, consult the "Saturn Placements" chart in order to learn what sign your Saturn was in when you were born. Use your sign and the traits associated with it to complete the exercise below.

Saturn Exercise

Refer to the Energetics Models (Charts 2 and 3 in Chapter 4) to determine the behavioral characteristics of your particular Saturn. For instance, I was born on December 13, 1942. My Saturn is in the sign of Gemini. Looking at the Soul Pattern Energetics Model (Chart 2 in Chapter 4), I find the characteristics that are more challenging; from the Soul Potential Energetics Model in Chart 3, I find the traits associated with Gemini that are more positive.

Using these traits, I can determine what kind of personality I had in a past life. I was bright, versatile, and articulate. I was probably a writer or speaker who used words to manipulate people to get what I wanted. I quite possibly told the truth when it suited me and lied when it suited me. I was inconsistent and had problems committing to one person. I could have had difficulty with emotions and been unable to express them. This exercise will guide you to complete your own karmic story as well as to glean some personal information meaningful to you.

STEP 1

My Saturn is in the sign of: _____
(refer to the "Saturn Placements" table).
Positive traits of this sign (refer to Chart 3 in Chapter 4) are:
Challenging traits of this sign (refer to Chart 2 in Chapter 4) are:

STEP 2

In order to better understand the type of male relationships you've created in this life, write a short story in your journal using the above words. The story should focus on problematic as well as positive aspects of a previous existence as a man. Each word could represent a career, an experience or event, or a possible conflict. Use your imagination to produce a story. Have fun with it. Even if you don't consider yourself a writer, or even a devout believer in past lives, many stories lie within you. Let your unconscious mind provide you with interesting ideas. Don't overanalyze: let the story flow, using the words as your guide.

For example, your "challenging" list might contain the word *aggressive* or perhaps *possessive* or *selfish*. For the purpose of this exercise, let's focus on aggression. Let your mind create a story in which being aggressive is the centerpiece. Create a character whose life was imbued with aggressive behavior. What aggressive act might he have done? What were the ramifications of that aggression? Who could he have hurt? Now work in the positive characteristics that refer to this man's personality strengths and depth of character. By making use of all the words, you will develop a powerful story about a male past life.

This exercise will help you build emotional, spiritual, and educational foundations. It is a means to an end: to yield a better understanding of yourself as well as those around you. Try not to get bogged down in deciding whether you have a definitive belief in past lives. Keep an open mind, complete the exercise, and after you've finished, ask yourself whether you have a more insightful view of yourself as well those closest to you.

STEP 3

How does this story affect your life today? Think about the experience you've just created. Could it have influenced relationships and situations in this life, particularly those that involve men? Using the aggression example (or whatever meaningful word you chose): Have you created soul contracts with men who are aggressive toward you? What are they trying to show you about yourself? Do you hate aggression? Why? Could it be that it is something that you hate about yourself from that old life? Is there an old conflict surrounding aggression that you need to resolve? An obligation that has to be met? Your story is filled with possibilities that you need to resolve in this life.

STEP 4

Once we are aware of our past, we can alter our present reality. We can resolve our old conflicts and pay back our old obligations. Utilizing our aggression example: Suppose you have a soul contract with a man who has been aggressive toward you. This person signed a soul contract with you to be aggressive, to show you a side of yourself you never knew you had. Realizing that you have an unresolved aggressive pattern in yourself will help you take responsibility for it and do something to change it. Most importantly, you will no longer be a victim to this soul contract's aggression. Perhaps one day you will learn so much about yourself from this relationship that you will actually feel gratitude to this person. You may even find yourself thanking him for this valuable soul reminder. Learning about our past actions, and accepting responsibility for them, enables us to put all of our current relationships in a healthier, more constructive context, rather than being imprisoned by them, providing us with the opportunity to create freedom.

For instance, whenever my stepfather Doug was angry with me, he would always scream part of a biblical reference at me: "You are a liar, and the truth is not in you." On a personality level, that sounds like an abusive thing to say to someone. But on a soul level, he was reminding me of a life where I had been very cavalier with the truth. Doug was a circle-one karmic relationship for me. My soul created the soul contract with him to learn about that past life of lying to get what I wanted. In this life telling the truth is almost a compulsion with me—an interesting symmetry.

For years I found myself falling in love with men who looked physically very similar. They were dark-haired men with beards. I wouldn't even look at a man who did not fit that description. Years later after a great deal of research into my past life as a Civil War soldier, I found a photograph of him. He was dark-haired with a beard. All of my lovers looked remarkably like this soldier. My soul was showing me a fairly accurate picture of what I had looked like.

CHAPTER 8

MARS: HANDLING ANGER WISELY

Anger is as much a part of the vast spectrum of human emotion as any other feeling, yet no emotion has been more maligned and misunderstood. Our most enduring social mores perpetuate the belief that anger is ugly. We've been conditioned to equate its expression with being reckless, abusive, and dangerous. Although holding back our emotions can lead to stress and its concomitant maladies—from heart disease to depression to unmitigated violence—we are still expected to neatly tuck away our rancor deep within the recesses of our psyche. It's acceptable to express ourselves, as long as we don't lose our temper.

Growing up, I was told that anger was unrefined, socially unacceptable, and certainly not ladylike—not to mention immature, childish, and irrational. Many of my students and clients were taught the same thing.

Yet contrary to this childhood lesson, expressing anger is healthy—in fact, it is necessary to our health—as long as we do it in an appropriate manner. To deny ourselves any expression of anger would be an impossibility, just as it would be for sadness, happiness, fear, or shame.

Anger motivates us, helps us sustain our determination and drive, and sometimes works as a healing agent. Anger helps us defend ourselves, keeping us from being weak and vulnerable. Anger is the internal fire that gives us the impetus to take action in tense or emotionally challenging situations.

Anger becomes problematic and justifies its traditionally negative connotations when we don't express it in a healthy way, or when we don't express it, period, or when we seethe until we can't hold our anger anymore and then we explode, directing our fury at someone in the form of a verbal barrage or, worse, a physical attack. Abusing people with anger is wrong, so we need to distinguish between telling someone that we are angry with them and actually venting on them. One is done with sheer hostility; the other is done with thought, emotion, and understanding. We can use our anger to be strong and assertive. However, projecting your anger onto someone else implies that someone else's actions have made you angry, or that you have relinquished to that person your responsibility for your own emotions.

Expressing Anger

Healthy	Unhealthy
1. Shout the word no repeatedly.	1. Scream judgments at someone.
2. Hit a whiffle bat on a pillow.	2. Blame someone for your anger.
3. Take a fast walk around the block.	3. Hit something alive.
4. Vigorously dig in the dirt.	4. Be sarcastic to someone.
5. Make a loud noise.	5. Drive your car too fast.
6. Rip something up.	6. Drive recklessly.

7. Throw a tennis ball against a wall.	7. Give someone the finger for cutting you off on the highway.
8. Exercise.	8. Run a red light.
9. Write an angry letter and burn it.	9. Plot revenge.

Mars is about taking responsibility for our anger, laying claim to it, saying, "My anger is my anger, and no one can make me angry." Many clients come to me claiming they're depressed. My first question to them is, "What are you so angry about?" Although they are initially surprised by my question, when we talk about their repressed anger, their depression begins to abate. They are now able to do something about their anger and its related depression.

Most people don't honestly believe that their anger is self-perpetuated. Most of us believe that someone else's behavior, or an exasperating event, is what triggers our anger. I'm challenging you to accept that no one can make you angry without your acquiescence. Have you ever become furious when your 2-year-old threw his dinner on the floor, following a day at work you'd rather forget? And yet at a different time in a different context, when perhaps you were more relaxed— maybe you had just returned from a fun family day at the beach—you handled his dinnertime antics with a laugh. Have you ever become irate while sitting in a traffic tie-up that will make you late for work, while that same traffic jam, on the way to a vacation in the mountains, would elicit a grimace at worst? We have not been taught to believe that we are responsible for our emotions.

"A wrathful man stirreth up strife: but he that is slow to anger appeaseth strife."

—Proverbs

HANDLING YOUR ANGER

Anger is a palpable and visceral energy that we would be hard-pressed to release without doing something physical. Some therapists prescribe writing an angry letter and burning it. That's better than doing nothing, but not nearly as effective as physical means.

So go buy a plastic bat, and scream and yell and bat things that are inanimate. Imagine the face of the person with whom you are angry on a pillow, and go to work on it with a plastic bat. Have a temper tantrum! Maybe you were forbidden to do that as a child. What's stopping you now? Perhaps you fear losing control, or that once you begin, you'll never stop. I always tell clients to time their anger work using a loud buzzer, to prove to themselves that they are in control of their angry outburst.

Another powerful exercise involves the use of the word no. No has a negative connotation in our culture. It means you're not in alignment with someone or something—be it a plan, a strategy, or a policy—and that you're not going to do what is expected of you. Shouting "No!" can catalyze change within us. I have a lot of clients screaming "No!" in their cars to bleed off their anger.

In fact, the late psychiatrist Milton H. Erickson developed two "indirection" exercises that I've found helpful in this context. One is called a Yes Set, the other a No Set. The purpose of the Yes Set exercise is to help someone create alignment by asking them questions to which they will have to answer yes. Let's say you have a friend who is in a terrible frame of mind: she is moody, pessimistic, and negative about all the aspects of her life. By eliciting yes responses and creating a more positive energy, you are helping her migrate to a more encouraging mindset.

On the other hand, you may have an extremely passive friend who is being taken advantage of repeatedly by a man she is seeing, but can't muster the energy to draw the line. In order to help her access and confront her anger, you would help her with a No Set exercise. If you ask her questions to which she will have to answer no, her anger will build. The more she answers no, the angrier she will get.

Think about when and why you say *no*: perhaps you don't want to do something, or you want to protect your own best interests. Most of us were reared by parents who ordained that no was an unacceptable response, so no becomes one of the most difficult things for us to say as adults. By the same token, developing the ability to say it is a sign of assertiveness and independence.

Exercise: Mature and Responsible Handling of Anger

When you're in a conflict with another person and begin to get angry:

Step 1: Be present to the feeling and aware of the intensity of it.

Step 2: File the content material—the specific cause of the anger—away somewhere in your conscience so you can look at it later, when you are more reflective, to help you understand some hidden part of yourself.

Step 3: Instead of reacting automatically in anger, give yourself and the other person a time-out. Leave the room for a few minutes, telling the other person that you will return shortly.

Step 4: Do some anger work. Release the toxic, emotional physical energy that belongs to you.

Step 5: Return to the person and the conversation. Begin with an "I" statement: "I was angry when you (fill in the blank). I would like to discuss that with you." You've already released a good deal of the physicality of your anger in step 4. Now you're able to discuss the situation calmly and rationally.

I know what you must be thinking: What's the other person doing, while I'm being so measured and rational? It doesn't matter. You are only responsible for your own reactions. It's my experience, personally and through my clients, that if you don't escalate the conflict, the other person will calm down also.

MARS'S ROLE IN ANGER

Mars, the planet that ruled the Age of Aries, Moses, and most of the Old Testament, represents physical energy, assertion, aggression, war, power, initiation, and will. It is the energy that embodies action, forward motion, and risk taking. It represents independence, boldness, and self-reliance. Our Mars energy is a selfish energy; it wants to win for itself and compete with itself. At its best, Mars represents focused determination and self-motivation. At its worst, it can be impulsive, reckless, impatient, short-sighted, destructive, and accident-prone.

Mars represents the way we understand and express anger. At its most organic level, it symbolizes the savage in us, the impulsive part that is about action and reaction: no thought, no social consequence or rules. Mars also reveals how we make others angry at us. Karmically, in an astrological chart, Mars tells us about the conflicts and the wars that we have experienced in other lifetimes. The placement of the planet Mars on the day you were born indicates the kinds of conflicts you've initiated, and the havoc you've wrought in the past.

"Anger is a weed; hate is the tree."

—**Augustine**

One of the most prominent ways our Mars energy affects us is in our ability or inability to take aggressive action. In past lifetimes we've taken actions that hurt ourselves or others. Now in this life, we're very reluctant to take an aggressive action again, fearing the same injurious result as before. So before we can be free to be more assertive in this life, we have to confront and resolve those previous experiences. If you are afraid of discovering and resolving your Mars conflicts, you've created a new conflict right there. This conflict can be resolved only by uncovering the life where a Mars conflict had an extremely adverse effect on you. Without resolving the conflict, you may be depressed without knowing why.

Thus Mars is extremely important in helping us find out how past life conflicts can cause vague feelings of depression. A powerful clue is anger that we feel in this life that seems to have no immediate cause. To learn more about the issues from which you may be sourcing your anger, consult the "Mars Placements" chart, which will tell you your Mars sign. Each sign possesses a different residue of karmic anger.

Marilyn, who lives in Seattle, was plagued by a deep despondency that she couldn't entirely overcome, until she discovered and confronted her anger, sourced from a traumatic event from her past.

I spent the first forty years of my life proud of my ability to control my emotions, especially anger. As a young child, I would have temper tantrums, but they were gone by the time I made it to middle school. I hadn't experienced any type of anger since then. Upon turning forty-one, I entered the most depressing time of my life: I gained weight, I could not socialize with my friends, I got my first mediocre job evaluation, and I cried a lot. All of my old intellectual skills failed me. At first I thought I was going through early menopause. My doctor discounted that possibility and suggested a therapist. I took her advice, and a year later I was almost back to being my old self. Yet I still felt a vague sense of discomfort that wouldn't go away.

I saw Linda when she made one of her trips to Seattle, because I was interested in my spiritual mission. One of my friends had suggested that my dissatisfaction might be due to my lack of a spiritual path. Linda told me that my spiritual mission was to learn to be Arian and that Aries was ruled by Mars. She asked me how easily I assessed and dealt with my anger. I told her my story.

"Would you be willing to change your mind about controlling your anger?" she asked.

"No," I said emphatically, "I will not go back to being an out-of-control child having tantrums."

"There are other ways," Linda said softly.

I have to say that at this point of the session, I was not happy. I had come to Linda to understand my spiritual mission, and here we were talking about anger. It made no sense to me. I'm not sure what she did or said that kept me in her office that day. But I'm extremely grateful that I did stay. I learned that my Mars in Aries was about more than anger, but to be able to accept its gifts, I would need to value anger as part of my experience.

We did a meditation. She asked me to remember what had made me so angry as a child. I couldn't think of anything. I was able to remember my reactions but not what caused them. Then she asked me to visualize a bright fire-engine red. The color came immediately. It had been my favorite color as a child. At her request I allowed the color to locate in my lower back.

"Just be with the color. Let it turn into a picture," she said in her soothing voice.

I saw the color swirl, then slow down. It was like a kaleidoscope, and then there was a scene. The red was now blood on the hands of what looked like a young man. He was running, very scared, and breathing very heavily. Behind him was the body of a young woman, lying in a pool of blood.

Linda's voice was coaching me to speak. Somehow I knew that the young man in the scene was me. I told her what the scene was.

"Where did the blood come from?" Linda asked.

"A knife. I killed her with a knife," I reported, aghast at what I was saying, because it felt so true.

"Why?" Linda asked.

"She didn't love me. She was going to marry someone else. I got so angry, I couldn't control it. I killed her because I loved her so much."

Tears flowed down my face. Then I opened my eyes and looked at Linda, who was smiling. It seemed so contradictory to me that she would be smiling. I had just remembered killing someone.

"Remember that vague discomfort that's been torturing you for the last year? You just found the source of it. Congratulations!" Linda said. "You also just figured out why you're so afraid of anger. You think it's not only dangerous but murderous."

I knew it was true. I felt strangely relieved and so very tired. I saw Linda twice more during her Seattle stay. We worked on how I could complete that old life and deal with anger more effectively in this one. At her suggestion, I bought red clothes and claimed my soul color. The discomfort left, never to return. Now I have the courage and the will to claim all my feelings, and my life is more exciting than it has ever been.

Mars rules our basic need to achieve our wants and desires, and sexuality is one of those basic needs. Thus Mars encompasses our sexual motivation and gratification. Its energy manifests as our need for physical excitement and stimulation, whether through exercise, physical assertion, or sexuality. It drives our primordial need to physically connect with another person on a sexual level. Our Mars energy contains the ingredient that drives us toward the erotic and to consummate our desire through sexual relations. In many ways it represents what we find physically attractive and sexually exciting in another person. Once we are stimulated by a carnal desire for someone, we use our Mars energy to take the actions necessary to become sexually active with that person.

Mars also symbolizes sharp objects and people who use those objects in their work: surgeons and soldiers, for example. Mars rules warfare, whether it occurs internally or externally. As the male archetype, it has a strong need to manifest its male energy through forward, directed action. Mars colors how we motivate ourselves, and how we initiate action.

"Anger is a short madness."

—Horace

In a woman's astrological chart Mars is one of the planets that symbolizes her animus (the hidden male side of herself). It is also the energy that romantically stimulates her and draws her sexually to another person. If a man's Mars is in a female astrological sign, he may manifest his Mars energy in a more feminine, passive-aggressive manner. The following story from Stacy, 34, will give you an idea of how this Mars energy can cause conflicts in a relationship until it is understood.

My husband Steve and I were having serious problems in our marriage. We were always angry at each other. I would get so irritated with him that I would literally scream at him. He would respond by staring at me, saying nothing. That made me madder; I would scream more. He would get colder and more remote. The cycle seemed irreversible. Things were so bad that we had even thought about divorcing. But with three young children, an expensive house, and plenty of bills, divorce didn't seem like a viable solution. I knew about Linda from other friends who had seen her. Steve refused to go with me, saying that it was a waste of time and money. However, he did let Linda do his chart in preparation for my appointment.

She and I spent the first half hour discussing the problems Steve and I were having. Then Linda explained that Steve and I had challenging Mars placements. My Mars was in Sagittarius; Steve's was in Cancer. My Mars was definitely male-oriented, while Steve's was more female. It had never occurred to me that a part of me could be "male-like" and that my masculine husband could have a female side.

That revelation in itself made seeing Linda worthwhile. I have to admit that I was usually the protagonist of our arguments. When I'm angry, I just say so. Having more male energy than Steve meant that I was blunt, more aggressive, impulsive, and direct than he was. For his part, he was more responsive, sensitive, and defensive of my male anger. He would close down and hide inside himself, because he felt so scared and unsafe. His inability to speak to me honestly and directly when he was upset about something would drive me nuts. I wanted him to be more like me. Learning that he had a different orientation toward anger helped me. I could stop expecting him to be a mirror image of me. I could also begin to appreciate his fears and insecurities and how abused he felt.

I told Steve about the session. Surprisingly, he decided to go with me to our next appointment. Linda explained our Mars placements to Steve and told him how he must have felt when I was so loud and forward. He was amazed. He later told me that Linda had very accurately described how he felt and why he felt so paralyzed during those moments. We spent several sessions striving to understand our differences and learning how to better deal with each other's anger styles. It worked. I have learned to think before I speak in anger, and Steve has learned to be a little more expressive. We slip once in a while, but the change in our marriage is dramatic because we're able to understand our reactions, and we have a better chance of altering them.

In this life we handle our past life Mars conflicts, or past life issues surrounding anger, in one of three ways:

1. Project our anger onto someone else. We create a soul contract with someone to help us unravel a past life conflict. Remember, the stronger the reaction, the more vital the information it contains. Suppose your husband's angry words to you are sarcastic and biting. Your reaction is to become extremely angry with him. Intellectually, you know you are overreacting, but it's automatic on your part. When you realize your reactions form this pattern, you can see that your husband is reflecting a residual conflict involving anger from a past life of yours. In the past, you yourself probably were very sarcastic and used your rapier wit to wound people.

2. Continue to exhibit negative aspects of our Mars energy. The "Mars Placements" chart will show you how you may be handling issues relating to anger and other Mars issues. As I've said earlier, we often repeat our mistakes—or create them—until we learn from them and resolve them.

3. Avoid positive aspects of our Mars energy. Normally people tend to avoid confronting their Mars energy in this life because of the way they've handled it in the past. In other words, when we've taken an aggressive action in the past, its negative consquences often foster a fear of assertion in this life.

MARS PLACEMENTS: SOURCING YOUR ANGER

Each astrological sign in Mars articulates its anger issues differently. Knowing your Mars sign will help you understand what you are angry about, so you can take responsibility for it. Your anger issues in this life are directly correlated to the conflicts you've created in the past. Until you discover and handle your past life conflicts, you won't be able to fully use the positive, assertive energy from your Mars placement. You'll find yourself unable to make a major decision that needs to be made quickly, to take a new action, to create a new beginning, or to take a risk. Your unconscious fear of repeating old behaviors caused by impulsivity, aggression, and rage may lead to immobilization and passivity in this life. In an effort to learn more about your anger as well as other aspects of your Mars energy, find your Mars sign by looking up your birth date in this chart.

Mars Placements

If you were born:	Your Mars is in:	If you were born:	Your Mars is in:
Jan. 1, 1915	Capricorn	Aug. 18–Oct. 1, 1918	Scorpio
Jan. 31–Mar. 9, 1915	Aquarius	Oct. 2–Nov. 11, 1918	Sagittarius
Mar. 10–April 16, 1915	Pisces	Nov. 12–Dec. 20, 1918	Capricorn
April 17–May 26, 1915	Aries	Dec. 21–Jan. 27, 1919	Aquarius
May 27–July 6, 1915	Taurus	Jan. 28–Mar. 6, 1919	Pisces
July 7–Aug. 19, 1915	Gemini	Mar. 7–April 15, 1919	Aries
Aug. 20–Oct. 7, 1915	Cancer	April 16–May 26, 1919	Taurus
Oct. 8–May 28, 1916	Leo	May 27–July 8, 1919	Gemini
May 29–July 23, 1916	Virgo	July 9–Aug. 23, 1919	Cancer
July 24–Sept. 8, 1916	Libra	Aug. 24–Oct. 10, 1919	Leo
Sept. 9–Oct. 22, 1916	Scorpio	Oct. 11–Nov. 30, 1919	Virgo
Oct. 23–Dec. 1, 1916	Sagittarius	Dec. 1–Jan. 31, 1920	Libra
Dec. 2–Jan. 9, 1917	Capricorn	Feb. 1–April 23, 1920	Scorpio
Jan. 10–Feb. 16, 1917	Aquarius	April 24–July 10, 1920	Libra
Feb. 17–Mar. 26, 1917	Pisces	July 11–Sept. 4, 1920	Scorpio
Mar. 27–May 4, 1917	Aries	Sept. 5–Oct. 18, 1920	Sagittarius
May 5–June 14, 1917	Taurus	Oct. 19–Nov. 27, 1920	Capricorn
June 15–July 28, 1917	Gemini	Nov. 28–Jan. 5, 1921	Aquarius
July 29–Sept. 12, 1917	Cancer	Jan. 6–Feb. 13, 1921	Pisces
Sept. 13–Nov. 2, 1917	Leo	Feb. 14–Mar. 25, 1921	Aries
Nov. 3–Jan. 11, 1918	Virgo	Mar. 26–May 6, 1921	Taurus
Jan. 12–Feb. 25, 1918	Libra	May 7–June 18, 1921	Gemini
Feb. 26–June 23, 1918	Virgo	June 19–Aug. 3, 1921	Cancer
June 24–Aug. 17, 1918	Libra	Aug. 4–Sept. 19, 1921	Leo

If you were born:	Your Mars is in:	If you were born:	Your Mars is in:
Sept. 20–Nov. 6, 1921	Virgo	Feb. 22–April 17, 1927	Gemini
Nov. 7–Dec. 26, 1921	Libra	April 18–June 6, 1927	Cancer
Dec. 27–Feb. 18, 1922	Scorpio	June 7–July 25, 1927	Leo
Feb. 19–Sept. 13, 1922	Sagittarius	July 26–Sept. 10, 1927	Virgo
Sept. 14–Oct. 30, 1922	Capricorn	Sept. 11–Oct. 25, 1927	Libra
Oct. 31–Dec. 11, 1922	Aquarius	Oct. 26–Dec. 8, 1927	Scorpio
Dec. 12–Jan. 21, 1923	Pisces	Dec. 9–Jan. 19, 1928	Sagittarius
Jan. 22–Mar. 4, 1923	Aries	Jan. 20–Feb. 28, 1928	Capricorn
Mar. 5–April 16, 1923	Taurus	Feb. 29–April 7, 1928	Aquarius
April 17–May 30, 1923	Gemini	April 8–May 16, 1928	Pisces
May 31–July 16, 1923	Cancer	May 17–June 26, 1928	Aries
July 17–Sept. 1, 1923	Leo	June 27–Aug. 9, 1928	Taurus
Sept. 2–Oct. 18, 1923	Virgo	Aug. 10–Oct. 3, 1928	Gemini
Oct. 19–Dec. 4, 1923	Libra	Oct. 4–Dec. 20, 1928	Cancer
Dec. 5–Jan. 19, 1924	Scorpio	Dec. 21–Mar. 10, 1929	Gemini
Jan. 20–Mar. 6, 1924	Sagittarius	Mar. 11–May 13, 1929	Cancer
Mar. 7–April 24, 1924	Capricorn	May 14–July 4, 1929	Leo
April 25–June 24, 1924	Aquarius	July 5–Aug. 21, 1929	Virgo
June 25–Aug. 24, 1924	Pisces	Aug. 22–Oct. 6, 1929	Libra
Aug. 25–Oct. 19, 1924	Aquarius	Oct. 7–Nov. 18, 1929	Scorpio
Oct. 20–Dec. 19, 1924	Pisces	Nov. 19–Dec. 29, 1929	Sagittarius
Dec. 20–Feb. 5, 1925	Aries	Dec. 30–Feb. 6, 1930	Capricorn
Feb. 6–Mar. 23, 1925	Taurus	Feb. 7–Mar. 17, 1930	Aquarius
Mar. 24–May 9, 1925	Gemini	Mar. 18–April 24, 1930	Pisces
May 10–June 26, 1925	Cancer	April 25–June 3, 1930	Aries
June 27–Aug. 12, 1925	Leo	June 4–July 14, 1930	Taurus
Aug. 13–Sept. 28, 1925	Virgo	July 15–Aug. 28, 1930	Gemini
Sept. 29–Nov. 13, 1925	Libra	Aug. 29–Oct. 20, 1930	Cancer
Nov. 14–Dec. 27, 1925	Scorpio	Oct. 21–Feb. 16, 1931	Leo
Dec. 28–Feb. 9, 1926	Sagittarius	Feb. 17–Mar. 30, 1931	Cancer
Feb. 10–Mar. 23, 1926	Capricorn	Mar. 31–June 10, 1931	Leo
Mar. 24–May 3, 1926	Aquarius	June 11–Aug. 1, 1931	Virgo
May 4–June 15, 1926	Pisces	Aug. 2–Sept. 17, 1931	Libra
June 16–Aug. 1, 1926	Aries	Sept. 18–Oct. 30, 1931	Scorpio
Aug. 2–Feb. 21, 1927	Taurus	Oct. 31–Dec. 10, 1931	Sagittarius

If you were born:	Your Mars is in:	If you were born:	Your Mars is in:
Dec. 11–Jan. 18, 1932	Capricorn	May 15–Aug. 8, 1937	Scorpio
Jan. 19–Feb. 25, 1932	Aquarius	Aug. 9–Sept. 30, 1937	Sagittarius
Feb. 26–April 3, 1932	Pisces	Oct. 1–Nov. 11, 1937	Capricorn
April 4–May 12, 1932	Aries	Nov. 12–Dec. 21, 1937	Aquarius
May 13–June 22, 1932	Taurus	Dec. 22–Jan. 30, 1938	Pisces
June 23–Aug. 4, 1932	Gemini	Feb. 1–Mar. 12, 1938	Aries
Aug. 5–Sept. 20, 1932	Cancer	Mar. 13–April 23, 1938	Taurus
Sept. 21–Nov. 13, 1932	Leo	April 24–June 7, 1938	Gemini
Nov. 14–July 6, 1933	Virgo	June 8–July 22, 1938	Cancer
July 7–Aug. 26, 1933	Libra	July 23–Sept. 7, 1938	Leo
Aug. 27–Oct. 9, 1933	Scorpio	Sept. 8–Oct. 25, 1938	Virgo
Oct. 10–Nov. 19, 1933	Sagittarius	Oct. 26–Dec. 11, 1938	Libra
Nov. 20–Dec. 28, 1933	Capricorn	Dec. 12–Jan. 29, 1939	Scorpio
Dec. 29–Feb. 4, 1934	Aquarius	Jan. 30–Mar. 21, 1939	Sagittarius
Feb. 5–Mar. 14, 1934	Pisces	Mar. 22–May 25, 1939	Capricorn
Mar. 15–April 22, 1934	Aries	May 26–July 21, 1939	Aquarius
April 23–June 2, 1934	Taurus	July 22–Sept. 24, 1939	Capricorn
June 3–July 15, 1934	Gemini	Sept. 25–Nov. 19, 1939	Aquarius
July 16–Aug. 30, 1934	Cancer	Nov. 20–Jan. 3, 1940	Pisces
Aug. 31–Oct. 18, 1934	Leo	Jan. 4–Feb. 17, 1940	Aries
Oct. 19–Dec. 11, 1934	Virgo	Feb. 18–April 1, 1940	Taurus
Dec. 12–July 29, 1935	Libra	April 2–May 17, 1940	Gemini
July 30–Sept. 16, 1935	Scorpio	May 18–July 3, 1940	Cancer
Sept. 17–Oct. 28, 1935	Sagittarius	July 4–Aug. 19, 1940	Leo
Oct. 29–Dec. 7, 1935	Capricorn	Aug. 20–Oct. 5, 1940	Virgo
Dec. 8–Jan. 14, 1936	Aquarius	Oct. 6–Nov. 20, 1940	Libra
Jan. 15–Feb. 22, 1936	Pisces	Nov. 21–Jan. 4, 1941	Scorpio
Feb. 23–April 1, 1936	Aries	Jan. 5–Feb. 17, 1941	Sagittarius
April 2–May 13, 1936	Taurus	Feb. 18–April 2, 1941	Capricorn
May 14–June 25, 1936	Gemini	April 3–May 16, 1941	Aquarius
June 26–Aug. 10, 1936	Cancer	May 17–July 2, 1941	Pisces
Aug. 11–Sept. 26, 1936	Leo	July 3–Jan. 11, 1942	Aries
Sept. 27–Nov. 14, 1936	Virgo	Jan. 12–Mar. 7, 1942	Taurus
Nov. 15–Jan. 5, 1937	Libra	Mar. 8–April 26, 1942	Gemini
Jan. 6–Mar. 13, 1937	Scorpio	April 27–June 14, 1942	Cancer
Mar. 14–May 14, 1937	Sagittarius	June 15–Aug. 1, 1942	Leo

If you were born:	Your Mars is in:	If you were born:	Your Mars is in:
Aug. 2–Sept. 17, 1942	Virgo	Aug. 14–Oct. 1, 1947	Cancer
Sept. 18–Nov. 1, 1942	Libra	Oct. 2–Dec. 1, 1947	Leo
Nov. 2–Dec. 15, 1942	Scorpio	Dec. 2–Feb. 12, 1948	Virgo
Dec. 16–Jan. 26, 1943	Sagittarius	Feb. 13–May 18, 1948	Leo
Jan. 27–Mar. 8, 1943	Capricorn	May 19–July 17, 1948	Virgo
Mar. 9–April 17, 1943	Aquarius	July 18–Sept. 3, 1948	Libra
April 18–May 27, 1943	Pisces	Sept. 4–Oct. 17, 1948	Scorpio
May 28–July 7, 1943	Aries	Oct. 18–Nov. 26, 1948	Sagittarius
July 8–Aug. 23, 1943	Taurus	Nov. 27–Jan. 4, 1949	Capricorn
Aug. 24–Mar. 28, 1944	Gemini	Jan. 5–Feb. 11, 1949	Aquarius
Mar. 29–May 22, 1944	Cancer	Feb. 12–Mar. 21, 1949	Pisces
May 23–July 12, 1944	Leo	Mar. 22–April 30, 1949	Aries
July 13–Aug. 28, 1944	Virgo	May 1–June 10, 1949	Taurus
Aug. 29–Oct. 13, 1944	Libra	June 11–July 23, 1949	Gemini
Oct. 14–Nov. 25, 1944	Scorpio	July 24–Sept. 7, 1949	Cancer
Nov. 26–Jan. 5, 1945	Sagittarius	Sept. 8–Oct. 27, 1949	Leo
Jan. 6–Feb. 14, 1945	Capricorn	Oct. 28–Dec. 26, 1949	Virgo
Feb. 15–Mar. 25, 1945	Aquarius	Dec. 27–Mar. 28, 1950	Libra
Mar. 26–May 2, 1945	Pisces	Mar. 29–June 11, 1950	Virgo
May 3–June 11, 1945	Aries	June 12–Aug. 10, 1950	Libra
June 12–July 23, 1945	Taurus	Aug. 11–Sept. 25, 1950	Scorpio
July 24–Sept. 7, 1945	Gemini	Sept. 26–Nov. 6, 1950	Sagittarius
Sept. 8–Nov. 11, 1945	Cancer	Nov. 7–Dec. 15, 1950	Capricorn
Nov. 12–Dec. 26, 1945	Leo	Dec. 16–Jan. 22, 1951	Aquarius
Dec. 27–April 22, 1946	Cancer	Jan. 23–Mar. 1, 1951	Pisces
April 23–June 20, 1946	Leo	Mar. 2–April 10, 1951	Aries
June 21–Aug. 9, 1946	Virgo	April 11–May 21, 1951	Taurus
Aug. 10–Sept. 24, 1946	Libra	May 22–July 3, 1951	Gemini
Sept. 25–Nov. 6, 1946	Scorpio	July 4–Aug. 18, 1951	Cancer
Nov. 7–Dec. 17, 1946	Sagittarius	Aug. 19–Oct. 4, 1951	Leo
Dec. 18–Jan. 25, 1947	Capricorn	Oct. 5–Nov. 24, 1951	Virgo
Jan. 26–Mar. 4, 1947	Aquarius	Nov. 25–Jan. 20, 1952	Libra
Mar. 5–April 11, 1947	Pisces	Jan. 21–Aug. 27, 1952	Scorpio
April 12–May 21, 1947	Aries	Aug. 28–Oct. 12, 1952	Sagittarius
May 22–July 1, 1947	Taurus	Oct. 13–Nov. 21, 1952	Capricorn
July 2–Aug. 13, 1947	Gemini	Nov. 22–Dec. 30, 1952	Aquarius

If you were born:	Your Mars is in:	If you were born:	Your Mars is in:
Dec. 31–Feb. 8, 1953	Pisces	Feb. 4–Mar. 17, 1958	Capricorn
Feb. 9–Mar. 20, 1953	Aries	Mar. 18–April 27, 1958	Aquarius
Mar. 21–May 1, 1953	Taurus	April 28–June 7, 1958	Pisces
May 2–June 14, 1953	Gemini	June 8–July 21, 1958	Aries
June 15–July 29, 1953	Cancer	July 22–Sept. 21, 1958	Taurus
July 30–Sept. 14, 1953	Leo	Sept. 22–Oct. 29, 1958	Gemini
Sept. 15–Nov. 1, 1953	Virgo	Oct. 30–Feb. 10, 1959	Taurus
Nov. 2–Dec. 20, 1953	Libra	Feb. 11–April 10, 1959	Gemini
Dec. 21–Feb. 9, 1954	Scorpio	April 11–June 1, 1959	Cancer
Feb. 10–April 12, 1954	Sagittarius	June 2–July 20, 1959	Libra
April 13–July 3, 1954	Capricorn	July 21–Sept. 5, 1959	Virgo
July 4–Aug. 24, 1954	Sagittarius	Sept. 6–Oct. 21, 1959	Leo
Aug. 25–Oct. 21, 1954	Capricorn	Oct. 22–Dec. 3, 1959	Scorpio
Oct. 22–Dec. 4, 1954	Aquarius	Dec. 4–Jan. 14, 1960	Sagittarius
Dec. 5–Jan. 15, 1955	Pisces	Jan. 15–Feb. 23, 1960	Capricorn
Jan. 16–Feb. 26, 1955	Aries	Feb. 24–April 2, 1960	Aquarius
Feb. 27–April 10, 1955	Taurus	April 3–May 11, 1960	Pisces
April 11–May 26, 1955	Gemini	May 12–June 20, 1960	Aries
May 27–July 11, 1955	Cancer	June 21–Aug. 2, 1960	Taurus
July 12–Aug. 27, 1955	Leo	Aug. 3–Sept. 21, 1960	Gemini
Aug. 28–Oct. 13, 1955	Virgo	Sept. 22–May 6, 1961	Cancer
Oct. 14–Nov. 29, 1955	Libra	May 7–June 28, 1961	Leo
Nov. 30–Jan. 14, 1956	Scorpio	June 29–Aug. 17, 1961	Virgo
Jan. 15–Feb. 28, 1956	Sagittarius	Aug. 18–Oct. 1, 1961	Libra
Feb. 29–April 14, 1956	Capricorn	Oct. 2–Nov. 13, 1961	Scorpio
April 15–June 3, 1956	Aquarius	Nov. 14–Dec. 24, 1961	Sagittarius
June 4–Dec. 6, 1956	Pisces	Dec. 25–Feb. 1, 1962	Capricorn
Dec. 7–Jan. 28, 1957	Aries	Feb. 2–Mar. 12, 1962	Aquarius
Jan. 29–Mar. 17, 1957	Taurus	Mar. 13–April 19, 1962	Pisces
Mar. 18–May 4, 1957	Gemini	April 20–May 28, 1962	Aries
May 5–June 21, 1957	Cancer	May 29–July 9, 1962	Taurus
June 22–Aug. 8, 1957	Leo	July 10–Aug. 22, 1962	Gemini
Aug. 9–Sept. 24, 1957	Virgo	Aug. 23–Oct. 11, 1962	Cancer
Sept. 25–Nov. 8, 1957	Libra	Oct. 12–June 3, 1963	Leo
Nov. 9–Dec. 23, 1957	Scorpio	June 4–July 27, 1963	Virgo
Dec. 24–Feb. 3, 1958	Sagittarius	July 28–Sept. 12, 1963	Libra

If you were born:	Your Mars is in:	If you were born:	Your Mars is in:
Sept. 13–Oct. 25, 1963	Scorpio	Sept. 22–Nov. 9, 1968	Virgo
Oct. 26–Dec. 5, 1963	Sagittarius	Nov. 10–Dec. 29, 1968	Libra
Dec. 6–Jan. 13, 1964	Capricorn	Dec. 30–Feb. 25, 1969	Scorpio
Jan. 14–Feb. 20, 1964	Aquarius	Feb. 26–Sept. 21, 1969	Sagittarius
Feb. 21–Mar. 29, 1964	Pisces	Sept. 22–Nov. 4, 1969	Capricorn
Mar. 30–May 7, 1964	Aries	Nov. 5–Dec. 15, 1969	Aquarius
May 8–June 17, 1964	Taurus	Dec. 16–Jan. 24, 1970	Pisces
June 18–July 31, 1964	Gemini	Jan. 25–Mar. 7, 1970	Aries
Aug. 1–Sept. 15, 1964	Cancer	Mar. 8–April 18, 1970	Taurus
Sept. 16–Nov. 6, 1964	Leo	April 19–June 2, 1970	Gemini
Nov. 7–June 29, 1965	Virgo	June 3–July 18, 1970	Cancer
June 30–Aug. 20, 1965	Libra	July 19–Sept. 3, 1970	Leo
Aug. 21–Oct. 4, 1965	Scorpio	Sept. 4–Oct. 20, 1970	Virgo
Oct. 5–Nov. 14, 1965	Sagittarius	Oct. 21–Dec. 6, 1970	Libra
Nov. 15–Dec. 23, 1965	Capricorn	Dec. 7–Jan. 23, 1971	Scorpio
Dec. 24–Jan. 30, 1966	Aquarius	Jan. 24–Mar. 12, 1971	Sagittarius
Jan. 31–Mar. 9, 1966	Pisces	Mar. 13–May 3, 1971	Capricorn
Mar. 10–April 17, 1966	Aries	May 4–Nov. 6, 1971	Aquarius
April 18–May 28, 1966	Taurus	Nov. 7–Dec. 26, 1971	Pisces
May 29–July 11, 1966	Gemini	Dec. 27–Feb. 10, 1972	Aries
July 12–Aug. 25, 1966	Cancer	Feb. 11–Mar. 27, 1972	Taurus
Aug. 26–Oct. 12, 1966	Leo	Mar. 28–May 12, 1972	Gemini
Dec. 5–Feb. 12, 1967	Libra	May 13–June 28, 1972	Cancer
Oct. 13–Dec. 4, 1966		June 29–Aug. 15, 1972	Leo
Feb. 13–Mar. 31, 1967	Scorpio	Aug. 16–Sept. 30, 1972	Virgo
April 1–July 19, 1967	Libra	Oct. 1–Nov. 15, 1972	Libra
July 20–Sept. 10, 1967	Scorpio	Nov. 16–Dec. 30, 1972	Scorpio
Sept. 11–Oct. 23, 1967	Sagittarius	Dec. 31–Feb. 12, 1973	Sagittarius
Oct. 24–Dec. 1, 1967	Capricorn	Feb. 13–Mar. 26, 1973	Capricorn
Dec. 2–Jan. 9, 1968	Aquarius	Mar. 27–May 8, 1973	Aquarius
Jan. 10–Feb. 17, 1968	Pisces	May 9–June 20, 1973	Pisces
Feb. 18–Mar. 27, 1968	Aries	June 21–Aug. 12, 1973	Aries
Mar. 28–May 8, 1968	Taurus	Aug. 13–Oct. 29, 1973	Taurus
May 9–June 21, 1968	Gemini	Oct. 30–Dec. 24, 1973	Aries
June 22–Aug. 5, 1968	Cancer	Dec. 25–Feb. 27, 1974	Taurus
Aug. 6–Sept. 21, 1968	Leo	Feb. 28–April 20, 1974	Gemini

If you were born:	Your Mars is in:	If you were born:	Your Mars is in:
April 21–June 9, 1974	Cancer	Feb. 28–April 7, 1979	Pisces
June 10–July 27, 1974	Leo	April 8–May 16, 1979	Aries
July 28–Sept. 12, 1974	Virgo	May 17–June 26, 1979	Taurus
Sept. 13–Oct. 28, 1974	Libra	June 27–Aug. 8, 1979	Gemini
Oct. 29–Dec. 10, 1974	Scorpio	Aug. 9–Sept. 24, 1979	Cancer
Dec. 11–Jan. 21, 1975	Sagittarius	Sept. 25–Nov. 19, 1979	Leo
Jan. 22–Mar. 3, 1975	Capricorn	Nov. 20–Mar. 11, 1980	Virgo
Mar. 4–April 11, 1975	Aquarius	Mar. 12–May 3, 1980	Leo
April 12–May 21, 1975	Pisces	May 4–July 10, 1980	Virgo
May 22–July 1, 1975	Aries	July 11–Aug. 29, 1980	Libra
July 2–Aug. 14, 1975	Taurus	Aug. 30–Oct. 12, 1980	Scorpio
Aug. 15–Oct. 17, 1975	Gemini	Oct. 13–Nov. 21, 1980	Sagittarius
Oct. 18–Nov. 25, 1975	Cancer	Nov. 22–Dec. 30, 1980	Capricorn
Nov. 26–Mar. 18, 1976	Gemini	Dec. 31–Feb. 6, 1981	Aquarius
Mar. 19–May 16, 1976	Cancer	Feb. 7–Mar. 16, 1981	Pisces
May 17–July 6, 1976	Leo	Mar. 17–April 25, 1981	Aries
July 7–Aug. 24, 1976	Virgo	April 26–June 5, 1981	Taurus
Aug. 25–Oct. 8, 1976	Libra	June 6–July 18, 1981	Gemini
Oct. 9–Nov. 20, 1976	Scorpio	July 19–Sept. 1, 1981	Cancer
Nov. 21–Jan. 1, 1977	Sagittarius	Sept. 2–Oct. 20, 1981	Leo
Jan. 2–Feb. 9, 1977	Capricorn	Oct. 21–Dec. 16, 1981	Virgo
Feb. 10–Mar. 20, 1977	Aquarius	Dec. 17–Aug. 3, 1982	Libra
Mar. 21–April 27, 1977	Pisces	Aries Aug. 4–Sept. 20, 1982	Scorpio
April 28–June 6, 1977	Aries	Sept. 21–Oct. 31, 1982	Sagittarius
June 7–July 17, 1977	Taurus	Nov. 1–Dec. 10, 1982	Capricorn
July 18–Aug. 31, 1977	Gemini	Dec. 11–Jan. 17, 1983	Aquarius
Sept. 1–Oct. 26, 1977	Cancer	Jan. 18–Feb. 25, 1983	Pisces
Oct. 27–Jan. 26, 1978	Leo	Feb. 26–April 5, 1983	Aries
Jan. 27–April 10, 1978	Cancer	April 6–May 16, 1983	Taurus
April 11–June 14, 1978	Leo	May 17–June 29, 1983	Gemini
June 15–Aug. 4, 1978	Virgo	June 30–Aug. 13, 1983	Cancer
Aug. 5–Sept. 19, 1978	Libra	Aug. 14–Sept. 29, 1983	Leo
Sept. 20–Nov. 2, 1978	Scorpio	Sept. 30–Nov. 18, 1983	Virgo
Nov. 3–Dec. 12, 1978	Sagittarius	Nov. 19–Jan. 11, 1984	Libra
Dec. 13–Jan. 20, 1979	Capricorn	Jan. 12–Aug. 17, 1984	Scorpio
Jan. 21–Feb. 27, 1979	Aquarius	Aug. 18–Oct. 5, 1984	Sagittarius

If you were born:	Your Mars is in:	If you were born:	Your Mars is in:
Oct. 6–Nov. 15, 1984	Capricorn	Nov. 5–Dec. 18, 1989	Scorpio
Nov. 16–Dec. 25, 1984	Aquarius	Dec. 19–Jan. 29, 1990	Sagittarius
Dec. 26–Feb. 2, 1985	Pisces	Jan. 30–Mar. 11, 1990	Capricorn
Feb. 3–Mar. 15, 1985	Aries	Mar. 12–April 20, 1990	Aquarius
Mar. 16–April 26, 1985	Taurus	April 21–May 31, 1990	Pisces
April 27–June 9, 1985	Gemini	June 1–July 12, 1990	Aries
June 10–July 24, 1985	Cancer	July 13–Aug. 31, 1990	Taurus
July 25–Sept. 10, 1985	Leo	Sept. 1–Dec. 14, 1990	Gemini
Sept. 11–Oct. 27, 1985	Virgo	Dec. 15–Jan. 21, 1991	Taurus
Oct. 28–Dec. 14, 1985	Libra	Jan. 22–April 3, 1991	Gemini
Dec. 15–Feb. 2, 1986	Scorpio	April 4–May 26, 1991	Cancer
Feb. 3–Mar. 28, 1986	Sagittarius	May 27–July 15, 1991	Leo
Mar. 29–Oct. 9, 1986	Capricorn	July 16–Sept. 1, 1991	Virgo
Oct. 10–Nov. 26, 1986	Aquarius	Sept. 2–Oct. 16, 1991	Libra
Nov. 27–Jan. 8, 1987	Pisces	Oct. 17–Nov. 29, 1991	Scorpio
Jan. 9–Feb. 20, 1987	Aries	Nov. 30–Jan. 9, 1992	Sagittarius
Feb. 21–April 5, 1987	Taurus	Jan. 10–Feb. 18, 1992	Capricorn
April 6–May 21, 1987	Gemini	Feb. 19–Mar. 28, 1992	Aquarius
May 22–July 6, 1987	Cancer	Mar. 29–May 5, 1992	Pisces
July 7–Aug. 22, 1987	Leo	May 6–June 14, 1992	Aries
Aug. 23–Oct. 8, 1987	Virgo	June 15–July 26, 1992	Taurus
Oct. 9–Nov. 24, 1987	Libra	July 27–Sept. 12, 1992	Gemini
Nov. 25–Jan. 8, 1988	Scorpio	Sept. 13–April 27, 1993	Cancer
Jan. 9–Feb. 22, 1988	Sagittarius	April 28–June 23, 1993	Leo
Feb. 23–April 6, 1988	Capricorn	June 24–Aug. 12, 1993	Virgo
April 7–May 22, 1988	Aquarius	Aug. 13–Sept. 27, 1993	Libra
May 23–July 13, 1988	Pisces	Sept. 28–Nov. 9, 1993	Scorpio
July 14–Oct. 23, 1988	Aries	Nov. 10–Dec. 20, 1993	Sagittarius
Oct. 24–Nov. 1, 1988	Pisces	Dec. 21–Jan. 28, 1994	Capricorn
Nov. 2–Jan. 19, 1989	Aries	Jan. 29–Mar. 7, 1994	Aquarius
Jan. 20–Mar. 11, 1989	Taurus	Mar. 8–April 14, 1994	Pisces
Mar. 12–April 29, 1989	Gemini	April 15–May 23, 1994	Aries
April 30–June 16, 1989	Cancer	May 24–July 3, 1994	Taurus
June 17–Aug. 3, 1989	Leo	July 4–Aug. 16, 1994	Gemini
Aug. 4–Sept. 19, 1989	Virgo	Aug. 17–Oct. 4, 1994	Cancer
Sept. 20–Nov. 4, 1989	Libra	Oct. 5–Dec. 12, 1994	Leo

If you were born:	Your Mars is in:	If you were born:	Your Mars is in:
Dec. 13–Jan. 22, 1995	Virgo	Jan. 5–Feb. 12, 2000	Pisces
Jan. 23–May 25, 1995	Leo	Feb. 13–Mar. 23, 2000	Aries
May 26–July 21, 1995	Virgo	Mar. 24–May 3, 2000	Taurus
July 22–Sept. 7, 1995	Libra	May 4–June 16, 2000	Gemini
Sept. 8–Oct. 20, 1995	Scorpio	June 17–Aug. 1, 2000	Cancer
Oct. 21–Nov. 30, 1995	Sagittarius	Aug. 2–Sept. 17, 2000	Leo
Dec. 1–Jan. 8, 1996	Capricorn	Sept. 18–Nov. 4, 2000	Virgo
Jan. 9–Feb. 15, 1996	Aquarius	Nov. 5, 2000–Dec. 23, 2000	Libra
Feb. 16–Mar. 24, 1996	Pisces	Dec. 24–Feb. 14, 2001	Scorpio
Mar. 25–May 2, 1996	Aries	Feb. 15, 2001–Sept. 8, 2001	Sagittarius
May 3–June 12, 1996	Taurus	Sept. 9, 2001–Oct. 27, 2001	Capricorn
June 13–July 25, 1996	Gemini	Oct. 28, 2001–Dec. 8, 2001	Aquarius
July 26–Sept. 9, 1996	Cancer	Dec. 9, 2001–Jan. 18, 2002	Pisces
Sept. 10–Oct. 30, 1996	Leo	Jan. 19, 2002–March 1, 2002	Aries
Oct. 31–Jan. 3, 1997	Virgo	March 2, 2002–April 13, 2002	Taurus
Jan. 4–Mar. 8, 1997	Libra	April 14, 2002–May 28, 2002	Gemini
Mar. 9–June 19, 1997	Virgo	May 29, 2002–July 13, 2002	Cancer
June 20–Aug. 14, 1997	Libra	July 14, 2002–Aug. 29, 2002	Leo
Aug. 15–Sept. 28, 1997	Scorpio	Aug. 30, 2002–Oct. 15, 2002	Virgo
Sept. 29–Nov. 9, 1997	Sagittarius	Oct. 16, 2002–Dec. 1, 2002	Libra
Nov. 10–Dec. 18, 1997	Capricorn	Dec. 2, 2002–Jan. 17, 2003	Scorpio
Dec. 19–Jan. 25, 1998	Aquarius	Jan. 18, 2002–March 4, 2003	Sagittarius
Jan. 26–Mar. 4, 1998	Pisces	March 5, 2003–April 21, 2003	Capricorn
Mar. 5–April 13, 1998	Aries	April 22, 2003–June 17, 2003	Aquarius
April 14–May 24, 1998	Taurus	June 18, 2003–Dec. 16, 2003	Pisces
May 25–July 6, 1998	Gemini	Dec. 17, 2003–Feb. 3, 2004	Aries
July 7–Aug. 20, 1998	Cancer	Feb. 4, 2004–March 21, 2004	Taurus
Aug. 21–Oct. 7, 1998	Leo	March 22, 2004–May 7, 2004	Gemini
Oct. 8–Nov. 27, 1998	Virgo	May 8, 2004–June 23, 2004	Cancer
Nov. 28–Jan. 26, 1999	Libra	June 24, 2003–Aug. 10, 2004	Leo
Jan. 27–May 5, 1999	Scorpio	Aug. 11, 2004–Sept. 26, 2004	Virgo
May 6–July 5, 1999	Libra	Sept. 27, 2004–Nov. 11, 2004	Libra
July 6–Sept. 2, 1999	Scorpio	Nov. 12, 2004–Dec. 25, 2004	Scorpio
Sept. 3–Oct. 17, 1999	Sagittarius	Dec. 26, 2004–Feb. 6, 2005	Sagittarius
Oct. 18–Nov. 26, 1999	Capricorn	Feb. 7, 2005–March 20, 2005	Capricorn
Nov. 27–Jan. 4, 2000	Aquarius	March 21, 2005–May 1, 2005	Aquarius

If you were born:	Your Mars is in:	If you were born:	Your Mars is in:
May 2, 2005–June 12, 2005	Pisces	Dec. 8, 2010–Jan. 15, 2011	Capricorn
June 13, 2005–July 28, 2005	Aries	Jan. 16, 2011–Feb. 23, 2011	Aquarius
July 29, 2005–Feb. 17, 2006	Taurus	Feb. 24, 2011–April 2, 2011	Pisces
Feb. 18, 2006–April 14, 2006	Gemini	April 3, 2011–May 11, 2011	Aries
April 15, 2006–June 3, 2006	Cancer	May 12, 2011–June 21, 2011	Taurus
June 4, 2006–July 22, 2006	Leo	June 22, 2011–Aug. 3, 2011	Gemini
July 23, 2006–Sept. 8, 2006	Virgo	Aug. 4, 2011–Sept. 19, 2011	Cancer
Sept. 9, 2006–Oct. 23, 2006	Libra	Sept. 20, 2011–Nov. 11, 2011	Leo
Oct. 24, 2006–Dec. 6, 2006	Scorpio	Nov. 12, 2011–July 3, 2012	Virgo
Dec. 7, 2006–Jan. 16, 2007	Sagittarius	July 4, 2012–Aug. 23, 2012	Libra
Jan. 17, 2007–Feb. 26, 2007	Capricorn	Aug. 24, 2012–Oct. 7, 2012	Scorpio
Feb. 27, 2007–April 6, 2007	Aquarius	Oct. 8, 2012–Nov. 17, 2012	Sagittarius
April 7, 2007–May 15, 2007	Pisces	Nov. 18, 2012–Dec. 26, 2012	Capricorn
May 16, 2007–June 24, 2007	Aries	Dec. 27, 2012–Feb. 2, 2013	Aquarius
June 25, 2007–Aug. 7, 2007	Taurus	Feb. 3, 2013–March 12, 2013	Pisces
Aug. 8, 2007–Sept. 28, 2007	Gemini	March 13, 2013–April 20, 2013	Aries
Sept. 29, 2007–Dec. 31, 2007	Cancer	April 21, 2013–May 31, 2013	Taurus
Jan. 1, 2008–March 4, 2008	Gemini	June 1, 2013–July 13, 2013	Gemini
March 5, 2008–May 9, 2008	Cancer	July 14, 2013–Aug. 28, 2013	Cancer
May 10, 2008–July 1, 2008	Leo	Aug. 29, 2013–Oct. 15, 2013	Leo
July 2, 2008–Aug. 19, 2008	Virgo	Oct. 16, 2013–Dec. 7, 2013	Virgo
Aug. 20, 2008–Oct. 3, 2008	Libra	Dec. 8, 2013–July 26, 2014	Libra
Oct. 4, 2008–Nov. 16, 2008	Scorpio	July 27, 2014–Sept. 13, 2014	Scorpio
Nov. 17- 2008–Dec. 27, 2008	Sagittarius	Sept. 14, 2014–Oct. 26, 2014	Sagittarius
Dec. 28, 2008–Feb. 4, 2009	Capricorn	Oct. 27, 2014–Dec. 4, 2014	Capricorn
Feb. 5, 2009–March 15, 2009	Aquarius	Dec. 5, 2014–Jan. 12, 2015	Aquarius
March 16, 2009–April 22, 2009	Pisces	Jan. 13, 2015–Feb. 20, 2015	Pisces
April 23, 2009–May 31, 2009	Aries	Feb. 21, 2015–March 31, 2015	Aries
June 1, 2009–July 12, 2009	Taurus	April 1, 2015–May 12, 2015	Taurus
July 13, 2009–Aug. 25, 2009	Gemini	May 13, 2015–June 24, 2015	Gemini
Aug. 26, 2009–Oct. 16, 2009	Cancer	June 25, 2015–Aug. 8, 2015	Cancer
Oct. 17, 2009–June 7, 2010	Leo	Aug. 9, 2015–Sept. 25, 2015	Leo
June 8, 2010–July 29, 2010	Virgo	Sept. 26, 2015–Nov. 12, 2015	Virgo
July 30, 2010–Sept. 14, 2010	Libra	Nov. 13, 2015–Jan. 3, 2016	Libra
Sept. 15, 2010–Oct. 28, 2010	Scorpio	Jan. 4, 2016–March 6, 2016	Scorpio
Oct. 29, 2010–Dec. 7, 2010	Sagittarius	March 7, 2016–May 27, 2016	Sagittarius

If you were born:	Your Mars is in:	If you were born:	Your Mars is in:
May 28, 2016–Aug. 2, 2016	Scorpio	June 12, 2021–July 29, 2021	Leo
Aug. 3, 2016–Sept. 27, 2016	Sagittarius	July 30, 2021–Sept. 15, 2021	Virgo
Sept. 28, 2016–Nov. 9, 2016	Capricorn	Sept. 16, 2021–Oct. 30, 2021	Libra
Nov. 10, 2016–Dec. 19, 2016	Aquarius	Oct. 31, 2021–Dec. 13, 2021	Scorpio
Dec. 20, 2016–Jan. 28, 2017	Pisces	Dec. 14, 2021–Jan. 24, 2022	Sagittarius
Jan. 29, 2016–March 10, 2017	Aries	Jan. 25, 2022–March 6, 2022	Capricorn
March 11, 2017–April 21, 2017	Taurus	March 7, 2022–April 15, 2022	Aquarius
April 22, 2017–June 4, 2017	Gemini	April 16, 2022–May 24, 2022	Pisces
June 5, 2017–July 20, 2017	Cancer	May 25, 2022–July 5, 2022	Aries
July 21, 2017–Sept. 5, 2017	Leo	July 6, 2022–Aug. 20, 2022	Taurus
Sept. 6, 2017–Oct. 22, 2017	Virgo	Aug. 21, 2022–March 25, 2023	Gemini
Oct. 23, 2017–Dec. 9, 2017	Libra	March 26, 2023–May 20, 2023	Cancer
Dec. 10, 2017–Jan. 26, 2018	Scorpio	May 21, 2023–July 10, 2023	Leo
Jan. 27, 2018–March 17, 2018	Sagittarius	July 11, 2023–Aug. 27, 2023	Virgo
March 18, 2018–May 16, 2018	Capricorn	Aug. 28, 2023–Oct. 12, 2023	Libra
May 17, 2018–Aug. 13, 2018	Aquarius	Oct. 13, 2023–Nov. 24, 2023	Scorpio
Aug. 14, 2018–Sept. 11, 2018	Capricorn	Nov. 25, 2023–Jan. 4, 2024	Sagittarius
Sept. 12, 2018–Nov. 15, 2018	Aquarius	Jan. 5, 2024–Feb. 13, 2024	Capricorn
Nov. 16, 2018–Jan. 1, 2019	Pisces	Feb. 14, 2024–March 22, 2024	Aquarius
Jan. 2, 2019–Feb. 14, 2019	Aries	March 23, 2024–April 30, 2024	Pisces
Feb. 15, 2019–March 31, 2019	Taurus	May 1, 2024–June 9, 2024	Aries
April 1, 2019–May 16, 2019	Gemini	June 10, 2024–July 20, 2024	Taurus
May 17, 2019–July 1, 2019	Cancer	July 21, 2024–Sept. 4, 2024	Gemini
July 2, 2019–August 18, 2019	Leo	Sept. 5, 2024–Nov. 4, 2024	Cancer
August 19, 2019–Oct. 4, 2019	Virgo	Nov. 5, 2024–Jan. 6, 2025	Leo
Oct. 5, 2019–Nov. 19, 2019	Libra	Jan. 7, 2025–April 18, 2025	Cancer
Nov. 20, 2019–Jan. 3, 2020	Scorpio	April 19, 2025–June 17, 2025	Leo
Jan. 4, 2020–Feb. 16, 2020	Sagittarius	June 18, 2025–Aug. 6, 2025	Virgo
Feb. 17, 2020–March 30, 2020	Capricorn	Aug. 7, 2025–Sept. 22, 2025	Libra
March 31, 2020–May 13, 2020	Aquarius	Sept. 23, 2025–Nov. 4, 2025	Scorpio
May 14, 2020–June 28, 2020	Pisces	Nov. 5, 2025–Dec. 15, 2025	Sagittarius
June 29, 2020–January 6, 2021	Aries	Jan. 7, 2025–April 18, 2025	Cancer
January 7, 2021–March 4, 2021	Taurus	June 18, 2025–Aug. 6, 2025	Virgo
March 5, 2021–April 23, 2021	Gemini	Aug. 7, 2025–April 18, 2025	Cancer
April 24, 2021–June 11, 2021	Cancer	April 19, 2025–June 17, 2025	Leo

If you were born:	Your Mars is in:	If you were born:	Your Mars is in:
June 18, 2025–Aug. 6, 2025	Virgo	Feb. 28, 2030–April 8, 2030	Aries
Aug. 7, 2025–Sept. 22, 2025	Libra	April 9, 2030–May 19, 2030	Taurus
Sept. 23, 2025–Nov. 4, 2025	Scorpio	May 20, 2030–July 1, 2030	Gemini
Nov. 5, 2025–Dec. 15, 2025	Sagittarius	July 2, 2030–Aug. 15, 2030	Cancer
Dec. 16, 2025–Jan. 23, 2026	Capricorn	Aug. 16, 2030–Oct. 2, 2030	Leo
Jan. 24, 2026–March 2, 2026	Aquarius	Oct. 3, 2030–Nov. 21, 2030	Virgo
March 3, 2026–April 9, 2026	Pisces	Nov. 22, 2030–Jan. 15, 2031	Libra
April 10, 2026–May 18, 2026	Aries	Jan. 16, 2031–Aug. 25, 2031	Scorpio
May 19, 2026–June 28, 2026	Taurus	Aug. 26, 2031–Oct. 10, 2031	Sagittarius
June 29, 2026–Aug. 11, 2026	Gemini	Oct. 11, 2031–Nov. 20, 2031	Capricorn
Aug. 12, 2026–Sept. 28, 2026	Cancer	Nov. 21, 2031–Dec. 29, 2031	Aquarius
Sept. 29, 2026–Nov. 25, 2026	Leo	Dec. 30, 2031–Feb. 6, 2032	Pisces
Nov. 26, 2026 –Feb. 21, 2027	Virgo	Feb. 7, 2032–March 18, 2032	Aries
Feb. 22, 2027–May 14, 2027	Leo	March 19, 2032–April 28, 2032	Taurus
May 15, 2027–July 15, 2027	Virgo	April 29, 2032–June 11, 2032	Gemini
July 16, 2027–Sept. 2, 2027	Libra	June 12, 2032–July 27, 2032	Cancer
Sept. 3, 2027–Oct. 15, 2027	Scorpio	July 28, 2032–Sept. 12, 2032	Leo
Oct. 16, 2027–Nov. 25, 2027	Sagittarius	Sept. 13, 2032–Oct. 30, 2032	Virgo
Nov. 26, 2028–Jan 3, 2028	Capricorn	Oct. 31, 2032–Dec. 17, 2032	Libra
Jan. 4, 2028–Feb. 10, 2028	Aquarius	Dec. 18, 2032–Feb. 6, 2033	Scorpio
Feb. 11, 2028–March 19, 2028	Pisces	Feb. 7, 2033–April 6, 2033	Sagittarius
March 20, 2028–April 27, 2028	Aries	April 7, 2033–Oct. 17, 2033	Capricorn
April 28, 2028–June 7, 2028	Taurus	Oct. 18, 2033–Dec. 1, 2033	Aquarius
June 8, 2028–July 20, 2028	Gemini	Dec. 2, 2033–Jan. 12, 2034	Pisces
July 21, 2028–Sept. 4, 2028	Cancer	Jan. 13, 2034–Feb. 23, 2034	Aries
Sept. 5, 2028–Oct. 24, 2028	Leo	Feb. 24, 2034–April 8, 2034	Taurus
Oct. 25, 2028–Dec. 21, 2028	Virgo	April 9, 2034–May 23, 2034	Gemini
Dec. 22, 2028–April 7, 2029	Libra	May 24, 2034–July 8, 2034	Cancer
April 8, 2029–June 5, 2029	Virgo	July 9, 2034–Aug. 24, 2034	Leo
June 6, 2029–Aug. 7, 2029	Libra	Aug. 25, 2034–Oct. 11, 2034	Virgo
Aug. 8, 2029–Sept. 23, 2029	Scorpio	Oct. 12, 2034–Nov. 26, 2034	Libra
Sept. 24, 2029–Nov. 4, 2029	Sagittarius	Nov. 27, 2034–Jan. 11, 2035	Scorpio
Nov. 5, 2029–Dec. 13, 2029	Capricorn		
Dec. 14, 2029–Jan. 20, 2030	Aquarius		
Jan. 21, 2030–Feb. 27, 2030	Pisces		

MARS IN THE ASTROLOGICAL SIGNS

Mars in Aries

Mars in Aries manifests itself through directed, focused physical action. Its physical energy is fueled by movement and confidence. Your positive characteristics include being action-oriented, assertive, ambitious, competitive, courageous, energetic, enthusiastic, and optimistic. You are a natural athlete, competing against yourself. You strive for new beginnings and possess an eagerness to try new things and take risks.

Possible Past Life Conflicts/Archetypes
- A Native American warrior who was alone most of his life, fighting overwhelming odds
- A solitary explorer or adventurer, who died alone
- Someone whose impulsive angry actions accidentally led to a death
- A military leader who led soldiers into battle, causing them to die
- A person whose impatience led to conflict
- A person injured by a sharp object, which led to the loss of much blood
- A male who was unable to have a relationship due to his self-centered, selfish nature
- Someone who died from inflammation or fever

Reactions/Phobias that May Have Surfaced
- Fear of being openly angry, impulsive, impatient, and spontaneous
- Aversion to war, fighting, blood, and any form of violence
- Fear of sharp objects, including scissors and knives
- Desperate need for a committed relationship
- Dread of dying alone

- Terror of taking action, any action, because it could lead to conflict or someone's death

Residue of Karmic Anger in Present Behavior

Karmic anger can manifest as impatience, frustration with physical limitations, irritability at being restricted, and anger at authority figures. You deal well with anger because you are able to access it and then can express it quickly: You get angry, take action, and then forget it. You don't hold a grudge. Your propensity to act is motivated by your strong will to fight for your ideals. As a result you are courageous and eager.

Sexually, you are assertive, ardent, and strong. Your challenging characteristics are being accident-prone, combative, easily bored, uncooperative, domineering, abusive, impulsive, and arrogant.

Your Transformed Self-Assertion

Spiritual self-awareness leads you to be willing to take the actions necessary to perform your soul's mission.

How to Handle Anger

Because you are able to understand anger as a physical emotion, you are able to release it more effectively. You claim your anger and are responsible for it. Because you are not inherently afraid of your own anger, you are able to transform it into physical energy, stamina, and power.

Mars in Taurus

Mars in Taurus manifests itself through practical, concrete success requiring creativity, patience, and endurance. Its physical energy is fueled by discipline, hard work, determination, and the acquisition of valued possessions. Your positive characteristics include building slowly, thoroughly, and patiently, and finishing what you start in a persistent, dependable, earthy manner.

Possible Past Life Conflicts/Archetypes

- A wealthy woman who was greedy and materialistic because she was obsessed with security
- A Native American who loved his land and had it taken away by U.S. soldiers
- Someone whose unrelenting resistance to change caused conflict with others
- Someone whose desires for material possessions interfered with his/her spiritual goals

Reactions/Phobias that May Have Surfaced

- Need for land as vital to security
- Need for security and possessions at all costs
- Fear of being materialistic and greedy, leading to over generosity
- Fear of being too fixed or stubborn, leading to "going with the flow" Denial of any material success or stability

Residue of Karmic Anger in Present Behavior

Karmic anger can manifest as a tacit refusal to alter your views or accept change. You dig in your heels and will not budge, especially when it comes to financial and security matters. You are slow to anger, but when you are angry, you have a temper and become furious. Because of your practical nature, you seek to resolve your anger, but it takes time. Your willingness to take action is fueled by your need to be enlightened by strong material and spiritual values.

Sexually you are romantic, earthy, sensual, and sensitive, and you may be possessive. Your challenging characteristics are being self-indulgent, stingy, stuck in old patterns, and resistant to change. Your physical movements may be slow and lazy. You can be argumentative and prone to temper tantrums, and you tend to either over- or undervalue your own worth.

Your Transformed Self-Assertion
By synthesizing your spiritual and material values, you can create serenity and peace in your life.

How to Handle Anger
Develop a habitual routine to assess anger, dealing with it when it shows up on a regular basis. Use your sensory experiences, including doing gardening, arts and crafts, and home repair, to utilize your anger in a constructive manner.

Mars in Gemini

Mars in Gemini manifests itself through the expression of ideas, and active communication, either verbal or written. You have an inertia driven by mental challenges, and a vast supply of ideas. Your positive characteristics include being endlessly curious, needful of a constant exchange of ideas; being an information gatherer, inquisitive in thought and action, mentally alert, and quick to grasp an idea. You are a writer or lecturer. You often try to integrate your thoughts and ideas into action. You are versatile and multifaceted as well as adroit at doing more than one thing at a time.

Sexually, you are versatile and imaginative. Your need for sexual diversity, however, impinges on your ability to remain faithful to one partner. You need to overcome your tendency to be mercurial, fickle, gossipy, overly talkative, restless, scattered, and inconsistent. At times you lack commitment, and sometimes you get lost in the moment. You tend to spread yourself too thin and become unfocused, because you are interested in so many things at one time.

Possible Past Life Conflicts/Archetypes
- An angry writer, journalist, or lecturer who spewed judgments or wrote for effect but not necessarily truth

- A salesman who skewed his words to sell anything to anybody
- Someone whose lack of commitment in a relationship led to infidelity
- Someone whose distracted, restless temperament caused conflict with others
- A liar who wasn't aware he or she was lying

Reactions/Phobias that May Have Surfaced

- Writer's block to such a degree that writing a simple letter is a chore
- Tactlessness, truthfulness at all costs, even when saying nothing would be more appropriate
- Fear of speaking out to such an extent that necessary communication fails
- Aversion to gossip
- Unexplained dislike of salespeople

Residue of Karmic Anger in Present Behavior

Karmic anger can manifest as incredible restlessness and inattentiveness. You can be argumentative and caustic. When angry, you may be sarcastic and petty, using vituperative words to attack; you are quick to gossip about a person who has incurred your wrath. When confronted about your mode of anger, you will say anything to absolve yourself, including lying. Your anger can yield sarcasm and a manipulative streak. Your Transformed Self-Assertion A more focused and committed effort to integrate thought and action will enable you to express new creative ideas.

How to Handle Anger

When you use your anger constructively, you deal with thought, words, and interactive communication to seek clarity, insight, and information.

Anger inspires you to want to discover more about your environment. Be honest, and report conflicts with fairness and precision.

Mars in Cancer

Mars in Cancer manifests itself in emotional tenacity, sensitivity, and connection with the emotional needs of others. Its physical energy is fueled by feeling needed by others, and by being sensitive. Your positive characteristics include being supportive, sympathetic, receptive, nurturing, and maternal. You collect valued items from the past and are devoted to your family, affectionate, and loyal. Your motivations are based on kindness, with a strong sensitivity to the emotional needs of others.

Possible Past Life Conflicts/Archetypes

- A brooding, insecure, guilt-inducing mother who smothered her children, causing them to leave
- A healer so obsessed with being needed that he created codependent relationships that hurt his patients
- A person who was so hypersensitive, moody, and emotional that he or she felt childish, fragile, and pathetic
- A woman who clung to the past, became lost in it, and lost opportunities to enjoy her current life

Reactions/Phobias that May Have Surfaced

- Fear of children's leaving
- Phobias relating to parenting issues
- Anger at mothers and other nurturing women, who remind you of what you once were
- Hypersensitivity to any guilt
- Paranoia about being overly emotional
- Avoidance of commitment in a relationship for fear of being codependent

- Strong desire to be serious, to overcompensate for past life childishness
- Dismissal of all connections to the past

Residue of Karmic Anger in Present Behavior

Karmic anger can manifest as frustration and discord with family members, especially women. You may become passive-aggressive. When angry, you may get sulky, moody, and depressed.

Sexually, you are gentle, loyal, faithful, and romantically sentimental. Your challenging characteristics include being possessive, smothering, sullen, overly cautious, brooding, and too nostalgic. Because you are ultrasensitive emotionally, you may be timid, temperamental, too easily hurt, and sometimes childishly pathetic. When you aren't feeling secure emotionally, you close down and withhold your feelings.

Your Transformed Self-Assertion

Destruction of past illusions yields emotional freedom.

How to Handle Anger

Value anger as a normal, healthy emotion not to be feared or repressed. You are aware that to be angry with another means there must be some attachment. Use your sensitivity to nurture that attachment, even when you are angry.

Mars in Leo

Mars in Leo manifests itself in inspired and charismatic leaders who pour out their heart-centered energy to others. Your energy is fueled by your affectionate, dramatic, loving, and creative connections with others. Your positive characteristics include being commanding, dignified, prone to take action zealously, and needful of the limelight. You perceive yourself to be a commanding and inspired leader. Your alacrity to take action relates to your ambitious and exuberant nature. You love to have fun, and you may be a born entertainer.

Possible Past Life Conflicts/Archetypes
- An aging actor who was terrified of getting old
- An autocratic king who was totally self-centered, demanding of adoration, and in complete disregard of his kingdom
- A bombastic male who had to be on center stage at all costs
- A performer who was assassinated onstage
- A childish, vulnerable adult who was obsessed with being loved and adored, never taking anything seriously, preferring to play and have fun

Reaction/Phobias that May Have Surfaced
- Discomfort with being too visible or the focus of any type of attention
- A fear of being assassinated by imagined enemies
- Excessive responsiveness to other people, compensating for the need never to be accused of disregarding anyone.

Residue of Karmic Anger in Present Behavior
Sexually, you are warm, dynamic, dramatic, and generous. Although you love to be in love, you may be inhibited in your expression of it. Your most challenging characteristics include being self-centered, self-absorbed, and demanding of love, adoration, and acknowledgment. You expect to be appreciated. You may be boastful, conceited, and childish, becoming belligerent when you are not getting the attention you think you deserve.

Your Transformed Self-Assertion
Being enthusiastic and enjoying life will lead to inspirational spiritual leadership.

How to Handle Anger
Use anger to buttress your confidence. Anger can inspire your powerful leadership nature. Realize that through your innate generosity, you can be a catalyst for helping others deal with their anger.

Mars in Virgo
Mars in Virgo manifests itself in your need to create order and high standards, in your efficient use of logic, and in your ability to analyze and discern. Your energy is fueled by a strong devotion and concern for service and a health orientation. Your positive characteristics include being scientific, discriminating, industrious, dependable, and conscientious. Your challenging characteristics include being too obsessive, too result-oriented, nervous, hypochondriacal, perfectionistic, judgmental, and critical. You project the impossibly high standards you have for yourself onto others. But you are also methodical, practical, organized, and thorough. You seek a perfect blend of mind and body, and you support that pursuit by being studious and exacting in your search for information.

Possible Past Life Conflicts/Archetypes
- A doctor or nurse whose entire motivation was martyrdom to his or her patients
- A doctor or nurse who overlooked an important detail that might have led to a patient's death or injury
- A workaholic obsessed with perfection, whose life was filled with pettiness, detail, and negative thoughts

- A leader of workers who was controlling, hypercritical, and pedantic
- A hypochondriac driven by fear of illness

Reactions/Phobias that May Have Surfaced
- Terror of making any mistake lest it damage self or others
- Eschewal of healers to avoid being positioned as a martyr
- Obsession with or abhorrence of details and order
- Strong bias toward being self-critical with impossibly high standards
- An overarching desire to have the "perfect" body

Residue of Karmic Anger in Present Behavior
Karmic anger can manifest in a picky, petty attitude when life is not going exactly as planned. When angry, you may be critical and judgmental. Anger brings out your pettiness. You will analyze your anger and at times discriminate about whether you should be angry. Therefore you are not spontaneous but are rather studied in your expression of anger. You are loyal and loving sexually, although not terribly passionate.

Your Transformed Self-Assertion
A disciplined mind delivers practical service with compassion.

How to Handle Anger
Utilize your anger to hone your logical abilities, in order to produce a clearer understanding of the essence of a conflict. Value conflict and the anger associated with it as a learning experience.

Mars in Libra
Mars in Libra manifests its energy in harmonious, cooperative, and satisfying interactions with other people. Your energy is fueled by social

connections, diplomacy, balanced communication, and a strong desire for justice. Your positive characteristics include a pleasant social manner, a desire to please, an ability to see both sides of a situation, and an appreciation for beauty, as well as refinement and peacefulness. You act based on your need for social fairness and compromise.

Possible Past Life Conflicts/Archetypes
- A self-serving judge whose partial decisions led to injustices in his court
- A vain society matron whose life revolved around status, superficiality, and phoniness
- A woman whose obsessive passion in a love affair created serious emotional and physical imbalances in her life

Reactions/Phobias that May Have Surfaced
- Obsession with fairness and justice
- Need for peace at any price to create harmony and balance
- Aversion to superficiality and need for status
- Anger with any person who appears disingenuous
- Strong commitment to the needs of others to the extent of unfairness to self

Residue of Karmic Anger in Present Behavior
Karmic anger can manifest as disgust with injustice, unfairness, and a lack of social refinement and grace. You dislike anger in any form, believing it disrupts the peace, disturbs harmony, and interferes with social interaction. You repress your angry feelings and may get depressed by turning your anger inward. You also have the ability to transform your anger into compromise.

Sexually, you are very affectionate and enjoy planning a romantic setting for lovemaking. Your challenging characteristics include being indecisive, ambivalent, willing to obtain peace at any price, superficial, cloying, and phony. Because you are so interested in what others think, you sometimes devalue yourself and do what will make someone else happy. You may allow others to define how you feel and what you think.

Your Transformed Self-Assertion

Your will to support balance and harmony in all relationships creates social and spiritual justice.

How to Handle Anger

Recognize that anger is a natural by-product of all human relationships, and that discord is a way to move a relationship to a higher level of resolution and harmony. Understand the true meaning of constructive conflict.

Mars in Scorpio

Mars in Scorpio manifests its energy in an intense desire to seek deeper meaning by transforming and regenerating emotions. Your energy is fueled by a passionate, probing need to understand the mysteries of life and death. Your positive characteristics include magnetism, as well as strength, resourcefulness, willfulness, and inquisitiveness. You are devoutly loyal, determined, idealistic, and imaginative, and you may be a powerful and convincing leader. Your initiative stems from your need to understand all levels of spiritual and emotional transformation.

Possible Past Life Conflicts/Archetypes

- An intense, brooding man whose passion, extremism, and jealousy lead him to stalk someone with whom he was involved
- A magician who performed black magic
- A dark, vengeful woman whose single-minded anger created volatile emotional reactions between herself and others

- A detective whose work centered on his suspicious and paranoid nature
- The head of a company whose controlling, manipulative, and unyielding personality stifled his employees' creativity and freedom

Reactions/Phobias that May Have Surfaced

- Fear of intensity and passion
- Repression of anger lest it become too much to handle
- Aversion to any type of controlling or manipulating behavior
- Passivity and stoicism, rather than risking the expression of feelings

Residue of Karmic Anger in Present Behavior

Karmic anger can manifest as a deep, all-consuming rage. You feel you must control this rage for fear of its potential damage to yourself and others. When angry, you gravitate toward very dark internal places that manifest as cold, remote, and intense demeanors. Your anger can turn vengeful and vindictive; you do not easily forget.

You are highly sexual and passionate. You view sex as a mystical, magical transforming experience, one of the mysteries of life. Your challenging characteristics include being secretive, jealous, possessive, intimidating, resentful, distrustful, and unforgiving. You have a tendency to be controlling and manipulative when you feel threatened.

Your Transformed Self-Assertion

The courage, passion, and will to understand death and transformation creates spiritual leadership.

How to Handle Anger

Be unafraid to go as far as is necessary in order to transform the experience of the conflict. Transmute anger into power and creativity. Know that it can be transformed into passion and internal control.

Mars in Sagittarius

Mars in Sagittarius exhibits its energy in a search for philosophical truth, expansion, and freedom. Your energy is fueled by traveling, nature, teaching, and exploring new horizons. Your positive characteristics include optimism, enlightenment, ethics, openmindedness, charm, and athleticism, as well as energy and boldness. You are motivated to take action by your desire and courage to fight for what you perceive as your visionary truth.

Possible Past Life Conflicts/Archetypes

- An itinerant preacher who traveled the country proselytizing his beliefs in the form of fire-and-brimstone sermons
- A cowboy who rode into town, had a love affair, and left without any commitment
- A traveler who led a peripatetic existence fueled by intense claustrophobia
- A philosopher who was pedantic and pushed his truth down the throat of his followers

Reactions/Phobias that May Have Surfaced

- Fear of open spaces
- Dislike of traveling, especially long distances
- Fear of expressing truth and philosophy, in the event of misunderstanding or misperception as pedantic
- Apprehension at being abandoned in relationships

- Preference for city to country
- Aversion to intense religious doctrine

Residue of Karmic Anger in Present Behavior

Karmic anger can manifest as frustration with travel, especially at long distances, irritability with religious authority, and any perceived limitation on freedom. You may be argumentative and preachy.

You are also an enthusiastic, open-hearted lover who can be charming and carefree. Your challenging characteristics include being bored by details, aggressive, extravagant, irresponsible, claustrophobic, dogmatic, afraid of commitment, and a gambler. Because you are interested in a multitude of journeys, you may often lack direction and follow-through.

Your Transformed Self-Assertion

The will to search for universal truth through an optimistic vision creates an inspired teacher.

How to Handle Anger

See anger and conflict as an opportunity for expanding your philosophical horizons; convert it into a quest for truth, freedom, and a symbolic open road. You can release anger quickly because of your optimistic nature.

Mars in Capricorn

Mars in Capricorn manifests its energy in the achievement of practical success as an archetypal good father and executive. You perpetuate your energy by persevering, and you will not stop until you reach your goals. Your positive characteristics include thrift, efficiency, independence, and loyalty, as well as an appreciation for integrity, history, and tradition. Your initiative and drive are based on your internal requirement to climb steadily to established heights.

Possible Past Life Conflicts/Archetypes

- A dictatorial, ruthless, demanding father who alienated his children because he was insensitive, cold, and inflexible
- An authoritarian businessman who dominated his subordinates, was indifferent to their emotional needs, and rigidly enforced all the rules
- A Scrooge-like personality who was stingy and selfish
- A person mired in self-righteous anger

Reactions/Phobias that May Have Surfaced

- Anger at dominant father or other authority figure
- Dissatisfaction with rules and regulations
- Obsession with issues of being too successful
- Leniency with children, failure to set boundaries
- Oversensitivity and emotionalism

Residue of Karmic Anger in Present Behavior

Karmic anger can manifest in a stern, unyielding, and punitive authority figure. You have difficulty expressing all emotions, particularly anger, so you rarely have angry outbursts. You're slow to anger, but when you're angry, you become cold, calculating, domineering, and inflexible. You transform your anger into severe discipline. You believe that your anger must be righteous in order to be justified.

You tend to be traditional and somewhat inhibited sexually, but you are very loyal and faithful in your sexual behavior. Your challenging characteristics include being compulsive about rules, intolerant, and rigid, as well as having an obsessive drive toward materialism.

Your Transformed Self-Assertion

Being responsible and self-disciplined will create a wise, more mature social organization.

How to Handle Anger

Be aware that there are appropriate, righteous times to be angry, and when those times come, you shouldn't hesitate to be assertive and strong. You tend to argue in a socially acceptable manner by imposing rules and structures onto a conflict.

Mars in Aquarius

Mars in Aquarius manifests itself in a tendency toward inventiveness and independence. Your energy is fueled by your fierce protection of your individuality, as well as your yearning for universal truth and equality. Your positive characteristics include your willingness to get behind a cause you believe in; you are humanistic, altruistic, progressive, and innovative, and you may be blessed with a refreshingly distinct thought-process. You lend your support for the ideals of freedom, equality, diversity, cooperation, and brotherhood. You may be highly imaginative and visionary. You may create a group dynamic to accommodate your cause-based existence. You take action based on the creative, revolutionary power of your mind.

Possible Past Life Conflicts/Archetypes

- An erratic rebel who led a revolution against his government for the sake of rebelling
- A lawless nonconformist who hurt others with his egocentric attitudes and his unwavering belief in a cause
- An inflexible, detached individualist who was unable to connect with others on an emotional level
- A brilliant yet tormented scientist who hid in his laboratory, far from society
- A leading-edge philosopher who was ostracized for his nonconforming beliefs.

Reactions/Phobias that May Have Surfaced
- Fear of anything that seems radical or revolutionary
- Aversion to causes requiring dedication
- Fear of adopting unorthodox views that could lead to ostracism
- Fear of standing alone behind a principle
- Need to fall in line with others

Residue of Karmic Anger in Present Behavior
Karmic anger can manifest as an erratic rebelliousness and irritability with any rules and regulations. When angry, you may become cold, remote, and detached, as well as argumentative with firm ideas that you refuse to modify. Sexually, you can adopt a more experimental approach, sometimes having somewhat radical ideas. Your challenging characteristics include being impersonal, intolerant, too logical, radical, internal, shy, remote, erratic, and rebellious. You tend to observe life rather than participate in it.

Your Transformed Self-Assertion
A progressive and distinctive approach will lead to group leadership that best serves the universal order and humanity.

How to Handle Anger
Focus your anger on community, political, and humanitarian concerns. Understand that anger can manifest on intellectual, emotional, and spiritual levels. You are detached enough to observe yourself when you are in those situations.

Mars in Pisces
Mars in Pisces expresses its energy in a devoted quest for emotional and spiritual connections with all people. You understand others with your superb intuition and compassionate nature. Your energy is fueled by kind actions, charitable acts, and sympathetic reactions to those who need them.

Your positive characteristics include being forgiving, flowing, humble, imaginative, artistic, musical, unselfish, devoted, and spiritual.

Possible Past Life Conflicts/Archetypes

- An alcoholic unable to handle the practical realities of the world
- A religious leader who martyred himself to his religion
- An early Christian who died at the hands of the Romans
- A woman who was totally codependent, naive, illusionary, escapist, and unable to care for herself
- A person who believed that to be "good," one must sacrifice himself or herself to others
- Someone who took actions on intuition without incorporating thought and reason

Reactions/Phobias that May Have Surfaced

- Aversion to any type of drugs and anger at those who are addicted to them
- Aversion to martyristic behavior
- Unexplained approach/avoidance issues with Christianity
- Fear of psychic experiences and distrust of intuition.

Residue of Karmic Anger in Present Behavior

Karmic anger can manifest as self-doubt, vulnerability, and distrust of emotional power. You're also afraid of anger, sometimes turning it inward, resulting in escapist and addictive behaviors toward food, drinking, and drugs. You may become depressed. Because you believe anger is not a spiritually correct feeling, you will refuse even to acknowledge it, perhaps resorting to passive-aggressive behavior.

Sexually, you are a sensitive romantic and poetic lover who craves the mystical experience that the sexual act can create. Your challenging characteristics include being overly sensitive, melancholy, martyristic, impractical, too submissive, self-pitying, and timid. Because of your kind nature and naiveté, you may be taken in by other people's hard-luck stories and be easily manipulated.

Your Transformed Self-Assertion

Devotion to an intuitional and compassionate will creates spiritual communion and leadership.

How to Handle Anger

Understand anger as a natural emotion, using your energy to drive you to be imaginative and creative. You know that anger can have intrinsic spiritual value; utilize it to understand your karmic past and conflicts for spiritual growth and resolution.

MARS AND CHILDREN

Many of us were taught not to be angry—not even to feel anger and certainly not to express it. As children, we were often punished for getting mad. Needless to say, our parents didn't know about our Mars energy! But your knowledge of your children's Mars placements will help you better understand how your child feels when he's angry and how he can transform his anger. Since you know the karmic anger buttons that your child may have, you can help her understand why certain behaviors or circumstances trigger her anger. Because you are a circle-one relationship in your child's life, you may even carry some of those triggers in your own personality.

Parents, please use the "Expressing Anger" techniques (shown at the start of this chapter) with your children. Model them in your own life. Buy a punching clown, and use it with your kids. They'll love it. Teach them how to remove anger from their bodies naturally and safely. They will learn to value their anger as a teaching tool, to discuss it, and they will learn more about themselves in the process.

Marty is 5 years old. Her Mars is in Pisces. Her mother, Irene, 38, is a lovely, forgiving woman who is devoted to her spiritual pursuits. Irene's Soul Pattern sign and her Mars are both Pisces. Irene can also be timid and shy, fearing intense feelings, especially anger. Because she believes that anger interferes with love and compassion, she has effectively erased it from her conscious emotional life. Irene is also a hundred pounds overweight, having struggled with a food addiction since she was a small child. Given the strong influence of Pisces in her Soul Pattern, she has spent much of her present life struggling with Pisces's challenging attributes: she is addictive, escapist, sacrificing, and overly sensitive.

Marty is very angry at her mother and has been since she was old enough to talk. Irene is devastated that her only child feels such hostility toward her and is totally perplexed by its intensity. She adores Marty with all her heart and in fact gave up a successful, lucrative career to stay home with her. From Irene's perspective, the more she did, the more cantankerous Marty got. When Irene brought her situation to me last year, I explained that Marty had her Mars in Pisces, which gave her an addictive escapistic personality, a personality like a Christian martyr who sacrificed herself for her spiritual beliefs, who put everyone else's needs before her own. I knew that Marty would one day be able to identify with that past life.

Marty's unconscious reactions were not to her mother so much as to what her mother symbolized: her own past life themes. Whenever Marty perceived her mother giving in to her food addiction, on an unconscious level it reminded her of her own past addictions. Nor could Marty tolerate her mother sacrificing for her. Because of her own lives of self-sacrifice, it rankled her that her mother was so martyristic. Thus, the more Irene gave to Marty, the more it reminded her of lives where her sacrifice had been to her own detriment.

I convinced Irene that however painful her relationship with her daughter was, it was also spiritually perfect. Marty created her relationship with her mother to deal with her Mars in Pisces past. Irene, for her part, needed a strong motivation to leave problematic Pisces behind, in order to achieve her Soul Potential in Virgo. The more balanced Irene became in her life, the less angry Marty would become. Irene understood this immediately, telling me the message resonated deeply in her body and soul. She saw the beautiful spiritual dance that she and Marty had created in their mutual soul contracts.

My advice to Irene was to learn to take care of herself. Her first step would be to return to work, something she had missed terribly for five years. The second would be to acknowledge and deal with her own anger and see it as an emotion given to her by God. She needed to understand that by repressing anger, she was in fact escaping it through food. Third would be to honor her physical body by creating a new approach to diet and exercise. Lastly, she would talk to her daughter about the value of taking care of herself, then model that for her in a positive way. Irene was nervous about this program, but her love for Marty gave her the courage and the will to begin.

One year later, I am happy to report that Irene is back at work, has lost twenty-five pounds, and has actually been able to claim her anger and express it a few times. Marty, in the first grade, is far less angry at her mother and is very happy that Irene is happy at work. Even though Marty was too young to understand or describe her anger at Irene, her mother was clearly a constant reminder of her past life conflict. Whenever Irene was kind and sacrificing,

Marty hated it because it unconsciously provoked her own memories of martyrdom and self-effacement in a previous incarnation. Seeing her mother taking better care of herself gave Marty hope for herself. She wanted and needed her mother to show her how to deal with Mars in Pisces. Irene's progress gave Marty a wonderful role model that would help her alter her old problematic Piscean behavior early in her life.

CHAPTER 9

URANUS: YOUR PERSONAL HURRICANE

U
ranus rules Aquarius and therefore rules the Age of Aquarius for the next 2,000 years. The glyph for Uranus (♅)is a derivation of the letter "H" for its discoverer Herschel in 1781. It is almost impossible to see Uranus with the naked eye; it required technological advances of the telescope to see it. Because it takes Uranus about 84 years to go around the Sun, the average individual will only experience one Uranus return. Uranus is the first of the transpersonal planets, which means it affects the collective as well as the individual. Uranus is associated with sudden, unexpected changes and events. It is the "awakener" and symbolizes the urge to freedom, intuition, individuation, originality and independence. It is our personal hurricane rushing

through our lives and taking down whatever structures have outlived their usefulness in our lives.

Uranus is always connected to the mind of God, from whence all creative invention comes. As intuitive connections are made with God, change occurs for the individual and for the world. Each generation will break with the traditions of the generation before it and take on the unique energy of its particular Uranus. It is the energy that generates opportunities to create freedom and independence. Through Uranus we will recognize the previously held beliefs that have enslaved us. Through Uranus we will find many opportunities to create freedom, autonomy and independence from previously held beliefs that might otherwise continue to enslave us. Uranus will also provide the intuition and the clarity to hear the voice of God, reminding us of the blessings that we would be wise to hold onto. Uranus is the tornado or the hurricane disrupting the foundations of our life.

THE LAST URANUS CYCLES

Uranus in Pisces
(Dec. 31, 2003–May 28, 2010 and Aug, 15, 2010–March 12, 2011)
Uranus creates an opportunity to create freedom and independence from previously held beliefs that would enslave or bless us. Therefore the final months of Uranus in Pisces brought us face to face with unexpected experiences meant to teach us what ancient Piscean values and beliefs we needed to claim or that no longer served us. Uranus in Pisces was a blessing in the disguise of the powerful personal hurricane. As it blew through our unconscious, extreme Piscean beliefs, it killed them off at a rapid rate. We were left with voids to fill and new emotions to recognize and handle. The voice of God became stronger for us and we reacted with fear, sorrow and shame, until we resolved the past from which they sprang.

Disruption, shifts in water, especially through floods and storms were prevalent to remind us of the power of the water element. Natural upheavals rocked the foundations of cities, states and countries.

We were challenged by our deep extreme natures and pushed to adapt and flow. Uranus in Pisces ultimately gave us the freedom to choose what Piscean beliefs worked and which ones kept us nailed to the cross. Astrology took its rightful place as a vehicle through which people could find spiritual grace, dignity and power. It has been seven years of external and internal, unexpected events which have brought us to now–the end of a transit and even more important–the end of the Age of Pisces.

It is an astrological truth that transits are strongest at their beginnings and at their ends. When we were one year away from the final end of the Uranus in Pisces transit, we were in the midst of one of the worst oil spills, floods and water contaminations in our history. I believe that in some universal way I and we have something to do with all of those tragedies. I believe that all of us collectively create what goes on in our world. I believe that we do that through the process of projection. Unconscious beliefs that we have are projected into our relationships and our environment. We then, in essence, wait for our reflections to come to us. I know that this sounds impossible and on a mundane level it is. Spiritually it makes perfect sense, though. We are all one, we are all of this earth, and there is a cause and effect.

If the ends of a transit are the strongest, imagine what the end of a 2,000 year cycle (like the Age of Pisces) could be. I think that we are seeing it every day. I also believe that one person can make a difference. If I stop projecting my contaminated emotions out into the world, and I convince you to do the same, then you will pay it forward, and on it goes. There is a tipping point when we can make a difference in our world. That is my hope and my vision. We are clearly at the cusp or in the transition between the ages so what about the last two thousand years? This question is still asked me by students and clients alike. How do we prepare for what is to come if we do not know what we are leaving? What are the blessings and the curses of that time? Uranus travelled through the sign of Pisces during Dec. 31, 2003–May 28, 2010 and Aug, 15, 2010–March 12, 2011 to help us clarify, discriminate and choose what we, as individuals, wish to bring from the last two thousand years into the next epoch: The Age of Aquarius.

Uranus in Aries (March 12, 2011 – March 7, 2019)

On March 12, 2011 the planet Uranus began its seven-year journey through the sign of Aries. Aries is a fire sign, and the burning bush is a constant fire that does not burn, which in my mind symbolizes the filter of God-given intuition. Moses came down the mountain with the Ten Commandments. During that time on the mountain top, God manifested Himself as a burning bush, saying, "I am that I am." Moses did not know that he had a burning bush within him that would provide him the courage to become the icon of the Age of Aries. His God was external. It is only now that we are evolving into the Age of Aquarius that we can claim our inner, powerful God. It is now with Uranus in Aries that we understand this new cosmic beginning.

Uranus represents the voice of the Universe coming to us as inspiration, intuition, disruptions and unexpected experiences. In Aries the Universe's voice will encourage and inspire us to become more confident, self-aware, self-contained, and assertive and action-oriented. This seven-year journey will give us a giant leap into the Age of Aquarius by providing us the desire to embrace the pioneer spirit; find our independent, confident integrated male and female selves; and claim our divine inner triangle: mind, body and soul. Today, we are witnessing the reemergence of an integrated philosophy marrying the material world with the metaphysical, the temporal with the eternal. This rational age, pregnant with possibility, will see us break new ground as we discover and revel in the relationship between our souls and the universe.

My God-given intuition tells me that the seven years of Uranus in Aries is the time we have all been waiting for. This is another new beginning of the Age of Aquarius and it is at hand! To create commitments to the pioneer spirit necessary to being leaders of the Age of Aquarius we need:

- To find our independent, confident, assertive male energy to aid in transforming our last 2,000 year experience.
- To become courageous and be free to take the actions that inspire ourselves and others.
- To learn what "I am" really means.
- To honor the excitement that comes from being a cosmic Arian warrior.
- To listen to our internal voice of God and use our intuition

A new beginning is here!

YOUR PERSONAL URANUS TABLE

Uranus takes seven years to go through an astrological sign. It, therefore, affects a generation of people born within 7 years of each other. Each Uranus generation can therefore help each other process the effects of this powerful planet.

If the date is:	The sign is:
Jan 1, 1931–Mar 27, 1935	Aries
Mar 28, 1935–May 14, 1942	Taurus
May 15, 1942–Aug. 30, 1948	Gemini
Aug. 31, 1948–Nov. 12, 1948	Cancer
Nov. 13, 1948–June 10, 1949	Retrograded into Gemini
June 11, 1949–June 10, 1956	Cancer
June 11, 1956–Aug. 9, 1962	Leo
Aug. 10, 1962–Sept. 28, 1968	Virgo
Sept. 29, 1968–May 21, 1969	Libra

May 22, 1969–June 24, 1969	Retrograded into Virgo
June 25, 1969–Nov. 21, 1974	Libra
Nov. 22, 1974–May 2, 1975	Scorpio
May 3, 1975–Sept 18, 1975	Retrograded into Libra
Sept. 19, 1975–Nov. 16, 1981	Scorpio
Nov. 17, 1981–Feb. 15, 1988	Sagittarius
Feb. 16, 1988–May 27, 1988	Capricorn
May 28, 1988–Dec 2, 1988	Retrograded in Sagittarius
Dec. 3, 1988–Jan 12, 1996	Capricorn
Jan. 13, 1996–Dec. 30, 2003	Aquarius
Dec. 31, 2003–May 28, 2010	Pisces
May 29, 2010–Aug. 14, 2010	Aries
Aug. 15, 2010–March 12, 2011	Retrograded into Pisces
Mar. 13, 2011–Mar 6, 2019	Aries
Mar. 7, 2019–Apr. 27, 2026	Taurus
Apr. 28, 2026–Aug. 3, 2032	Gemini

URANUS IN THE ASTROLOGICAL SIGNS

Once you have identified where Uranus was located during the date of your birth (see previous table), you can read on to learn how this placement of Uranus is likely to affect you and those in your peer group over the course of your lives.

Uranus in Aries

With Uranus in Aries the Universe's voice will encourage and inspire you to become more confident, self-aware, self-contained, assertive, and action oriented. You may experience a deep urge to be uniquely creative and inventive. Uranus in Aries represents will, assertion and our need for action. It stimulates warms, excites and cheers. It provides quick energy, counteracts feeling depressed, encourages constructive anger, and increases physical strength. It symbolizes the spiritual warrior that promotes the pioneer spirit in all of us. Through this energy you will find your independent, confident, male side and be free to take the actions that inspire you.

Your personal hurricane might cause accidents that are caused by repressed anger, recklessness and impulsivity. This would encourage you to take conscious actions that lead to more spontaneity and freedom. You need to find creative, innovative way to finish your projects.

Uranus in Taurus

With Uranus in Taurus, the Universe's voice will encourage, inspire and awaken you to become more self-valued with a strong connection to your intrinsic self-worth and talents. Your urge to unique creativity is expressed through practical realities. Your love of the earth manifests through innovations in cooking and creating usable art like pottery. You could have a unique, inventive approach to financial matters in the banking and investment fields as well as banking and real estate.

Your personal hurricane could create disruptions in your financial life to promote the freedom that comes from releasing tangible possessions. Foundations based on external security might be interrupted to promote more internal confidence and safety. Your tendency to be stuck in the mud will be washed away by the winds of Uranus.

Uranus in Gemini

With Uranus in Gemini the Universe's voice will encourage, inspire and awaken you to become a brilliant, innovator communicator who supports the holistic model of mind, body, soul paradigm. Your urge to unique creativity is expressed through mental and verbal originality and a drive towards enlightenment. You create new thoughts, new philosophies and new languages that support the Aquarian consciousness. Freedom comes from a connection to the universal mind, which creates intellectual insight and change. This would occur by being so present to the moment that you are actively listening to everything around you.

Your personal hurricane could create an existential crisis between old foundational beliefs and new, innovative ideas. Once these challenges are resolved you will communicate your philosophy to serve others. This Uranus placement is the gateway to the Age of Aquarius.

Uranus in Cancer

With Uranus in Cancer the Universe's voice will encourage,inspire and awaken you to understand and control your emotional foundations. This would enable you to nurture yourself and others in unique and unusual ways. You would break away from traditional values regarding parenting and your family of origin. You might rebel against your family of origin if their values differ from your own. You could alter attitudes about feeling abandoned and emotionally rejected by understanding Aquarian models in why we create our parents. This unique philosophy would provide you an opportunity to become emotionally independent. You also have an ability to become a rational human being utilizing and integrating your emotional and intellectual filters as you respond to life's experiences. Freedom would come as you use your powerful emotions to fuel your passions for humanistic concerns.

Your personal hurricane could disrupt your clinging to old emotional patterns that no longer serve you. You might have a family crisis that challenges you to create more freedom in your life. It might push you to use your unique approach to rationality to solve the problem.

Uranus in Leo

With Uranus in Leo the Universe's voice will encourage, inspire and awaken you to giving love in unexpected and unique ways. You might find yourself creating unconventional opportunities to express your affection and generosity. You are a citizen of the world, opening your heart to those who need compassion. You know you have an inner child that wants to shine and be happy. You will have the courage to explore new age ways to heal your little internal person. You might use astrology as a language to connect to and make the inner child a reality. Your love of your inner child gives you the freedom to play and explore child-like pleasures. This might seem inappropriate to others who might reject your manner of self-expression. You need to maintain your independence and confidence to find inspired ways to connect with the naysayers.

Your personal hurricane could disrupt your life by causing conflict between your need for freedom and pleasures and how dependent you are on other people's attitudes toward you. Your inner child might have temper tantrums to create disruption in your adult relationships if you are not paying it the attention it requires.

Uranus in Virgo

With Uranus in Virgo the Universe's voice will encourage,inspire and awaken you to holistic forms of health,healing and service. You want to be free to develop unconventional treatment programs that incorporate natural medicine, meditation, yoga, nutrition and other alternate systems. You are an innovator whose out-of-the-box analytical thinking will improve all areas of work and service. You are a trouble shooter using your unique abilities to discriminate and glean problems; you are an environmentalist finding unique ways to protect and serve the earth and the creatures on it. You might even want to be a new age veterinarian using alternate healing techniques to bring health to the animals you love so much. On a personal level you need to be free of an inner desire for perfection that could create an extreme right/wrong paradigm.

Your personal hurricane could cause you to have a health problem that traditional medicine is unable to cure. This would cause you to find an alternate healing source. Finding a new solution would change the course of your work and service. Your body could have been hurt by contamination, leading you to become an activist for the environment. Your life could be disrupted by periods of procrastination, causing you to learn about your perfectionism. Wanting outcomes to be perfect will often cause fear, which will prevent you from acting.

Uranus in Libra

With Uranus in Libra the Universe's voice will encourage, inspire and awaken you to create a unique and innovative approach to partner relationships. With freedom and independence tugging at your responses, traditional marriage and partnership must change. You will rebel at any relationship that requires you giving up your space. You need to be a pioneer in finding a way to be in relationship with others and yourself. You will break away and rebel against any relationship that feels suffocating to you. Libra requires harmony and balance in your life, and Uranus desires a sense of adventure and liberation. So balance must include both. You want fairness and justice for the world and will work on finding new ways to promote it. The creative side of you will be happy discovering new ways to produce unusual social experiences. If you are artistic, making art will be a novel and freeing adventure in color and balance.

Your personal hurricane would disrupt relationships that are too co-dependent and smothering. This would result in your rebelling against traditional relationship values. You might have experiences which you feel are unfair and not just. They would cause you to look at how important fairness and justice are to you. You might also be confronted with issues that make you angry and throw you off balance. You want harmony but need to find freedom in being able to be angry and showing it.

Uranus in Scorpio

With Uranus in Scorpio the Universe's voice will encourage, inspire and awaken you to find unconventional methods to become a master of your emotional life. You are passionate and intense and need to find new and innovative methods to manifest these deep feelings. You are sexual and desire intimacy, yet you also want freedom and independence. You want to explore your sexual life outside of the conventional box. You crave change and transformation to maintain the intensity that continues to awaken you. You tend to live life in a black/white paradigm, which creates its own form of intensity. You are a pioneer in discovering and understanding the mysteries of life, especially life and death. You would love to create a scientific approach to proving life after death. You want to be in control of your relationships and yet you will not be controlled. You hold your cards close to your vest.

Your personal hurricane would cause you to examine your emotions and to be able to express them to someone important to you. You could be challenged to bring your deeper emotions to the surface. This will conflict with your desire to be in control and maintain a certain detachment. You might experience the death of someone close to you. That would cause you to investigate death, change and transformation.

Uranus in Sagittarius

With Uranus in Sagittarius the Universe's voice will encourage, inspire and awaken you to use your powerful intuition and to seek changes in religion, philosophy, higher education and the law. You will rebel against traditional thought in each of those arenas. Your intuitive connection to your own unique truth will rebel against any structures you find confining and outdated. You are optimistic and expansive as long as you are allowed to be free and independent in your thoughts and actions. You love travel and learning about different cultures. Your generous spirit will want to help those in need of enlightenment. You might have a unique, pantheistic approach to understanding God, nature and animals. You would love teaching this innovative approach to those of like mind.

Your personal hurricane would disrupt any structure that feels too rigid and confining. Your erratic approach to pushing your truth onto others might cause challenges in your personal relationships. Discovering your truth is not necessarily everyone's truth will create more freedom for you. You may not always listen to others' opinions and therefore limit more understanding. Your need for the freedom to travel and create new experiences could lead to being commitment phobic.

Uranus in Capricorn

With Uranus in Capricorn the Universe's voice will encourage, inspire and awaken you to merging success and ambition into new, innovative practices. You want to be successful and make money to be secure and you want to be free and independent. You want to be your own boss and will thrive in pioneering a company you built from the ground up. You can be parental and often find yourself in the good father role. You like organization and structure if you have created them. You will rebel if someone tries to impose their system onto you.

Your personal hurricane would create sudden changes in employment because of your need for independence. You care about people and they trust you because you are responsible. You are capable of seeing how future trends can affect your current business. You create goals and are materially successful in work that does not offer you freedom. You might have a boss that does not honor your individuality. You may have to have many jobs to find your niche. You want to be safe and secure in work that you can succeed in but it cramps your style. People might criticize you for giving them unsolicited advice that feels dictatorial to them. You have innovative ideas that traditional people cannot understand.

Uranus in Aquarius

With Uranus in Aquarius the Universe's voice will encourage, inspire and awaken you to being the unconventional, unique person you really are. You are one of the leaders of the Age of Aquarius because Uranus is the planet that rules Aquarius. You believe in the holistic model of mind/body/spirit. You think thoughts no one has thought before. You are a progressive thinker. You are open-minded and tolerant of all people.

You associate with groups of like-minded people to further your shared political, cultural, and holistically spiritual goals. You are a true "citizen of the world," networking within symbiotic groups to further raise global consciousness. You will be a leader of humanity, knowing that the attainable goals of freedom, brotherhood, and tolerance will become an ever-increasing point of convergence and kindred social activism across our planet. You understand astrology as a universal language to promote cross-cultural understanding. You are a true friend, honoring your friends' uniqueness and individuality. You do not judge. You do not care too much what others think about you.

Your personal hurricane comes as you push ahead into a tomorrow your family and friends cannot foresee and understand. You might have to detach from old beliefs that no longer serve you. Their lack of tolerance baffles you because it is not your nature to be intolerant. They might criticize you for being a Utopian with impractical goals.

Uranus in Pisces
With Uranus in Pisces the Universe's voice will encourage, inspire and awaken you to transcending the material to the spiritual. You will create opportunities for personal sacrifice to create your own redemption. This is accomplished by the spiritual need to enter into the suffering of human experience in order to become compassionate and empathetic. You are highly creative and artistic, striving to create a perfect world through your art and music. You are a dreamer and a romantic, wanting peace and tranquility in all of your relationships. You believe you are the person that can fix problematic situations and love to be needed to resolve them. You often care more about others than you do yourself. You believe their needs are more important than your own. You are quick to forgive and believe in the importance of forgiveness.

Your personal hurricane will bring you face to face with unexpected experiences that will teach you what ancient Piscean values and beliefs that you need to claim or that no longer serve you. This hurricane is a blessing blowing through your unconscious, extreme Piscean beliefs. You will have experiences that confront your sacrificial nature and cause you to find more value for yourself. Your co-dependence will probably be challenged as you realize these relationships are fraught with difficulties and inequalities.

YOUR URANUS WORKBOOK

Now that you have read my brief description of your personal Uranus placement, it is time for you to do your own work. The following questions will guide you to a better understanding of how Uranus operates in your life. The astrological words that describe your Uranus placement will give you a starting point that will begin your journey to connecting with and understanding your Uranus.

Step 1. Find your Uranus placement from Your Personal Uranus Table.

Step 2.   Answer the following questions using the astrological words pertaining to your Uranus sign (see the "Soul Potential Energetic Models" section in Chapter 4). I have provided some examples from my Uranus in Gemini to help you find your own.

1.   How can I claim my unique talents and express them to improve my world?

     My Example: Uranus in Gemini helps me be present to the moments of my life. I actively listen to people's words and learn from them. I talk to them about my holistic philosophy. I communicate my ideas about the Aquarian Age through writing and speaking.

2.   How do I allow myself the space to change direction?

     My Example: Uranus in Gemini helps me pay attention to the ebbs and flows of life around me. I have learned what positive change really is. It has led me to the philosophy of Serendipity which I have written about in Chapter 1.

3. How can I prepare for the sudden and unexpected circumstances that Uranus will bring?

    My Example: Uranus in Gemini helps me understand the Aquarian principle of soul creation. It brings sudden and unexpected challenges for my best interest.

4. What do I need to do to claim my independence and be wholly free?

    My Example: Uranus in Gemini honors my Soul and my relationship with it. I am free to use its knowledge and power to aid my personality with life's challenges. Internal freedom and independence comes from that knowledge.

5. How do I honor my unique path to individuation?

    My Example: Uranus in Gemini honors individuation. That energy aids me in being a person who thinks and speaks the Aquarian truths. These truths exemplify uniqueness and innovation that are the foundations of the Aquarian Age.

6. What must I do to satisfy my need for stimulation and excitement?

    My Example: Uranus in Gemini loves new thoughts, new philosophies and new methods of communicating them. Uranus rules astrology and I am an astrologer who loves my work. Each day is a new discovery.

7. How do I connect with my generation and its need to change and create progress in the world?

    My Example: Uranus in Gemini provides my generation the desire to break free of old beliefs and illusions that no longer serve us. We are the leaders and teachers of the Age of Aquarius. I am honored to be an integral part of that experience.

Journal your answers and use them as your guide to becoming friends with Uranus. Through this practice you can begin to predict the unpredictable. You will discover the meaning of the curve balls that life throws at you. Your personal hurricane creates a different change. A hurricane occurs—Uranus—and blows us off of our intended course. You can see this as Serendipity in action. The outcome is better than any you would have expected. You feel in control again and happier. Processing Uranus experiences as a Serendipitous opportunity will put you back into feeling in control and connecting with your Soul.

CHAPTER 10

PLUTO: OVERCOMING GUILT AND FOSTERING FORGIVENESS

E very day, whether we care to accept it or not, most of us are motivated by the desire to avoid feeling guilty. This unfortunate grounding is reflected in the way we act toward others and the decisions we make. For example, when faced with the prospect of doing something you'd rather not do, like visit a family member, how do you decide whether to do it? Do you call your mother, or perhaps the sibling who is causing you angst? Chances are the avoidance of guilt will play a central role in whatever action you take. Perhaps the following thought processes sound familiar to you:

- Mother's all alone, and if I don't call her, who will? After all, she depends on me.

- We have to go see him this weekend. If we don't, he'll make me feel guilty that we "don't see our nieces and nephews enough."
- Everyone else is putting in extra hours at the office on the project, and if I don't, I'll look like I'm slacking off.

All of these sentiments above are contaminated by the perception that if we don't take action, someone or something else will "make us feel guilty." Thus, instead of being motivated by want or need to some perceived beneficial end for others or ourselves, we are motivated to do something in order to avoid feeling guilty. By allowing guilt to skew our thought processes and decision-making ability, we're manifesting negative, lose-lose thinking. If you cede control of what you truly want to a value system based on guilt, you will never do what you want to do, but rather what you should do. Sometimes, of course, you are confronted with things you have to do. But whether you follow through should be based on the perceived benefits or opportunity cost of taking action, not on the ramifications of possible guilt. We become frustrated and dissatisfied when we know we are doing something primarily to appease someone and avoid guilt. Yet if we don't take that action, we are forced to confront our guilty feelings. Thus if we fall victim to the demands of a guilty conscience, then ultimately we will be dissatisfied and frustrated, because we will resent whatever decision we make.

We all allow guilt to contaminate our decision-making processes to some degree, but those of us who have learned to absolve our guilt-laden inclinations are leading healthier, more productive, and more stress-free lives.

DISTINGUISHING BETWEEN GUILT AND SHAME

As a legal term, guilt means one's culpability in a court of law. But guilt is also a counterproductive phenomenon that we create ourselves, independent of other people and events. This definition clashes with most people's perception of guilt: they perceive it as generated by someone else's disappointment in them. In fact, Webster's *New World Dictionary* defines *guilt* as "a painful feeling of self-reproach resulting from a belief that one has done something wrong or immoral." By contrast, *Webster's* defines *shame* as "a painful feeling of having lost the respect of others because of the improper behavior, incompetence, etc., of oneself or another."

Interestingly, guilt is defined as being based on a *belief*, while shame is based on an actual *behavior* or *event*. Taking it a step further, we may say that guilt is based on a perception, while shame is based on something that has actually transpired. Shame is an emotion, like fear or sadness, while guilt is a *perceived* emotion.

Most people use the words interchangeably, failing to see any difference. But distinguishing between guilt and shame is essential to the effort to eradicate guilt from relationships and daily behavior. Guilt subverts our purest intentions to do what makes us happy. It causes us to abdicate responsibility for our shame to somebody else whom we claim "is *making* us feel guilty." Getting to the source of our guilty feelings by confronting our shame enables us to take responsibility for our actions and learn from them.

Shame is an emotion that we own. When we feel ashamed, it's because of an action we've taken or a behavior we've exhibited. We can't shift the onus onto anyone else. But "feeling guilty" implies that someone or something else made us feel that way, thus shifting the burden of responsibility away from us. Once we understand that we are the source of our guilt and the reasons why, we can take the steps necessary to correct it.

Let's say you're at the dinner table with your fiancée's parents. You pick up an intricately designed wine decanter cut from crystal, to admire its workmanship. Suddenly it slips from your hands and falls to the floor, spilling wine all over their Oriental rug. The hundred-year-old family heirloom is fractured into a dozen pieces. Picture this, and pay attention to your body's reaction. My guess is that you will experience shame. It's a hot emotion that you feel in your heart or stomach. Your face may get red, and you want to crawl away as quickly as you can. That strong emotion produces a need to apologize and do whatever it takes to rectify the situation. Assuming your hosts are gracious, you will live through the moment and will forget about it. Shame is normal.

Now let's take the same experience, but let's change your age. You're 6 years old when the decanter breaks. The adults immediately scream at you for being "stupid and clumsy." They send you from the table in disgrace. You feel inadequate and embarrassed, and you have no chance to apologize. Two months later, you break something else—getting the same reaction. Now you feel shame, plus all the judgments that have been heaped upon you since the first time. The guilty feelings internalize and grow over time. The original experience is long forgotten, but the guilt remains. It builds over time and is paired with an emerging belief that you are bad.

The primary difference between guilt and shame is that guilt impedes us and keeps us stuck, while shame teaches us what we need to know about being in the world in an appropriate manner. Shame marks an experience or event in which you really did something wrong; guilt is based not on an actual experience but on a perception or belief that you did something wrong. If you are ashamed of something, you can deal with it, but guilt can fester in perpetuity. Ironically, most people have no compunction about acknowledging their feelings of guilt: "I'm feeling guilty; my cousin called two weeks ago and I've yet to return her call." But you hardly ever hear someone say they're ashamed of a specific behavior or action they've taken: "I'm ashamed of the way I've treated my cousin lately." Because once we say we're ashamed of something, we are more likely to take responsibility for it and do something about it.

GUILT AND OUR PAST

Many of my clients say that they were born feeling guilty. They have memories from their earliest years of feeling deeply guilty about something, but they are unable to pinpoint it. That ineffable feeling is actually the karmic guilt that transcends our lives, waiting to be dealt with and resolved. I believe that our souls use this very uncomfortable sensation to remind us of a karmic experience that needs handling. It is a cosmic two-by-four that keeps hitting us over the head until we take responsibility for it.

Mary had an extremely close relationship with her mother. They enjoyed the same interests and saw each other almost every day. They went everywhere together. Then Mary, who was in her late thirties, met a man, Chris, of whom she became very fond. They began spending a lot of time together. Mary's mother felt somewhat betrayed and tried to pull Mary closer to her—just when Mary needed space to explore her budding relationship with Chris.

In an effort to maintain the relationship they once had, the mother made demanding requests of Mary. Mary felt a miserable sense of guilt when she could not accommodate her mother. In fact, she found herself racked with guilt. Mary's guilt became so intense that it had a deleterious effect on how she related to her mother: she found herself lying or pretending not to be home when the phone rang, to avoid having to talk to her. Her torment was not lost on Chris, who became concerned that Mary would never have the autonomy to take part in a normal, healthy relationship. "It's tearing me apart," Mary cried one day in my office. "I love this man, and I love my mother. I can't stand this awful feeling in the pit of my stomach when I have to say no to her. I'm afraid of what this is doing to me and to my relationship with both of them."

After Mary told me her story, my first question to her was: "What are you ashamed of?" Mary looked at me, obviously miffed. "I didn't say I was ashamed of anything. I do feel guilty about abandoning my mother."

I explained that her guilt feeling is a prostitution of an old shame that she hadn't confronted, and that in order to remove the guilt, we had to find the old shame.

Mary absorbed the words, ruminating over them in silence. I waited for her to collect her thoughts. "You know my dad left us when I was only ten," she finally replied. "The night he left, I was standing in the hall, listening to him screaming at my mother. I felt so scared, but now that I look back, I remember feeling something else too. Maybe it was shame. I felt bad that I was listening, and real bad that my mother was being humiliated like that."

Mary had sourced a feeling of shame, for hearing something she shouldn't have heard. "I know that I have always felt guilty for not standing up for my mom. Or to use your word, maybe I felt ashamed that I wasn't strong enough to tell my dad to stop yelling at her." I asked Mary if she had ever told her mother what she had just told me. She shook her head. "What if you did, Mary? Don't you think it would alter some of the guilty feelings you have?" Mary agreed that she had nothing to lose and everything to gain. She left the session determined to talk to her mother.

A week later Mary came back. "We talked about that night," she reported to me. "My mother was shocked to learn that I had overheard the fight she had had so long ago with my father. She was amazed that I had spent all this time feeling so bad over not intervening. Then I told her that I felt guilty when she had asked me to do something that would interfere with a date with Chris. She told me about the guilt she had always felt when her mother had wanted her to do things with her. We actually laughed about it. I felt as if the weight of the world was lifted off my shoulders. My mother and I decided that guilt was one of the less desirable traditions that had been passed down from mother to daughter. We decided that it would stop here."

I wish I could count the number of clients who attribute some source of guilt to their families: sons feeling guilty about not pleasing their fathers, daughters about not being what their mothers want. Most of us have a story about guilt that includes our mother or father.

We often joke about "Jewish guilt" or "Italian guilt," by-products of cultures that are as traditionally enmeshed as matzo ball soup and Sunday pasta. But we can't all rectify our familial guilt as cleanly and neatly as Mary did. Our souls have often chosen our parents in order to help us deal with old karmic guilt. We created those circle-one parental relationships and soul contracts in order to discover the sources of our deepest shame. If no original shame exists in this life, then it exists somewhere in the past.

Think of a situation with your mother that produces guilt regularly. Is there something you are ashamed of that might be at the heart of it? Talk to her about the shame you're feeling, and see if the guilt dissipates. If it doesn't, chances are the source of the guilt is older than your relationship with her. For example, maybe you always feel guilty when your mother says you are mean-spirited toward your younger brother. You know that you've always been kind or at least neutral toward him. Perhaps your mother is reminding you of a time in a previous incarnation when you were hateful toward this person who is now your brother. Now you'll have the opportunity to apologize to your brother, therefore resolving the conflict and fulfilling your karmic obligation.

GUILT AS A CONTROLLING MECHANISM

As essential as it is to understand our propensity to foster guilt and to work toward ridding ourselves of it, we must also be aware of how we ourselves wield guilt as a tool to control others.

Becoming acutely aware of our history of fostering guilt in this life and in past lives gives us a chance to change our ingrained guilt-laden patterns so we don't perpetuate them in our children. Whenever we don't give our children an opportunity to deal with their shame and apologize for it, we are perpetuating guilt in them. Whenever we've paired their accidents with unintentionally harmful and demeaning statements—"You're always so clumsy" or "Didn't I teach you how to hold a glass? You never pay attention"—we're not allowing them to handle shame and say they're sorry. We're contaminating the shame process and creating problems with their self-esteem, self-worth, and sense of adequacy.

Can you recall any instance from your childhood when you felt humiliated and had no chance to resolve it? Give your children the time and the coaching they need to deal with shame in a healthy way. Let them feel complete with the process. Never allow them to leave a broken dish feeling broken themselves. Give them a chance to feel good about taking responsibility for things that they've done, and teach them the value of saying "I'm sorry." Watch how you might be using guilt to control your child's behavior. Think about how you were controlled by guilt, by either your teachers, parents, or other close relatives. Write down the situations in your early childhood that perpetuated that horrible belief. Try not to forget those times, especially when dealing with your own children. I have noticed that rarely do parents say they're sorry to a child. You're their role model. If you can't say you're sorry, you can't expect them to do it. As adults working through our guilt, taking responsibility for our shame, and becoming free of old thought patterns, we can keep our children from having to experience the same problem.

LIVING WITHOUT GUILT

Try to conjure what your life would be like without guilt. You would be free to discriminate among life's choices without someone's expectations or judgments weighing heavily on you. You would be free to be prosperous; free to take risks; free to explore your feelings; free to feel good about yourself; free to be happy; free to realize your potential. You would be less restrained in your dreams and aspirations. Being free to do things because you want to do them, not because you should, would clearly promote more honesty in your relationships.

At the age of 39, Cindy went through a difficult divorce, feeling as though the entire experience was her fault. Once she shed her sense of overwhelming guilt, she was able to turn her life around.

Five years ago, my marriage of fifteen years imploded. I had been a dutiful, stay-at-home wife to a successful business owner. In fact, my relationship with Phil very much resembled that of an employee and a boss, with me in the subordinate role. Now I felt that my world was collapsing. I had done nothing to deserve this. I was scared to death. Yet I also felt this overwhelming sense of guilt.

Had I done something to cause him to say it was over? He had been suffering from depression for years and had systematically closed off all sources of discomfort from his life: his job, his mother, our church, certain friends. I felt that I had been supportive, but perhaps he was right; it really was my fault. While I know intellectually that that couldn't be the whole truth, emotionally I felt consumed with dread, remorse, and guilt. About exactly what, I wasn't sure.

I underwent therapy with a Christian psychologist. I attended Alanon meetings to develop a sense of detachment. I went to monthly support meetings for families of manic-depressives. (My husband had been properly diagnosed by now.) And I thought I had begun to heal.

My first several sessions with Linda were filled with my bitching about Phil and his problems. But Linda gently steered me toward another perspective. What if all I was experiencing was my soul creating exactly the events I needed in order to learn and grow in this lifetime? I had certainly made great headway in my personal work, yet I still blamed my soon-to-be ex for my lack of internal peace. His leaving had made me sad, and I had the illusion that only his return would make me happy.

After almost two years, things were finally getting better in my life. Yet I still had a vague sense of guilt, as though I had done something I had forgotten but that I should feel sorry about. Linda took me through some exercises in which I visualized two past lives, which allowed me to recount experiences that were the source of my guilty feelings. I do not proclaim that the two "lives" I glimpsed actually occurred. Perhaps they did, perhaps not. But both shed light on my relationship with my ex-husband. Could the events I "saw" really be memories of past lives? I don't think those questions are nearly as important as the results of the session itself.

I experienced an immediate physical relief from that pervasive sense of guilt. In fact, I had nothing to feel guilty about any longer. My ex and I had done what we had done and had been doing for lifetimes. I began to feel a sense of internal strength unlike anything previously experienced in my life. I had a soul that was greater than circumstances, more powerful than emotions, unlimited by earthly time, and not limited to my earthly form.

Now I experience joy daily and in abundant quantities. I have a strong sense of purpose and a passion for life. I have remarried, and most importantly, I have healed the relationship with my former husband. I see him as a valuable part of my life, a man worthy of respect. I've also imbued this attitude in my two sons, who last year began living with their father when I moved to Toronto.

Last month, almost five years to the day since our split, my boys, my ex-husband, my new husband, and I spent time on an island on vacation. It was a truly remarkable experience. I have learned that I have the power to create any experience of life that I wish, and that honoring the soul's path is the most effective approach to a truly empowering joyful journey. I don't remember the last time I felt really angry—I believe it was about a year ago. I no longer live under the influence of guilt, a development that has propelled me forward in an exponential way. Life is indeed what we choose to make it.

Guilt is so pervasive that it often obfuscates how we really feel. Absolving ourselves of guilt gives us the opportunity to investigate and express our true feelings, allowing us to experience relationships with more profundity. But some find the unknown—life without guilt—so problematic and scary that they prefer the guilt.

Many of my clients have voiced their concern that life without guilt would be chaos. Their reasoning is that guilt controls us on a societal level. But I think of all the issues from the Age of Pisces that have haunted us for the last two thousand years: our need for redemption, our inadequacy, our need for perfection, our extremism, our mutual exclusion, and perhaps most of all, our guilt. I think about walking through a door into the world called Aquarius and closing that door behind me, leaving the Age of Pisces behind.

Let's assume for a moment that guilt was simply a belief system that we needed during those two thousand years, as a means simply to grow and evolve: to become more aware of the consequences of our actions and to gain more control over our impulsive behavior. As we move into the Age of Aquarius and evolve as loving, sensitive, responsible adults, we don't need guilt anymore to provide a social and moral boundary.

Now we must learn to appreciate what taking responsibility for our shame can do for us. Being ashamed is not just a sentiment reserved for childhood, but rather an emotion that allows us to resolve experiences that we feel bad about, so they don't fester into guilty feelings. If we determine what we did that made us feel ashamed and overcome it by making amends, then we learn not to take that action again. It sounds so simple, and it is. Yet most of us still don't follow that process. We are so uncomfortable with the feeling of shame that we will repress it, disregard it, blame someone else for it, and in time create our own guilt over it. Becoming more responsible for our actions is the cornerstone philosophy of the dawning Age of Aquarius. Guilt will dissipate as we become more conscious and more aware of our own feelings and actions. As we leave the Age of Pisces and enter the Age of Aquarius, we want to leave behind these parts of the Piscean personality, even as we take other parts with us.

Leave Behind…

- **A need to prove we can be redeemed for something.** This underpinning belief of the Piscean personality holds that something is inherently wrong with us and that we need some external influence to "fix" us. We have believed for centuries that if we prayed enough, some force of God would forgive us and make it all better. Perhaps it is the atavistic belief that we were born with sin and that only God would exonerate us and forgive that sin. Hence we join churches, synagogues, and mosques that promise us forgiveness and redemption.

- **A need to understand the difference between good and evil.** Our preoccupation with good and evil is thousands of years old. I believe that our souls created this dichotomy as a projection of ourselves. Each of us has a shadowy side that we may perceive as evil. Since most of us can't bear to confront that painful part of our psyche, we create it outside ourselves. When we are prepared to explore those unseemly aspects, we can work on changing them. Then our need to externalize what we see as evil will wane.

- **A need to aspire to heaven and avoid hell.** Each religion has its own teachings about the afterlife and its own specific "requirements" for admission to that ethereal bastion that Christians call heaven. Going to hell is unthinkable. Interestingly, the Random House Unabridged Dictionary defines heaven as "the abode of God, the angels, and the spirits of the righteous after death." In turn, hell is defined as "the place or state of punishment of the wicked after death; the abode of evil and condemned spirits." In today's more complex world, where would the spirits of those who are considered neither particularly righteous nor evil go? Once again, most religions supply us with an either/or philosophy of extremes, with no room for alternatives.

- A strong need to value ourselves as victims and a symbolic desire to be martyrs. I equate the failure to choose to make a change that we know is beneficial for us with self-martyrdom. Even though we know that the change will make us happier, we don't do it. We are more comfortable with the suffering that staying "stuck" brings. You might, for example, have a skewed belief that you don't deserve to feel good.

- A strong need to value Godliness and devalue earthly concerns, including personal gratification. "My reward will be heaven." A traditional Piscean way of thinking holds that living a comfortable life on earth will keep us from entering heaven. We must not love the earth and what it can give us, because to do so means we are hedonistic, materialistic, and ungodly. The Piscean personality sees things as either black or white, good or bad, right or wrong. Through this filter they would have to choose either earth over spirit or conversely spirit over earth, when in fact they can have both. How many times have you heard someone say, "I just want to have enough money to be comfortable. That's all I need." Many of us perpetuate the religious belief that God wants us to live a spartan existence and for doing so will reward us. But God has given us the earth and all it contains. God wants us to be happy.

- A need to feel guilty to remind us of what is bad. Clients have told me that guilt represents their personal border of acceptable behavior. Several have said that the absence of guilt would foster immorality. Guilt becomes their moral barometer.

Take with Us…

- A strong need to be introspective: to have quiet moments to find inner peace. Increasing numbers of people are turning to some form of meditation and introspection to find quiet and inner peace. Self-help books abound, offering great ideas to help us center and regroup in a world of noise, chaos, irritability, and confusion. People are taking these ideas to heart and putting them into practice. Solitary exercise is also becoming more popular, because it gives us time to be with ourselves. We're also seeking various forms of coaching to better analyze our behavior and its effects on others. Through Pisces we learned we have a spirit, and now, as we move from the Age of Pisces to Aquarius, we are learning how to understand it and communicate with it.

- A need to value our feelings. We need to understand our feelings: how they affect our life, how to express them, how they can control our lives, and how to integrate them into the totality of our personality. Our five basic emotions are mad, glad, sad, scared, and ashamed. Yet we have hundreds of words that mean the same thing. We can say that we feel frustrated, irritable, peeved, annoyed, enraged, irate, exasperated, and furious, but they all boil down to feeling angry. Many of us use these other words instead of simply saying "I'm angry; I'm ashamed; I'm sad; I'm scared." We even have trouble saying "I'm glad." If we honor and understand our basic feelings, we take responsibility for them. Taking responsibility for our feelings can be frightening. After a few years of denial, we lose touch with most of our emotions. Few of us, in any given moment, stop to ask the question, "How am I feeling right now?"

- Use the five fundamental basic emotions to get more in touch with your own feelings. Stop a few times a day and ask yourself how you're feeling. Discriminate among the different sensations.

Anger and fear can feel very similar. Sadness and shame may also feel nearly the same. The more you practice gauging your emotions internally, the more likely you will be to express them externally.

- A need to control your aggressive and impulsive actions that could hurt yourself and others. Aggression flares when we ignore our anger over time and it escalates. News reports chronicle the most extreme examples: those tormented people who have leaped out of their quiet, controlled personas to commit unspeakable acts of random violence. Taking the time to source our anger, understand it, and be responsible for it helps put us in control and makes us less prone to lashing out. As we understand how to act more constructively, we will have fewer causes of shame and hence guilt.

LEARNING MORE ABOUT GUILT THROUGH PLUTO

The planet Pluto in your astrological chart can help explain your guilty inclinations. The interesting component of Pluto is that it rules not only our individual past, but our generational past. Those of us born within twenty years of each other may share deep memories that seem similar.

Pluto urges us to focus on personal transformation and our Soul Potential. It helps us face our deepest desires and obsessions and alter them. It gives us a strong motivation to let go of past guilt so we can be reborn, spiritually and emotionally. In order to become free of past life karma and the need to resist changing our Soul Patterns, we must understand what Pluto represents.

The astrological sign in which your Pluto is placed can suggest how you can act on your desire for personal transformation. The following discussion of Pluto will help you answer the following questions: How do you develop the courage to confront the parts of yourself about which you feel guilty? What do you need to do to transform your old fears into internal strength and confidence? How do you delve into your deepest obsessions and destroy them?

Pluto Placements

If you were born:	Your Pluto is in:	If you were born:	Your Pluto is in:
Jan. 1, 1915–Oct. 7, 1937	Cancer	May 19, 1984–Aug. 28, 1984	Libra
Oct. 8, 1937–Nov. 25, 1937	Leo	Aug. 29, 1984–Jan. 17, 1995	Scorpio
Nov. 26, 1937–Aug. 3, 1938	Cancer	Jan. 18, 1995–April 21, 1995	Sagittarius
Aug. 4, 1938–Feb. 8, 1939	Leo	April 22, 1995–Nov. 10, 1995	Scorpio
Feb. 9, 1939–June 14, 1939	Cancer	Nov. 11, 1995–Jan. 26, 2008	Sagittarius
June 15, 1939–Oct. 19, 1956	Leo	Jan. 27, 2008–June 14, 2008	Capricorn
Oct. 20, 1956–Jan. 15, 1957	Virgo	June 15, 2008–Nov. 27, 2008	Sagittarius
Jan. 16, 1957–Aug. 19, 1957	Leo	Nov. 28, 2008–Mar. 23, 2023	Capricorn
Aug. 20, 1957–April 11, 1958	Virgo	Mar. 24, 2023–June 11, 2023	Aquarius
April 12, 1958–June 10, 1958	Leo	June 12, 2023–Jan. 21, 2024	Capricorn
June 11, 1958–Oct. 5, 1971	Virgo	Jan 22, 2024–Sept. 2, 2024	Aquarius
Oct. 6, 1971–April 17, 1972	Libra	Sept. 3, 2024–Nov. 19, 2024	Capricorn
April 18, 1972–July 30, 1972	Virgo	Nov. 20, 2024–Mar. 9, 2043	Aquarius
July 31, 1972–Nov. 5, 1983	Libra	Mar. 10, 2043–Sept. 1, 2043	Pisces
Nov. 6, 1983–May 18, 1984	Scorpio	Sept. 2, 2043–Jan. 19, 2044	Aquarius
		Jan. 20, 2044–Dec. 31, 2050	Pisces

PLUTO IN THE ASTROLOGICAL SIGNS

Pluto in Cancer

Members of the Pluto in Cancer generation share past lives of fear, insecurity, and loss. You may have experienced lives where you had no permanent home or roots and no emotional or financial security. You probably lived in passivity or subordination, with little power to effect change. Others changed their life circumstances with little regard for what it did to you. In some dire circumstances you could have lost your family or those closest to you. An archetypal Pluto in Cancer lifetime would be that of a slave, with no home and no power, whose family could have been sold and sent away. In this life, you and the rest of your generation are terrified of change because of your powerlessness in other incarnations. The karmic guilt you experienced by being subject to the whims of the powerful, and being powerless and fearful to do anything about it, has created obsessions for you in this life. You fight for your family and hold it together at all costs. You value home, tradition, and foundations. You cling incessantly to what feels secure, haunted by issues that you perceive as having a debilitating impact on your family. You are obsessed with the immediate past because it represents cohesiveness and stability. You are loyal to government, your employers, and your religion because they represent a part of your stable "family." You were born into the Depression or thereabouts and survived it by being frugal and cautious. You learned about the value of families sticking together to survive. If you were born early in this generation, you fought in World War II to defend all that is important to you: home and country.

Pluto in Leo

The Pluto in Leo generation shares past lives of understanding power and control. You've been in various roles of power, ranging from rulers of small countries to owners of land. Your vainglorious and self-centered approach kept you from seeing other people's needs. You ignored your subordinates, seeing them as having little meaning other than as workers or servants, an attitude that has no doubt fostered unconscious guilt in this life. This unconscious guilt could create a need for service, a karmic symmetry that could lead you to want to dedicate your life to others. Each person you meet in this life could potentially have been one of those poor servants with whom you have an unresolved obligation. What better way to resolve your obligation to them than to care for them as a doctor, nurse, counselor, teacher, or social worker. Many people who are healers in this life have had past lives of opulence, during which they held a blatant disregard for others. For hundreds of years those in power were born into power. They were royal and were trained to be separate from the lower classes. Now, as a member of the Pluto in Leo generation, you feel ashamed and even guilty for the way you were. Thus you've created a life to redeem yourself from the insensitivities and abuses you so ruthlessly exhibited from a previous incarnation.

Pluto in Virgo

The Pluto in Virgo generation shares past lives of being Godlike healers, well ordered, and structured. As a member of this generation, you judged those who were not as ordered and rigid as you were. The archetype here is the doctor or other medically prominent member of the community who could do no wrong. You were adored, lionized, and revered. You were the healer, and everyone needed you. You believed yourself infallible: you did not make mistakes. Your mission was to be a perfect healer and to be respected as such. But one day you did something imperfect. You made a terrible mistake that cost someone their life—and you your reputation. Your shameful responsibility for the demise of someone who had placed their trust in you has manifested itself in an intense guilt yielding the type of personality that overanalyzes every move and seeks internal and external perfection to the point that it is immobilizing. Terror of making a mistake, no matter how small, keeps you and your generation in procrastination and caution. The guilt also creates a strong need to do service, but you don't derive any satisfaction from it unless you perform it flawlessly.

Pluto in Libra

Members of the Pluto in Libra generation share past life memories of being codependent in relationships, a tendency that has weakened you and led to your indecisiveness and ambivalence. Because of your inability to articulate your needs, you constantly find yourself in situations that seem unfair to you. Your cloying ways undermine your quest for independence, yet at the same time satisfy your perverse need to climb the social ladder. Socially adept to the point of being phony, you are currently very sensitive to situations and people that appear disingenuous or dishonest.

Guilty about your own relational superficiality, you are intensely absorbed with justice and honesty in all your human relationships. You and other members of this generation often created your parents to be divorced, which allowed you to view the destruction of marriage firsthand. Your task is to transform relationships so they will endure through fairness, equality, cooperation, and balance.

Pluto in Scorpio

At this writing, the Pluto in Scorpio generation are young adults, several of whom I am seeing in my practice. From what I have observed so far, they share past life memories of intensity and chaos, fueled by a tendency toward extremes. These extremes can create a paralysis in making choices, afraid they will make a mistake. Deeply paranoid, they are secretive about their innermost feelings and have difficulty trusting. They have memories of being totally in control and are relentless in their approach to getting what they want but vindictive if thwarted. They passionately love mystery, especially pertaining to sexuality and death. Their guilt feelings over their anger and fear will fuel their quest to play a major role as transformational healers. They will help others understand and transform themselves in the areas of emotions, sexuality, and fear of death.

They will relentlessly strive to alter the power structure. Because of their past-life guilt about sexual misuse, they will learn to honor sex. Because of their past-life paranoia, they will hone their insights into human nature and help the healing process by probing and investigating the human condition. Because of their preoccupation with death, they might even overcome their fear of it. Because of their guilt over controlling others in other lives, they will learn the true meaning of controlling their own lives and creating their destiny. This generation knows exactly what it wants and will do whatever it can to get it.

Pluto in Sagittarius

Members of this generation are from 7-20 years old; I have worked with many of these children since they were very young. I know they are the incarnation of many philosophers, scientists and religious leaders, primarily those that lived during the Renaissance. They were alive during the major split between the Church and the Illuminati. I believe their path to significance is to heal that old wound and integrate religion and science.

They share past lives of total freedom and adventure, symbolized by the archetype of the cowboy wandering the Old West in happy solitude and on his only reliable friend, his horse. They will value nature, space, and their own thoughts. They will not be interested in committed relationships, although they like experiencing other people. They will wander into a relationship, have a brief affair, and move on, unencumbered. They may have claustrophobia in big cities, and they may be restless when not on the move. They will probably be brutally honest and outspoken, possessing little diplomacy. They know when they are being lied to and find it demeaning when others try to protect them by lying.

They will learn how to thrive in society and still appreciate nature. They will transform their need for physical space and freedom into a need for spiritual regeneration and freedom of thought. They will learn to share their thoughts by teaching and inspiring others. This generation is thrilling to watch as they grow into their awesome potential.

Pluto in Capricorn

As of this writing members of this generation are under 7 years old. They share past lives of power, financial success and authority in the government, the church and in business. They were in positions of power over many people. They were seen as the good father that held their children's very lives in their hands. They were traditional, structured and rigid in their approach to ruling. They were wise at their best and pedantic and dictatorial at their worst. They controlled everything around them. In this life they were born older than their years and definitely feel like old souls. They are angry because they remember lives in which they were completely dominant and resent that they do not possess that same dominance now. They probably bring in very old, historic beliefs that will be different from their parents and other authority figures. These attitudes need to be transformed into a more benevolent and compassionate view of their world.

They can become wonderful, wise leaders who wish to give others a hand. Some may be very irresponsible in their youth as a reaction to lifetimes where they were obsessed with responsibility. Organized religions were their only connection to an external God so they believed all external authority figures were an outside force that shaped their daily lives. There was a time when they unquestioningly accepted the beliefs of their families and lived their lives in their shadows. They may believe in hierarchical systems that provide security and stability. They may have lived many lives when the corporate bottom line was more important than the needs of individuals. There was a time when security was measured by their health insurance, their retirement plans and their financial bottom-lines. Pluto will teach them to be more self-contained and self-empowered to become truly successful.

Capricorn honors self-reliance, and Pluto wants this group of individuals to use all of their resources. Success occurs when they fully engage in life with strength, courage and commitment. They will live as adults in the Aquarian Age where equality, humanism and grass roots movements will be the name of the game. Their conservative traditions will no longer serve them as they move into their Aquarian adulthood. They will need to transform concrete standards and structures to create new, practical and wise rules for the new age.

Pluto in Aquarius

This is the generation of the future. They will not begin to be born until 2023. They will be the leaders of the Age of Aquarius. Much that I have written about the Age of Aquarius pertains to this group. I believe they were a part of the creation of the United States, actually helping in crafting the Constitution and the Bill of Rights. They know what freedom for the individual really means. They will transform old-boy networks, big business, and big government. They will fight to honor "a government of the people, by the people and for the people." They are citizens of the world, wanting peace and harmony for that world. Their karmic understanding of technology will bring about an opportunity for people to vote from their homes. No longer would a candidate need millions of dollars and special interest groups to be elected. They will be elected by the people using their computers. Big government will be a thing of the past. Hierarchical systems will be destroyed. Committees are formed to deal with the needs of the people. Their inherent love of freedom and independence will create a world not hampered by old-world beliefs. Their spiritual triangle of understanding the mind, body and spirit will instill God's power within the individual.

GUILT AND FORGIVENESS

Religion preaches the importance of our being forgiven by God. We go to our respective houses of worship to pray for that forgiveness. We ask our spiritual leaders to forgive us and are significantly buoyed when they do.

We confess our sins and take our penances with faith, in hope that we will be freed from our guilty impulses. We open our mind, heart, and spirit to God's forgiveness. It is a receptive process: we are the recipients of that holy forgiveness.

After being forgiven, we feel cleansed, revitalized—as if a weight has been lifted off our chests. In the Lord's Prayer, Christ asked us to pray to forgive others who "trespass against us, as we are forgiven by God for our sins." Asking to be forgiven and forgiving others liberates us from the weighty throes of guilt. Both are equally important. If we are unable to forgive, we are holding back and continuing to feel guilty because we haven't been living "in forgiveness."

I believe it's easier to ask for forgiveness than to grant it. To ask for forgiveness requires acknowledging your guilt or shame. Moreover, waiting for acceptance of your bid can be wrenching. However, the most challenging aspect of the forgiveness process is forgiving someone else who either denies that they did anything to hurt you in the first place, or who shows no remorse for their action. Taking the first step and forgiving that person—before they've sought your forgiveness—is an emotional risk. Still, just because they aren't contrite—or deny they transgressed at all— doesn't mean you should abandon your gift of forgiving and the liberating qualities it can have. By forgiving, your soul is making peace with that person and the hurtful experience they conjured, regardless of whether they agree to be willing participants. But if you refuse to forgive someone based on their attitude, you are ceding your power—to heal and to move on and live a healthy and productive life—to them.

Living in forgiveness gives us a sense of completion and resolution. When we're not living in forgiveness, we tend to hold on to our grief and sadness, which can later manifest themselves as depression. Probably three hundred people in my practice over the years have written letters to those dearest to them—some alive, some long departed—asking for forgiveness.

Often they shed tears of relief when they burned their letters, thereby sending their poignant messages out to the respective souls for whom they were intended.

One of my clients, Claire, wrote a letter of forgiveness to her father, who had been dead for more than twenty years. She burned it in my office in a brass pot. As it was turning to ash, she broke out into contagious, unbridled laughter. Her father had always made her laugh. In this moment she had remembered a funny story he used to tell her. Since she had been angry at her father for so long, she had forgotten his humorous side. She wrote her letter to ask him to forgive her for being so selfish and angry. She had not visited him in the hospital when he was dying and had not said good-bye to him. She had been furious that he was dying at the age of 40. She was only 15. When she remembered the funny story and laughed, she knew he had heard her and forgiven her. She felt renewed and giddy, free from the nagging pain of guilt and incompletion. She had a clean slate and was on her way to healing that place in her heart that had been so wounded.

This exercise will help you learn more about sourcing your own personal guilt via Pluto. Part of the process of letting go of guilt is to be able to elicit forgiveness, as well as to give it.

Pluto Exercise

1. My Pluto is in the sign of: _____ (refer to the "Pluto Placements" chart).

2. Words for that sign from the Soul Pattern Energetics Model (Chart 2 in Chapter 4) that bother me are:

    Remember that for this exercise the words that create the deepest emotional reaction in you are the vital ones. They are most likely to symbolize situations in which you did something that you might be ashamed of, things you'd consider "bad" or "wrong."

For example, if your Pluto is in the sign of Leo, you might use the following words from the Energetics Model: *melodramatic, self-centered, disdainful, autocratic, dictating,* and *needs attention.*

3. Using these words, write a story about yourself living the kind of life you could have had where guilt conceivably could have surfaced. Each word from the Energetics Model can symbolize a lifestyle, a career, an interaction with others, a relationship—a total mode and philosophy of living during a particular time in history. Use your imagination to figure out what you might feel guilty about. Relax and allow your imagination to flow. Have fun with the story and see what happens.

Again supposing your Pluto is in Leo, here's how a story might unfold:

The source of my guilt comes from a life where I was in a position *to* dominate *others. I was probably a ruler of some kind with many servants. I believed that my power was all that mattered, so I was* disdainful *and* autocratic. *I was* self-centered *and* needed attention. *When I did not get what I wanted, I could be* melodramatic.

4. Having considered the kind of life you could have had, the source of your guilt may be:

Exercise: Eliminating Guilt

Here is how you can deal with an experience that has taken place in another time, in another place, and through another personality.

Step 1: Become conscious. You cannot confront something if you don't know what it is.

Step 2: Take responsibility for the behavior you feel guilty about. Nothing will change if you blame someone else for your own behavior.

Step 3: Forgive yourself by asking someone for forgiveness. Let's explore Step 3. How do you ask for forgiveness from a person who is from your past? You may not even know who that person is. Review the story you wrote in the Pluto Exercise. Meditate on that life; think of one person who could embody all the people you might have hurt in that life. Now make that image more real: give it a sex, a name, a physical identity, and a personality. Now create a situation between both of you that would necessitate an apology from you. The following Forgiveness Exercise will help you do your own.

Forgiveness Exercise

1. I karmically wish to be forgiven for (refer to the Pluto Exercise, Step 3):

   Example: I wish to be forgiven for using my position of power to dominate others. In my arrogance, I disregarded people who served me well. I was autocratic and did not listen to anyone. I am so sorry that I did not understand the depth of my self-absorption and self-centeredness. It makes me ashamed that I expected and required people to bow before me and surrender their dignity for my need for constant adoration. I wish to be forgiven for my childish use of power.

2. Someone in that past life whom I need to ask to forgive me is:

   Example: I had many servants whom were loyal and trustworthy and truly cared about me. One young woman symbolizes them all. She was only 16 when she was pressed into service as one of my concubines. I ignored her unless I wanted her favors. She loved me, but I held her in contempt. I would ask her to forgive me.

3. Someone in this life whom I need to forgive is:

   Example: I need to forgive my father for being arrogant and self-absorbed. He was, in fact, showing me pieces of myself that I needed to see. I not only forgive him for his behavior, I thank him for helping me see a part of my past.

4. Someone in this life whom I need to ask to forgive me is:
    Example: I need to ask my older child to forgive me for being so self-involved. I had wanted his unconditional approval and would get angry when I felt he was being critical of me.

Once you have identified someone whose forgiveness you need, write that person a letter.

Exercise: Forgiveness Letter

Dear Someone,

It has taken me many lifetimes to write this letter. For much of that time I have felt very guilty for the way that I treated you then. I just did not know how to talk to you. I now know how poorly I treated you. I disregarded you as a human being. I accepted your love as my divine right and forgot that you might have needed something in return. I want you to know that I am so very sorry for what I did. I want you to know that I have changed and that the guilt I have felt over you has produced that change. Will you forgive me?

Love,

Exercise: Freedom from Guilt

The following steps will help you learn to live without guilt.

- **Pay attention to your feelings, especially the feeling of shame.** Dealing with shame means rectifying whatever led to the feeling in the first place, in order to take responsibility for it and put it behind you. Get past your embarrassment and say, "I'm sorry." Some people will say they're sorry about everything under the sun, except when they've done something truly hurtful—then they say nothing or project the blame onto someone else. Remember, shame that is not resolved sooner or later turns into guilt. To live guilt-free, we must resolve the shame.

- **Understand that you no longer need guilt to keep you on a moral road, to keep you from noxious behavior.** We are capable of being good people without the specter of a negative taskmaster shaking its long, bony finger at us. We are moving into the Age of Aquarius, when guilt will be totally inappropriate.
- Love and honor yourself enough to be excited about filling the void once occupied by guilt—no matter how frightening that prospect may be.

CHAPTER 11

NEPTUNE: ILLUSION VERSUS ASPIRATION

O ver the years scores of my clients have insisted on maintaining illusions that are nonetheless destined to make them unhappy. They tell me, "If only I had more money, I'd be happier," or "If I got married, then things would be better." By perpetuating such illusions, they unwittingly set themselves up to fail.

When we feel guilty about something we've done or failed to do in the past, we foster a belief that we don't deserve to get what we want. As an unhealthy response to our guilt, we create the illusion that the thing we want is unobtainable. As unconscious belief systems, illusions are often totally irrelevant to authentic happiness. They represent our desire to accomplish or obtain something in order to rid ourselves of a specific guilt, even though we may frame the purpose as "to be happy."

All of us, to varying degrees, foster and perpetuate illusions. These illusions give rise to anxious yearnings that we feel we must satisfy in order to be happy. We live with the misguided and inexplicable feeling that only through this one thing will life be fulfilling. Our sadness comes with the realization that we can't seem to satisfy this nebulous and insatiable desire—it always exists beyond us. When I first began studying illusion, I was confounded by people's obsessions with things that lie just beyond their grasp. But once I understood that these illusions or unfulfilled dreams are created from old beliefs of inadequacy, guilt, and self-loathing, they made perfect sense.

ILLUSIONS VERSUS ASPIRATIONS

Unlike illusions, however, hopes and aspirations are not by-products of guilt. As our conscious creations, they can indeed be fulfilled. If our illusions are what we wallow in, our aspirations and goals are what we seek to attain.

Illusion	Hope/Aspiration
Unconscious	Conscious
A pensive longing	Something we strive for
Set up to fail	Plan to succeed
Wallow	Work
A disappointment	A goal

Illusions and aspirations are sometimes difficult to distinguish. We can make an aspiration or hope come true. We can set a goal or objective, then take action to accomplish it. Let's say as a child you always aspired to be a doctor; you took that dream seriously, prepared for it through years of study, and made it happen. Conversely, an illusion is a dream that does not come true, is rife with regret, and is fraught with shadowy "should haves" and "what ifs."

Let's say that when you were a child, your father told you he wanted you to become a doctor. You felt you should be a doctor, and you perpetuated a myth that you wouldn't be happy unless you practiced medicine. Yet you did nothing to prepare for it. You eventually became a college professor, but your existence is plagued by the gnawing illusion that you have "failed," that you are inadequate because you didn't fulfill your father's expectation. You cultivated your own illusion by internalizing your father's dream, in the belief that being a doctor would make him happy and garner his approval. Despite the rewarding aspects of your job and your high professional standing, you continue to feel unsatisfied and vaguely discontented. We all would feel better about who we are and what we do if we could identify the illusions that torment us, confront what they represent, and resolve them.

REALIZING OUR ILLUSIONS THROUGH NEPTUNE

A powerful and effective way to bring our illusions to consciousness is to understand the influence of the planet Neptune. Neptune is the planet that ruled the Piscean Age. Everything we have said about Pisces is true of Neptune: It is mystical, psychic, a healer, devotional, inspirational, idealistic, compassionate, empathetic, and creative. It is the energy that best symbolizes Christ. Its challenging aspects include escapism, addiction, self-indulgence, self-deception, delusion, irresponsibility, being noncommittal, and martyrdom. Neptune gives us information about Soul Patterns that keep us mired in self-deception, allowing our illusions to thrive. It sheds light on skewed belief systems and unrealistic standards that can cause serious disappointments.

Neptune also supplies us with information about how we can redeem ourselves for past life mistakes. At its best, it shows us how to become one with the universe, experience our greatest joy through spiritual awakening, and transform our illusions into spiritual experiences. It symbolizes how we can realize our ideals with great love, compassion, and vitality. Neptune urges us to move from the limitations of our personality into our spiritual selves.

Aligning ourselves with the highest energetic manifestation of Neptune gives us the spiritual faith and energy to achieve our Soul Potential. This planet exposes us to the joys and the freedom of living in our soul's experience, of gravitating toward our soul mission. It helps us realize and manifest our most poignant ideals. It pushes us to uncover our illusions and discover the truth. It helps us realize our creativity. Neptune shows us that being at one with our spirit is our most joyful experience. Knowing your Neptune placement will provide you with answers to the following spiritual questions:

- How do you create a vision that will help you connect to the universal order?
- What are your true ideals, and how do you manifest them?
- How do you live in forgiveness and be compassionate with yourself and others?
- How do you change your beliefs so that you do not always live in failed expectation and disappointment?

On a much larger scale, each generation has an illusion or belief system that constitutes a retribution for a previous life experience. You can locate your Neptune in the following chart.

Neptune Placements

If you were born in:	Your Neptune is	If you were born in:	Your Neptune is
Jan. 1, 1915–July 19, 1915	Cancer	Sept. 22, 1928–Feb. 19, 1929	Virgo
July 20, 1915–Mar. 19, 1916	Leo	Feb. 20, 1929–July 24, 1929	Leo
Mar. 20, 1916–May 1, 1916	Cancer	July 25, 1929–Oct. 3, 1942	Virgo
May 2, 1916–Sept. 21, 1928	Leo	Oct. 4, 1942–April 17, 1943	Libra

If you were born in:	Your Neptune is	If you were born in:	Your Neptune is
April 18, 1943–Aug. 2, 1943	Virgo	Nov. 22, 1984–Jan. 27, 1998	Capricorn
Aug. 3, 1943–Oct. 19, 1956	Libra	Jan. 28, 1998–April 4, 2011	Aquarius
Oct. 20, 1956–June 16, 1957	Scorpio	April 5, 2011–August 5, 2011	Pisces
June 17, 1957–Aug. 6, 1957	Libra	August 6–February 4, 2012	Aquarius
Aug. 7, 1957–Nov. 6, 1970	Scorpio	February 5, 2012–March 31, 2025	Pisces
Nov. 7, 1970–Jan. 18, 1984	Sagittarius	April 1, 2025–October 23, 2025	Aries
Jan. 19, 1984–June 22, 1984	Capricorn	October 24, 2025-January 27, 2026	Pisces
June 23, 1984–Nov. 21, 1984	Sagittarius	Jan. 28, 2026–May 22, 2038	Aries

Here is a brief description of your generational illusions:

- **Neptune in Cancer**: Only when my family loves and needs me will I be happy.

- **Neptune in Leo**: Only when I am honored, loved, and respected will I be happy.

- **Neptune in Virgo**: Only when I am perfect in the service I provide will I be happy.

- **Neptune in Libra**: Only when I am in a relationship of harmony, fairness, and balance will I be happy.

- **Neptune in Scorpio**: Only when I have power and control over myself and others will I be happy.

- **Neptune in Sagittarius**: Only when I have total freedom and space to think about what I want will I be happy.

- **Neptune in Capricorn**: Only when I have obtained wealth and success will I be happy.

- **Neptune in Aquarius**: Only when I can live by my own rules and manifest my own individuality will I be happy.

- **Neptune in Pisces**: Only when I am suffering and giving to others will I be happy.

- **Neptune in Aries**: Only when I am independent, assertive and self-expressed will I be happy.

The problem with all of these belief systems is that they are impossible to fulfill. People in the various generations never have enough love, money, success, power, or harmony to be content. At some point in our past, we set up our illusions so they will never be attained, punishing ourselves and creating a lifetime of disappointment.

THE OTHER SIDE OF THE RUBBER BAND

Picture your Pluto placement—which represents guilt—at one end of a rubber band. Your Neptune placement—your illusions—is stretching the rubber band at the other end. This image shows their relationships well. Pluto is about the source of our guilt, while Neptune is about manifesting it as illusion. Our residual guilt keeps us from creating dreams that actually come true. We feel bad about ourselves, so we create failures, resulting in further unhappiness. Our old guilt, rotting within us, sets in place a vicious and self-perpetuating cycle of illusion, ensuring that we will never have the life we want.

Taking control of and ultimately reversing this discouraging trend is a two-step process. The first step is to discover what our illusions are. Many of them are so deeply imbedded in our unconscious and so intertwined among our old belief systems that we have no idea they exist. Consciously, we realize that these illusions do not come true, cultivating an aching ambivalence. The second step is to reframe our illusions into aspirations that really can come true. Let's examine how this process played itself out with one of my clients.

Lucy harbored the illusion that unless she had a loving and romantic relationship that was "perfect," she would be inadequate. But neither of her two failed marriages nor her many relationships were what she would call perfect. She wished they had been; in fact, she had needed them to be perfect. But none of her affairs of the heart were loving enough and certainly not romantic enough to meet her lofty and virtually unattainable criteria for perfection.

Thus at the age of 45, because she had not yet found the "perfect" relationship, Lucy continued to foster a feeling of worthlessness. The cycle became self-perpetuating because the more inadequate she felt, the less likely she was to create a healthy, meaningful relationship. This illusion had kept her from exploring many potentially significant relationships because she anticipated that they wouldn't meet her demanding criteria. Her illusion also kept her from discovering the most important relationship of all: the one with herself.

In order to help Lucy deal with her illusion, we first had to discover its source. What guilt had driven her to feel that she couldn't be happy without a man in her life? On the other end of the rubber band, opposite Neptune, is Pluto, the issues related to guilt. Lucy's Pluto is in Leo, which is based on being self-absorbed and focused on oneself, so she learned that she had some past guilt about being too selfish or self-involved. This guilt activated the dynamic Neptune process, fostering the illusion that the only way to overcome that guilt was through having a relationship; without it she considered herself worthless—a common illusion for those with Neptune in Libra. Lucy's illusion was thus a reaction to the guilt produced by an old karmic experience.

Uncovering your illusions by understanding your Neptune placement gives you another opportunity to understand Pluto and therefore issues from the past that need to be resolved. Once Lucy understood this principle, she could deal with her Pluto issues of guilt without creating severe illusions that could have kept her discontented for the rest of her life. As an extreme reaction to old guilt, an illusion is seductive, usually unconscious, and difficult to discern, because it's something we think we need to be happy. Although we may perceive it as a path to happiness, an illusion insidiously creates disappointment.

The next exercise will help you uncover your illusions. Concentrate first on your illusions sourced from your parents, since they represent circle-one soul contracts. You chose your parents to show you your unconscious illusions, based on karmic guilt left over from past life experiences. Observing and analyzing their illusions is a lot easier than consciously analyzing your own, and it allows you to uncover the illusions they've perpetuated within you. Each part of the exercise has a sample answer to give you an idea of how to respond.

Illusion Exercise

1. When I chose my mother, I chose the following illusions (illusions that your mother perpetuated within you):

Examples:

- Peace and harmony are the most important personal values.
- Protect the sanctity of the family at all costs.
- Showing anger is not socially acceptable.
- Being pretty, charming, and pleasant will get you a man who will take care of you.
- When in doubt, don't!
- Take care of others before yourself, and you will be rewarded.
- It is a woman's job to hold on to her man.
- Security comes from being married.

2. When I chose my father, I chose the following illusions (illusions that your father perpetuated within you):

Examples:

- If you don't have anything nice to say, say nothing.
- A man's job is to support his woman.
- Be ladylike, and people will like you.
- Taking risks is dangerous.
- When you're upset, drink. You'll feel better.

- Men don't like assertive women.
- Don't rock the boat, and you'll get along.

3. What hope/aspiration do I have that I've not yet realized? *Example*: I have always hoped that one day I would not have to work so hard, that a man would come into my life and support me, so that I wouldn't have to work if I didn't choose to. We would live happily ever after, travel extensively, and life would be safe, comfortable, and secure.

4. Which of my parent-based illusions supports this dream? *Examples*:
- A man's job is to support his woman. (father)
- Being pretty, charming, and pleasant will get you a man who will take care of you. (mother)
- Security comes from being married. (mother)

5. What previous experience or belief system and resultant feeling of guilt caused me to create this present-life illusion? (Analyze each illusion using this rule. Remember the rubber band theory: illusion as a by-product of guilt.) The following are examples of possible scenarios to answer Step 5:

    Past Experience: *One's personal value is measured by the ability to get what one wants. Aggression and war bring power and strength.*

    Associated Guilt: *Guilt at being selfish and self-absorbed, at being warlike and aggressive, at taking what I wanted from others without remorse, and in fact being proud of my ability to do it.*

    Present-Life Illusion: Peace and harmony are the most important personal values.

    Past Experience: *Family cohesiveness is not important. Individual wants and desires outweigh those of family.*

Associated Guilt: *Guilt at disregarding people who loved and nurtured me, at not honoring and valuing family relationships.*

Present-Life Illusion: Protect the sanctity of the family at all costs.

Past Experience: *Expressing anger causes others to cower and makes me intimidating.*

Associated Guilt: *Guilt at making others afraid, at being abusive and combative with no concern about how it makes them feel.*

Present-Life Illusion: Showing anger is not socially acceptable.

Past Experience: *Being commanding and dominating will get me anyone I want. I am totally independent and need no one to take care of me.*

Associated Guilt: *Guilt at hurting people who cared about me, at not being able to love, at dominating those who were weaker than myself.*

Present-Life Illusion: Being pretty, charming, and pleasant will yield a man who will take care of you.

Past Experience: *Security comes from my personal power and my ability to control others. Relationships have no meaning other than to provide me pleasure.*

Associated Guilt: *Guilt at not valuing and understanding the importance of relationships. Guilt, once again, at my selfishness.*

Present-Life Illusion: Security comes from being married.

THE TRICKSTER

One of our greatest illusions is sourced by the Trickster, another voice of Neptune. I call it the henchman of Chiron. Chiron symbolizes our lifetimes of victimization, fear and suffering. It is our emotional, cautionary tale of how excellence has destroyed us in the past (please refer to "Chapter 12: Chiron: In Quest of Real Change") The trickster hears Chiron's call and tells us what Chiron want us to hear. It speaks to us about how inadequate we are, how small we are, how stupid we are, how little we really know and how we can never be successful. We believe it because this voice is often projected onto other people of authority. Our parents and teachers often tell us the same things.

The trickster is the part of us that lies. Why? To keep us safe from the remembered harm that destroyed us. Its job is to keep us safe by stopping us from being excellent, successful and exceptional; these are the same qualities that betrayed us in the first place. The Neptune illusion is based on the idea that what has happened to us before will, in fact, happen again. This is the epitome of contaminated feelings driving our lives without any bases in reality. Whatever sign your Neptune is in will tell you more about the voice. The more we know about the voice and the more conscious we are, the more we will be able to confront and silence it. One exercise I give my clients and students is to write down all conversations that you have heard either from your inner voice or others about how incapable you are. You will know the voice by its critical, judgmental and condescending tone. Having the conversations written down will remind you of who is talking to you when he returns. At this phase after he has been recognized and named, you will be able to challenge and fight him. I have used every weapon I can think of to destroy him. I have succeeded for the most part to silence it. The following will give you a few possible examples of Trickster conversations that may have tormented you over the years. It is important that you add to this list, using your particular Neptune placement, as you get more familiar with the voice of the Trickster. This will help you recognize it as an illusion when it arises and empower you to defeat it.

The Trickster in the Astrological Signs

ARIES NEPTUNE TRICKSTER: "You can't take any actions. Being assertive has caused you pain. Being angry will get you in trouble. Never be self-centered; it will cause others to betray you."

TAURUS NEPTUNE TRICKSTER: "Don't you dare become too successful. Having money and security will be taken away. The rug will be pulled out from under you if you become too peaceful and serene."

GEMINI NEPTUNE TRICKSTER: "Be careful what you write down. Others would be ready to accuse you of lying or stealing others' work. Don't express your ideas for it could cause someone to betray you."

CANCER NEPTUNE TRICKSTER: "Don't get too attached to others; they will abandon you. You cannot be too emotional. It could betray you. Watch out when you feel too sensitive. Create a shell that will protect you."

LEO NEPTUNE TRICKSTER: "Being too visible will destroy you; remember, you have been assassinated. People betrayed you when you were a leader with confidence and pride. Don't be too full of yourself."

VIRGO NEPTUNE TRICKSTER: "You are not a perfect person. You are inadequate. You make mistakes so don't you dare try to help anyone. You cannot serve humanity so you cannot be a healer. You are not smart enough."

LIBRA NEPTUNE TRICKSTER: "You are not attractive enough. No one will ever want you. Don't voice your opinion; it will hurt others and they will harm you."

SCORPIO NEPTUNE TRICKSTER: "Be careful with your feelings. You cannot trust anyone. You will never get what you want, so why try? There is no controlling anything so everything is chaos."

SAGITTARIUS NEPTUNE TRICKSTER: "Don't live in the country, and please never ride a horse. Never speak what you believe is true. Being too honest has hurt you. You will never be free."

CAPRICORN NEPTUNE TRICKSTER: "Climbing your personal mountain of success will lead to people's disrespecting, humiliating and ultimately destroying you. You will not make the kind of money you want. Authority figures cannot be trusted."

AQUARIUS NEPTUNE TRICKSTER: "Don't be too different. Being unique and out of the box will cause your tribe to abandon you. Any group will be a problem. Don't trust your friends; they will betray you."

PISCES NEPTUNE TRICKSTER: "Being too emotionally sensitive will never work. You will never feel forgiven. Your creativity is not good enough. You cannot trust your faith."

NEPTUNE IN THE ASTROLOGICAL SIGNS

What follows is a brief description of Neptune in the different signs, replete with the illusions that need to be understood. Chances are you are perpetuating some of the illusions listed under your Neptune sign.

Neptune in Cancer

You become one with the universe by being sensitive to the emotional needs of yourself and your family. Family is a broad concept encompassing all that you love. You nurture everyone who is close and wishes to be needed. You are capable of extraordinary acts of devotion and sympathetic support. You redeem yourself by your preoccupation with home, family, culture, and country at the expense of your own needs and desires. But your protection of others may be smothering and disabling. You deceive yourself by staying steadfastly with the traditions of past cultures and memories, unable to relinquish them for a more productive and freer present and future. At your most illusionary, you believe you must manifest extreme acts of sacrifice in the spirit of martyrdom to be accepted as emotionally understanding. Your illusions that need to be understood:

- I must be devoted to my family to be redeemed.
- I must always be supportive of my children.
- I must be there for those who need me, or I will die.
- I must value the traditions of the past to be happy.
- I must never be disloyal to friends and family.
- I must be sensitive to others' feelings over my own.

Neptune in Leo

You become one with the universe through inspired, courageous leadership, especially connecting to the joyful, creative, spiritual child. You share ideals of self-love and honor, drama, fun, and spontaneity, and you inspire these traits in others through your role modeling. You redeem yourself by putting aside your need for constant visibility, approval, and self-indulgence. You are probably status conscious and desperately need everyone to love you. You deceive yourself by being arrogant and overly dominating. You suffer the most when not being honored or respected. Your illusions that need to be understood:

- I must be a powerful, inspiring leader to be redeemed.
- I must be respected by everyone.
- I must never lose my youthful appearance.
- I must have everyone's approval to be happy.
- I must maintain a proud, commanding presence at all times.
- I must constantly prove that I am secure and confident, or I will die.

Neptune in Virgo

You become one with the universe and spiritually, physically, and mentally healthy by serving others. You share ideals of purity, efficiency, discrimination, and organization. You are a practical healer. You redeem yourself by helping others to create the personal structure and organization that will produce the greatest results on all levels, especially in the area of physical health. You deceive yourself by feeling you must martyr yourself in service to be perfect enough. You strive to create external perfect order and can be judgmental and critical of others who do not conform to your high expectations. You suffer the most by being judged for not "doing it right." Your illusions that need to be understood:

- I must serve mankind's needs over my own to redeem myself.
- I must strive for perfect order in my life to be happy.
- I must be totally efficient and dependable.
- I must never make a mistake, or I will die.
- I must worry about my health to be healthy.
- I must be perfectly organized to be productive.

Neptune in Libra

You become one with the universe by communicating compassion and sensitivity toward all people. You share ideals of cooperation and have a strong sense of justice and fair play. You are creative in establishing harmony and balance within yourself and for others. You believe in romance but can be codependent and illusionary in relationships. You redeem yourself by caring more for others than for yourself. You deceive yourself by believing that a relationship with another is more important than a relationship with yourself. You suffer the most when others are out of harmony with you. You abhor being the recipient of others' anger. Your illusions that need to be understood:

- I must compromise myself in order to redeem myself.
- I must always be fair.

- I must be pleasing and cooperate with everyone.
- I must maintain harmony at all costs.
- I must not rock the boat.
- I must not be angry at anyone.
- I must have a relationship to be socially appropriate.

Neptune in Scorpio

You become one with the universe by probing the depths of life's mysteries. You strive toward transformation and regeneration, sharing your ideals through a powerful intensity that leads to emotional insight and healing. You redeem yourself by suffering the agonies of your extremist, paranoid, and jealous nature. You deceive yourself by believing you must be in total control of yourself and others. You can be inscrutable, secretive, withholding, and distrustful. In extreme cases, you are obsessed with the darker sides of magic and sexuality. You suffer the most when out of control. Your illusions that need to be understood:

- I must have control, or I will die.
- I must always seek personal transformation.
- I must not express any powerful feelings.
- I must have intense sexual experiences to be happy.
- I must be powerfully insightful with self and others.
- I must suffer in order to redeem myself.

Neptune in Sagittarius

You become one with the universe by exploring truth, spiritual ethics, and the law, and by being an inspired teacher of philosophical thought. You share your ideals of freedom, optimism, and serendipity and teach them. You value education and are constantly in search of more enlightened teaching methods. You redeem yourself by being too expansive and unrealistic. You are overly abstract and Pollyanna-ish, with a tendency toward claustrophobia and a fear of commitment. You deceive yourself by being too pedantic and dogmatic, believing that your truth is the only truth. You can be preachy and extravagant. You are the restless traveler seeking freedom at all costs. You suffer the most when someone else restricts you. Your illusions that need to be understood:

- I must be totally honest with myself and others.
- I must have freedom, or I will die.
- I must always inspire and teach others to be redeemed.
- I must constantly travel to expand my philosophy to be happy.
- I must be more generous with others than with myself.
- I must focus on the future instead of the present.

Neptune in Capricorn

You become one with the universe by seeking practical wisdom and maturity with the responsibility and commitment of the good father. You bring spiritual values into the realm of the realistic and into the daily environment. You share traditional ideals of integrity, self-reliance, and discipline. You redeem yourself by being too cautious, inflexible, and rigid. You can be authoritarian and materialistic. You deceive yourself by being obsessed with rules that can be severe and outmoded. You can be fearful of change, addicted to the old ways of doing things. You suffer the most when your integrity is questioned. Your illusions that need to be understood:

- I must be totally responsible to be redeemed.
- I must always be disciplined and structured.
- I must live by the rules, or I will die.
- I must maintain the traditions of my family and country.

- I must always be realistic and practical to be happy.
- I must be the good father to all who rely on me.

Neptune in Aquarius

You become one with the universe by communicating humanitarian and universal concepts to reestablish a peaceful world order. You represent the holistic triangle of mind, body, and spirit and the symbolic beginning of the Age of Aquarius. You share ideals of individual mastery, rationality, innovation, reformation, and cooperation. You truly believe that one committed individual can make a difference in the world. You redeem yourself by being detached and observing and sometimes by being too impersonal. You deceive yourself by being too logical, remote, and intolerant (especially of others' intolerance). At your most illusionary, you are the erratic rebel who breaks rules just because they exist. You suffer the most when you are unable to understand a situation rationally.

Your illusions that need to be understood:

- I must be the detached observer to be redeemed.
- I must always be logical and rational.
- I must be impersonal to achieve reformation for myself and others.
- I must maintain the ideals of equality at all costs.
- I must always be innovative and an individualist to be happy.
- I must be self-possessed and internal to be strong.

Once you know more about your illusions and the guilt that perpetuates them, you can begin to strive for attainable hopes and aspirations, free from the burden and pain of self-deception.

Neptune in Pisces

You become one with the universe by finding compassion without judgment. You will learn to flow with your emotions, not being controlled by them. Finding compassion and being gentle with yourself is part of the Neptune in Pisces experience. Spiritual practices need to become more disciplined to create needed retreats from the material world. Neptune is at home in the sign of Pisces so it is a powerful conduit for using the power of the unconscious mind to bring you symbolic solutions to daily challenges. The power of dreams and your ability to interpret them is a wonderful opportunity to connect with your Soul's voice. You redeem yourself by understanding the importance of forgiveness. You need to learn that forgiveness is an act of love and freedom for you. You are the most illusionary when you believe others' needs are more important than your needs. You believe you must suffer because you believe it is your way to emulate the Christ.

Your illusions that need to be understood:

- I believe I need to sacrifice my needs to be redeemed.
- I must be humble and compassionate to be morally correct.
- I must emulate the Christ and be a martyr and a victim.
- I must be perfect to be okay.
- I am sinful and filled with guilt.
- I believe that God exists outside of us.
- I am basically inadequate and child-like and need an external God to guide me.
- I desire the spiritual plane so I renounce earthly pleasures.
- I believe Heaven (good) and Hell (evil) are the only choices of our earthly experience.
- I want love to conquer all, so we must never be self-centered I will suffer enough so I can be redeemed and forgiven.

Neptune in Aries

You become one with the universe by creating new beginnings and finding new spiritual ideas and philosophies. You belong to a generation of spiritual warriors. Since Aries is a sign of action, you will revolutionize whatever old Neptune in Pisces beliefs that persist in the transition to the Age of Aquarius. Caring about others' needs before your own would be one of those antiquated beliefs that you will alter. Your independent nature will want to change any old, dogmatic religious attitudes that you intuit will not work for you. One of your illusions is not caring if few share your ideals because you are an individual who cares only for your views. Your illusions might cause you to be impulsive and reckless. Your illusions might cause you to be easily bored. Finishing a project might not happen if new worlds to explore show up and seduce you to change directions. You will be redeemed if you transmute Aries to its most spiritual warrior aspect. When you are a leader whose actions inspire humanity to honor its highest ideals, you will be forgiven for any old, aggressive, and self-centered behaviors you might have displayed. When you care about others as much as you care about yourself, you are being a spiritual Aries. You will find personal crusades that you believe will be a rebirth of a spiritual philosophy that could alter the course of humanity.

Your illusions that need to be understood:

- You are independent and do not need others.
- Your needs take precedence over others.
- You know what spiritual values are important for everyone.
- You do not need to finish projects you have started.
- Actions are more important than thoughts.
- Going to war is the best solution for societal problems.
- Changing people's minds or changing the world occurs simply by taking action.
- Altering things should not take very long.

CHAPTER 12

CHIRON: IN QUEST
OF REAL CHANGE

Many years ago, after publishing *Discovering Your Soul Mission*, I began questioning my strategies in helping my clients as I saw that many of them remained reluctant to making the changes necessary to have more congruent, balanced and happy lives. I was tired of talking about the changes they needed to make. I wanted to help them create actions that would lead them to real and enduring change. My mission for 40 years has been to inspire my clients and students to make the changes they needed to live the life they would love. I have taught them how emotions must be understood and altered to grow and change. I have encouraged them to embrace their Soul's energy in order to become more integrated on a mind, body and spirit level.

I have coached my clients to discriminate the differences between natural and contaminated feelings. I have taught that natural feelings were responses to real life situations. For example, you have a flat tire in the middle of the night in a dangerous part of a big city and three young men approach you with tire irons. My guess is that you will be scared. You have read the papers, watched television and seen horrible crimes being committed in that part of town. Yet, when they arrive they volunteer to help you change the tire. At that moment you cease to be afraid. They are not going to hurt you. Your feelings as they were approaching you were contaminated based on previous knowledge and experience. The reality was very different than your feelings indicated. We all have preconceived notions that give rise to emotional states that interfere with our lives. Many of these feelings come from past lives and so are absolutely contaminated.

I have observed many clients having immense emotional reactions to what other people might perceive as small life challenges. When I have suggested that these feelings are contaminated and are not, therefore, realistic responses to their current life, they have gotten angry at me for not honoring their emotions. Now it was my turn to feel their fear and frustration. It happened after my book, *Discovering Your Soul Mission*, was published. It should have been the happiest day of my life. Instead I felt the deepest fear that I had ever experienced. For three weeks I was overwhelmed and paralyzed by fear. I was haunted by horrific imaginings of people's possible responses to the book. People would hate, judge, scorn and humiliate me. I was not safe and everyone I loved would be at risk. Now I could feel what my people had shared with me about their fear and frustration. Now the shoe was on the other foot. I was in a conflict. I really wanted the book to be successful, and yet I was terrified to make that happen.

My coauthor, Evan St. Lifer, and I had worked on *Discovering Your Soul Mission* for years, mostly at night after work, from 10 PM to 12 AM. We were determined that the book would be excellent all around:

easy to read for the novice and informational for the advanced reader. Now I was afraid to promote the book. So many hours and so many dreams could disappear because of my unnamed fear. I was in conflict and my emotions were winning. I believed, as David Spangler wrote in *Revelation*, that emotion would interfere with and precede any thought. I knew that I was in trouble. My fear could undermine the success of our book.

I LEARN ABOUT CHIRON

On December 31, 1998, one month after my book was published I received an email from someone who had read the book and was wondering why Chiron was not included. I had to admit to him that I was not familiar with Chiron other than its being an asteroid, and I promised to research it and let him know my opinion. I learned that the mystical Chiron was the centaur (half man, half horse) who was a wounded healer.

> *"There is a Native American prophecy which states that when the planet of healing is discovered in the sky, this is when the sacred warrior teachings will return to the earth."*
> —**Larry Williamson**

Chiron was discovered in 1977 by Charles Kowal. It is a large comet, which orbits between Saturn and Uranus. Astrologically it symbolizes the "Wounded Healer." The mythological Chiron's father was Saturn and his mother was called Philyra. Philyra rejected Chiron because of his appearance and begged the gods to take him away. The gods obliged and took Chiron to their heavenly home where they instructed him in the healing arts. Chiron returned to Earth and became a great healer, astrologer and oracle. He used crystals in healing and was thought to be the teacher of heroes, helping them discover their destiny.

Chiron's pupils came to him to learn the pragmatic way to fulfill their highest destiny. He taught Jason how to undertake his journey to find the Golden Fleece. He taught Asclepios the art of healing and is in myth the father of ancient medicine. So powerful was his influence that today many of the root words of the ancient healing arts incorporate his name. Chirurgery is an ancient Greek word that became the word *surgery*. *Chiron* is the root word of *chiropractics;* chiropractors heal joints and bones by means of manipulation.

In *Chiron 2001* (Part 1), Eric Francis tells us about the asteroid of Chiron:

> *Astronomically, Chiron bears attributes of a comet (harbinger or messenger of change), an asteroid (a seemingly minor influence, though of great importance—yet often ignored), [and] a planet (a recognizable element in the consciousness of many people). Chiron functions as an inner planet, piercing through the realm of Saturn at its closest point to the Sun and an outer planet, going way beyond Saturn, almost to Uranus. He is, in this way, a bridge between the outer planets and the transpersonal planets.*

This last piece led the astrologers involved to settle on the name Chiron. Astrologically, Francis explained:

> *It closes the space between phases of growth, layers of awareness, people, beliefs systems, countries and phases of history. It provides a link between the celestial and earthly orders of consciousness, to the extent these seem to be separate realities from our viewpoint here. Thus, its function is as a healer, since healing is always about closing separation.*

Chiron: The Martyr

The mythological Chiron became a martyr by poisoning himself in the foot using an arrow from the quill of Hercules. He allowed himself to die and go into the underworld so that Prometheus could be released. Chiron was the last of the Centaurs. Chiron symbolizes the area in an astrological chart where we remember being deeply wounded. This covers all sorts of experiences like rejection, abandonment, deprivation, abuse, loss and so on. The wound is karmic and that emotional pain occurs not only in the past but also in our current life. We chose the family, the situations and the soul contracts that bring this pain to the surface. That wound is continued throughout our lives until we finally seek relief and heal.

I believe that Chiron's journey began with the Age of Pisces with 2,000 years of symbols of wounded healers, victims and sacrifice. We have lived for 2,000 years under the cosmic umbrella of Piscean martyrdom, extremism and a child-like need to be taken care of. Up to this point in my life, my experience of Chiron had been an intellectual, mythological investigation. Now I needed much more. I needed to understand the emotional aspect of Chiron.

My Personal Chiron

Over time I learned that the Chiron's astrological sign in our natal chart would give us valuable information about the manner in which we have been the most victimized in the past. This victimization would leave its mark and result in unnamed and visceral fear. I spent years working on uncovering lives where I had been the perpetrator and the villain. The contaminated feelings from those lives were shame and guilt. But this was different; I only felt fear. Now I needed to figure out what I was afraid of and how to resolve it. It was feeling the fear that helped me distinguish my experience as Chironic.

My Chiron in Leo gave me the words and symbols to further understand Chiron's role, and my husband, Michael, was able to help me deepen my understanding by doing many past-life regressions. I uncovered lifetimes of attacks on my heart center—real and symbolic. I was humiliated and tortured and made to witness unimaginable horrors.

I was not a bad person. As a matter of fact, I was probably a powerful, visible person who was too heart-connected to my people. My childlike naiveté and loving nature put me and those that I loved at risk. Fear and shame are two distinctive emotions. Fear comes from being overpowered and victimized, and shame comes from doing something bad to someone else. Clearly I was in a Chiron moment! I began to realize that Chiron is always about the past, and the associated feelings of fear are always contaminated. I did the work. I forgave those that hurt me. I did book talks and book tours. I felt freer than ever.

REAL CHANGE IS OUR BIRTHRIGHT

Real change requires a deep abiding belief that it is not only possible but that it is our birth right. Real change is a conscious resolution of emotional and sensory blocks that occur in the body. The largest block is fear, which does not allow success, only failure. Chiron is the astrological energy that symbolizes our deepest fear. Chiron's energy resides deeply in our body, creating lifetimes of procrastinating and failure, resulting in lack of self-love. Without self-love there is difficulty in loving and trusting others. Disconnection from love keeps us from embracing the divine spark of our Soul. Without that connection we are without divine will. Without divine will there is no real change. The faint of heart cannot find happiness in this time. We need the courage that divine will can provide.

As I continued on my journey of discovery of Chiron, I found that I needed to explore my body to uncover where my karmic poisons were hidden. These poisons take on a life of their own and manifest as deep fear. They become very seductive, believing they are keeping us safe from having experiences that destroyed us over lifetimes. In reality these old karmic poisons are keeping us from facing and resolving the old fears. This is our time if we have the courage to destroy any old beliefs that no longer serve us. This is our time if we personally accept and are responsible for our past history and want to honor and resolve it. If we do not, we will not achieve our Soul's mission. Embracing our Soul's mission requires change— probably the most important change we will ever make--and Chiron does not want us to make that change. We need to resolve this issue to live a spiritually rewarding life. Answer the following questions:

1. Do you experience deep emotional fears without any external reality?
2. Do you have anxiety attacks?
3. Have you had reoccurring nightmares or night terrors?
4. Do you feel alienated from your Soul?
5. Are you afraid of intimacy?
6. Are you afraid of being betrayed or hurt, but without a cause?
7. Do you feel paralyzed by some life events?
8. Do you have a desire that you have always want to manifest, but were afraid to create?

Understanding Chiron will give us the specific karmic information that we need to find the manner in which we have been victimized. This is the first time in history that we have had the consciousness, awareness and courage to complete and resolve those lives. Doing so will allow us to create our lives without old contaminated fear. The Age of Aquarius is the time where we will be able to fully comprehend who we really are— holistic people who know that the kingdom of God is within us, honoring our place on the sacred earth. We are no longer hopeless or helpless; we are certainly not victims, and we no longer need to sacrifice ourselves to be in sacred service.

Understanding Chiron changed my life. I now feel more integrated and complete, I am not afraid, and my heart is more open than ever. Without fear I am looking more to my Soul and its infinite blessings. I use its divine will and courage every day. I feel free for the first time in my life. My fear had created a disconnection from love that had kept me from embracing the divine spark of my Soul; now I am ready to transcend to the highest level of my Chiron. I sent my reader a profound thank you for asking me why Chiron was not discussed in my original book!

I have often said that the planet Saturn is the conductor of the train to our north node destination. I think that Chiron provides that conductor the karmic memories, skills and fortitude to turn on the train. Imagine the greatness, power, success, and competence that people envied to such a degree that they betrayed us. Imagine being able to use these energies again to help yourselves and others. Well, we can—this is Chiron's role in your spiritual achievement. The more we understand the energy of our Chiron, the more we can transform the outmoded "wounded healer" into the fearless, sacred teacher. The following exercises worked for me and my clients to accomplish that.

"And if it is a fear you would dispel, the seat of that fear is in your heart and not in the hand of the feared."

—**Kahlil Gibran**, *The Prophet*

TECHNIQUES TO RESOLVE CHIRON

Choose a fear that has plagued you throughout your life. Take time to experience this fear through your body sensations–taste, sound, smell, hearing, location in your body, pulse rate and any other visceral reactions. After you feel it, identify what sensory comforts that you use to feel better–music, food, alcohol, comfortable environment or any others. Finally think about what you have always said you want to *change* in your life but have not changed. Think about what you have always longed for and never created.

I believe that we are born with Chiron fears that tend to be catalyzed by experiences in our current life so that we can remember our past. Close your eyes, sit back and relax. Picture the cause of your fear inside your mind. What are you thinking about? Which memories does it bring back? Which faces, images, sounds, smells, places, faces, colors, voices or people does it make you think of? Which situations? What did you feel at the time? How does that relate to what you feel when you are scared? How does it help you uncover your past? How does it help you claim your fear?

After you have done this personal work, check out the important words that describe your personal Chiron. Astrology came to my rescue. Now I want it to come to yours. An astrological chart is divided into twelve sections that rule different signs. Imagine that one of these astrological signs has been contaminated to such an extent that you become terrified of it. At this point you would eliminate a major segment of your life in order to avoid what you fear. How so? In my experience you would repress it, deny it and vow to never become it again. Your feelings of fear would be as strong today as they were when you were first wounded and victimized. Answer the following questions and see how old Chiron lifetimes affect you today.

Describe your deepest fear and how it relates to your Chiron. *(Example: I have been terrified of being too visible because I have been afraid of assassination. I stopped performing on stage as a 7-year-old singer because I felt unsafe and humiliated. I have Chiron in Leo which means that I have been killed because I was a powerful leader who lived a big visible life.)*

What strategies can you employ to resolve this fear and transform your Chiron? (Example: *I had faith and courage that my Soul would not recreate these experiences. I put myself in situations on stages, TV and radio to see what would happen. I not only survived, I flourished and proved to myself that my Chiron emotions were truly in the past.)*

In addition to engaging in the previous exercise, you can also program your dreams using this mantra: *Dear Soul, please protect me as I rest. I have the courage to be free of my Chiron fears. Please help me discover my Chiron core life. (Read Chapter 6 on dream symbolism to provide you symbols to aid in your interpretation of your dreams.)*

CHIRON: THE HEALER AND SACRED TEACHER

Healing is a process that leads to wholeness and integration. Through our lives we encounter experiences that replay the old wounds so we can have an opportunity to be released from them. We need to understand that pain can be a gift to help us learn about our Chiron. Through that resolution we may become more creative in learning how to serve ourselves and others. This is the path of Chiron. Where we feel wounded, we seek healing, and from this experience we seek to help others. Teaching others through our own intense experiences is an act of generosity and compassion.

Through Chiron we find our vehicle for an expression to our higher purpose. We heal our personal wound by facing our fear and by doing what we fear. This takes courage and willpower because we need to become that which we have felt destroyed us in the past. It takes courage and faith to become that scared teacher *again*. The good news is that is exactly what we need to fill a void that has been a part of us for lifetimes. This is the time to become free of the past to create our future! The "Wounded One" when conscious can transform into the sacred healer/teacher. It is at this time that we are able to embrace, integrate and celebrate our Soul's intentions for our lives—our Soul's mission.

YOUR PERSONAL CHIRON TABLES

Date of Change	Sign
Jan 1, 1915	Chiron in Pisces
April 11, 1918	Chiron in Aries
May 24, 1926	Chiron enters Taurus
Oct 20, 1926	Chiron retrogrades back into Aries

Mar 25, 1927	Chiron enters Taurus
June 6, 1933	Chiron enters Gemini
June 6, 1933	Chiron enters Gemini
Dec 22, 1933	Chiron Retrogrades back into Taurus
Mar 23, 1934	Chiron enters Gemini
Aug 27, 1937	Chiron enters Cancer
Nov 22, 1937	Chiron Retrogrades back into Gemini
May 28, 1938	Chiron enters Cancer
Sep 29, 1940	Chiron enters Leo
Dec 27, 1940	Chiron Retrogrades back into Cancer
June 16, 1941	Chiron enters Leo
July 26, 1943	Chiron enters Virgo
Nov 17, 1944	Chiron enters Libra
Mar 23, 1945	Chiron Retrogrades back into Virgo
July 22, 1945	Chiron enters Libra
Nov 10, 1946	Chiron enters Scorpio
Nov 28, 1948	Chiron enters Sagittarius
Feb 8, 1951	Chiron enters Capricorn
June 18, 1951	Chiron Retrogrades back into Sagittarius
Nov 8, 1951	Chiron enters Capricorn
Jan 27, 1955	Chiron enters Aquarius
Mar 2 1960	Chiron enters Pisces
Aug 19, 1960	Chiron Retrogrades back into Aquarius
Jan 20, 1961	Chiron enters Pisces
Apr 1, 1968	Chiron enters Aries
Oct 18, 1968	Chiron Retrogrades back into Pisces
Jan 30, 1969	Chiron enters Aries
May 28, 1976	Chiron enters Taurus
Oct 13, 1976	Chiron Retrogrades back into Aries
Mar 28, 1977	Chiron enters Taurus
June 21, 1983	Chiron enters Gemini
Nov 29, 1983	Chiron Retrogrades back into Taurus
Apr 10, 1984	Chiron enters Gemini
June 21, 1988	Chiron enters Cancer
July 21, 1991	Chiron enters Leo
Sep 3, 1993	Chiron enters Virgo

Sep 9, 1995	Chiron enters Libra
Dec 29, 1996	Chiron enters Scorpio
Apr 4, 1997	Chiron enters Sagittarius
June 1, 1999	Chiron Retrogrades back into Scorpio
Sep 21, 1999	Chiron enters Sagittarius
Dec 11, 2001	Chiron enters Capricorn
Feb 21, 2005	Chiron enters Aquarius
July 31, 2005	Chiron Retrogrades back into Capricorn
Dec 5, 2005	Chiron enters Aquarius
Apr 20, 2010	Chiron enters Pisces
July 20, 2010	Chiron Retrogrades back into Aquarius
Feb 8, 2011	Chiron enters Pisces
Apr 17, 2018	Chiron enters Aries
Sep 25, 2018	Chiron Retrogrades back into Pisces
Feb 18, 2019	Chiron enters Aries
Jun 19, 2026	Chiron enters Taurus
Sep 17, 2026	Chiron Retrogrades back into Aries
Apr 14, 2027	Chiron enters Taurus
Jul 19, 2033	Chiron enters Gemini
Oct 23, 2033	Chiron Retrogrades back into Taurus
May 5, 2034	Chiron enters Gemini
Jul 22, 2038	Chiron enters Cancer
Jan 8, 2039	Chiron Retrogrades back into Gemini
Apr 26, 2039	Chiron enters Cancer

CHIRON IN THE ASTROLOGICAL SIGNS

Several years ago I conducted my first Chiron workshop. I gave each participant an archetypal karmic view of their Chiron placements. I used their astrological charts, my previous experience with clients with the same placement and my intuition. The results were amazing. I hope the following descriptions will lead you to a better understanding of your personal Chiron. It is a start. You need to become a master at the sign which contains your Chiron. The more you know, the more you can understand the qualities that were a significant part of your past lives as a victim.

Many of my clients still have difficulty accessing their dreams to find Chiron lifetimes. When this occurs I advise them to seek a reputable past-life therapist to assist them. Often people need a sacred place to feel safe enough to discover these painful lives.

Chiron in Aries

Chiron in Aries people are afraid to take action when there are possible risks involved in the experience. You tend not to know and honor your Selfness. It is hard for you to claim your excellence. You are afraid for others to think you are proud of your accomplishments. You often denigrate your accomplishments. You fear anything that is, in your view, impetuous and impulsive. You may feel insecure and lack confidence in your abilities to lead others. New, innovative ideas make you feel nervous. You have difficulty acknowledging your anger. Repressed anger may create accidents and health issues such as sinus problems, headaches, back problems and skin eruptions. I see you as a powerful tribal leader whose courageous actions kept your people safe from harm. You were an assertive warrior who took risks and led from the front. You were independent, with a strong will. You were strong of body and very physically fit. You were betrayed by one of your tribe who was in competition for your position. He hated you because you were an assertive, powerful proud warrior king and he was not. He assassinated you by stabbing you in the back as you were leading your warriors into battle.

Chiron in Aries Sacred Teacher

You become healed by taking small actions and paying attention to the outcomes which will most likely be positive. Soon you take larger risks and relish your more assertive self. You learn to take pride in yourself and honor your individuated personality. You begin to claim your physical body and become active in ways to make it strong and agile. You learn to access your anger and find creative ways to release it. In expressing your anger you will be healthier and less accident prone. You aid others in becoming their assertive, adventurous, active self.

Suzanne's Chiron in Aries Story

"Today, we're going to deal with your Chiron in Aries," Linda said to me as we started the second day of my weekend retreat with her and Michael. I was clueless about what Chiron was, but soon enough I got it. Chiron was the part of my astrological chart that represented how I had been victimized in past lives. My Chiron was in Aries which meant I had been harmed in a past life for displaying Arian behaviors like assertiveness, leadership, will, ambition, and risk taking.

Here's how Chiron could be so destructive to me in my current life. Whenever I started to engage or even imagine engaging in Arian behaviors, a voice in my head would pop up and discourage me from proceeding. In fact, the voice could be downright mean, sometimes like a negative Aunt Nelly, sometimes as bad as a parent who was verbally abusive. When I dreamed about writing my own book, my voice of Chiron said, "Get back in your place, girl! No one will want to read your book." When I imagined getting on stage and speaking to audiences in the next phase of my career, the voice said, "You're not good enough to be on stage; sit back down!"

To help me better understand why Chiron showed up in my chart associated with Arian behavior, Michael engaged me in a past-life regression to a time in my past when I was most victimized for being Arian--assertive, willful, confident, independent, masculine, etc. This exploration revealed to me that I was once the daughter of a Native American chieftain--his only child--to whom he had taught everything. Under my father's protection and special privilege, I had my own horse and could ride faster than most in the *tribe. I knew everything my father had taught me about being a good leader, and I was sure that I would be my father's successor upon his death. But my confidence was foolhardy and led to my downfall. After my father died, I rode my horse into the midst of my tribe to claim the leadership I thought was mine, and I was quickly executed for my bravado as a woman displaying the strength and aggression of a man.*

After the regression experience, Michael shared that I looked like a different person. Linda told me that the earlier look of ambivalence on my face had been replaced with confidence and certainty. I knew they were right. I had reconnected with a positive experience of my Arian energy—before I lost my life for being too Arian--and remembered how wonderful it felt to be assertive, masculine, and unafraid of taking risks. I felt strong, fearless, and ready to pursue my Soul Mission regardless of how others might judge me.

Chiron in Taurus

Chiron in Taurus people feel frightened of having the rug pulled out from them when they achieve a certain modicum of financial success. Often they shoot themselves in the foot when success appears to be right around the corner. Imagine you are a successful person, who was an innovator and pioneer in your field. You received acclaim and financial rewards for your talents. You had a peaceful, serene life, secure in your abilities to build a life for your family. You had financial security and knew money would always come because of the value you had in the world. Your self-worth and self-esteem was high and life was good. You did not expect anything bad to happen. But something bad did happen. A friend or a close business acquaintance became very jealous of your life. He could not emulate your life, your brilliance, your innovation and your financial success. Your life was destroyed by this betrayal. So in your unconscious memories you might be fearful of being too relaxed, creating too much financial success and being too visible.

Chiron in Taurus Sacred Teacher

You become healed as you embrace your talents that will create a comfortable, happy life. As you do this, your self-esteem and self-worth will increase and your love of self will be profoundly heightened. You will allow yourself to feel the sensual pleasures of life. You will create a beautiful environment for yourself and your family. You will learn to understand that spiritual values can integrate into the material world and provide a safe, secure and serene life. You will be able to help others embrace their self-value and inner security.

Jessica's Chiron in Taurus Story

The ultimate theme of my Chiron experience is dealing with my personal insecurities. I am insecure about how I present myself to the world and about how others perceive me, and I certainly do not want anyone to expect anything from me. I try not to put myself "out there" for fear of personal rejection. My insecurities have told me my whole life that I am not good enough for anything. I do not want anyone to expect anything from me. I do not like the feeling of performing on command; I usually freeze and cannot complete the task on their terms (in college I turned most of my work in late, with good excuses.) In turn I then feel insecure and embarrassed that I did not deliver. For example, Linda asked me to write on this topic for her book. I stalled, thinking about how it would probably suck; even though I was excited to be included, I felt frozen and stuck. I had a million reasons for why I could not complete this piece: stay-at-home mom of two toddlers, no time, I'm always tired etc. Michael mentioned it had to be done in a timely fashion, meaning within a couple of days. That created the pressure I spoke of. I froze, felt embarrassed, and worried I was going to let down two of the most important people in my life. I then felt ashamed of myself. They wanted me to perform on command and produce something insightful and raw. What if they read my experience and it wasn't good enough? Oh crap, vicious cycle, here we go again.

It weighed heavily on my mind after Linda reminded me she was on a deadline. I felt like such a loser to let her down. I explained in a brief text that I wouldn't be able to produce for her. I even wondered/ and obsessed about what she was thinking about me. I figured she didn't expect me to pull through anyway, thought that I had always been a bit flaky, and knew she couldn't depend on me. I couldn't stop thinking about what she was thinking about me. I sort of let it go and the pressure alleviated; I was now under no deadline and no one expected anything from me anymore. Ahh, I could breathe again.

I have been hurt by Chiron many times; as soon as I put myself "out there," mostly publically, and when there is the slightest feeling of rejection, fear consumes me and I retreat back into my very safe shell. I now know that this is my deepest wound from my past lives, whereby putting myself out there, in public and saying or being too much has killed me. Being too confident and bold—standing for something—has cost me my life. I am learning about the other end of the spectrum: that by not taking chances or risking anything, my life has become very mundane, very boring, and very safe. I need some excitement, damn it. I decided to start by writing this passage for Linda and to go from there, one step at a time, with caution of course. So, as I'm having this diatribe in my head while driving home, I saw the word Taurus on the back of some mobile home camper; that was my soul speaking to me or maybe shouting at me. "You better do this, you asshole!"

Even though I struggle with being stuck in old patterns (not being dependable, flaking out, all based on fear of not being good enough), my Taurus loyalty to Linda kicked in! My Taurus has made me fearful that the rug will be pulled out from under me as soon as I put forth effort or try to do something that would make me feel proud of myself. I know this familiar feeling. How I am working through this experience is one foot in front of the other. I am slowly and conservatively trying to manage my Chiron. I have to be patient and kind to myself. The only person who can validate or take anything away from me is me. I am learning to not need validation from anyone in order to feel confident and gently trying to value myself as a mother, wife, friend, daughter and most of all me.

Chiron in Gemini

Chiron in Gemini people have had many lives where being a brilliant communicator and writer caused others to have powerful emotional reactions to them. If your Chiron is in Gemini, your intellectual curiosity and intense nature formed the cornerstone for how you expressed your views about education, religion and philosophy. Your new ideas and strength of beliefs brought you up against the traditional wisdom of the day. I can imagine your being a college professor, charming and popular with a dramatic and powerful view of the world. You expressed your ideas with courage and resolve. You may now hold an old belief that being too intellectual is dangerous. You were betrayed by those who could not understand what you thought or what you said. I can imagine you as an orator and journalist whose unorthodox ideas challenged the status quo.

Chiron in Gemini Sacred Teacher

You become healed as you claim your inner speaker and writer. You remember how well you can express your ideas without worrying about other people's reactions. You journal and begin to take pride in your inherent love of words. You find ways to test your intelligence and discover you are very bright. You will create opportunities to express your views and be amazed when people agree with you. You will encourage others in finding their voice.

Ron's Chiron in Gemini Story

Several years ago as I was sweating out my senior year in college, my sister wanted to give me a gift certificate to see Linda Brady. I knew she was an astrologer because my sister had studied with her. I was not interested in wasting my time or my sister's money to make an appointment. I was on

Spring break, with my Senior thesis due in three weeks. To say I had writer's block was an understatement; I was frozen. I had spent three years doing anything other than write papers. I even paid for several of them. I had to write this one. And I couldn't. I called my sister with my tale of woe, asking her for any advice she might have. "Call Linda" was her best answer. I hung up feeling angry and scared. The next day in desperation I called and made an appointment with Linda Brady. She took me right away; I guess she could feel my anxiety. I gave her my date, time and place of birth and left for her home in a town in Vermont near me.

She met me at the door, asked me to sit down and asked me what she could do for me. I told her about my inability to write my paper. She had my astrological chart on her lap. She spent a couple of minutes reviewing it and then looked up. "You have Chiron in Gemini. That is why you are so terrified to write this paper or any paper," she said. "I never said I was scared," I retorted. "Really?" she said. "I believe that you are scared and we need to figure out why. How do you feel about reincarnation? Do you believe you have lived before?" she queried. Inside I was trying to figure out a way to leave without offending her, when she said. "Your silence is your answer, so let me tell you a little story and you tell me how you feel when you are listening to it, okay?" "Sure," I answered, feeling let off the hook.

"I see you as a successful writer in New York City. You wrote novels loosely based on real people, telling their secrets to a world eager to know them. No one could prove you were doing that and you became quite famous essentially being a gossip. Soon you tired of this game and decided to write a serious and important work that had real meaning. You found your talent and finished your book. On a book tour as you were lecturing about your work you were shot. Someone from your past whose life you ruined by your words found you and killed you. Your last dying thought was you would never write again. You would never be visible talking about your ideas again."

I was stunned. I felt tears running down my face. I was scared and relieved at the same time. The story felt so right. I hated New York. I had been there once on a class trip and felt claustrophobic and scared there. I also hated gossipy rags that I saw in grocery stores. Linda had hit on those issues. "So, if you are right about this Chiron thing causing me this fear, what do I do about it?" Linda gave me the techniques I needed to ultimately resolve my fear of writing. I saw her husband for past-life regression, found the writer in me that had been betrayed and tortured and forgave the one who had hurt me. I learned I could write without being afraid I would be hurt. I got an A on my senior paper, graduated and am now an attorney. I write a lot in my profession and I am not scared.

Chiron in Cancer

People with Chiron in Cancer are terrified of being abandoned. You may feel unloved and unwanted and very much alone. You do not trust anyone to nurture you because that nurturing will not last anyway. So it becomes difficult for you to allow anyone into your emotional space. You are very nurturing to others, providing for them what you cannot allow for yourself. As a matter of fact you are a magnet for strays. You believe you do not deserve to be loved. I can see you as a small child being taken from your ill mother who was unable to care for you. You are taken to an orphan's hospital, placed in a crib and given basic care. You are not held or loved. You end up with a couple who are emotionally unavailable. Once again you are fed, clothed and housed but little else. You are a good child doing anything you can to not be given away again. You learn to take care of people so they will like you and want you around. You build a shell around yourself to protect you from hurt. You do not want anyone to see the pain you feel. As an adult you choose a career where you can take care of others.

Chiron in Cancer Sacred Teacher

You are healed when you become the good Mother to your own inner, sad child. You will be the one to love that child in a way no one else has been able to. You will know their needs and provide for them. You will give them the promise that you will never leave them. You will help them heal their fears of abandonment day to day. Many hugs later and you and your inner child are emotionally secure. Now you are ready to allow others into your heart. You are no longer afraid to be hurt by others because you and your child are safe and happy. You will continue to know and handle your emotional needs, and the old fears of being left alone will dissipate. You will teach others to be emotionally available to themselves and their inner children.

Ruth's Chiron in Cancer Story

Learning about my Chiron in Cancer saved my life. Really, I am not being dramatic. My fiancé of 2 years broke up with me as we were planning our wedding. That was bad enough but what made it worse was it was the third time a man I was emotionally involved with left me. I was not sure I wanted to live. I had studied enough about Jungian psychology to know I was the common denominator so there must be something really wrong with me. I had heard that Linda Brady did Jungian astrology so I made a telephone appointment with her. I had never done something like that before but I was desperate. I was nervous before she answered her phone with "Hi Ruth, How may I help you today?" Then I relaxed. It was not her words but her voice that made me feel comfortable and safe. She reminded me of my Grandmother. I was crying when I told her my story. "Can you help me make some sense of this?" I said through my tears.

Linda said that she could. She asked me to take a few deep breaths and anchor my consciousness in my heart by putting my right hand on my chest. She wanted me to stay in my body and pay attention to my feelings, not my head and my thoughts. I found that easy because my heart was hurting so bad that putting my hand there helped. She then told me about my Chiron in Cancer. "0*Ruth, you are terrified to be in an emotionally vulnerable relationship. As soon as you get close to having a marriage you "create your partner to leave you. I know this sounds strange to you, but because you are the common denominator it is your pattern. You have had many lives where you totally trusted your partner. In one life you actually had your dream of home and children. He left you and your children. You were unable to take care of them. You gave them away so they would have a better life. You died swearing you would never love and trust that way again."*

I was totally blown away. She was right. I was terrified of being abandoned, even as a little girl. I thought my parents would be gone when I woke up. I also thought about the three men I had chosen to marry. Each one had a history of commitment phobias. Maybe I had unconsciously brought these men into my life because I knew I could not trust them. It made perfect sense. She helped me through the karmic process of finding the core past life, dealing with emotions generated from that life and finally helping me forgive those who had betrayed me. I am now free to find a person who is ready to commit to me. I know I am.

Chiron in Leo

Chiron in Leo people are terrified of being too visible in roles of leadership and power. You have had many lives as a ruler and leader who was a shining star. You used your powerful, divine, heart-centered courage to inspire your followers to be great also. Your childlike wonder and creativity created happiness and joy for those around you. I can imagine you behind a podium on a stage in front of thousands of people strongly articulating your beliefs. I can see an assassin standing with a gun in his hand shooting you in the heart. You died knowing the person who killed you. He was your best friend. His betrayal broke your heart physically, spiritually and emotionally. Your family never recovered from the shock of your loss.

Chiron in Leo Sacred Teacher

You become healed as you claim your joyful child and realize you can have fun in your life without fear. Your heart is generous and full when you have integrated your child and your adult selves. You need to find the divine will that can provide you with the courage to shine in your world. Finding opportunities to put yourself on stage will generate old fears that you can now transform into courageous actions. You will inspire others to be courageous and heart-centered.

Linda's Chiron in Leo Story (repeated from earlier, for convenience)

My coauthor, Evan St. Lifer, and I had worked on Discovering Your Soul Mission *for years, mostly at night after work, from 10 PM to 12 AM. We were determined that the book would be excellent all around: easy to read for the novice and informational for the advanced reader. But upon publication of the book, I discovered that I was deeply afraid to promote it. So many hours and so many dreams could disappear because of my unnamed fear. I was in conflict and my emotions were winning. I knew that I was in trouble. My fear could undermine the success of our book.*

Through past-life regression with my husband, Michael, I uncovered lifetimes of attacks on my heart center – real and symbolic. I was humiliated and tortured and made to witness unimaginable horrors. I was not a bad person. As a matter of fact, I was probably a powerful, visible person who was too heart-connected to my people. My childlike naiveté and loving nature put me and those that I loved at risk. Fear and shame are two distinctive emotions. Fear comes from being overpowered and victimized, and shame comes from doing something bad to someone else. Clearly when I feared promoting my new book, I was in a Chiron moment! I began to realize that Chiron is always about the past and the associated feelings of fear are always contaminated. I did the work. I forgave those that hurt me. I was no longer afraid I would be assassinated because people would read my book. I did book talks and book tours. I felt freer than ever.

Chiron in Virgo

People with Chiron in Virgo are terrified that their physical body will fail them. You might be obsessed with illness and fears of being misdiagnosed by doctors. You believe they will miss details and you will be victimized by them. You are extreme and a perfectionist by nature and can become anal about the smallest details yourself. You may believe that forgetting details can be dangerous to you. You might want to heal others and in turn find ways to heal yourself. Unfortunately, you may feel that you may never be truly healed. If you do that you might totally overlook your health because you feel it is no use and you feel helpless and out of control. In this life you may have a dislike for doctors and nurses because of what a doctor did to you in the past.

I can imagine a life where you were taken to a hospital with a fairly insignificant illness. You were a young, healthy man when you were admitted. You were treated by a doctor who was incapacitated in some way and who totally misdiagnosed you. And then he overlooked details in your history and gave you the wrong medicine. You became critically ill. You suffered for a long time before you died. You watched your young wife and child suffer by your bedside every day until you took your last breath. You died filled with rage at the doctor who made such a stupid, life-ending mistake.

Chiron in Virgo Sacred Teacher

You become healed by learning to handle imperfection. Finding perfection in your spiritual life and being the best you can be in your mundane life will help you find peace. Forgiving the doctor who made such a mistake would allow you to release your obsession with your not making a mistake. You need to understand that extremism causes psychological and physical problems of its own. Healing will come from finding a balance between your mind, body and soul. Doing some work in the medical field would help you reclaim respect for the medical profession. You will aid others in finding their service.

Sue's Chiron in Virgo Story

I am allergic to just about everything, including the medicines that are supposed to help me. I hated the Spring when the allergens abounded. I wanted a dog, but I couldn't be around them. I was miserable most of the time. I spent years of my life in doctors' offices. I would dread each visit. I never knew why I felt so uncomfortable around people who were there to provide me medical advice. As I got older I began reading about holistic medicine and started seeing a wonderful chiropractor/healer. I learned my allergies could be healed from the inside out. He sent me to see Linda Brady to understand the spiritual reasons for my medical challenges.

I found out that I had Chiron in the sign of Virgo. Linda, her husband, Michael, and I discovered a past life where I had been a young woman whose doctor operated on her when he was intoxicated. The operation left me paralyzed. The doctor refused to take responsibility for the mistake, blaming his nurse for doing something wrong during the procedure. I had no recourse but to live with my Mother until I passed, very angry and bitter.

This made perfect sense to me. It explained my distrust of doctors. It also helped me see that my allergies had a karmic base in deep anger. I forgave the doctor who had hurt me. I let go of my anger. I am an avid proponent of holistic health and continue to heal more every day. I am writing this with my little puppy beside me! I have decided to become a nurse practitioner specializing in holistic medicine.

Chiron in Libra

Chiron in Libra people are terrified that other people will think ill of them. You automatically think you will be treated unfairly by others. You have lifetimes being highly creative and were surrounded by great beauty. You felt a strong sense of self-value and self-worth because of your talents. Many of your relationships came from others honoring those talents. Your life was all about art and the relationships they produced. You were defined by others' opinions of you, leaving you vulnerable and off balance.

One day they loved you, and the next day they hated you. The vagaries of others' behaviors caused you great pain and insecurity. They were the "beautiful people" living in the upper stratus of society. Much of your life was measured by those people, leaving you with a deep sense of unfairness and injustice. Without them you were nothing. You saw them being all that you wanted for yourself. They had the beauty, balance and harmony you desired. Because you hated conflicts and were overly compromising, you never spoke up for yourself.

Chiron in Libra Sacred Teacher

You will be healed when you manifest your artistic talents just for yourself. Others' opinions are not necessarily important nor would they change your mind about your work. Being able to believe "what they think about me is none of my business" will help you define yourself with any co-dependent relationship you might engage in. Learning justice and fair play requires you to engage occasionally in conflict to take care of yourself. Finding equality in a relationship would be a healing balm to your spirit. You will teach others about the need for balance and harmony.

Julie Harbin's Chiron in Libra Story

My Chiron is in Libra, and in my chart it highlights the issue of my immensely fragile sense of personal value. As a young teenager, I didn't know about Chiron, but I certainly knew I had relationship problems in my family and with school friends. I felt that there was something wrong with me, but I did not know how to fix myself. I was outwardly intelligent, athletic, friendly, and helpful, but within, I had a fragile inner sense of personal value. Depression and anxiety began to creep in.

After college graduation, I took a job in the aerospace industry that would eventually turn into a career. Hindsight is always 20/20. So, looking back, it's now clear how I unconsciously chose an environment where my fragile sense of personal worth was mirrored back to me in the faces of the men I worked for.

Oh, they liked me a lot, but they didn't know what to do with me once I was dissatisfied as a secretary.

Eventually, a couple of things happened where my personal value began to grow. The vice president of our office had quite a reputation for liking the ladies, and (I heard) he took pride in hiring attractive secretaries. All the other secretaries were quite attractive. I was hired so, ergo, I must be attractive too! That is actually how I decided I was attractive—very Chiron in Libra of me!! Secondly, when the CEO of the company came to town, he occasionally required secretarial assistance. This duty normally fell to the Office Administrator's secretary; however, she was not confident in her shorthand and begged me to take her place. Round the corner I went to the Executive Suite armed with my newly discovered sense of attractiveness and my more-than-competent shorthand. Soon I was the only one the CEO wanted for secretarial assistance. Eventually he offered to move me from Washington, DC, to Los Angeles, CA, to become his full-time Staff Assistant (aka chief secretary). I was divorced and fighting a difficult relationship with my mother who lived relatively nearby, so I packed my bags and left before anyone could change their mind!

In those early days, I based my sense of self on others' opinion of me. Thankfully, it didn't take me long after college to find the personal counseling I needed. That was followed by ten years of Landmark Education's intensely transformational seminars, two years of studying astrology, and twenty plus more years of working with my favorite astrologers, Linda and Michael Brady, as counselors, mentors, guides, and friends to eventually produce the result I wanted—an internally generated, strong, healthy, and peace-loving sense of personal value. All it took was courage.

Chiron in Scorpio

People with Chiron in Scorpio are terrified of emotional loss. These fears feel like death to you--as does any betrayal that leads to loss. You live your life in extremes: black and white, right or wrong, good or evil. You are that extreme. You have intense emotional reactions, which you may not express to others. You might become depressed, which is essentially anger and rage turned inward. Often those feelings may seem dangerous to you and so you repress them. Passion and desire can lead to deep disappointment when they do not manifest and that feels overwhelming to you. Being betrayed in sexual relationships has led to paranoia around intimacy. You innately understand life mysteries but are afraid of the power that could come from them. You may be afraid of financial situations where you are not in control and you need to trust others. Trust does not come easy for you around money and other people whose values are different than your own.

You have been betrayed and tortured for being a person of great power and wealth. A person who you were in an intimate relationship with could have been the one who set you up to be hurt. They might have felt you had too much control over them and they fought back in a vindictive, underhanded way. You clearly thought you had exactly what you wanted in a relationship and then you found yourself in a torture chamber because of them.

Chiron in Scorpio Sacred Teacher

You will be healed when you find ways to create balance in your life. Understanding how inherently problematic extremes are can lead you to practice techniques to capture and resolve these thoughts and feelings. You can study a mystical art form and discover how it can feel powerful without being dangerous. Learning to desire something and finding creative ways to manifest it can alter old beliefs that having what you want is impossible. Being grateful for what you have can help here too. Becoming a master of your emotions, especially around anger and rage, will be very liberating to you. You need to be able to trust and be in control of yourself so you create a relationship that you trust. Helping others go through the grief of loss could help you heal your own.

Carol's Chiron in Scorpio Story

How could she—that Linda Brady—burst my Chiron bubble? He was my idol, my hero: part man and part horse and the wounded healer. He was everything I loved and worshipped and aspired to be. I had to challenge her on this one. I did not want to see the other negative side of Chiron— the Chiron in Scorpio part. I struggled until she continued to explain that is how Chiron works. She said he seduces you, knows how to sink his hooks into you and pushes all of your buttons. My Chiron is in Scorpio, so these hooks are buried deep in my unconscious. Chiron in Scorpio sabotaged me by relentlessly urging me to be extreme in my reactions to my life. I needed to be perfect all of the time, especially with my horses. I worried and fretted constantly.

My extreme passion with horses was my priority, leaving time for little else. I had tunnel vision; horses were all that mattered! My Chiron also warned me every day not to trust anyone around my horses, so I became obsessed with their care. I could not rely on anyone else. Chiron would not let go, even after accidents and surgeries damaged me, causing far-reaching physical challenges. Linda and I worked through all of this over time. It was not easy, even when I learned to recognize Chiron and his trickery. I persevered and I am winning my battle with Chiron. I learned to seek out other interests beyond my horses and find balance, an anathema to Chiron in Scorpio. Now I feel softer, more relaxed, more versatile and well rounded. Chiron may still be riding in tandem with me, but now he is in the back seat. And I intend to keep it that way!

Chiron in Sagittarius

Chiron in Sagittarius people are terrified of speaking their truth to others for fear of reprisals. You believe that others will betray you for your religious or philosophic opinions. You believe that having an optimistic view of life is dangerous. You have issues with God and religion. You might experience emotional and physical claustrophobia. You desire travel and may do a lot of it, yet problems may occur during trips that cause unnamed fears.

You could have been a powerful traveling minister who had a large following that you visited regularly. You owned a ranch where you raised horses and cattle. You were a large, optimistic man who believed in all that he preached. You had faith in positive outcomes and you served your congregation well. You always believed that keeping the faith and believing in the power of God would keep you and your family safe. You were passionate about taking care of your parishioners. You often had to leave your family to help them in their times of crisis. You never expected your family to be in danger. One night while you were ministering to a dying parishioner, raiders killed your family, stole your horses and burned your home. You were left totally alone and blaming yourself for not being there to protect them. You believed God had turned on you while you were out doing His work. You turned away from Him and your church and disappeared. You died alone, bitter and angry without your faith to sustain you.

Chiron in Sagittarius Sacred Teacher

You will be healed when you rekindle your relationship with God and find your divine source: your Soul. You will be free of your anger at God when you have found it in your heart to forgive the men who destroyed your life. Learning alternative philosophies like serendipity will aid you in regaining your faith. Finding life situations that give you a sense of optimism is also helpful. Creating a relationship with a horse will mend the loss of the other horses. You might find yourself wanting to teach or minister again as an opportunity to share your truth with others.

JCM's Chiron in Sagittarius Story

In past lives, I was a teacher and philosopher, wanting to share what I considered my greatest gift—my knowledge—with the world. Over many lives my truth was not received well by those in power. My messages were counter-cultural regarding societal mores, religious doctrines, philosophical norms, etc. I was often ahead of my time and not understood by those around me. My punishments went from being imprisoned with no one to speak to, to having my tongue ripped out; I was literally gagged for long periods of time and my head was cut off. In other words I had no voice, literally and figuratively. I was unable to speak my truths. I suppose I would not have been made to suffer if I had not begun to attract a following that threatened the power structure. So there was some sort of collective acknowledgment experienced.

My in life situation: After months of my asking for us to go into counseling, I found that my husband's rage-filled outbursts became more frequent and more frightening, so I stood my ground. We had planned to go on vacation. My timing of this experience with my husband challenged me to reject a phenomenal Sagittarius once-in-this-lifetime opportunity to see the Orient. I wanted to ride an elephant. And yet I told him I was too afraid of him to go away on that preplanned, prepaid, two-week vacation to the Orient.

My husband's verbal rage; animated, violent flailing; and visceral resentment (because I would not move to Florida with him and live together, which was the original agreement of our four-year marriage) had reached a new intensity. I stood my ground and refused to go on the vacation to the Orient. I spoke my truth; I would not be forced to leave my home, even though I knew it would end the marriage. The pattern was broken. The wound was healed by manifesting this needed change, to be free of this tyrant.

My Soul was also demanding that I listen to my intuition, which was saying that it was unsafe to go. As it turned out, the Japanese tsunami hit that part of the world just then on 3/13/11. Our hotel was evacuated and seriously damaged.

Also, interestingly, I had a "collective writer and astrologer breakthrough" when my article on the topic of listening was published. I now have my voice!

Chiron in Capricorn

People with Chiron in Capricorn are terrified that they will not be respected for what they do. You might choose work as a way to give yourself an organizational structure that gives you a sense of status. You might be afraid of making too much money and being too successful; yet you are driven toward those things at the same time. You probably have issues with authority figures that you feel do not acknowledge your achievements. However, you want to be certified and sanctioned by those same people. You get very scared when your schedules get screwed up or your plans go awry. Controlling your life is critically important.

I can imagine that you were a powerful leader whose life supported and nurtured many people. You were the elder of the tribe, the priest of your city, the executive whose factory employed a whole town. You were respected and honored for your integrity and wisdom. Your reputation was beyond reproach. Unfortunately there were those who were jealous of your success, hated your financial good fortune and envied your exemplary relationships. Often people hate what they cannot emulate. They betrayed you by destroying your reputation and removing you from your position of authority.

Chiron in Capricorn Sacred Teacher

You are healed when you know that you are your own authority and no one can take that from you. You will learn that respecting yourself is all that matters, regardless of position and status. You will be free to be successful, knowing that respect and success cannot be taken from you if you are self-contained and self-aware. You find that being a workaholic does not create a serene life and being overly organized does not leave room for relationships, fun and childlike wonder. You will provide wise counsel to others needing a good father.

GC's Chiron in Capricorn Story

Early on, my Chiron in Capricorn manifested as my controlling others in an effort to protect those close to me, or so I thought. I was highly motivated to succeed, which I have done in many areas throughout my life. I am a healer and very proficient in the profession of helping others. However, I have come to realize that while I have always been the nurturer of others, I have neglected myself in this very area—until very recently.

I had not fully realized the imbalance between success in my life and allowing myself to be nurtured, particularly by a partner. I do allow nurturing from family and friends, but the controlling personality is always lurking in the background, on guard, ready to protect. Protect from what? I fear some dark, impending doom will overtake me if I become fully vulnerable and unattached, allowing serendipity to do its part on this area of my being. So here I am, alone, in this one facet of my life. I am brought to tears by this realization.

Chiron in Aquarius

People with Chiron in Aquarius are terrified of being too individualistic and different from the norm. You want to fit in at all costs so no one will point their finger at you. If you are rejected you will likely disconnect and isolate yourself. You have an innate fear of large groups, feeling they will band together against you. You ultimately believe you just don't fit in anywhere. You are in constant search for those like-minded people that will help you feel safe.

Living as a native in a position as a Shaman over many lives, you were never accepted or tolerated for who you were, only what you could do. They needed you to be their healer but kept you on the periphery of their lives. They feared and needed you at the same time. You were also a teacher that shared your knowledge with the tribe but your truth fell on deaf ears. They did not have the consciousness and intelligence to understand you. They wanted you to be quiet, take care of them and that was all! You had deep emotional sensitivities that made you an excellent Shaman, but you were very alone. You had no friends. You did have a wife and a male child that you loved beyond measure, but they were ostracized from the tribe too. You felt responsible for their emotional pain. You finally decided to leave the tribe and find another tribe that would accept you and your family. You misjudged the weather and the distance you would need to travel and you all perished on the way. Your wife and child died first, leaving you outraged at the unfairness of the tribe that had used you so badly and had destroyed your life.

Chiron in Aquarius Sacred Teacher

You will be healed when you acknowledge that being unique and different is a wonderful thing. You are a child of Aquarius, which rules the next 2,000 years. Individuation, freedom, independence and personal uniqueness will be the rule, not the exception. Your search for a like-minded tribe is important. Finding people with new, innovative ideas will heal your fear of large groups; they will honor you for your ideas by listening to you and your innovative thoughts. Together you and your likeminded group will create common purposes that will do great things. You will aid others by honoring their uniqueness.

Monica's Chiron in Aquarius Story

My Chiron placement is Aquarius. I describe my Chiron wound as being a misfit among misfits, unable to see the meaning of life and powerless to find purpose on this planet. Before my Chiron retreat and healing with Linda and Michael Brady, I lived a life that was slowly corroding me from the inside out. For years I navigated the conservative 9 to 5 life in entry-level jobs, underemployed (and bored), proving my unhealed Chiron wound was working perfectly to keep me hidden and small and living with a constant background noise of fear. However, the Aquarian quality of rebellion in

Chiron would eventually explode, and I would either quit the job or get fired but only to repeat the pattern over and over.

I became used to not fitting in, but the question "What is the meaning of Life?" was not a Monty Python joke to me but a tightrope on which I walked a fine line between staying on this planet and leaving through suicide. I did not know what to believe, but I was sure to not believe what other people said about meaning, purpose, god, faith, religion or spirituality. What other people said made no sense. Their actions did not fit their words of belief. A small voice inside kept telling me the universe had more common sense than the average person or the average god.

Through my Chiron healing I was introduced to and am becoming more familiar with that small voice. That small voice, known to me now as my higher self, is slowly healing me from the inside out. My wound started to heal when I understood that another way of saying a "misfit among misfits" is to say I am a "black diamond"; in other words, a "rare diamond among rare diamonds."

I also know that my Extraordinary Self lives in Astrology and in the Holistic Arts. After my Chiron retreat I now work on something more important to my "thrival." I work my relationship to my higher power. This relationship gives me a view of the universe that suits me. It allows me to jump off that tightrope. It is slowly answering any question I have and filling in my empty spaces with a meaning and a purpose that gives me inner peace.

Karen's Chiron in Aquarius Story

I used to think that Chiron in my chart reflected a wound about being my Aquarian authentic self. Now I know it's about being terrified of opening my heart and being rejected again, just like with my father. In every attempt I made as a child to reach out and love my father, he crushed my heart. He could be cruel, insensitive, mean and abusive. It broke my heart that my dad, the one who was supposed to be my protector, the man I loved and cherished, could treat me with such contempt.

When I was 11 years old, babysitting my six brothers and sisters, I invited a boy I liked and his friend over without my parents' permission. Mom and Dad came home early. My friends tried leaving out the back door but the lock jammed. They panicked and ran upstairs just before my parents walked in the front door. Innocently, we fell asleep in my bedroom waiting for my parents to fall asleep in theirs. I woke up shocked to see it was 4am! While sneaking them down the stairs, my mother heard us and all hell broke loose! My father called the police. Raging uncontrollably, he screamed at me in front of the detectives that I was a whore, calling me names, swearing and accusing me of explicit sexual acts. I felt like I was being raped in front of everyone. I begged him to stop saying those horrible things, but he went right on. They wanted me to see a doctor and I didn't even know why. I'd never been taught anything about my sexuality!

When the police left, my father came into my bedroom, pulled off my panties and beat my bare buttocks with his belt. Mom insisted I go into their bedroom and apologize to Dad for hurting his feelings! I was dazed, traumatized and had pretty much left my body. I said I was sorry, still not knowing what I had done that was so awful. With tears in his eyes, my father walked towards me, put his arms around me, and said "I love you". At that very moment I froze my heart! With intense loathing, I thought "You will never hurt me again!" feeling my heart slowly squeeze shut, becoming as hard as stone.

I could not understand how something so innocent had suddenly turned so ugly. I was utterly ashamed of my body, my heart and my soul. I felt alone, terrified, and completely abandoned. I just wanted them to love me. Why didn't they love me? It seemed I had betrayed them somehow by just being me. *My heart was injured and as a young child, I didn't know how to heal it! From that night on I was true to my word; my heart was impenetrable, that is, until around age 32, when I became very sick. I stumbled upon a homeopathic woman doctor who for the first time in all those years uncovered the repressed feelings I had locked up that night when I was 11 years old.*

As the memories surfaced, I felt pins and needles all over, like when your arm falls asleep and the blood begins to flow again. I was afraid of what was happening. I didn't know how to deal with all those powerful feelings of rage, fear, sadness and hatred. In order to protect her heart (Leo), my inner child did what Aquarius does: she detached from her feelings. I'd tried to stay in my mind for so long, but it hadn't worked. Aquarius (mind) and Leo (heart) need each other to be whole. I believe my soul gave me this experience as an opportunity to heal and bring an end to lifetimes of suffering. With a north node in Sagittarius, my soul wants to experience the freedom of sharing expressions of heart-felt love, laughter and joy in an intimate way with another person.

I've never given up. I've known somehow the love inside my heart is still there for me. With courage and faith I keep taking baby steps gently around the raw edges of my heart, moving closer to peace with each go round. This has been my life-long Chiron experience: helping my inner child to heal her wounded heart and believe in her ability to reach out and love again.

Chiron in Pisces

You are terrified to access your emotions and have essentially lost your faith in people and God. You do not trust people easily. You feel guilty often without understanding why. You want to do everything perfectly and are disappointed when you can't. You have suffered a lot, and in some ways believe it is what you need to do to emulate Christ. You could feel that the suffering is caused by your not working hard enough to heal others. You then might draw people to you that need healing and you want to fix and take care of them. Your empathetic nature could leave you with their pain in addition to your own, which continues the suffering. Your life could be spent as a victim to life because it feels too harsh for your sensitive nature.

People with Chiron in Pisces have been wounded and tortured for being open, empathetic, compassionate, emotionally sensitive and totally open. Your feminine nature welcomed others into your open arms and was totally betrayed in the process. You were a spiritual woman who was naïve, idealistic and totally guileless. You were totally open with your feelings and wanted to love and heal everyone. You had the emotional development of a child. Yet you are a beautiful and very sexually attractive woman. Your implicit trust of men could leave you vulnerable to those who would take advantage of you.

Chiron in Pisces Sacred Teacher

You will be healed when you realize that all people need to learn to heal themselves. It is not your job to take on their pain as it disables them when you do. You need to figure out the ways you have been wounded and forgive the perpetrators. Doing that helps you realize the power of your emotions and your need to become a master of them. You will learn to discriminate and decide the people you can trust from those you can't. Using your intellectual skills will help you find clarity in your motivations to help and fix others. When you learn that perfection only exists in your Soul and excellence is good enough in the real world, you will feel less disappointed in yourself and certainly less guilty. You will help others find their faith.

Peter's Chiron in Pisces Story

I have Chiron in Pisces. All my life I have worried about being separated from my family and being alone. This persistent concern began to make sense to me when I experienced the following past life memory:

I am a six-year-old child in a prehistoric clan. The clan is my family. Every part of my life feels as though it fits together and flows in harmony with nature. Life is beautiful; it changes with the seasons and I am happy. Our village is in a meadow next to the mountains. There is a cave at the foot of the mountain with a spiritual hot spring. Inside the cave there are wall paintings showing the living history of my family. I often go to the cave with my mother and look at the paintings. I think when I grow up I will become part of the painting.

One day I wander from the village to the cave. I sit there for hours just imagining being part of the adventure. I realize I am hungry. My mother has not come looking for me. I get up and head back to the village. As I am walking there is a slight drizzle of rain. I smell smoke--not the smoke of the cooking fires but a different smoke. As I approach the village I see the huts are all burned. Everyone is gone. I call out for my mother. No one replies. I am all alone. It starts to rain harder. I feel the cold rain stinging my face. I don't feel my tears. I am scared. I am hungry. I call out. No one is there. No one is coming. It is getting darker. I am alone. I am afraid. I am cold. In my mind I hear, "Go back to the cave. It is warmer and dry in the cave." I run back to the cave and huddle in the corner, just looking at the paintings. No one is coming for me. I am hungry. I am tired. As I look at the paintings I see myself in them. I am so tired. I go to sleep, escape, and don't wake up. I die alone in the cave.

Learning about Chiron has helped me recognize when I feel emotions come up that I often shut down, zone out, detach or fall asleep to escape from the fear of feeling emotionally overwhelmed and feeling the extreme pain of that loneliness and sadness. Understanding my Chiron has allowed me to see what is real in this life and what is an exaggerated over reaction.

More Chiron Poignancy

Your astrological chart is divided into 12 segments called Houses. Each House has a relationship to one of the 12 astrological signs or constellations. It is a living example of the old truism, "as above, so below." Houses are the earthly manifestation of an astrological experience. Each of the 12 Houses is influenced or ruled by a related energy from a constellation or sign.

When you are born, you symbolically enter the first house of your astrological chart and begin your personal earthly journey. Each house has hundreds of life issues contained within it. Each issue can be turned into a question which is answered by the sign that rules that house and the planets within it. For example, the first House relates to issues of self. So if Chiron appears in the first House of your chart, it will show up quite a bit in your life involving issues of self, identity, self-esteem, etc. The tenth House relates to career, so if Chiron appears in the tenth House of your chart, you can expect to see fears related to your Chiron showing up in areas related to your workplace, job, vocation, etc.

You may recall the story of Carol, whose Chiron appeared in Scorpio. We can learn even more about the symbolic implications of Carol's Chiron placement by seeing that it appeared in the first House of her astrological chart. As Carol described,

> *Knowing my Chiron was in Scorpio was important. But what was pivotal for me was knowing he resided in my first House, the House of self and the body. That's when he became real. He was ruthless: he attacked my body, my strength, through injuries and surgeries. Now I could see how devious he was. He often used my passion and love for horses to attack my body via horse-related injuries. I can see that clearly now. No more rose-colored glasses. He is indeed, the Trickster.*

I originally deleted the house placements from stories like Carol's because I was not going to write about the astrological Houses in this book. However, based on my conversation with Carol, which underscored how valuable this piece of information was to her on her journey, I decided to address their importance here in brief. To learn your particular house placement for Chiron, you will need to have your astrological chart prepared, using your date, time and place of birth, and I encourage you to work with a reputable astrologer to do so.

What I can share in this chapter, as we close, is a broader view of the astrological houses and your astrological chart at large. Imagine yourself as a Soul sitting in a garden on the Other Side with a view of the earth. You are getting ready to return to the earth for another physical incarnation. You are preparing your astrological chart that will serve as a guide and a script throughout your life. With this in mind you know that the earth is a reflection of the sky and that each constellation has its image on the earth. The earth is a grid that is divided into twelve equal segments, called Houses, each one reflecting an astrological sign. This grid will become the earthly base of your astrological chart.

When you are ready, say goodbye to your heavenly friends and teachers. Imagine yourself being born into the physical world. You have the ability to see a huge circle around you. This is your astrological chart and you are at its center. Each House is there to provide you with all of the questions that your Soul wants you to answer. It is your Soul's guidebook.

Identifying what astrological sign your Chiron is associated with—and further identifying which House it resides in—will provide you with essential information to resolving fears that hold you back in this lifetime. Learn where your Chiron is placed and you can start on the path to moving from victim to actor.

CONCLUSION

THE AGE OF AQUARIUS IS HERE: BECOMING SPIRITUAL ADULTS

have said before that we have one foot in the Age of Pisces and the other foot in the Age of Aquarius. We are in the Age of Transition now.

PLUTO IN CAPRICORN: THE TRANSITION

The planet Pluto is creating the transitional changes necessary to help us develop the attitudes and beliefs necessary for us to be fully planted in the Age of Aquarius. Pluto moved into Capricorn on January 25, 2008, and will leave in November of 2024. During the next nine years we will continue to be challenged to become the spiritual Aquarian adults that our souls want us to be. The more self-contained and self-empowered we are, the more successful we will be; we also need strength, courage and commitment. Capricorn honors self-reliance and Pluto wants us to use all of our resources. Success occurs when we fully engage in life with those attributes.

Old age Capricorn represents time-honored conservative traditions that no longer serve us. There was a time when hierarchical systems provided security and stability. There was a time that corporate bottom lines were more important than the needs of individuals. There was a time when many authority figures were an outside force that shaped our daily lives. There was a time when personal responsibility meant taking care of others and not ourselves. There was a time when God was perceived as an external force—the ultimate authority that only tended to weaken and disable our personal power. There was a time when organized religions were our only connection to God. There was a time when security was measured by our health insurance, our retirement plans and our financial bottom lines. There was a time when we unquestioningly accepted the beliefs of our families and lived our lives in their shadows.

The planet Pluto represents the force of will needed to destroy these outmoded beliefs. Capricorn is a cardinal earth sign that takes action from a deep sense of personal responsibility and maturity. Together Pluto in Capricorn will help us purge these deeply entrenched beliefs.

As cosmic, irresponsible children we were weighed down based on ideas and truths imposed on us before we had the intellectual power to disagree. These foundations may be shaky and will probably not withstand the earthquake rumblings of Pluto in Capricorn. The next nine years gives us the opportunity to review and make changes that will aid us in becoming the cosmic adults the Aquarian Age requires.

Since Capricorn represents the earth and our bodies are our connection to the earth, these beliefs live in our bodies and can be felt if we pay attention to the physical sensations that our bodies provide when asked the right questions. Our bodies never lie. I developed a practice for my students to help them understand the physical heaviness of their personal beliefs.

Personal Beliefs Exercise

You have an imaginary 15 lbs. of weight on your ankles; get up and walk around, feeling how very heavy this is. Then think about an old, rigid belief that you have incorporated into your life. Do this practice twice a week for a month. Feel the weight of that belief. Record your thoughts and feelings.

Soon you will want to release these weights and walk with freedom and lightness. You will accomplish this transformation by letting go of the belief. You can then strew your path with the seeds of magnificent Aquarian truths that support your new holistic structure.

We have the power and potential to create these changes within our own lives *now*! One person can make a difference. We are the microcosm of the macrocosm. As we change, so can our world community. Each restrictive, archaic imposed belief we allow to die brings freedom to ourselves, our families, our community and ultimately our world. This is the Aquarian way!

There will be a time when equality and community-based government and corporations provide stability and security. There will be a time when honoring individuals' needs will help manifest strong financial bottom lines. There will be a time when our inner authority and strong character will be the force that shapes our lives. There will be a time when we are the "man" and the "woman" to our inner family and good parents to our younger selves. There will be a time when we honor and respect ourselves as much as we do others. There will be a time when we claim our gift from God—our soul—to strengthen and empower us to greatness. There will be a time when we and our souls are the foundations of our spiritual lives and that our religious community is sourced by that knowledge. There will be a time when security is measured by our will to succeed and to pursue our spiritual missions.

I believe that spiritual adulthood is also predicated on understanding the incredible diversity of our inner lives. To me one of the most important parts we need to investigate, welcome and nurture is the child who lives within.

Have you ever said or done something so automatic that it surprised and embarrassed you? Well, look over your shoulder; it is probably your inner child needing attention. When we do not understand this child, what results is a life that is out of control and chaotic. These automatic experiences provide excellent clues to the wants and needs of your little children. They were born in traumas in our early lives, which creates inner children that become fixated, or stuck, at that age. Emotions that were felt then can still be felt now. In his book *Revelation*, David Spangler wrote that no matter how much you may want on an intellectual level to accomplish something, if your feelings run counter to your conscious wishes, you will not succeed. This scared me when I first read it, because I knew that emotions are often unconscious and deeply hidden.

I place emotions into two distinct categories: contaminated (from the past) and natural (of the moment). Have you ever noticed the difference? Mad still feels like mad, doesn't it? Yet the distinction is very important. You need to understand the source of your feelings, especially if you cannot accomplish your goals because your feelings interfere. There are five basic emotions—mad, glad, sad, scared and ashamed.

Emotions located in your body and early experiences may still be unresolved and can cause constant trouble with contamination. Needless to say, these contaminated emotions can create issues in our daily lives: depression, relationship problems, eating disorders, etc. Our inner children contain our emotions, so exploring them will assist us in discovering their personality.

Emotions and Inner Child Exercise

I would like each of you to commit to paying close attention to your body and its emotions. Five times a day stop whatever you are doing, go inside of your body, asking the question: "What am I feeling right now—mad, glad, sad, scared, or ashamed?" Pay attention to your body's reactions, and you will learn how to determine the emotion and learn more about your inner child's emotional personality. The following questions will help you determine the power of your relationship with your inner child.

- Do you know why your inner child needs to eat unhealthy foods?
- Have you embraced your adult self to create good boundaries for your inner child?
- Have you created healthy food alternatives for your inner child?
- Do you love exercise?
- Are you able to label, embrace and express your emotions?
- Are you in touch with your unconscious mind?
- Do you remember your dreams?
- Do you know how to play?
- Are you in connection with your Inner Mother?
- Are you in connection with your Inner Father?
- Do you experience child-like creativity?

As an astrologer I rely on the Moon sign in an astrological chart to give me valuable information concerning our inner child's personality. The Moon represents our emotional life, which is built on instincts, moods, feelings and early mothering. The Moon also shows us the probable nature of our earliest imprints that create our unique inner child. Understanding the Moon sign in our astrological chart helps us to know and help our little ones. We cannot parent—or reparent—a child that we do not know. Many of my clients in their quest to become spiritual adults have become responsible, good parents to their inner children. They have had remarkable successes. They have lost weight, learned to love exercise (after all, most healthy children like to run and play), and have found joy in life's wonderful moments. They understand their emotional lives more deeply. They come from compassion and do not automatically judge or denigrate themselves, because they now know that it is hurtful to the little one inside. How often do we berate ourselves with terrible words? Our little ones hear these words. Worse than that, they *believe* what we say and bear the emotional impact of our self-contempt. We would call it child abuse if we said denigrating and demeaning things to "outside" children, would we not?

I have cautioned many of my clients not to make a half-hearted commitment to developing a relationship with their inner child. I have had many clients tell me they did inner child work in the 90's. I say, "Great what did you do for your inner child today?" I believe it is a relationship that we need to have with our inner child, not an intellectual exercise. If you are serious, the commitment will last the rest of your life. When you are ready I recommend writing a letter to your inner child telling them how much you love them and want to be their good parent. You will create the wholeness and integration necessary to living in the Age of Aquarius.

I love baby books. I have mine and have given many to friends as baby gifts. I decided to create a baby book for the inner child. *Through the Eyes of a Child: A Baby Book for Your Inner Child* is available with information on your Moon sign and strategies and techniques to aid you in becoming the best parent your little one will ever have.

Lastly, Capricorn symbolizes the surefooted goat that climbs mountains, reaches the top and then climbs another mountain. It represents the steady climb to success that is Capricorn's mandate. Its surefootedness is the integrity and character upon which Capricorn's reputation is built. Liz Greene wrote in *Astrology for Lovers*:

in the Eastern teaching of Bodhisattva, having reached the portal of the divine, the enlightened soul turns back and sees the rest of humanity suffering and wandering in darkness. He chooses voluntarily to return and travel back into the dense, dark world of the mundane world, in order to help those who are imprisoned. Only when they are free does he feel free to leave his self-imposed prison.

This portrays the real destiny of Capricorn—whatever mountaintop he seeks, material or spiritual—he cannot remain at the top. He must descend again into the world while his skills are still needed. This is the true leadership of Capricorn. Pluto provides Capricorn the intensity of emotion and through it the relentless striving to accomplish its goals for itself and for others. During this time of Pluto in Capricorn we need to eliminate anything that would stand in our way of climbing our metaphoric mountains. We will need to garner and honor our personal resources that will create our success in the climb to the top. Pluto is the harbinger of this transition, the agent of profound change into the Aquarian Age.

BECOMING SPIRITUAL ADULTS

"The Age of Aquarius fulfills the promise of the previous Golden Age of Leo, which occurred 12,000 years ago. From an individual's struggle for survival through will, which is Leo, emerges an age of democracy, equality and brotherhood for all people on the planet."

—Linda Brady

The Aquarian Age symbolizes our ability to understand God with more maturity by integrating His power into our hearts and minds. It is an awesome responsibility, but we are preparing for it. This new cycle will provide us the tools to create a life free of old restrictions. We will become cognizant of past-life memories that have kept us immobilized for so long. We will take appropriate actions to create the internal balance to heal pain left over from the past. We will create our own divine path to spiritual freedom by actively considering the full spectrum of possibilities that exist for each of us. We will claim our soul, not as a mystery, but as a spiritual companion. We will listen to its messages and follow its mission. Through that process we will be co-creating our life with God.

Although I believe the Age of Aquarius officially began in January of 1998, the Age of Pisces had already been winding down for some time, as evidenced by cataclysmic changes in corporate America and the explosion of technology. The gradual integration into the medical orthodoxy of holistic practices is further evidence that the Age of Aquarius has begun to manifest itself. Poised to enter and embrace the Age of Aquarius – the age of spiritual adulthood – we recognize that no biblical scenario will be played out for us; no spiritual leader will symbolize the meaning of this era. Being Aquarian is about being equal, about groups of people who are like-minded with a common goal, sitting in a circle with no leader. Community is the cornerstone of this Age of Aquarius.

There is no stronger proof that the Age of Aquarius has dawned than the proliferation of the Internet, a technological breakthrough affording people the world over unprecedented networking capabilities and access to information they never could have obtained otherwise. Virtual communities organized around grassroots causes are the ultimate Aquarian symbol. It is no accident that the Age of Aquarius coincides with what has been coined by the scholarly and research community as the Information Age. The implications and potential of the Aquarian Age have already begun to take root. The rise in alternative medicine and self-employment, our enhanced ability to inform and educate ourselves, our willingness to shed the yoke of victim hood, and the meteoric growth of the self-help market, are key indicators confirming the transition from an old age to a new one. Our deliberate effort to be more humane by fostering compassion and kindness serves as another Aquarian symbol, as evidenced by its increasing priority as a stated goal in schools.

AQUARIUS: A SEARCH FOR BALANCE

Aquarius' canons are equality, personal responsibility, and self-creation. During this time we will discover that personal creation leads to internal balance. Blaming others for the misfortunes of our lives demeans our respective spirits and causes us to feel hopeless and powerless. Too often we relish the feeling of righteous indignation that comes with victimhood. Thousands of years of indoctrination and socialization are slow to change. Taking the ultimate responsibility for our creations and learning from them is a day to day experience of empowerment, an approach to life drastically different from the doctrines that we accepted for so long.

It is certainly easier to be a victim. But although it is natural for us to blame someone else for the condition of our life, it weakens the fabric of our being and makes us fearful. Our lives today are increasingly complex and confusing, with a mind numbing array of variables more diffuse than ever before. We can no longer afford to apply simple, pat solutions to the conflicts of modern life. Growing up clinging to the dusty rule that every situation can be measured in an either-or framework becomes limiting, stressful—even maddening. It's not surprising that people seek counseling simply to hear that more than one option exists.

A counselor or therapist may say, "Have you thought about doing this?" and suddenly life doesn't seem as bleak. It sounds simple enough, but breaking out of the absolute mode of mutual exclusivity is terrifying, because thinking creatively means taking personal responsibility for our new options.

The Scientist's View

Fred Alan Wolfe, Ph.D. and physicist, in his book *The Spiritual Universe* wrote, "in a manner similar to Moses, Kepler, and Pauli, I believe that we are in a unique period of rediscovery of the soul." Some of science's most innovative minds have published work that applies quantum theory to cosmological precepts to explain the existence of soul as well as a higher level of consciousness or connectedness that transcends the material plane.

Science concerns itself only with what can be proven materially, yet we know spiritual matters cannot be studied using the same criteria. Colgate University Astrophysicist Victor Mansfield in his book, *Synchronicity, Science and Soul-Making* said, "Descartes, with his principles on cause and effect, laid the foundation for the philosophic view that guided the development of classical science. Still, his radical separation of the mind or the thinking subject from nature, or our body from the world surrounding us, is a deeply troubling legacy." Mansfield went on to say that this Cartesian dualism, this separation of science from the self and therefore the soul, makes understanding spiritual matters "impossible." Yet it is this exclusionary and anti-Aquarian theory that our early schooling and science 101 classes continue to ingrain in us.

In his book on Galileo, James Reston wrote,

science and faith clashed, and in their terrible conflict, the two were severed, to continue in divergent directions and to lose their common ground. In its insistence on the total victory of theology, the Catholic Church branded itself to the modern world as anti-science...It is still struggling to overcome the curse of 1616. And science fearing the spiritual became increasingly dry and bloodless, to the point that even the fantastic discoveries in today's heavens have lost the power to move the soul and spirit of mortals.

Physicist Will Keepin, in a 1996 interview, referred to a line of which he is most fond: "The greatest discovery of modern science is the discovery of its own limitations." He said he loved the line, because it indicates that there is an opening now "for the mystery, for the unknown to enter." Keepin said that the next greatest challenge for science is to not only recognize its own limitations, but to recognize the limitations of its principal instrument of inquiry, the human mind. "When we fully recognize that, for which the spiritual traditions are providing data in spades," said Keepin, "there will be the beginnings of a true science of the heart and the development of an interior epistemology to complement the one we've got of the exterior."

The Sixties Revolution

The 1960s saw the emergence of a new generation that staked its claim to a set of revolutionary values and social morays that differed defiantly from the Establishment's. The song Aquarius, from the 1968 stage classic "Hair," evoked liberation by embracing peace, love, and understanding—grass roots societal concepts that a dismissive America was loathe to confront. Ironically, the show was 30 years ahead of its time. One Saturn cycle—30 years later—the Age of Aquarius began with little fanfare on January 28, 1998, signaling one of the beginnings of the 2000-year epoch known as the Age of Aquarius.

The *Random House Unabridged Dictionary*, Second Edition, defines the Age of Aquarius as "an astrological era believed to bring increased spirituality and harmony on earth." Largely due to the millennial fervor and Y2K hype stoked by the media, most of us are conscious that a new time has emerged; we know that we have entered a new chapter in our history, but we haven't been able to comprehend or articulate what it all means. Now, with the dawning of the Age of Aquarius, we can. Aquarius is depicted by a man carrying an urn of water, from which flows rational thought, universal love, and equality for all humanity.

Seeking Spiritual Maturity

Spiritual maturity is the most prominent quality distinguishing the Aquarian Age from the previous epoch. For the past 2000 years, humankind has grappled with finding a mid-level point for its morality. Guilt was a primary behavioral determinant and remains today as an enduring Piscean vestige we need to shed. We demonstrated our need for leaders, institutions and armies to set our moral compass for us. Empires, dictatorships, monarchies, and papal rule characterized this earlier time. Thus our move into Aquarian times is wholly consistent with the democratic ideal—a government by the people, for the people—at the end of the 20th century. The United States of America, a dominant force for democracy, has a Moon and South Node in the sign of Aquarius.

The Internet as an Aquarian Technology

The emergence of the Internet—the ultimate Aquarian technological model due to its far-reaching networking capacity—is well timed. Internet pundits analyze successful web sites or portals based on their ability to "build community." Reva Basch, commentator on the evolution of online community, talks about the growing "importance of place" on the web, in which some sites serve as a "virtual town commons where people can meet." The Internet has enabled millions across the globe to participate in like-minded groups: from support groups that help members handle grief and addictions to professional list servers to social groups and clubs.

While the commercial machinations of the largest web companies—Google, Amazon, Microsoft—continue to make headlines, the Internet is closing the digital divide between the haves and have-nots by providing the poor with unprecedented opportunities to access information. Urban public libraries are jammed with users looking for job opportunities, health information, and research for every phase of their lives.

Heeding the Lessons of the Aquarian Age

Despite living during the Aquarian Age in its infancy, we are realizing the power and the infinite fairness of our soul and its wisdom to create our lives with God-like perfection. Because Aquarius is the embodiment of the holistic model—integration of the mind, body and soul—conscious cocreation can only begin with a commitment to pursuing our soul mission, starting with the development of our personality. Aquarius honors the countless striations of the human personality and loves the spiritual connection it has with all humankind. World harmony through unified nations will promote the exploration of our inner and outer space.

The importance of this age occurs on the individual level with the integration of our soul and personality, which must take place for each of us to influence and fulfill the promise of this glorious age. Universal brotherhood based in rationality will solve social problems in a manner equitable to all. For that reason, Aquarius might be described as the principle of cosmic rationality or cosmic mind, the ability to perceive or make connections of the most abstract and cosmic sort. Aquarius isn't simply concerned with ideas and theoretical relations; it is concerned with ideas and relationships that are global or universal in scope. Religion and science will be married to create a religious science and a scientific religion.

The Dominance of the Air Element

The deeper meaning of the Age can be understood by studying the underlying element involved. In the case of Aquarius, the influence of air is dominant. This is reflected in a literal way with the startling rise of aviation technologies over the past two centuries; humans are increasingly learning how to master the air realm, not only through aviation but in the construction of ever-taller buildings, which allow us to live higher up off the ground. The media employs metaphors that reflect this elemental shift. A show is "on the air," or a broadcaster is "taking to the airwaves." What this means is that the Aquarian Age will undoubtedly witness major advances in humanity's intellectual growth. Terms like the "information superhighway" and the "information revolution," especially with the advent of the Internet, are examples of how the impending Aquarian influence has already begun to propel our world toward more mental values and modes of experience. Indicators of the new Age that are upon us are quite obvious and include recent breakthroughs in genetic engineering, computer technology, telecommunications, space technology, and developments in medicine, surgery and world politics and government.

BECOMING CITIZENS OF THE WORLD

Aquarius symbolizes citizenship that encompasses the whole world. Teamwork may become the keyword for the new age. Social organizations and institutions may gain more power in the coming years. Mass movements may reach across national boundaries. Sudden and radical changes may shape the lives of millions. Looking at others as friends instead of strangers may become more prevalent as barriers are broken down. We may become a more spiritual community.

A culture of higher consciousness may arise. The sharing of information may bring knowledge to the masses and hopefully allow more people in the world opportunities to be the best they can be. Conversely, there is so much information that we can become overwhelmed by it. We need to be discriminating and use our intuition to know what we accept and use and what we do not.

"Creativity is paradoxical. To create, a person must have knowledge but forget the knowledge, must see unexpected connections in things but not have a mental disorder, must work hard but spend time doing nothing as information incubates, must create many ideas yet most of them are useless, must look at the same thing as everyone else, yet see something different, must desire success but embrace failure, must be persistent but not stubborn, and must listen to experts but know how to disregard them."

—**Michael Michalko**, "Twelve Things
You Were Not Taught in School about Creative Thinking,"
The Creativity Post, December 6, 2011

The Aquarian Personality

On a personality level, Aquarian energy reminds us to value the singular, open-minded, holistic part of ourselves. It encourages us to associate with groups of like-minded people to further our shared political, cultural, and holistically spiritual goals. As Aquarian "citizens of the world," we will network within these symbiotic groups to further raise global consciousness. In doing so, we will be living the holistic model of mind-body-soul integration by creating harmonious, congruent lives of our own. As humanity enters this new age, a universal, spiritually driven urgency to rededicate ourselves to the attainable goals of freedom, brotherhood, and tolerance will become an ever-increasing point of convergence and kindred social activism across our planet.

The Aquarian Challenge

As I said we all have one foot in the Age of Pisces and another one in the Age of Aquarius, and we may find ourselves caught between in, as

Shakespeare said, "a drama of cosmic proportions." Our value systems collide, our old beliefs and precious illusions are being threatened and destroyed, disagreements abound, terrorism flourishes, extremism escalates and political polarization causes anger and fear. We are the microcosm of a world going crazy.

Feeling confused, unhappy, inadequate, helpless or hopeless? We *all* are. The world is undergoing massive economic instability, political upheaval, and cultural and religious conflict. In addition "coincidentally," self-aware people are experiencing their greatest spiritual challenges. Because of all of this humankind is in the midst of its greatest potential for spiritual integration, actualization and evolution. We need to be integrated, centered and balanced using our knowledge of Pisces and Aquarius to find the integration that we seek and to really make a difference in our world. With Aquarius change is eminent; suffering is optional.

Many years ago one of my interns suggested that I write a Bible for the Age of Aquarius. I laughed and told her that I would be happy to do that but that it would only be a poster, not a book. Learning a few basic truths is really all that we need to navigate the next 2,000 years. I challenge each of you to take one of the statements and incorporate it into your life for a month and see how it changes your responses to life's experiences and challenges.

My Aquarian Poster

*I know that my soul creates my
life experiences for my highest good.*

*I love feeling empowered when I take
personal responsibility for my life.*

I pursue my soul's mission with commitment and action.

*I love the excitement and wonder
of living a life of Serendipity.*

I understand that my soul and
personality need to be integrated.

I know that my mind, body and
spirit need to be understood equally.

I honor my soul contracts and learn from them every day.

I resolve past life conflicts and
free myself from guilt and shame.

I know that my soul connects to all souls with love.

I love and honor myself as I love and honor others.

We are now in the "end of days" the last years of the Age of Pisces as recorded by the New Testament. We need to discover more truth about the Age we are leaving to more fully understand the Age we are beginning. Please refer again to "The Age of Pisces Revisited" section in the Prologue and read books like *The Secret Gospel, Holy Blood, Holy Grail, The Jesus Papers, The Gospel According to Thomas,* and *The Gospel According to Judas* that are all asking the same question: Who was Jesus and what was his impact on the Age of Pisces.

I am asking another relevant question: What is Jesus' impact on the age we are moving into – the Age of Aquarius? We are currently living in two worlds ruled by two distinct ways of life dominated by the energies of Pisces and Aquarius. Aquarians tend to deride and criticize Pisceans for being too reliant on an external God that is characterized as too fundamental, too extreme and too rigid, while Pisceans tend to see Aquarians as secular humanists who are blasphemers, anti-Christ and anti-God. Aquarians tend to be liberal; Pisceans tend to be conservative.

We are in a time of intense Polarization: conservatives against liberals, liberals against conservatives, Christians and Jews against Muslims, Muslims against the infidels and on it goes. I believe the key is integrating the cycles. I believe that by taking the compassion and love of Pisces into the rational maturity of Aquarius, we have the potential to create heaven on earth.

CHRIST: THE FIRST AQUARIAN

I believe that Jesus fulfilled the Old Testament prophesies and ushered in the Age of Pisces when he was born. I also believe that he was the first true Aquarian. The most important tenet of the Aquarian Way is the holistic triangle of mind, body and spirit. This level of integration is based on our knowledge that God has presented to all of us his greatest gift – a piece of Himself – our soul. That makes us a creation in His image. With that gift we truly live in His kingdom each day of our lives. This was Christ's message, spoken in parables to uneducated people, whose bias was to take his stories quite literally. As more sophisticated, rational Aquarians, 2,000 years older and wiser, we are able to look to the real truth of his words.

The Kingdom of God

In the book *The Jesus Papers*, Michael Baigent quoted Father Loisy, saying, "Jesus proclaimed the coming of the Kingdom, but what came was the Church." How many of us have railed against the rigid structures and rituals of organized religions and have lost Jesus' words in the process? The basic difference between the Age of Pisces and the Age of Aquarius is whether or not man worships an external God or an internal God. During the time of Jesus his followers thought that he meant that the Kingdom of God was in the heavens and that mankind would only reach it after his earthly life was over. Yet Jesus said in many ways throughout his ministry: For behold the kingdom of God is within you. We as Aquarians know that God is an integral part of us through our understanding of the holistic triangle of mind, body and spirit. Jesus was speaking to us across 2,000 years and we now have the wisdom to hear.

In Luke 17:20-21, Jesus declares that one need not go on a search for signs to find the Kingdom:

> Once, having been asked by the Pharisees when the kingdom of God would come, Jesus replied, "The kingdom of God does not come with your careful observation, nor will people say, 'Here it is,' or 'There it is,' because *the kingdom of God is within you."* (New International Version)
>
> Now having been questioned by the Pharisees as to when the kingdom of God was coming, He answered them and said, "The kingdom of God is not coming with signs to be observed; nor will they say, 'Look, here *it is!*' or, 'There *it is!*' For behold, *the kingdom of God is in your midst."* (New American Standard Bible)

This reinforces a point that Jesus has already raised in his teaching in the rebuke about being able to read the weather but not the signs of the times (Luke 12:54-56 par.). It also parallels the warning about the sign of his preaching being the only sign this wicked generation must respond to (Luke 11:29-32 par.). The Kingdom does not come, in this phase, with such heavenly portents. Rather it is "in your midst."

We are exploring the Kingdom of Heaven and returning feeling renewed and transformed, bringing the Kingdom of God from the depths of our unconscious to consciousness. The Kingdom of God exists within us to be remembered through meditation and through a deep understanding of our gift from God – our beloved Soul. We must then be of God. Jesus said those words 2,000 years ago. In John 10:31 Jesus responded to the crowd that was stoning him because he claimed to be the son of God, by saying, "I said, 'You are gods, and all of you are sons of the Most High'" (New American Standard Bible).

In *The Gospel of Thomas*, which was a part of the Gnostic texts found at Nag Hammadi, it was written that, "When you come to know yourselves, then you will become known and you will realize that it is you who are the sons of the living Father" and in Romans 8:14 "for as many as are led by the Spirit of God, they are the sons of God" (King James Bible).

Christ Foretells the Age of Aquarius

Mark 14:13 states "And he sendeth forth two of his disciples, and saith unto them, Go ye into the city, and there shall meet you a man bearing a pitcher of water: follow him" (King James Bible). This was an odd thing for Jesus to say since carrying water was strictly women's work. As Morton Smith says in *The Secret Gospel*, it would be akin to asking his disciples to look for a man wearing lipstick.

The disciples obey this command and follow him to the place where Jesus was to hold the Last Supper. Therefore this could be interpreted as meaning that Jesus (who represents the age of Pisces) will "die" when the "man bearing a pitcher of water" appears, an apparent allusion to the coming Age of Aquarius. He was referring to the Age of Aquarius that is symbolized by the cosmic man bearing the pitcher of the living waters of life, pouring it throughout the universe. In this sign [Aquarius] the waters of the Piscean age will, symbolically speaking, be absorbed into the water-pot carried on the shoulder of Aquarius in the symbol that is distinctive of this sign, for Aquarius is the water-carrier.

The Aquarian Age is the Golden Age of the universal man. It will be a holistic age marked by a deeper understanding of the powerful meaning of Christ's teachings. We can all be exalted in our knowledge that we are sons and daughters of God and live within the Kingdom of God with happiness and peace. John Onyido says,

> As we come to the end of this millennium and as we look forward to the dawn of a new era, it is prudent and in our interest to make an informed decision which results in a marked shift from our old, familiar ways. The responsibility of making ourselves worthy

and prepared for the demands of our time as always remains an individual one. It involves stepping-up higher than before on the evolutionary scale; it involves a positive change for the better.

The Aquarian Christ

Perhaps the most important way to integrate the Pisces and Aquarius Ages is through an understanding of the Aquarian Christ. Alice Bailey in her *Destiny of the Nation* says, "In the Aquarian Age, the Risen Christ is Himself the Water-Carrier; He will not this time demonstrate the perfected life of a Son of God, which was His main mission before; He will appear as the supreme Head of the Spiritual Hierarchy, meeting the need of the thirsty nations of the world—thirsty for truth, for right human relations and for loving understanding."

As Aquarians, I believe it is our mission to actively pursue reconciliation with all people, after all, we believe that our souls lovingly connect with all souls. If we can connect with people who are not like us, our communities, states and governments can ultimately do the same. I believe that it is our responsibility to create a model of divine integration that could generate peace and harmony in our lifetime. It begins with us!

EPILOGUE

We all must have the courage and fortitude to listen to our souls and follow the path that will make our hearts sing, even when that path portends substantive reframing, transformation, and tumult. This book has supplied you with tools to help you learn more about yourself and your soul in order to discover your life's purpose and live it with greater meaning and profundity.

We are beginning to understand with greater certainty how important it is to embrace and be aware of our soul. In order to become the most complete human beings possible, we must be in touch with our soul on a daily basis.

Put simply, when we strive to fulfill our soul mission, our life's work, we get what we want; when we don't, we often find ourselves mired in significant crises. Our soul missions provide us with all the things for which we yearn: happiness, fulfillment, meaning, purpose, direction and motivation. Most importantly, living our soul mission gives us peace. We must remind those who are less spiritually cognizant that they too have a soul and explain what it does and what it means.

In essence, we're teaching people to be more reflective, to approach their lives with honor so they mean something. We're asking them to be observers, to see the world with a broader and sharper focus. Once they've overcome their myopia, their fears and insecurities will begin to subside. If we're in love with our soul, we're in love with abundance—in love with the universe. If we're consumed with fear, we're left with scarcity. At some point in our lives, we've all felt like victims, enslaved to our families, our mates, our culture, our economy or even our own feelings. We must first gain the perspective to envision the opportunity, then dedicate ourselves to creating the freedom in our lives where none currently exists.

In reading this book and applying its principles, you have begun an adventure in self-discovery that will bring to your life an unprecedented lucidity, focus and fulfillment. Once you make it a priority to align your personality's desires with your soul mission, you will sense your life taking on more meaning and joy. Your life work is now beginning: using the book as a foundation, you can lay the groundwork for living your soul mission on a daily basis.

It is my hope that you will continue to use the new and expanded version of *Discovering Your Soul Mission: New Rules for a New Age* as a reference tool, accessing it to deal with any particularly challenging relationship or experience in any given moment. Staying conscious of your soul mission is the key to success. It is all too easy to slip imperceptibly back into old behaviors and thought processes. Continue gathering pertinent astrological information relating to your Soul Potential. Journalizing your experiences and spending reflective quality time with yourself every day remain essential.

Michael and I would like to acknowledge you, the reader, for having the courage to look at your life from a different vantage point, and for wanting to confront issues that may be painful but from which you can evolve, grow, and even heal. We all deserve to learn our ultimate truth: who we are and why we are here. Unfortunately, many of us are too fearful of what we might unearth. We encourage you to "play" with the information you've gleaned from the book for at least a month. Then you can decide for yourself whether it has made a significant difference in your life. If you make the commitment, you will undoubtedly find more meaning and gain more strength, not to mention enjoy a more thrilling and satisfying journey than you ever imagined possible.

GLOSSARY OF TERMS

anger processing How we deal with anger.

astrological symbolism Every symbol in our world corresponds to an astrological sign, house, or planet.

Chiron The comet discovered in 1977 and touted as the comet of healing by Native Americans. Chiron is symbolized by the "wounded healer." It was named after the centaur in Greek mythology who was a healer and teacher who could not heal himself. It represents lifetimes of being wounded and victimized. It offers us the information to heal those old wounds and become the sacred teacher.

color healing/meditation/symbology Each color vibrates to a specific level, which corresponds to a life-enhancing energy. This energy aids us in altering our consciousness, calming or intensifying our feelings, and helps in healing our mind, body, and spirit. Bringing color into our energetic bodies helps stimulate understanding and clarity.

cosmic two-by-four An experience our soul creates to stop us in our tracks and draw our attention to a behavior or habit we had been unable to detect previously.

dream interpretation Every symbol in a dream comes from our unconscious minds. Our chart provides specific information regarding the unconscious process. Correlating our dream symbols with astrological symbols gives us a wealth of information not normally gleaned from a dream.

inner child A memory of the children we've been. It represents information and experiences in this life that we remember upon intense introspection. It's an unconscious part of us that, when released, can cause havoc.

journalizing A writing exercise that helps you elicit information that may otherwise be hidden. Often unconscious memories surface when we write.

karma An energetic, universal, and physical law described by the axioms "What goes around, comes around," and "You reap what you sow." Karma continues from one life to another and is only complete when you have balanced your previous actions through consciousness, commitment, and new actions.

karmic amalgam An opportunity to see ourselves through the people we create; an aggregate image comprised of the people most meaningful to us.

karmic astrology Utilizing the information obtained through the study of our past lives, karmic relationships, and soul processes to create the lives we want.

karmic debts Actions you need to take in this life to balance an action you took in a past life.

karmic forgiveness To forgive ourselves for what we think we've done wrong.

karmic memory Memories of our previous lifetime experiences that are part of our unconscious mind and our soul.

karmic retribution When we have taken an action in a previous life, and have not balanced that action out in this life. It is what we do to balance our karmic debt.

karmic warning bells The heady emotions, the passionate rush, that accompanies our initial foray with someone special. What feels like "love" in many cases is really a cosmic two-by-four meant to get our attention and prepare us for a major karmic insight.

mandala The astrological chart circle and the symbols it represents.

Mars The planet that represents the way we understand and express anger. It is the energy that embodies action, forward motion, and risk taking. At its best, Mars represents focused determination and self-motivation. At its worst, it can be impulsive, reckless, impatient, shortsighted, destructive, and accident prone.

Mercury The planet that represents our orientation to the world. Its energy helps us determine who we are, how we receive and perceive information, and what we do with it and how we express ourselves once we have it.

Neptune The planet that gives us information about the Soul Patterns we have that keep us mired in self-deception, allowing our illusions to thrive. It sheds light on the skewed belief systems that perpetuate the unrealistic standards we've set that can cause serious disappointments.

North Node (Soul Potential) The point where the moon orbiting its way to earth's northern hemisphere intercepts the earth's orbit around the sun. It represents all for which you strive. Your North Node offers you a road map of words and concepts helping you to understand whom you need to be to achieve your soul's potential. Once embraced, your North Node provides you with a clear path to a life of profound joy, purpose, and congruence.

obsession A negative thought we can't let go of. Something that has no basis in reality but still drives us.

personality Our social and emotional DNA, helping us to distinguish who we are. The part of us that responds, often impulsively, to the ebbs and flows of life. It encompasses our thoughts, feelings, senses, motivations, dreams, and the way we emote, and it carries the indelible stamp of our family and history. Unlike our soul, our personality does not transcend this life.

Pluto The planet that represents our guilty inclinations. Pluto urges us to have the courage to focus our will on personal transformation, enabling us to focus on our Soul Potential. It helps us face our deepest desires and obsessions and alter them.

projection/reflection Both Jungian concepts. Projection is a process by which we deny an ugly part of ourselves and our souls impart it to another person, so that we can observe it in them. Reflection is the process by which that other person sends this information back to us for our review.

Saturn Our karmic conductor on the journey to our soul mission. It teaches us the truth about ourselves and helps us create order and structure in our lives. Without it we could not accomplish our soul mission.

serendipity Making a commitment, taking an action, and expecting the unexpected that your soul and the universe create with you.

soul The essence of our spiritual core; the primary, never-ending force behind us forging our destiny.

soul circles of life The sum total of our relationships—hundreds or more—that are linked to us from one life to the next in order to help our soul evolve and learn the lessons it needs to learn.

soul contracts Agreements we make with souls we've known from other lifetimes to work through situations in this life that need special attention. Souls reincarnate with other souls they are closely related to in order to overcome conflict, repay an obligation, or perpetuate love.

soul creation The practice of taking ultimate responsibility for the way our lives transpire given the fact that our souls create exactly the lives we need in order for us to learn and evolve to a higher spiritual order.

soul mates Karmic relationships that have been resolved: deep conflicts that have been settled, obligations that have been fulfilled, and love that has replaced fear and anger.

soul mission Your reason for being; your grand purpose, transcending the here and now.

soul/personality integration The aligning and meshing of our oft-divergent soul and personality to achieve our soul mission.

South Node (Soul Pattern) The South Node is the point where the moon, on its way to earth's southern hemisphere, intercepts earth's orbit around the sun. It represents your default mechanism, the type of person you become when you regress into old, predictable patterns and behaviors. The memories of your South Node run deep within you, representing your most familiar thoughts, feelings, and beliefs.

synchronicity A condition allowing your soul to create perfect timing and interactions with the world in perfect ways.

traditional astrology The study of how planetary positions and the alignment of the stars affect human affairs.

Uranus Uranus is the first of the transpersonal planets, which means it affects the collective as well as the individual. Uranus is associated with sudden unexpected changes and events. It is the "awakener" and symbolizes the urge to freedom, intuition, individuation, originality and independence. It is our personal hurricane rushing through our lives and taking down whatever structures have outlived their usefulness to us.

Suggested Reading

Arroyo, Stephen. *Astrology and the Four Elements*. Sebastopol, CA: CRCS Publications, 1975.

———. *Astrology, Karma and Transformation*. Sebastopol, CA: CRCS Publications, 1978.

Bach, Marcus. *The World of Serendipity*. Marina del Rey, CA: DeVoss & Co., 1970.

Baigent, Michael. *Jesus Papers*. San Francisco, CA: Harpers, 2006

Campbell, Joseph. *Myths to Live By*. New York: Viking, 1972.

Casey, Caroline W. *Inner and Outer Space*. Boulder, CO: Sounds True, 1996.

Cayce, Edgar. *God's Other Door and the Continuity of Life*. Virginia Beach, VA: A.R.E. Press, 1977.

Cayce, Edgar, and Mary Ann Woodward. *Edgar Cayce's Story of Karma*. New York: Berkley Publishing Group, 1994.

Christensen, Andrew, Brian Doss, and Neil Jacobson. *Reconcilable Differences: Rebuild Your Relationship by Rediscovering the Partner You Love--without Losing Yourself* (2nd ed.). New York: The Guilford Press, 2014.

Erickson, Milton, et al. *Hypnotic Realities.* New York: Irvington Publishers, 1976.

Einstein, Albert. *Merging of Spirit and Science,* 1954.

Francis, Eric. "Chiron: Part 1," *Astrology News* (Planetwaves.net).

Gawain, Shakti. *Creative Visualizations.* San Rafael, CA: New World Library, 1995.

Greene, Liz. *Saturn: A New Look at an Old Devil.* York Beach, ME: Samuel Weiser, 1976.

Hay, Louise. *You Can Heal Your Life.* Carlsbad, CA: Hay House, 1984.

Herbert, Nick. *Quantum Reality.* New York: Doubleday, 1987.

Jung, C. G. *Memories, Dreams, Reflections.* New York: Pantheon, 1961.

———. *The Structure and Dynamics of the Psyche.* Princeton, NJ: Princeton University Press, 1970.

Jung, C. G., ed. *Man and His Symbols.* New York: Dell, 1968.

March, Marion, and Joan McEvers. *The Only Way to Learn Astrology, vol. 1.* San Diego, CA: ACS Publications, 1980.

———. *The Only Way to Learn About Relationships.* San Diego, CA: ACS Publications, 1992.

Marks, Tracy. *The Astrology of Self-Discovery.* Sebastopol, CA: CRCS Publications, 1985.

———. *Your Secret Self: Illuminating the Mysteries of the Twelfth House.* Sebastopol, CA: CRCS Publications, 1989.

Maslow, Abraham. *Motivation and Personality.* New York: Harper, 1954.

Mansfield, Victor. *Synchronicity, Science and Soul Making.* Chicago: Open Court Publishing, 1995.

Reston, James. *Galileo.* Beard Books, 2000.

Russell, Bertram. In a speech given 3/6/1927 to the Battersea Town Hall South London Branch of the National Secular Society.

Schulman, Martin. *Karmic Astrology*. York Beach, ME: Samuel Weiser, 1975.

Singer, Julie, ed. *Boundaries of the Soul: The Practice of Jung's Psychology*, rev. ed. New York: Anchor, 1994.

Spangler, David. *Revelations: The Birth of a New Age*. Boulder, CO: Lorian Press, 1976.

Spiller, Jan, and Karen McCoy. *Spiritual Astrology*. New York: Simon & Schuster, 1988.

Wallace, Amy, and Bill Henkin. *Psychic Healing Book*. Oakland, CA: Wingbow Press, 1981.

Walsch, Neale Donald. *Conversations with God: An Uncommon Dialogue*. New York: Putnam Publishing Group, 1996.

Wilber, Ken. *No Boundary*. Boston: Shambhala, 1979.

Wolfe, Fred Alan. *Spiritual Universe: How Quantum Physics Proves the Existence of the Soul*. New York: Simon and Schuster, 1996.

Zukav, Gary. *The Dancing Wu Li Masters*. New York: Bantam Books, 1979.

———. *The Seat of the Soul*. New York: Simon & Schuster, Fireside Books, 1989.

INDEX

Printed in Great
Britain
by Amazon

32027527R00248